BLACK RESONANCE

BLACK RESONANCE

Iconic Women Singers
and African American Literature

EMILY J. LORDI

Rutgers University Press
NEW BRUNSWICK, NEW JERSEY, AND LONDON

LIBRARY OF CONGRESS CATALOGING-IN-PUBLICATION DATA

Lordi, Emily J., 1979–
    Black resonance : iconic women singers and African American literature /
Emily J. Lordi.
        pages cm. — (American Literatures Initiative)
        Includes bibliographical references and index.
        ISBN 978-0-8135-6250-6 (hardcover : alk. paper)
        ISBN 978-0-8135-6249-0 (pbk. : alk. paper)
        ISBN 978-0-8135-6251-3 (e-book)
        1. American fiction—African American authors—History and criticism. 2. African
American women singers—In literature. 3. African American women in literature.
4. Music in literature. I. Title.
PS153.N5L68 2013
810.9'896073—dc23

                                                                    2012051444

A British Cataloging-in-Publication record for this book is available
from the British Library.

Visit our website: http://rutgerspress.rutgers.edu

Manufactured in the United States of America

THE
AMERICAN
LITERATURES
INITIATIVE

A book in the American Literatures Initiative (ALI), a collaborative
publishing project of NYU Press, Fordham University Press, Rutgers
University Press, Temple University Press, and the University of Virginia
Press. The Initiative is supported by The Andrew W. Mellon Foundation.
For more information, please visit www.americanliteratures.org.

For my parents

CONTENTS

Acknowledgments

A recent book by Anthony Heilbut quotes Aretha Franklin as saying, "I'm sentimental, I don't forget." I know what she means and for that reason have looked forward to writing these acknowledgments for years.

I am proud that this project began at Columbia University. Robert G. O'Meally, Farah Jasmine Griffin, Ann Douglas, Brent Hayes Edwards, Robin D. G. Kelley, Marcellus Blount, and Monica Miller not only fostered this particular work but also continue to inspire me with their exemplary scholarship, writing, teaching, and *style*. To have trained with them is to never have to wonder if what we do matters; their political commitments are as clear as they are complex. My debt to Bob O'Meally is happily profound. A mentor in the truest sense of the word, he spent hours in conversation, invited me into intellectual and artistic communities, and essentially made a place for me in this profession long before I warranted one. He is the most generous scholar I know and the best example of Ralph Ellison's dictum that the secret of the game is to make life swing. Thank you.

Several colleagues at Cornell, where I worked as a visiting assistant professor in the English Department from 2009 to 2011, gave me well-timed support and valuable advice. Thanks to Ellis Hanson, Grant Farred, Shirley Samuels, Dagmawi Woubshet, Rayna Kalas, Jeremy Braddock, and Margo Crawford. Thanks especially to my students at Cornell, who provided such a rich foundation for my teaching career. Since coming to UMass Amherst in 2011, I have been welcomed and supported by too many people to name, but I especially appreciate the guidance of

Joe Bartolomeo, Stephen Clingman, Laura Doyle, Nick Bromell, James Smethurst, and Ron Welburn and the friendship of Tanya Fernando, Jane Degenhardt, and Asha Nadkarni. Britt Rusert and Tanisha Ford, I'm glad you're here. Many thanks as well to my students for making the teaching part of my job a pleasure even when the writing part is hard.

I am very grateful to my editor, Katie Keeran, at Rutgers University Press for taking a chance on a first-time author and for being exceedingly good at what she does. Lisa Boyajian answered many questions about permissions; Andrew Katz copyedited the manuscript; Tim Roberts guided the book through production. Thanks to archivists at the Schomburg Center for Research in Black Culture; the Harry Ransom Humanities Research Center at the University of Texas; the Howard Gotlieb Archival Research Center at Boston University; the Beinecke Rare Book and Manuscript Library at Yale; the Library of Congress Manuscript and Motion Picture Divisions in Washington, D.C. Thanks to the many artists and executors who granted me permission to reproduce images, song lyrics, and text, especially Julia Wright. Thanks to George Avakian, John Sommerville, and Linda Susan Jackson for interviews; speaking with Linda Susan about her poetry and Etta James was a highlight of this process.

This book is a chorus of other people's voices in a sense that my citations do not fully convey. In an effort to mark these contributions and to acknowledge, as Elizabeth Alexander writes, "how much thinking [and] theorizing . . . happens in talk," I want to cite the people whose brilliant questions, comments, and even direct language are in some way represented in the following pages. Thank you Lloyd Pratt, Courtney Thorsson, Nijah Cunningham, Douglas Field, Paul Peppis, Ann Douglas, Carter Mathes, Matt Sandler, Farah Griffin, Bob O'Meally, Ashraf Rushdy, Ann duCille, Monica Miller, Sangita Gopal, Scott Saul, Joel Pfister, Dag Woubshet, Patricia Akhime, Amanda Alexander, Jean-Christophe Cloutier, Brent Edwards, Steve Rachman, Greg Tate, Miles Parks Grier, Bakari Kitwana, José Limón, Jim Smethurst, Stephen Clingman, TreaAndrea Russworm, and Anthony Reed. Thanks to anonymous readers for their incisive feedback on portions of this book; thanks to the many institutions that gave me a platform to share it, including most recently the University of Denver, Michigan State, and Notre Dame. Thanks to Tony Bolden for organizing the remarkable Eruptions of Funk Symposium at the University of Alabama in 2007. Thanks to scholars I have not yet met but whose work helped shape what I've tried to do here: Angela Davis, Henry Louis Gates Jr., Nathaniel Mackey, Marisa Parham, and Tricia Rose.

I was extremely fortunate to have two of my "ideal readers" become the actual readers of this manuscript. At an early stage, Cheryl Wall articulated this book's significance as I could not have done; I am grateful to her for showing me what I was actually doing and what I could do better. I'm not sure I can adequately convey how much Daphne Brooks's detailed comments meant to me, except to thank her for taking the time to help me write a better book and for offering critical affirmation at a crucial stage. Despite the assistance I have received, it should go without saying that the flaws in this work are "nobody's fault but mine."

I am so happy to have Courtney Thorsson as a colleague in this profession; I cherish our friendship. Thanks to New York friends Daniel Menely, Josh Cohen, Rob Goldberg, Hiie Saumaa, and Miles Davis for making things fun and to Brad Lawrence, without whom the idea of spending my twenties in Butler Library would have seemed questionable. Thanks to my wonderful friend Sarah Schlein for seeing me through this and so much else. I met Anthony Reed as this thesis was becoming a book and I marvel at the love and support he has shown me every day since. He has brought so much music into my life that the only word for it is "blessed."

My extended and immediate family has pulled me through with love and laughter every step of this sometimes tedious way. I am incredibly proud of my brothers, Joe and Jeff, both true leaders and charismatic people who are a joy to be around. Catherine Lordi is the loveliest sister-in-law I could imagine. Thanks to my father, Larry Lordi, for being a model of hard work and determination and for always making me feel like I was someone special—such a gift. My mother, Lorraine Lordi—writer, teacher, musician, overall force of creativity and love—was my first and best teacher. It's because of her that I wanted to be a writer and was able to take for granted the value of a life devoted to the arts. There is really too much to thank her for, but this book is dedicated to her and to my dad, with endless thanks for all they've given me.

Finally, to the artists in this study: it has been such a challenging pleasure to live with your work all these years, and I hope I've done right by you all.

Copyrights and Permissions

Following is a list of copyright and permissions acknowledgments for works quoted herein:

"a/coltrane/poem" reprinted by permission of Sonia Sanchez, © 1970.

"All I Could Do Was Cry." Words and Music by Gwen Gordy Fuqua, Berry Gordy, and Roquel Davis. © 1959 (Renewed 1987) Jobete Music Co., Inc. All rights controlled and administered by EMI April Music Inc. and EMI Blackwood Music Inc. on behalf of Jobete Music Co., Inc.and Stone Agate Music (a division of Jobete Music Co., Inc.) All Rights Reserved. International Copyright Secured. Used by Permission. Reprinted with permission of Hal Leonard Corporation.

Draft excerpts from "As the Spirit Moves Mahalia" and *Invisible Man* reprinted by permission of the Ralph and Fanny Ellison Charitable Trust.

"At Last." Music by Harry Warren. Lyrics by Mack Gordon. Copyright © 1942 (Renewed) Twentieth Century Music Corporation. All Rights Controlled by EMI Feist Catalog Inc. (Publishing) and Alfred Music Publishing Co., Inc. (Print). All Rights Reserved. Used by Permission.

"At Last," "The Muse Speaks," "What Yellow Sounds Like," "Yellow and Blues," "Yellow Privilege" by Linda Susan Jackson. From *What Yellow Sounds Like*, published by Tia Chucha Press. © 2007 by Linda Susan Jackson. Reprinted by permission of the author.

"Backwater Blues" and "Preaching the Blues." By Bessie Smith. ©1927 (Renewed), 1974 Frenk Music Corp. All Rights Reserved. Reprinted with permission of Hal Leonard Corporation.

"Billie" and "Dark Lady of the Sonnets" reprinted by permission of SLL/ Sterling Lord Literistic, Inc. Copyright by Amiri Baraka.

"Billie's Blues." Written by Billie Holiday. Used by permission of Edward B. Marks Music Company.

"A Change is Gonna Come." Words and Music by Sam Cooke. Copyright © 1964 (Renewed) ABKCO Music, Inc., 85 Fifth Avenue, New York, NY 10003. All Rights Reserved. Used by Permission.

"Dear John, Dear Coltrane." From *Songlines in Michaeltree: New and Collected Poems*. Copyright 2000 by Michael S. Harper. Used with permission of the poet and the University of Illinois Press.

"Dreams" and "Poem for Aretha" by Nikki Giovanni. Reprinted by permission of the author, © 1968.

"Empty Bed Blues." By J.C. Johnson. © Copyright. Record Music Publishing Co./ASCAP. All rights reserved. Used by permission.

"FB Eye Blues," "Memories of My Grandmother," "So Long, Big Bill Broonzy." Copyright © 2013 by Estate of Richard Wright. Reprinted by permission of John Hawkins & Associates, Inc., and the Estate of Richard Wright.

"I Am A Black Woman" by Mari Evans. Published by Wm. Morrow & Co., 1970, reprinted by permission of the author.

"Move On Up a Little Higher." Words and Music by Herbert W. Brewster. Copyright © 1946 (Renewed) Unichappell Music Inc. (BMI). All Rights Reserved. Used by Permission.

"Reckless Blues." By Bessie Smith. ©1925 (Renewed), 1974 Frank Music Corp. All Rights Reserved. Reprinted with permission of Hal Leonard Corporation.

"Respect." Words and Music by Otis Redding. Copyright © 1965 (Renewed) Irving Music, Inc. All Rights Reserved. Used By Permission. Reprinted with permission of Hal Leonard Corporation. All Rights For the World Outside of the U.S. Controlled by Irving Music, Inc. and Warner-Temerlane Publishing Corp. All Rights Reserved. Used by Permission of Alfred Music Publishing Co., Inc.

"Something's Got a Hold On Me." Words and Music by Etta James, Leroy Kirkland, and Pearl Woods. ©1962 (Renewed 1990) EMI Longitude Music. All Rights Reserved. International Copyright Secured. Used by Permission. Reprinted with permission of Hal Leonard Corporation.

"Strange Fruit." Words and Music by Lewis Allan. Copyright © 1939 (Renewed) by Music Sales Corporation (ASCAP). All Rights for the United States controlled by Music Sales Corporation (ASCAP). International Copyright Secured. All Rights Reserved. Reprinted by Permission.

"Threats." Composed by Jean Grae. Reprinted by permission of Jean Grae.

BLACK RESONANCE

Introduction: Black Resonance

Creole began to tell us what the blues were all about. They were not about anything very new. He and his boys up there were keeping it new . . . in order to find new ways to make us listen.

—JAMES BALDWIN, "SONNY'S BLUES," 1957

Just listen to what the woman can do with a line.

—NIKKI GIOVANNI, SPEAKING TO MARGARET WALKER
ABOUT ARETHA FRANKLIN, 1974

Bessie Smith, the Empress of the Blues; Billie Holiday, Lady Day; Mahalia Jackson, the Queen of Gospel; Aretha Franklin, the Queen of Soul. As these artists' titles suggest, black women singers have dominated the major forms of twentieth-century American music. Revered as black royalty and also cited with the familiarity of kinship—as simply "Bessie," "Billie," "Mahalia," "Aretha"—these singers occupy a unique place in the national imagination.

This book centralizes their place in the African American literary imagination. It highlights the fact that, ever since Bessie Smith's improbably powerful voice conspired with the emerging "race records" industry to make her "the first real 'superstar' in African-American popular culture," black writers have memorialized the sounds and detailed the politics of black women's singing.[1] And it uses these engagements to tell a new story about how the African American literary tradition is made, who makes it, and how it sounds. I show that black women singers are not just muses for writers but innovative artists whose expressive breakthroughs illuminate literary works, which in turn reattune us to music. So the mode of analysis, and indeed the relationship between black music and literature that I propose here, is profoundly reciprocal.

Black Resonance chronicles two generations of African American artists from the 1920s to the 1970s, focusing on five writers' respective engagements with Smith, Holiday, Jackson, and Franklin. Richard Wright, Ralph Ellison, James Baldwin, Nikki Giovanni, and Gayl Jones have explored the non-narrative logic of Smith's blues, the unmistakable timbre of Holiday's voice, Franklin's signature style, and the way Jackson's gospel singing could make an audience feel like a congregation. Beginning with Smith's and Wright's landmark achievements in the recording and publishing industries—two moments when black artists spectacularly desegregate the cultural landscape of a segregated nation— I isolate the shared expressive strategies through which these artists perform new relationships to audience, community, race, gender, and each other through the end of the Black Arts Movement. As I discuss at more length in what follows, this trajectory allows me to trace and trouble the exaltation of music over text that is one of the Black Arts Movement's most enduring literary and critical legacies. This study is illustrative, not definitive; I aim to offer new directions for reading any number of writer-singer engagements not highlighted here. And there are several, for black and white American writers have cited the singers in this book and their peers with uncanny frequency throughout the twentieth century. In fiction, nonfiction, and poetry, writers have consistently figured black female singers as inspiring voices, cultural heroes, beloved mothers, imposing icons, radical stars.

Langston Hughes hails "the bellowing voice of Bessie Smith" in his seminal essay "The Negro Artist and the Racial Mountain" (1926).[2] He recounts meeting Smith with Zora Neale Hurston in his memoir *The Big Sea* (1940) and includes an "Ode to Dinah" (Washington) in *Ask Your Mama: 12 Moods for Jazz* (1961).[3] Carl Van Vechten writes a startling review of a Smith performance in "Negro 'Blues' Singers" (1926).[4] Sterling Brown and Al Young write poems for Ma Rainey (1932, 1969).[5] Jack Kerouac's Sal Paradise sings Holiday's "Lover Man" to himself in a California vineyard in *On the Road* (1957).[6] Edward Albee stages *The Death of Bessie Smith* in 1960.[7] Frank O'Hara elegizes Holiday in 1964.[8] Amiri Baraka (LeRoi Jones) famously imagines Smith's desire to "[kill] some white people" in *Dutchman* (1964); he writes several poems for Holiday, as well as one for Sarah Vaughan (1999).[9] Holiday is featured in *The Autobiography of Malcolm X* (1965), Maya Angelou's *I Know Why the Caged Bird Sings* (1969), Alice Adams's *Listening to Billie* (1977), Elizabeth Hardwick's *Sleepless Nights* (1979), and Ntozake Shange's *Sassafrass, Cypress and Indigo* (1982).[10] Sonia Sanchez writes a poem for Nina Simone in 1970.[11] Sherley Anne Williams writes a poetic meditation on Smith and a poem for Franklin "to set to music" in 1982—the same year August Wilson stages *Ma Rainey's Black Bottom*.[12] Wilson cites Smith as a key influence on his work in his preface to *Three Plays* (1991).[13] E. Ethelbert Miller's poem "Billie Holiday" appears in 1994; Fred Moten's poem

"Bessie Smith" appears in 2004.[14] Barack Obama structures a chapter of his memoir *Dreams from My Father* (1995) around listening to Holiday's recordings.[15] This list is far from exhaustive; many readers would no doubt wish to supplement it with important examples of their own.

Black Resonance began with my desire to account for this powerful refrain in American literature. A study of black music and writing that centralized the music of African American *women* seemed (as it still seems) imperative as increasingly common studies of black music and literature continued to figure music as a masculine domain best represented by male jazz and blues artists.[16] Yet my empirical, corrective impulse soon provoked a deeper conceptual aim, as I also felt it was crucial to foreground singer-writer engagements without simply celebrating female singers as inspiring muses for writers. I wanted a critical practice that would study these vocalists as artists-at-work, not only as cultural icons, and that would take their intellectual labor seriously enough to analyze their formalistic and performative choices. By "intellectual labor," I mean the intentional nature of singers' work—the fact that vocalists have specific ideas about what they want to do and make choices that produce meaningful effects. Setting women singers at the center of the story and locating the power of their music in discrete decisions should, moreover, affect the assumptions and procedures of literary criticism as well. As I explain at more length, this approach invites us to revise critical paradigms that privilege music as the culturally authenticating "source" of or model for black writing—a lasting legacy of Black Arts theorists—and thus to overturn not only the masculinist but also the musical biases extant in most studies of black music and writing.[17] My decision to centralize female singers is therefore not merely a recuperative gesture designed to "fill in the gaps" in our critical narratives—to show, for example, that black writers have always been as invested in Billie Holiday as they are in Charlie Parker and John Coltrane. Instead, my focus on female vocalists is meant to shift the grounds on which we conduct interdisciplinary analyses of black music and literature more generally.

As black feminist literary critics such as Hazel Carby, Valerie Smith, Cheryl Wall, and Deborah McDowell have long argued, we cannot simply highlight black women's contributions to male-dominated expressive traditions without developing new modes of reading those traditions—by considering, for instance, that the very notion of female "influence" may limit women more than it empowers them.[18] Such reconsiderations prompt new understandings of tradition, which are not exclusively relevant to black female subjects, although they emerge from black feminist forms of analysis. In this case, a study of female singers and writers threatens to enforce the masculinist trope of the muse, by which the female singer's value resides in her capacity to inspire male writing. This study thus necessitates—or at the very least occasions—an approach to cross-media interplay that eschews that paradigm. We might begin by recognizing that the writers in this study invoke specific singers not because black writers consistently inherit an elusive connection with the muse of black music but because these singers are *masterful artists* with whom writers choose to align themselves. We can appreciate singers' artistry when we analyze their sonic practices instead of celebrating their idealized power (the power of the muse). And this more rigorous approach to singers' art in turn encourages us to revalue writing—to see that writers do not simply absorb or respond to the power of music but instead perform their own uniquely valuable feats of analysis, expression, and effect. In short, *Black Resonance* denaturalizes the link between music and writing in order to revalue both.

Authors' accounts of iconic singers are a vital archive here. These "music writings" (the phrase mainly denotes nonfiction accounts but includes printed interviews) illuminate singers' choices and help us read the politics of vocal practice. But they also give us an interpretive language for some of the most enigmatic and innovative moves that these writers make in their own fiction and poetry. The notion that authors' commentaries on singers elucidate their own literary work should not be surprising, in the sense that any artist's commentary on another artist reflects his or her own values and aims. That we have not read these authors' particular metalanguage as such is largely due to the conceptual barriers between popular culture and more academically legitimized forms of art. In addition to deeply entrenched distinctions between "high" and "low" culture, racist and sexist tendencies to neglect the value of black women's creativity have obscured the connections between popular singers and canonized authors.

What makes the links between my chosen artists especially clear is that the writers all demonstrate a sustained preoccupation with specific singers throughout their work in multiple genres.[19] Wright relates one of his early short stories to Smith's music, dramatizes a singer named Bessie in his film of *Native Son* (1951), and quotes Smith's "Backwater Blues" in a lecture. Ellison not only writes a music review of Jackson's recordings and her performance at the 1958 Newport Jazz Festival, but he also depicts a black female "singer of spirituals" and alludes to Jackson's

"Move On Up a Little Higher" in two key moments of *Invisible Man* (1952). Baldwin claims that Smith's recordings helped him write his first novel; he cites Smith and Holiday in several essays and features recordings by Smith, Holiday, and Jackson in *Another Country* (1962). Jones has her characters in *Corregidora* (1975) invoke Holiday; she links her technique with Holiday's in an interview and titles a poem, dedicated to "BH," after Holiday's "Deep Song" (1979).[20] Giovanni writes poetic and prose works about Franklin and discusses the singer in interviews throughout her career.

Again, as these authors write (or speak) about female singers, they are always telling us something not only about music but also about their own writing. But they are never telling us everything about either. The writers in this book at times neglect important components of singers' artistry or offer misleading statements on their own. Quite simply, essays about music are not music, just as comments about novels are not novels, and citations of lyrics in poems are not songs. But when we read musical and literary works critically and on their own terms, we can better apprehend their complex imbrications, their specific points of coming together and moving apart.[21] This book is concerned with the edges between literary and vocal practice. As a genre, writings about music occupy that middle space. Emerging from the breaks between music and literature, these music commentaries offer a lexicon for writers' and singers' shared practices and thus reveal new facets of twentieth-century black aesthetics.

The shared practices that these mediating texts help me to theorize are not a product of influence. I am not suggesting that listening to female singers helps the writers in this book develop their literary techniques. What I argue is that music writings give us a lexicon that illuminates both literary and vocal practices. Thus, it is not that *music itself* enables or shapes writers' work but that authors' writings about music enable and shape our own. Ultimately, I hope this book offers a compelling view of writers and singers as equal partners in the creation of black aesthetics. I stage them as collaborators, in the etymological sense of "laboring together," as they develop analogous expressive techniques. It is not necessary that they know each other, or that vocalists sing about writers, in order for writers and singers to collaborate in this way. Their collaboration is not literal; nor is it perfectly symmetrical.[22] Writers discursively co-create musical meaning when they write about singers. As Ronald Radano writes, "The stories we tell do not simply surround the sound [of black music] but are inextricably linked to it."[23] At the same time, as Simon Frith reminds us, "'listening' itself is a performance," and the writers in this study perform their listening in different ways at different moments—which is why, as we'll see, Baldwin's Mahalia Jackson is different from Ellison's, and Jones's Holiday is different from Baldwin's.[24] Reading authors' commentaries not as timeless truths about music but as contingent, partial accounts helps us hear the many ways in which singers' work is *more* dynamic than writers may acknowledge. Authors' accounts tune us back into musical recordings themselves, inviting us to hear what writers hear *and* to listen for what they miss.[25] Both what they hear and what they miss is fair game, in my view, for elucidating literary aesthetics. As may be clear, my critical methodology in staging this collaboration involves what Houston Baker calls "inventive attention."[26] Rather than a study of influence, then, this book is best described as a search for *resonances*.

Resonance connotes reverberation, echo, the sounding again that "resound" implies. It names a "sympathetic response" or vibration between things, an elusive relationship that averts narratives of cause-and-effect but may be more diffuse and wide ranging for that.[27] What I have in mind is akin to Ellison's assertion of homologies between T. S. Eliot's poetry and Louis Armstrong's jazz:

> Consider that at least as early as T. S. Eliot's creation of a new aesthetic for poetry through the artful juxtapositioning of earlier styles, Louis Armstrong, way down the river in New Orleans, was working out a similar technique for jazz. This is not a matter of giving the music fine airs—it doesn't need them—but of saying that whatever touches our highly conscious creators of culture is apt to be reflected here.[28]

Because resonance, as a concept, signals relationships that are not causal or inevitable but are nevertheless *there*, it invites us to tease music and writing apart so as to realign them in fresh ways. Following Ellison, I contend that the aim of underscoring the creative interplay between canonized writers and popular women singers is not to confer the latter with a legitimacy they would not otherwise have, or to "give [them] airs" they don't need. It is rather to enrich our own sense of black aesthetics as a function of musical-literary reciprocity, while redressing the fact that women artists are often discursively excluded from such statements about cultural milieu as Ellison makes here.

While the formal resonances I theorize may seem elusive, I should say that these two generations of artists are closely connected and that one might certainly trace influences *within* these musical and literary lines, although I do not posit relations of influence between them. Wright helps launch Ellison's and Baldwin's careers, and however strained their personal relationships might eventually become, these writers form a kind of literary "triumvirate" by virtue of their stand-out success and their explicit and implicit responses to each other's work.[29] Although Wright dies in 1961—about seven years before Nikki Giovanni publishes her first collection of poems—Wright's essays on community-centered, vernacular-based literature are key texts for Giovanni's Black Arts contemporaries. As poet and critic Lorenzo Thomas puts it, "In the early 1960s Wright's words came to us in cheap paperback editions, but they might just as well have been engraved on tablets of stone. Many of us took them as commandments." Indeed, literary critic Stephen Henderson credits Wright (not Shakespeare) with the title of his own seminal 1973 analysis of black poetry, "The Forms of Things Unknown."[30] In the early 1970s, Giovanni conducts a remarkable televised conversation with Baldwin, whom she deems "the Dean of American Writing."[31] A few years later, Gayl Jones publishes *Corregidora*, a novel which amplifies the ambiguity of Ellison's *Invisible Man* while granting that complexity to a black female narrator. Although Giovanni and Jones are less widely celebrated than their male predecessors, they are equally central to the internally differentiated yet cohesive musical-literary tradition this book presents.

Artistically if not personally, the singers in this book are as interconnected as are their literary peers. Bessie Smith's blues recordings are formative practice tools for both Holiday and Jackson, who tell of singing along to her music while growing up. Although Smith died in 1937, five years before Aretha Franklin was born, the Empress's legacy was so potent that people would compare Franklin with Smith well into the 1970s. Franklin recorded her own cover version of Holiday's original composition "God Bless the Child" (1941), just as Holiday had covered Smith's blues. John Hammond recorded Smith's last session and Holiday's first; he later signed Jackson as well as Franklin, the young singer who would inherit Jackson's "gospel queen" mantle in the secular guise of soul.

To crystallize the foregoing claims: by theorizing aesthetic connections between these singers' and writers' work, this book makes three main interventions in the study of African American music and literature that we might broadly designate as topical, methodological, and theoretical. First, iconic black female singers are innovative artists who should be studied alongside more academically legitimized artists such as canonized African American authors. Second, whereas current approaches to black music and literature tend to treat entire genres of music like the blues as metaphors for culturally specific values like community, I focus on writers' accounts of specific singers' vocal practices, and I use these accounts to read the nuances of vocal and textual practice that standard critical narratives often miss. Finally, I propose a theoretical revaluation of the relationship between music and writing in black expressive culture by staging singers and writers as collaborators in the creation of twentieth-century black aesthetics. These interventions are interrelated, again, by my belief that centralizing black female singers necessitates new methods, which engender new theories. I elaborate these points in what follows.

The Myth of the Muse

According to stereotypical representations of black women's songs, representations that are as old as accounts of slave songs and as current as depictions of artists like Beyoncé Knowles, black women naturally sing what they feel. This reductive view of vocalists' art is especially clear when it comes to a singer such as Mary J. Blige, who publicly foregrounds the link between her biography and her music (not least by titling two of her albums *My Life* [1994, 2011]). Music critics, content to let Blige's commentary do their work for them, continually figure Blige's songs as an extension of her lived experience instead of examining the details of her musical craft.[32] Even a singer like Beyoncé, whose shape-shifting persona makes it harder to read her music as a direct conduit of biographical phenomena, is described as a force of nature instead of the technically outstanding "hardest working woman" in pop music that she is. Rich Juzwiak's laudatory review of Beyoncé's latest album, *4* (2011), for instance, compares the singer to a "hummingbird" and a "storm"; even when Juzwiak claims that Beyoncé "brims with creativity," he figures her as pure vessel rather than agent.[33] Reading this review, one would not think that Beyoncé had made a single decision about any aspect of her album, whether in terms of performance, production, composition, or design. This wholesale neglect of artistic agency is typical of discourse on black women's music.

Such representations are shaped by a discursive history throughout which the singing of black women has been coded as natural on a number of levels. First, singing itself has conventionally been figured as natural because the ability to sing, like the ability to speak, is presumed to be universal; according to this logic, everyone can sing, and some people "naturally" have good voices.[34] African Americans have historically been represented as "naturally" gifted singers and dancers. And female expression has been marked as a matter of the (sexualized) body rather than the reasoning mind.[35] These myths of song, race, and gender mean that to be a black female singer is to be coded as anti-intellectual on three different and related counts.

These myths have contributed to what Meta DuEwa Jones describes as the "gendered bias in the jazz tradition wherein singers were typically not viewed as *musicians*, let alone as skilled artists or intellectuals."[36] The deep-seated assumption that a singer is something other than a "musician" is enforced by jazz instrumentalists and also by the language singers use to describe their own work—for example, when Betty Carter states, "When it's all over for me, I would like it said that [I] was . . . a jazz musician *and* a singer."[37] Nevertheless, recent scholarship has underscored the expert musicianship—indeed, the genius—of black women singers. Robert O'Meally's and Farah Jasmine Griffin's studies of Billie Holiday are early models of scholarly works designed to dismantle the myth that black women singers naturally express their hard lives through their songs.[38] I follow these scholars in arguing that, while female vocalists' personal feelings may inform their singing in important ways, these singers are also what Ellison calls "highly conscious creators of culture." Singers' roles as culture workers become apparent when they participate in social movements, as when Mahalia Jackson sings at the March on Washington in 1963 and when Aretha Franklin headlines the "Soul Together" Concert to benefit the Martin Luther King Jr. Memorial Fund on June 28, 1968—a performance captured in this book's cover image. But singers also create culture through their subtle yet inimitable musical choices, which expand our understanding of what can be expressed, and how. These choices are the focus of my analyses.

I should perhaps say here that I certainly believe in the concept of natural talent. I believe that some singers are born prodigies, just as I support Randall Kenan's characterization of James Baldwin as a "literary prodigy."[39] What I would stress is, first, that the notion of natural "gifts" is extremely limited as an interpretive analytic and, second, that natural talent only becomes significant through conscious practice. While it is not my intention to explain how these singers (or, for that matter, writers) developed their prodigious expressive skills—although the lack of information about this process shapes my discussion of Billie Holiday in chapter 4—it is imperative to analyze the practices that years of training allow singers to effect. To analyze these practices, I draw on writers' and singers' commentaries, the work of musicologists and popular music critics, and my own vocal training. Because of this training, I approach singers' work as, in Avery Gordon's description of haunting (discussed in chapter 4), "something you have to try for yourself."[40] My own vocal limitations help me appreciate these singers' remarkable skill, some of which insight I hope to convey.

Analyzing singers' creative choices allows us to see that these artists are sources, not objects, of knowledge. When Bessie Smith sings the tragic narrative of "Backwater Blues" (1927) against a comic piano accompaniment, she creates a rich musical testament to the hazards and promises of raced and gendered alienation. When Billie Holiday insists on "pouncing" on the lyrics to "Strange Fruit" (1939), she disrupts common constellations of life, song, and voice.[41] When Mahalia Jackson combines vocal traditions such as the blues, spirituals, and opera, she reveals that gospel music might express spiritual conviction as well as a radical resourcefulness that defies creative and semantic limitations. When Aretha Franklin, in her words, "Aretha-ize[s]" a song like Otis Redding's "Respect" (1965), she shows how an artist might stamp her signature voice on another artist's lyrics—and, in the process, issue a call for black feminist collaboration, if not solidarity.[42] If these singers can be said to "inspire" twentieth-century African American writing, they do so less by providing writers with subjects for fiction and poetry than by prompting analysis of their expressive effects.[43] Here I bring writers' analyses together with singers' own comments about their work. However, because we do not have singers' extended accounts of their artistic development and techniques—in part because they have seldom been asked about either—their music itself is often the richest record of both. (This is especially true of Bessie Smith, who, unlike the other singers, did not write a memoir.) Writers crucially illuminate this musical record. At the same time, as I have said, their writings tune us back into the music itself.

The singers in this study composed the music and lyrics to roughly half of the songs I will discuss. Even when they did not, however, I understand their performances as acts of authorship. Performance is generally considered the stepchild of composition, denoting "mere" execution instead of agency and origination. But if we take seriously the idea that execution *creates*—and does not simply "enhance"—meaning, then we can see performance as creative authorship. We need not collapse literary and vocal authorship in order to do this. Writers compose text; singers often do not. But for singers whose repertoire is composed mainly of songs written (and performed) by other artists, authorship resides in inventive execution. Giovanni asserts the porous relation between origination and innovation through the title of the book in which her "Poem for Aretha" appears, *Re:Creation* (1970). The title references creation (re: creation) and also *sounds* re-creation, making seen and sounded meanings close kin. As Zora Neale Hurston argues in "Characteristics of Negro Expression" (1934), "What we really mean by originality is the modification of ideas. The most ardent admirer of the great Shakespeare cannot claim first source even for him. [His originality lies in] his treatment of the borrowed material."[44] Like the other singers in this book, Franklin performs her own original "treatment of borrowed material" as she covers songs originally written and performed by other artists. Her brilliant approach to this process makes it possible for Giovanni to claim that "Aretha has made *another statement* in terms of music" and explains why Ray Charles insists she be ranked "among the creators . . . , people who genuinely create the sound that other people wish they could do."[45]

It should be said, however, that the writers in this study have not always expressed this understanding of singers' artistry, even as they have figured singers as inspirations for their own. Instead, writers at times enforce a long tradition of figuring authorship as male and inspiration as female; this tradition "excludes woman from the creation of culture" while objectifying her as "an artifact within culture."[46] In making this point, I hope to check the critical tendency to celebrate African American writers' invocations of women singers without examining the often troubling gender dynamics such invocations advance. Here it is necessary to repeat Deborah McDowell's assertion that black feminist critique operates not against but rather "in clear service of a transformative [racial] politics."[47] We must ask, for instance, how rigid notions of black masculinity limit male authors' ability to identify with female singers. Feminist scholars have shown that the trope of the muse represents female vocality as an otherworldly, irrational force that exists to inspire, and to be mastered by, the male author's writing.[48] Identification with feminized music is a risk for black men themselves historically figured as, in Robert Park's infamous formulation, "the lady among the races."[49] A male writer who explicitly identifies with female song, as Baldwin does, runs the risk of symbolic emasculation—*especially* in the earlier part of the twentieth century, before Baraka and others (hetero-)normalize this gesture. This risk partly explains why Wright and Ellison, rather than explicitly link singers'

techniques with their own, hint at these connections through a reflex-
ively illuminating metalanguage about black female song. If Baldwin's
more fluid approach to sexuality can be seen to enable his identification with Smith,[50] I am convinced that Jones and Giovanni voice their
alliances with Holiday and Franklin because these women writers are
relatively unfettered by the gender biases that compel Wright and Ellison to keep such identifications oblique.

Singular Collaborations

Whether implicit or overt, the connections between singers and
writers that most interest me regard the formal, stylistic, and performative details of these artists' work. By highlighting the performative
facets of singers' art, I address an aspect of music that literary critics
tend to neglect, which is how it sounds. Insofar as critics examine lyrics, themes, structural principles, and musicians' biographies in lieu of
musical sound, "black music" still names a kind of negative imprint or
outline, an absence captured in Wright's phrase for black oral folklore,
"the Forms of Things Unknown." Indeed, critics' occlusion of sonic
detail may reflect a political view akin to Wright's: that music signifies
the generic, undifferentiated "voice of the people." This view of music is
not unique to African American culture, but for our purposes, we can
trace it back to W. E. B. Du Bois's discussion of the "sorrow songs" in *The
Souls of Black Folk* (1903) and forward to Amiri Baraka's contention that
the blues remain the "exact replication of the Black Man In The West."[51]
Thanks especially to Black Arts theorists like Baraka, critical approaches
to black music and literature still tend to treat entire genres of music,
such as the blues, as central metaphors for black life and African American "social ideas, concepts, and ideals."[52] According to this paradigm,
music itself expresses culturally specific values and imperatives—for
example, the importance of community and improvisation—that we
can also find in, or map onto, African American literature. Blues-related
ambiguity (the refusal of "either-or" binaries) and structures of call and
response are central concepts in this hermeneutic, which continues to
yield interesting literary interpretations especially with regard to theme.
Moreover, as I will discuss in more detail, this methodology has been
instrumental in establishing the discipline of African American literary
criticism and building its institutional homes.

At present, however, the practice of treating black music as a metaphor for black life and literature often obscures the very nuances that

interdisciplinary scholarship should reveal. This is because abstracting and idealizing music is a bit like idealizing people: it simplifies them and thereby diminishes their connections with others. But listening to specific singers' vocal practices encourages us to theorize more precise connections between these vocalists and the writers who engage their work. So while lyrics, themes, and structural principles like repetition will certainly play a part in my analyses, it is hard to overstate my critical investment in the details of musical sound. In addition to O'Meally and Griffin, several scholars in the fields of popular music, jazz, and performance studies—among them Sherrie Tucker, Gayle Wald, Daphne Brooks, Jayna Brown, and Alexandra Vazquez—demonstrate similar investments,[53] and I aim to bring African American literary criticism into closer alignment with the exciting developments in the study of black women's performance that these scholars' work represents. At the same time, if scholars of popular music and sound studies have something to teach literary critics about the importance of musical sound, then black feminist literary criticism and theory—as well as literary language itself—should further attune popular music and sound studies scholars to black female singers' complex art, as well as temper performance studies' longstanding skepticism toward print culture. The written texts I examine elucidate the nuances of vocal as well as literary art and reveal more specific links between singers and writers than do thematic and structural principles like blues ambiguity and call-and-response. I use these texts to develop metaphors for shared vocal and literary aesthetics—"lyricism," "understatement," "haunting"—and in this way I propose an alternative to the traditional method of reading music itself as a metaphor for all other black art.

I develop this critical lexicon by taking writers at their word and beyond it and reading for the singularity of the writer-singer engagement. Taking Ellison at his word means, for instance, assuming that he has unique and specific reasons for writing a review of Jackson's performance at the Newport Jazz Festival in 1958—rather than folding his essay on Jackson into the superstructure of his other music writings on male jazz musicians such as Louis Armstrong and Charlie Parker. Taking Ellison *beyond* his word means asking what he is describing when he invokes Jackson's "timbre of sincerity," why he feminizes this quality, and how this concept elucidates his own work. This approach does not deny consonances between what Ellison says about Jackson and what he says about other musicians (there are some). Nor does it suggest that female singers are *more* important to the writers in this study than are any other musicians they cite (although I believe they are, for Baldwin, Jones, and Giovanni). But I isolate these specific connections in order to alter standard critical narratives about these writers and their musical counterparts.

These authors' necessarily inventive linguistic responses to musical sound compel a newly attentive—if not inventive—critical practice. What does Wright mean when he says Smith's blues lift everyday details "to a plane of vividness that strikes one with wonderment"? What is Ellison responding to when he invokes Jackson's "timbre of sincerity"? Why does Baldwin praise Smith's "understatement"? Why do Holiday's listeners call her voice "haunting"? And what is Giovanni describing when she speaks of Franklin's "signature voice"?[54] I theorize these statements in order to develop a new vocabulary for reading musical and literary aesthetics. This vocabulary helps us see that there is a "vividly lyrical" aspect of Wright's supposedly naturalistic prose, a "timbre of sincerity" in Ellison's narrative voice that counters the practice of masking he privileged, a theory of understatement that shapes Baldwin's supposedly "overstated" work, a concrete narrative strategy that makes Jones's work "haunting," a "signature voice" that for Giovanni relies more on exploiting print than it does on aspiring to speech or song. These terms are not exclusively relevant to the artists who inspire their theorization. Ellison and Jackson deploy "vivid lyricism" along with Wright and Smith; we could analyze other artists' signature voices. But I associate specific artists with specific terms for the sake of clarity and in order to accent the aesthetic variation among this ensemble.

The methodology of each chapter also varies, alternately foregrounding unpublished archival material and well-circulated ideas and striking different balances between musical and literary analyses. First, because the writers in this book become increasingly candid about identifying with female singers, these alliances become rather more likely (and less dependent on unpublished work) as we proceed. Further, singers occupy a greater portion of each subsequent chapter, a structure that reflects what I take to be the growing importance of each singer to each writer's literary imagination. Thus, my discussion of Bessie Smith is subordinated to my reading of Richard Wright's work in the first chapter; equal space and analysis is afforded Gayl Jones and Billie Holiday in chapter 4 and Aretha Franklin and Nikki Giovanni in chapter 5. Finally, while I establish a reciprocal relationship between singer and writer in each chapter, the book's overall trajectory enacts this reciprocity on a broader scale. The first two chapters use Wright's and Ellison's nonfiction writings about Smith and Jackson to reread these writers' creative works. Chapter 3 serves as a hinge into the more musically oriented analyses of chapters 4 and 5 because this middle chapter engages and deepens the notion that writers' work reattunes us to singers' vocal art. My last two chapters accordingly take Jones's fiction and Giovanni's poetry as a lens through which to analyze Holiday's and Franklin's work, respectively.

While dominant critical narratives stress Wright's sexism and obscure his investment in black music, chapter 1 foregrounds his engagement with black women singers. Here I show how Wright's discussion of Bessie Smith's blues in an unpublished 1941 essay gives us a language for Wright's own "vividly lyrical" prose style and also illuminates the role of black women singers in Wright's film adaptation of *Native Son*, which stars Wright himself as Bigger Thomas and transforms Bigger's lover, Bessie, into a singer. The film represents black song as a medium of alliance between black men and women. This new vision is enabled by Wright's collaboration with visual artists and by his work outside the United States, both of which diminish his anxiety about inviting sentimental readings of his work. Overall, this chapter aligns Smith and Wright on the basis of their shared expressive style and lifelong creative improvisations on the condition of exile or marginalization.

Chapter 2 likewise links Ralph Ellison and Mahalia Jackson on the basis of their similar artistic techniques, but it moves these complex expressive techniques from margin to center by contending that these artists aim to create, instead of reacting to, imagined audience. When we read Ellison's narrative voice in *Invisible Man* for the complex and ambivalent "timbre of sincerity" he ascribes to Jackson, we can see that the practice of masking before an imagined opposition is only part of Ellison's literary aesthetic. The other part is his centralization of black expressive ambivalence before an audience that is not determined in advance.

Chapter 3 shows Baldwin re-privileging black listeners at a moment of integration when black music is perhaps too thoroughly "centered" in American culture. I bring Baldwin into conversation with Smith and Holiday less by theorizing their shared literary and musical practice than by studying Baldwin's interpretive listening, which I figure as literary accompaniment. Whereas Baldwin's comments on Smith's and Holiday's musical "understatement" assert a gendered power to decode these singers' music, his novel *Another Country* suggests that the writer's role is not only to detect but also to co-create understatement, and indeed Baldwin's later work increasingly makes him a co-creator of musical meaning, rather than a privileged decoder or beneficiary of it.

Chapter 4 elaborates the notion of writer as collaborative supporting figure while also returning to an analysis of shared literary and vocal techniques. Here I show that Jones's "haunting" practice in her novel *Corregidora* illuminates Holiday's "haunting" practice in her changing renditions of "Strange Fruit." Reversing the usual procedure by which critics start with set ideas about the blues to interpret Jones's "blues novel," I instead contend that the novel provokes questions about music and specifically asks us to rethink what we already "know" about Holiday's art. In short, *Corregidora* reanimates the cultural archive of stories about Holiday's life and work.

The final chapter turns back to the late 1960s to tell a new story about the Black Arts Movement itself. In this effort, I join a wave of scholars who are challenging the "caricature" of the movement that is the product of our own more conservative moment.[55] Staging this book's most bidirectional analysis, I read Nikki Giovanni and Aretha Franklin's mutual support or accompaniment of each other through the figure of the backup singer. By positioning Giovanni and Franklin as interdependent Black Arts leaders and by arguing that both artists' "signature voices" exploit the interplay between speech, song, and print, I revise the paradigm that privileges music over writing during Black Arts and thereafter. Put differently, this chapter aims to prompt new ways of conceiving the relationship between writing and song by showing that their relationship was never fixed even within the movement that inaugurated our current bias toward the latter. Finally, my epilogue offers a brief analysis of twenty-first-century poetry, hip hop, and classic soul in order to show how contemporary black women artists such as poet Linda Susan Jackson and rapper Jean Grae are expanding the musical-literary canon to include relatively unsung heroines such as the late, great Etta James.

Reciprocal Songs

That this musical-literary canon is mutable, contingent, and flexible is among the most basic tenets of this book. As Hortense Spillers reminds us, "Traditions are not born. They are made."[56] A brief genealogy will elucidate this "making" as it pertains to the dominant critical narrative about black music and literature that I aim to revise. This genealogy will remind us that the theorists and writers who initially privileged orality and music in discussions of black writing did so as a matter of strategy, not fact. They did so in order to make a political and institutional case for the cultural specificity and disobedient dynamism of African American fiction and poetry. As this strategy settles into received disciplinary wisdom, however, as engagement with black music comes to seem like a *feature* of African American writing instead of a practice black writers perform, we can lose sight of the dynamic alliances that the case for a music-literature continuum was initially designed to highlight and promote. So it is useful to contextualize current scholarly assumptions in order to recall their motivating politics and to revitalize those politics for our own time.

First, as I have discussed this project, people have asked how my approach squares with the historical primacy of black oral and musical forms: doesn't it make sense to privilege music given that prohibitions on black literacy meant that the vast majority of black people in America were singing, preaching, and so on before they wrote books and poems? There are several ways to answer this question, for example by noting that African American vernacular culture itself synthesizes print and oral technologies and that the notion that music "comes first" only nominally illuminates the work of those who choose print literature as their primary medium.[57] However, a more direct response to what I have come to consider "the history question" is that the question is itself the product of a particular and powerful narrative about African American literature's oral foundations that was developed in the mid-1960s. The point of this narrative was to explain that art created by black Americans was culturally distinct, vital, and beautiful on its own terms—in short, to codify "the Black Aesthetic."

Black writers and theorists of the 1960s were the first in the history of African American literature to collectively figure music as the superior alternative to what was increasingly viewed as the oppressive and elitist medium of print. Writers now associated with the Harlem Renaissance of the 1920s and '30s did not advance this view. While many Renaissance writers innovated literature by representing black "folk" expression in fiction and poetry, they rarely framed print culture itself as a problem. Instead, what we see in writing from this period is the use of print literature to archive, evoke, and celebrate musical and oral vernacular practices—whether through the poetry-prose form of Jean Toomer's *Cane* (1923) (a "swan-song" for the "folk spirit" that Toomer believed spirituals and work songs expressed),[58] the "speakerly text" of Hurston's *Their Eyes Were Watching God* (1937),[59] or the blues poems of Hughes's *Weary Blues* (1926) and *Fine Clothes to the Jew* (1927). When Hughes formalizes the blues on the page, he invents a new literary genre; he thus expands the possibilities of literature while also valorizing the blues as a poetic form. (This figuration of the blues as poetry anticipates current conversations about hip hop, as I discuss in the epilogue.) In short, the writers associated with the Harlem Renaissance do not, as a general rule, posit print culture as the domain of white supremacy and black music as the medium of black revolutionary agency. Stephen Henderson is thus onto something rather different from his forebears when, in 1973, he asks "wherein" the "Blackness" of very different black poets lies, ventures to locate it "in Black speech, and in the movement toward the forms of Black music," and so concludes that "structurally speaking . . . , whenever Black poetry is most distinctly and effectively Black, it derives its form from two basic sources, Black speech and Black music."[60]

Through such analyses, Henderson and his contemporaries generate what I term the *music-text hierarchy*. This hierarchy establishes a binary opposition between "(black) orality" and "(white) literacy," while privileging music over writing as the more immediate, authentic form of expression. This binary too cleanly separates orality from literacy and falsely constructs "black expression" as oral instead of written. Yet there are several viable grounds on which Black Arts–era theorists instantiate it. According to these theorists: historically, print embodied the medium through which black history had been systematically erased or distorted; economically, print signified a literary marketplace owned and dominated by white people; sociologically, print constituted the province of the bourgeoisie, who could afford to buy books and spend time reading them—if, that is, they possessed the requisite print literacy (poetry becomes the movement's chosen genre in part because it costs less, requires less time, and can be performed verbally); philosophically, print represented Enlightenment conceptions of rationality and, indeed, humanity constructed to exclude black people; anthropologically, print represented a Western focus on product, individualism, and disembodiment, in contrast to the process, community, and living embodiment of "oral" African cultures; ontologically, print signified stasis and fixity, as opposed to the dynamism of sound.

These are all compelling grounds on which to advance a bias toward music—or, in Cheryl Clarke's memorable formulation, to cast black poetry of the Black Arts era as "a poor relation of black music."[61] The problem is that, instead of seeing this bias as the product of a particular moment—as *ideology*—we tend to reify it as truth. We are apt to point to Frederick Douglass's claim that the slave songs better express "the soul-killing effects of slavery" than "whole volumes . . . on the subject" might do—less apt to see that ideology is what sifts such passages to the tradition's surface.[62] So it is helpful to recall, as Evie Shockley points out, that Houston Baker's and Henry Louis Gates Jr.'s influential theories of the black literary aesthetic follow closely on the heels of Black Arts. Like their immediate predecessors, Baker and Gates privilege orality in their quest to identify, as Gates writes in *The Signifying Monkey* (1988), "whatever is black about black American literature."[63] Moreover, the practice of invoking culturally black expressive forms such as "signifying" as models and metaphors for literature was a key strategy through which scholars in the field argued that writings by black people constituted a distinctive literary tradition—and not only because of authors' shared "melanin and subject matter," in Toni Morrison's terms.[64] At once authenticating and denaturalizing (in its appeals to *culture*), this strategy helped literary critics contribute to the broader argument that any true understanding of African American and, by extension, American life would require expert faculty, specialized courses of study, and autonomous Black Studies departments. In short, the Black Arts and Black Power Movements precipitated the institutionalization of the study of black literature, and African American literary criticism remains indebted to ideas about the primacy of oral culture that were generated as that critical practice was being institutionalized.[65]

Thus, in 1984, Baker theorizes the "blues matrix" as the foundational feature of black literature and culture.[66] In 1988, Gates asserts that the problem which confronts the authors of slave narratives—and, consequently, each writer in the African American literary tradition—is that of "recording an authentic black voice" in the "white written text," so that the "Talking Book" is the "ur-trope of the Anglo-African tradition."[67] Cornel West later claims that "music and rhetorical practices, especially black preaching practices, have been the two major traditions owing to the exclusion of black people in other spheres, even though many of us venture in those fields."[68] Paul Gilroy posits black music "as a cipher for the ineffable, sublime, pre-discursive and anti-discursive elements in black expressive culture," a "cipher" that becomes crucial for "racially subordinated people who are denied access to . . . the world of written communication."[69] Even as more recent theorists have sought to unsettle the binary between black orality and literacy, their attempts to deconstruct the difference—for instance, by suggesting that black oral forms phonographically reproduce themselves without writing— often create an imbalanced equation whereby print is phonographic only when it evokes (through musical structure or speakerliness) a sound that is inherently so.[70] Put simply, the suggestion is that black writing depends on music in a way that music has never depended on writing.

Moreover, such a view is often supported by writers themselves—who, though by definition *not* "denied access to . . . the world of written communication," have nonetheless valorized music as a model for their work with printed language since the 1960s. As Gayl Jones states, "Many African American fiction writers and poets acknowledge the superiority of the black musician as artist."[71] In 1961, Baldwin tells Studs Terkel that he wants to write the way Bessie Smith sings; in 1968, he tells his siblings the same thing about Aretha Franklin.[72] Baraka claims that Black Arts poets "wanted our poetry to *be* black music."[73] Toni Cade Bambara suggests that "music is probably the only mode we have used to speak of [the complexity of the black experience]."[74] Alice Walker asserts that in her writing, she is "trying to arrive at that place where black music already is; to arrive at that unself-conscious sense of collective oneness; that naturalness, that (even when anguished) grace."[75] And Toni Morrison offers the characteristically compelling prophecy that "what has already happened with [black] music in the States, the literature will do one day and when that happens it's all over."[76]

Black Resonance is methodologically designed to offer alternatives to this musical bias and is structurally designed to denaturalize it: the following chapters read music and writing reciprocally while tracing the historical process by which music gains ascendancy over literature in the writerly imagination. I mark this shift to Baldwin, who must be seen as a forerunner of and participant in the Black Arts Movement.[77] Baldwin's aspirational claims about black women singers not only extend a tradition of gay men's engagements with (black) female vocalists but also promote a vision of music as a source of culturally specific knowledge through which to imagine black community.[78] This vision of music continues to perform important cultural work today. By privileging music as a sign of collective struggle, post–Black Arts writers such as Gayl Jones, Walker, and Morrison seek to maintain a sense of black community at a time when African Americans are increasingly fractured along class lines and still imperiled by unjust sentencing, housing, education, and hiring practices—but now amid a dominant culture that tends to believe such problems were eradicated decades ago, by the Civil Rights Movement (to say nothing, yet, of the election of a black president).

These conditions help explain why the music-text hierarchy established in the 1960s still shapes contemporary scholarship. It is not just that critics take their interpretive cues from the commentary of writers, regarding the importance of music to their work. The deeper reason is that black artists and scholars often share historical precedents and political aims. If the argument that African American writers evoke speech and music entered the academy as a strategy of canon formation, the notion of music's radical primacy persists in part due to scholars' ambivalence toward historically white academic institutions and the class and generational divides they exploit and perpetuate. In such contexts, it becomes important for scholars to mark off black music as that which cannot be institutionalized—*even if* it can be taught, for instance, in the hip hop courses that are currently in demand at universities all over the country. Like Black Arts activists before them, contemporary scholars in the field of African American Studies posit music as a sign of racial unity—a culturally specific medium of community building and resistance that has always been relatively free from creative and social restrictions. This image of music continues to resonate as Black Studies is "embraced" by institutions that have historically rejected black people— and, more precisely, as key aims of Black Studies, such as fostering community activism and antiracism, clash with key values of predominantly white institutions, such as promoting diversity and "tolerance."[79]

When applied to African American literary criticism, the notion that music is uniquely free from systemic constraints risks implying that engagement with music consistently helps black writers, in approximately the same way, to resist restrictive (white) literary forms. The problem, as I see it, is less that this view essentializes musicians and writers—as Gayatri Spivak reminds us, essentialism can be a powerful political tool[80]—and more that it *divides* them. Again, to idealize music is to abstract and separate it from writing. One of the aims of this study is to show that neither black writers *nor* musicians have ever been free from social restrictions, but that both have nonetheless performed their own insurgent acts of expression and effect. When we cease idealizing music as a generic model for literature, we can attend to the material practices through which vocalists craft innovative musical performances and to the analogous practices through which writers advance their own literary voices. We can recover the sounds that make writers want to align themselves with musicians in the first place and the literary effects that could make such an effort worthwhile. So whether or not one believes music to be the supreme (black) art form, my point is that this view has outworn its utility for *literary* criticism. It is time to include writers as full partners in the complex narratives of community, resistance, and transformation that we tell about black music. I hope that the collaborative process I stage here will make a case for deeper, more precise connections between artists working in these media without privileging either one.

For a basic example of what this would mean, we might turn to the canon-establishing *Norton Anthology of African American Literature* (1997; 2nd ed., 2003), edited by Henry Louis Gates Jr., Nellie McKay, and other leading scholars in the field.[81] The text is a paragon of the music-text hierarchy I have described, as well as a proof of the claim that an idealized image of music as "source" segregates it from writing. The anthology presents literary works in chronological order, from "The Literature of Slavery and Freedom" to "Literature since 1975." But it begins with a section called "The Vernacular Tradition," which features texts of sermons, folktales, and blues and hip hop songs. Along with the introductory essay, "Talking Books" (much redacted from a section of *The Signifying Monkey*), the anthology's structure serves to propose that, in the closing words of the editors' preface,

> The authors of these works . . . have made the text of Western letters speak in voices and timbres resonant, resplendent, and variously "black." Taken together, they form a literary tradition in which African American authors collectively affirm that the will to power is the will to write and to testify eloquently in aesthetic forms never far removed from the language of music and the rhythmic resonance of the spoken word.[82]

Or, as Stephen Henderson had put it thirty years earlier, "Structurally speaking . . . , whenever Black poetry is most distinctly and effectively Black, it derives its form from two basic sources, Black speech and Black music." With the *Norton Anthology*, we see how effective such claims would ultimately be for delineating "a literary tradition."

In the preface to the volume, Gates and McKay explain that they place the oral material at the beginning of the anthology "because, historically, anonymous vernacular literature certainly preceded the tradition of written letters among African Americans, and because *all* of the world's literatures have developed from an oral base"—a statement that would be hard to quibble with if "anonymous vernacular literature" were the only kind of oral expression the editors included in the opening section.[83] But that section also includes works by Bessie Smith, Duke

Ellington, C. L. Franklin, Malcolm X, and Queen Latifah. Because *all* the book's oral material—from traditional work-song lyrics to classic hip hop rhymes—is placed at the start of the volume, the book makes the chronologically impossible suggestion that all black music is the source of all modern African American writing. But this structure not only produces a wrenched chronology. It also undermines the editors' own claim that "oral expression—the dozens, signifying, rap poetry—surrounds the written tradition rather as a Möbius strip intertwines above and below a plane," "continu[ing] to nurture it, comment upon it, and criticize it in a dialectical, reciprocal relation."[84] Oral expression does not "surround" the written in this volume; it births it.

My prior discussion will have indicated that I support the female representation among the musicians in the anthology as well as the inclusion of a CD that allows us to hear the music itself. But one practical extension of this book's argument is that, if musical texts are to be included in an anthology of African American literature at all, they must be integrated with literary selections: Jean Toomer should appear alongside his contemporary Bessie Smith, Chuck D alongside Rita Dove. This format would *amplify* "the role of the vernacular in shaping our written tradition," while also signaling the role of writing in shaping black music.[85] It would acknowledge that the literary tradition must be the other side of the "dialectical, reciprocal relation" that Gates and McKay describe. Writers continue "to nurture . . . , comment upon . . . , and criticize" the musicians who inform their work. By responding to singers' unique expressive skills—"Just listen to what [Franklin] can do with a *line*"—writers consistently create, in Baldwin's words, "new ways to make us listen."

Finally, acknowledging writers' discursive contributions to this tradition allows us to see that they have collectively helped canonize musicians whose iconicity we now take for granted. What made the women's blues of the 1920s and '30s the "classic blues," according to Baraka, was that these artists' recordings circulated so widely as to shape a generation of singers' styles: "The phonograph record increased one thousandfold the . . . popularity and imitation of certain blues singers" and thus "*created* whole styles of blues-singing."[86] Baraka is describing a form of active and generative (rather than passive) consumption, whereby U.S. consumers help *make* singers "classic" by adopting their musical styles—and here we might think of a young Billie Holiday singing along with Bessie Smith's recordings in Baltimore, and Mahalia Jackson doing the same in New Orleans. Writers participate in this consecrating process as well. The authors in this book often write about singers whom they have studied through recordings, and often do so after the singers have died. In this sense, they sustain and reanimate a tradition that arrives as an archive, in Diana Taylor's sense of "supposedly enduring materials"—and, in the case of Baldwin and Jones, as a reissued archive.[87] This process is complex. In a 1959 essay, Baldwin explains that he once regarded Smith as an embarrassingly brash figure and never listened to her music "in the same way that, for years, [he] would not touch watermelon."[88] But he ultimately helped revive her reputation. To recall Spillers's point, traditions are made, not born, and one reason why Smith has enjoyed an iconic afterlife since the 1960s is that writers like Baldwin, Baraka, singer-critic Abbey Lincoln, and poet Sherley Anne Williams have made the archive of her recordings signify anew. In ways that are dependent on yet distinct from market forces, these writers help figure these singers as icons, reinvesting value in titles, such as "Empress" and "Queen," that always begin as promotional strategies. Taken together, their work constitutes an alternative historiography. This book is at once a study and a result of their labors.

Earlier, I cited Ellison's statement about T. S. Eliot's and Louis Armstrong's contemporaneous development of modernist aesthetics. Ellison insists that to make a case for their relationship "is not a matter of giving the music fine airs—it doesn't need them—but of saying that whatever touches our highly conscious creators of culture is apt to be reflected here [in jazz, as well as in poetry]." I stressed the need to recognize that female musicians, whom Ellison rarely cites in such discussions, are equally key participants in the "conscious creation" of an era's aesthetics. Indeed, while I have said a great deal about denaturalizing Black Arts–era conceptions of music, I hope this study also honors and extends the Black Arts project of canon expansion. Namely, by showing that popular singers like Billie Holiday and Aretha Franklin have done as much to revolutionize expressive language as canonized writers like Richard Wright and Ralph Ellison have, I hope to expand our sense of who counts as cultural innovators and as legitimate subjects of intellectual inquiry.

In a post-Ellison moment, it also becomes necessary to reverse Ellison's formulation—to stress that black writers innovate these aesthetics just as black musicians do. The point of claiming singers and writers' shared ground is not to give literature airs—it doesn't need them. It is rather to show that writers and singers both maximize the expressive resources available to them, in their chosen media. None of these media say it all. A song is not a novel, and a printed poem is not a live performance. Yet the sheer fact of each medium's limited expressive resources means that each medium is *as good a site as any* to try to make language account for experience. In sending their attempts to capture and create experience out into the world, both writers and singers have always called out for a response they are never assured of effecting. But I suggest they have done so together.

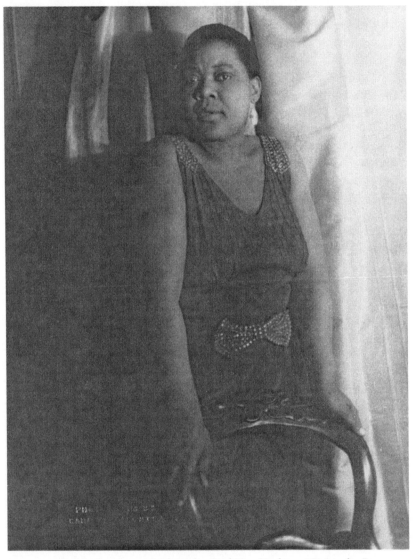

FIGURE 1. Bessie Smith, 1936. Photo by Carl Van Vechten / Beinecke Rare Book and Manuscript Library.

1 / Vivid Lyricism: Richard Wright and Bessie Smith's Blues

This chapter highlights Richard Wright's alignment of his work with Bessie Smith's, thus establishing the relationship between male writers and female singers that the next two chapters will also explore. Although Wright's fiction often depicts black song as a feminized threat to black male resistance, his unpublished 1941 essay "Memories of My Grandmother" attunes us to moments in Wright's work when feminized lyricism itself functions as a medium of resistance. Wright uses such lyricism to protest black alienation from U.S. society in general and from the domain of the literary in particular. His widely neglected film of *Native Son* (1951) takes this revalorization of feminized song a step further by granting black female singers themselves the voice of critique, or what I term *outsider's insight*. Hence, even Wright, whose work is generally thought to devalue both black women *and* black music, creates nonfictional and cinematic works in which song becomes the medium of expressive alliance between black men and women. Wright does not imagine that either singers or writers can escape social restrictions. But what aligns him with blues singers like Smith is that they creatively manipulate racialized social exclusion in similar ways—namely, by joining forces with other "exiles" to create incisive, vivid responses to disenfranchisement.

In 1949, Wright traveled to Buenos Aires to film the novel that, nine years earlier, had made him the biggest mainstream African American literary celebrity since Frederick Douglass. Wright himself starred as *Native Son*'s protagonist, Bigger Thomas, the young black Chicagoan who inadvertently murders his white employer's daughter, goes into hiding, murders his own lover, Bessie, and is captured, tried, and sentenced to death. Wright's starring role alone made the film a landmark event—as Kyle Westphal notes, it's hard to think of "another film where an American author literally enacts his major novel"—and, despite the dubious decision to have Wright play a character who was by then twenty years his junior, the film received rave reviews when it opened in Argentina in 1951.[1] But when it opened in New York three months later, critics panned it, and its U.S. reception has determined its fate ever since.[2] James Baldwin, a master of the elegant assault, may have delivered the most memorable blow in his essay on Wright, "Alas, Poor Richard" (1961). There Baldwin simply notes that he and a friend ran into Wright one day, shortly after Wright had "returned from wherever he had been to film *Native Son*. (In which, to our horror, later abundantly justified, he himself played Bigger Thomas.)"[3] Aside from this glib (and, I would say, unjustified) review of Wright's acting, the few scholars who have addressed *Native Son*'s cinematic incarnation have generally framed it as a "filmic fiasco"—or, at best, a "fascinating failure."[4]

It is unclear whether Baldwin actually saw *Native Son*, but if he had, one wonders what he would have made of the "makeover" the film gives Bigger's girlfriend, Bessie Mears. Especially considering Baldwin's own persistent engagement with black women singers like Bessie Smith and Billie Holiday, he may have been intrigued to see that Bessie, a long-suffering victim in the novel, becomes a beautiful singer (played by Gloria Madison) in the film. A pivotal scene dramatizes Bessie's transformation from page to screen. In the novel, Bigger accompanies his employer's daughter, Mary Dalton, and her white boyfriend, Jan Erlone, to a South Side restaurant called Ernie's Kitchen Shack; he dolefully encounters Bessie there, drinking at the bar. In the film, the Kitchen Shack becomes a stylish nightclub at which Bessie is the featured performer. Dressed in a lovely white evening gown, Bessie performs a sensual song while encircling Bigger and his new "friends." Bigger's mother, Hannah, though not as radically transformed as Bessie, also acquires a new unsentimental grandeur in the film, particularly through another scene of song. In the novel, Hannah sings a hymn that "irks" Bigger; we are meant to understand that the song represents a fatalistic response to black suffering that Bigger can neither accept nor effectively challenge.[5] Yet in the film, when Hannah prays along to a hymn at a church service, the congregation seems to threaten not Bigger's agency but rather the white policemen and investigators who have entered the church to hunt him down.

These scenes of black women and song are surprising because they simultaneously unsettle two rather basic critical assumptions about Wright and his work. The first is that, as feminist critics have long pointed out, Wright consistently denigrates black female authority.[6] The second is that he does not value African American music.[7] The latter assumption thrives in spite of Wright's thorough and supportive engagement with black music in "Blueprint for Negro Writing" (1937) and *White Man, Listen!* (1957)—works which, as I noted in the introduction, were important to Black Arts theorists. In light of influential writings by critics like Ralph Ellison and, later, Henry Louis Gates Jr., both of whom downplay Wright's investment in the blues, it is easy to forget that Wright himself is a key force behind Black Arts valorizations of music—and, indeed, that it is *Wright's* work which occasions Ellison's seminal definition of the blues, in "Richard Wright's Blues" (1945), as "an autobiographical chronicle of personal catastrophe expressed lyrically."[8] Still, the notion that Wright devalues black music is not entirely misguided, for Wright's treatment of this subject is ambivalent, and even his positive readings of the spirituals and blues do not express the proud love of black music that animates the work of Langston Hughes, Zora Neale Hurston, and his other contemporaries. Indeed, as Wright's depiction of Hannah's hymns in the novel *Native Son* suggests, his work often problematizes the black musical practices from which Ellison would claim Wright was tragically alienated.[9]

Standard accounts of Wright's work constellate his sexism, his supposed neglect of black music, and his writerly style. Lyricism is not a quality for which Wright is known—this despite the fact that Wright himself rejects "simple literary realism" in "Blueprint for Negro Writing" and encourages black writers to engage the "complexity, the strangeness, the magic wonder of life."[10] Such comments notwithstanding, Wright is framed as a naturalist-cum-existentialist whose writing expresses the dire facts of black life in hard-boiled prose. There is no place in such a project for the celebration of music or the stylization of what might be termed "musical" writing. Thus, Gates locates "the great divide" in African American literature in the "fissure" between the "lyrical shape" of Hurston's *Their Eyes Were Watching God* (1937) and the "naturalism" of (the novel) *Native Son* (1940).[11] Wright's supposedly amusical prose can appear to be an extension of his supposed machismo. This interpretation is especially tempting if one takes his scathing (and sexist) critique of Hurston's novel, in which he claims that Hurston's "prose is cloaked in that facile sensuality that has dogged Negro expression since the days of Phillis Wheatley," as a countermanifesto for his own work.[12]

The impulse to associate Wright's masculinism with hard-boiled writing would comport with early twentieth-century developments in the gendering of prose styles. As John Dudley points out, lyrical or highly wrought prose was marked as effeminate and decadent by influential U.S. naturalists like Frank Norris and Jack London, for whom "the figure of the aesthete . . . came to represent the ineffectual languor of a feminized aristocracy."[13] Wright's own influential predecessors, in other words, coded no-frills realism as "masculine" writing and rejected the soft lyricism of "feminine" prose. Yet this chapter is sparked by my own conviction that Bessie's and Hannah's cinematic incarnations encourage us to develop an alternative critical narrative about Wright's musical, gender, and prose politics—one that could account for these powerful cinematic scenes in which Wright literally makes his work sing, as well as for figuratively "songlike" passages in his writing. What do we make, for instance, of the sonorous, visionary writing—even purple prose—Wright deploys in texts like his memoir *Black Boy* (1945), when he describes "the quiet terror that suffused [his] senses when vast hazes of gold washed earthward from star-heavy skies on silent nights"?[14] What does it mean that Ellison calls such moments in *Black Boy* and in Wright's valedictory account of the Great Migration, *12 Million Black Voices* (1941), "lyrical," that David Bradley claims that "in *12 Million Black Voices* Richard Wright sang," and that both Ellison and Baldwin compare Wright's work with Bessie Smith's blues?[15]

I address these questions through Wright's analysis of Smith's blues in "Memories of My Grandmother," which is perhaps the only work in which Wright expresses unqualified admiration for a black female artist. Although the essay was intended as a preface to Wright's short story "The Man Who Lived Underground" (1941), it has never been published. Indeed, its "underground" status reflects the extent to which Wright's engagement with Smith (like his several depictions of female singers) remains muted in the critical imagination. Although Wright habitually treats black folk expression as a generic body of "authorless utterances" created by "nameless millions," his citations of Smith's work are an important exception to this rule.[16] For instance, as I discuss at the end of this chapter, Wright extensively cites Smith's "Backwater Blues" (1927) in *White Man, Listen!*, and he even allegedly planned to write Smith's biography. It is in "Memories," however, that Wright most fully engages with Smith's work. Writing about Smith's "Empty Bed Blues" (1928), he asserts that the details in blues songs "have poured into them . . . a degree of that over-emphasis that lifts them out of their everyday context and exalts them to a plane of vividness that strikes one with wonderment."[17] Wright suggests that the intensity of this vision is produced by and bears witness to black Americans' "enforced severance" from dominant society; the "everyday" looks different, even extraordinary, from the margins.[18] This claim demonstrates the rhetorical process that Paul Gilroy describes with regard to black Atlantic expressive cultures, by which "what was initially felt to be a curse—the curse of homelessness or the curse of enforced exile—gets repossessed. It becomes affirmed and is reconstructed as the basis of a privileged standpoint from which certain useful and critical perceptions about the modern world become more likely."[19] For Gilroy, this affirmation of alienation is a social philosophy that can illuminate literary thematics. I contend that this subversive affirmation also helps us reread—and even re-gender—Wright's literary style.

In Smith's music, Wright identifies a quality that I call *vivid lyricism*. The phrase refers to the practice of exploiting the sound of language to enhance visual description. The concept allows us to theorize the sonorous descriptive prose style Wright effects in *Black Boy* and *12 Million Black Voices*.[20] I see this prose style as enacting the promise Wright hears in Smith's blues: that social exclusion might yield uniquely intense, *musical* visions of the world. As I have noted, Wright resists "simple literary realism" in "Blueprint." He states that the black writer's "vision need not be . . . rendered in primer-like terms; for the life of the Negro people is not simple."[21] "Memories" helps us see that when Wright encourages writers to capture the "complexity, the strangeness, the magic wonder of life that plays like a bright sheen over the most sordid existence," what is at stake is not just fidelity to the complexity of black life but fidelity to an intensified vision of the world that Wright associates with social exclusion.[22] Wright's vividly lyrical prose style dramatizes the "oblique vision" Wright suggests such exclusion produces; it also showcases the author's struggle for and extravagant achievement of the literary.[23] Thus, this style both critiques and embraces the author's enforced "severance" from dominant U.S. society generally and the domain of the literary specifically.

While this literary style may be linked with W. E. B. Du Bois's oft-noted (and sometimes disparaged) "high Victorian" prose, the difference is that Wright deploys this style at a moment when it has passed out of literary currency, thanks in part to new aesthetics of proletarian art. In this context, Wright's use of the style becomes all the more unusual and makes its own statement. Namely, at a moment when descriptive expressionism is coded as "feminine," Wright revises the valence of "feminine" writing by decoupling "feminine" from "decadent." In short, whatever Wright's intentions, he uses a feminized form of expression to stylistically protest racial exclusion.

His collaborative work in visual media moves the power of feminized song from the level of style to that of representation, thus revising Wright's earlier fictional depictions of black women's songs. *12 Million Black Voices*, the photo-text project on which Wright collaborated with photographer Edwin Rosskam, ascribes the power to embrace and protest exclusion to black women singers themselves. Wright's film of *Native Son*, an independent production directed by Pierre Chenal, likewise represents the sustaining, subversive potential of female song. But in the film, black female characters embody their own outsider's insight, which is precisely the vision Wright's lyrical prose in *Black Boy* and *12 Million* serves to dramatize, and the vision Wright hears in Smith's blues.

These collaborative projects revise the musical and gender politics of Wright's earlier fiction in part because they release Wright from the singular responsibility of making meaning in words and thus diminish his fear of misrepresenting himself and his subjects—specifically, of inviting sentimental, emasculating readings of his work. What I am suggesting is that Wright's ambivalent relationship to feminized forms of expression (whether literary or musical) has at least as much to do with his anxiety about audience as it does with his own feelings about women. Fear of figurative emasculation may be hard to separate from misogyny, but what I call Wright's "reception anxiety" may go further in helping us make sense of his changing style and depictions of black women's songs than do charges of his masculinism and sexism. His complex relationship to audience may explain why, that is, both *12 Million* and the film of *Native Son* valorize "feminized" songs. If his collaborative projects in visual media diminish Wright's anxiety about misrepresentation, so too does his literal distance from the audience that might potentially misread (or misview) his work. As I have said, *Native Son* was filmed mainly in Buenos Aires (with some street scenes shot on location in Chicago). The film's revisionary gender and musical politics indicate that the collaborative medium of film, as well as *Native Son*'s creation outside the United States, transform the "burden" of representation into an opportunity to improvise.

In what follows, I briefly discuss Wright's portrayals of black women's songs in the novel *Native Son*. I show how "Memories" illuminates these portrayals, while also providing an interpretive language for Wright's own vividly lyrical prose style and his depictions of song in *12 Million* and the film of *Native Son*. I end by showing that Wright's representation of Smith not only elucidates his work but also attunes us to Smith's own—namely, to the unique form of vivid lyricism Smith creates through vocal performance.

Feminizing Black Song

To read the novel *Native Son* through the language of singing is to hear a protagonist afflicted by literal and figurative songs: his mother's hymns shame and annoy him; his employer's daughter, Mary, enters the novel through "singing" speech ("'Oh, Father!' a girl's voice sang out"); Mary embarrasses him by asking him to sing a spiritual with her; the fire in the furnace where he has burned her body "[sings] in his ears"; and three gunshots later "[sing] past his head" (*NS*, 9, 57, 88, 178, 308).

The singing starts early. The first sound of the novel is the famous elongated "BRING!" that, as many commentators have noted, not only signals the start of another difficult day for the Thomas family but also frames Wright's novel itself as a jarring wake-up call to white America. But the first *human voice* we hear is a woman singing, after a fashion: "A woman's voice sang out impatiently: 'Bigger, shut that thing off!'" (*NS*, 1). Thus are we introduced to Bigger's mother, Hannah. Later, when Bigger is hiding out in a vacant building after murdering Bessie, he awakens to a literal, but still feminized, song. Outside, black men and women are "singing, clapping hands, and rolling their heads," and Bigger muses that "the music sang of surrender, resignation. *Steal away, Steal away, Steal away to Jesus.*" This is the music of "his mother's world," and its "richness" contrasts dramatically with Bigger's own feeling of "emptiness." Yet embracing the music means "[giving] up his hope of living in the world. And he would never do that" (*NS*, 293–294). Here, the sacred song that awakens Bigger ironically represents the alluring possibility of putting his struggle to sleep.

Wright seems to justify Bigger's resentment of sacred songs by having Mary appropriate them. As if eager to test her new education in Negro culture, Mary asks Bigger to join her in her boozy rendition of "Swing Low, Sweet Chariot" after a night out (Bigger refuses) (*NS*, 88).[24] Wright himself may have recognized that both "Steal Away" and "Swing Low" were songs through which slaves expressed not only desire for heavenly comfort but also ambitions to "steal away" from slavery; to call for the chariot was often to call for the Underground Railroad.[25] However, the novel does not admit this alternative reading, instead framing sacred songs through Bigger's consciousness as feminized threats to male resistance or invitations to play the Uncle Tom. As Wright explains in "How 'Bigger' Was Born" (1940), "Throughout [the novel] there is but one point of view: Bigger's."[26] Yet Wright's own use of the language of singing to describe forces that afflict Bigger (from ominous female voices to bullets) subtly affirms his protagonist's position. In this context, Wright himself seems to figure Hannah's initial "song" of retaliation against the alarm clock as a threat to his own metaproject of consciousness raising.[27]

Yet "Memories of My Grandmother" offers a far more nuanced vision of song, particularly by affirming the subversive expressive potential of black women's blues. The essay also suggests that Wright's ambivalent, if not condescending, representations of black sacred song are partly meant to thwart sentimental misreadings of his work. In "Memories," Wright details the oppressive rule of his grandmother, Margaret Wilson, a Seventh-Day Adventist who forbade the young Wright to read any books other than the Bible and to sing any songs other than hymns: "If my grandmother had ever heard me so much as hum a blues song," he writes, the penalty would have been a beating with whatever was closest to hand, "be it a broom or an eight-pound, cast-iron skillet."[28] But I am less concerned with Wright's personally conflicted relationship to his grandmother and her songs than with the anxiety about artistic representation his essay reveals. As Wright proceeds to explain, he was unsure how to represent the power of religious song without catering to white fantasies of black servility and emotionalism. He writes that he was "afraid" that if he "depicted that *something*" that sustained his grandmother, white audiences would view his representation through the lens of stereotype, "a la GREEN PASTURES," and would "laugh instead of being enthralled."[29] *The Green Pastures*, a play by Marc Connelly that featured an all-black cast of guileless sinners and saints, won the Pulitzer Prize for Drama in 1930 and was adapted into a popular film in 1936. Wright's allusion to this work indicates that his representations of sacred song in *Native Son* may have been informed as much by his "reception anxiety" as by his purported sexism, traumatizing Adventist upbringing, or even Marxist skepticism regarding the political efficacy of religious belief. He problematizes sacred song in the novel partly in an effort to defy the sentimental readings of black worship associated with the *Green Pastures* stereotype.

In "Blueprint for Negro Writing," Wright laments the fact that "Negro writing has been addressed in the main to a small white audience rather than to a Negro one," but his own work was of course addressed to both.[30] His anxiety about being misread by his majority white readership is evident in Wright's famous declaration of his "awfully naïve mistake": writing a first book (*Uncle Tom's Children* [1938]) that "even bankers' daughters could read and weep over and feel good about."[31] With this statement, Gilroy rightly notes, Wright characterizes his "ideal misreader as a white woman."[32] Further, the locus of Wright's resentment here is the way that the feminized cathartic response would feminize *him*. Much later, in *White Man, Listen!*, Wright continues to reject such feminization by setting his own stoic masculine image against a feminized emotional foil; he ends his introduction to that work by relating his response to a concerned female interlocutor: "'My dear, I do not deal in happiness; I deal in meaning.'"[33] The implication is that, if Wright is to confront readers with the reality of life in America (and, later, in Ghana and Indonesia and Spain), he must resist a readerly desire for comfort that he genders as female. Wright's standard no-frills prose style must be understood in part as the stylistic analogue to his rhetorical critique of the "bankers' daughters'" cathartic response—and, perhaps, to his fictional portrayal of Bigger's refusal to sing for Mary. Wright's spare prose refutes the aestheticized portraits of black life Wright viewed as emasculating concessions to sentimental white female readers.

Yet "Memories" also reveals Wright's more expansive sense of how he might express that "*something*" that sustained his grandmother, if not through explicit representation then through compositional form. Wright claims that the nonlinear narrative form of "The Man Who Lived Underground" itself represents an "oblique vision" produced by racialized social exclusion, and he relates the nonlinear form of his story to Smith's blues. He links his work with Smith's music instead of Wilson's hymns because he believes religious hymns only embrace social exclusion, while the blues also protest it. As I will show, Wright's film of *Native Son* underscores the deeper connections between the spirituals and the blues (indeed, as early as *12 Million*, Wright calls the blues the "'spirituals' of [our] city pavements").[34] Yet the salient point here is that, according to Wright, the nonlinear form of Smith's blues itself reflects the power of perception that exclusion might generate: "If you should read the words to Bessie Smith's THE EMPTY BED BLUES, you would find no logic or progression between the verses; they are merely a series of incidents of domestic discord and defeated love thrown seemingly carelessly together." But this very form, Wright insists, reflects a view of reality as it is witnessed "from a position of enforced severance."[35]

Recorded in 1928, "Empty Bed Blues" was one of Smith's biggest hits, a crowd favorite and a best seller. According to pianist Lovie Austin, musical director of Chicago's Monogram Theater, "You could hear that record all over the South Side"—to which Wright had recently arrived, in 1927.[36] Whether or not one accepts Wright's claim that the song's verses seem to be "thrown carelessly together"—a point to which I will return at the end of this chapter—Wright is correct in saying that Smith's lyrics describe a non-narrative "series of incidents." Several scholars have identified this aspect of the blues, which Susan McClary describes with particular clarity when assessing Smith's "Thinking Blues" (1928): "The blues convention . . . minimizes the narrative component of the music," so that "what we get instead is a series of meditations on a single situation, as Smith returns to the problem nagging her with a new approach in each verse."[37] In "Empty Bed Blues," the trouble is the loss of an unforgettably skilled lover, and yet Smith's intricate vocal variations on this theme seem to revel in the loss even as they lament it. Smith's persona exploits the only thing that is useful about this particular abandonment, which is that it gives her the time to sing a mournful praise song for the days when her bed was full. The expressive engine here is a mood, or a series of moods, rather than a developing storyline.

I will say more about the song later, but for now I want to highlight Wright's claim that the associative logic of the blues reflects a unique social vision. As he writes, "Empty Bed Blues" expresses a view of life produced by "enforced severance." This "oblique vision" relates seemingly unconnected objects and experiences.[38] Describing this process—and *feminizing* it—Wright explains how "*a black woman, singing the blues*," will sing about a rainy day, a pair of red shoes, and her "lowdown" feeling, before turning to other such disparate subjects as murder, theft, and "tender love."[39] Similarly, Wright explains, his own story "The Man Who Lived Underground" moves swiftly from one vivid image to another: once the protagonist, Daniels, descends underground, he encounters a church congregation, a dead baby, a locked safe. What ties these seemingly arbitrary elements together is, as in the blues, a mood. The mood is the desperation generated by Daniels's false accusation of murder. Wright claims that false accusation defines the condition of black people in America—"Negroes in America are accused and branded and treated as though they are guilty of something"—and he suggests that the nonlinear form of his story itself dramatizes the "oblique vision" such alienation engenders.[40] Wright's alignment of his own narrative logic with Smith's may constitute the most explicit connection he would ever make between black male and female artistic responses to racialized exclusion.

Crucially, both musician and writer refuse to take exclusion as a curse. On the contrary, to recall Gilroy's point, Wright "affirm[s] and reconstruct[s]" alienation "as the basis of a privileged standpoint." Explaining both an experiential and a compositional principle, Wright asserts, "The moment one takes . . . a terrible lot for granted" and then "improvise[s]" on it, it is possible to create an artistic statement that is all the more exciting for being wholly unpredictable.[41] Wright compares this improvisatory process to jazz. Once the beat is established, the musician can introduce "surprise rhythms" or variations on it, and these surprises generate a dramatic tension. Both Wright and Smith improvise on the "terrible lot" of enforced severance ("the beat"), both in their lives and in the stories they compose. Their improvisations produce an anticipatory uncertainty—which, in writing as in music, creates "the *drama* of the thing" and a transient freedom.[42]

While Wright compares his work with Smith's blues primarily to highlight the relationship between exhilarating creative pressure and nonlinear form, his meditations on Smith allow us to hear his engagement with her work in a different register, attuning us to the "sound" of his prose. For when Wright claims that intricate blues details "have poured into them through the sheer emotional intensity of the participants a degree of that over-emphasis that lifts them out of their everyday context and exalts them to a plane of vividness," the "over-emphasis" generated by the "emotional intensity of the participants" is necessarily musical.[43] Insofar as this sonorous "over-emphasis" serves to "exalt" details to "a plane of vividness," we can see Wright suggesting that the sonorous properties of language—what Albert Murray calls "the music inherent in language as such"—might be deployed in the service of generating intense vision.[44]

To describe written expression as "lyrical" is always to imply the sonorous aspect of poetry or prose. Yet Wright underscores the visual aspect of Smith's lyricism when he speaks of the blues as lifting details to a new "plane of *vividness*." His language invites us to see his own lyrical prose as writing that generates vision. A sense of the spectacular is central to Wright, who often conceptualizes his art through visual metaphor. For instance, he tells of wanting *Native Son's* reader to "feel that Bigger's story . . . was a special premiere given in his own private theater . . . , that it was happening *now*, like a play upon the stage or a movie unfolding upon the screen."[45] Wright's visual imagination compels one to conceive the term "lyrical" beyond its traditional association with sound and to recognize that lyrical writing—especially as Wright performs it—often functions as descriptive expressionism. Wright's vividly lyrical prose exploits the kind of sonic intensity "poured into" each detail of a blues song, in order to conjure vibrant images.

Wright's Vivid Lyricism

It is this quality of expressionism that Ellison is getting at when, in his review of *Black Boy*, he writes, "like a blues sung by such an artist as Bessie Smith, [*Black Boy*'s] lyrical prose evokes the paradoxical, almost surreal image of a black boy singing lustily as he probes his own grievous wound."[46] When comparing Wright's memoir with Smith's blues, Ellison particularly cites Wright's descriptions of his childhood awakening to the natural world: the "cosmic cruelty that I felt when I saw the curved timbers of a wooden shack that had been warped in the summer sun, . . . the quiet terror that suffused my senses when vast hazes of gold washed earthward from star-heavy skies on silent nights."[47] As Wright describes "the aching glory in masses of clouds burning gold and purple from an invisible sun," he tempers the sonic weight of "aching" with the lighter, gliding "masses," and thus generates vivid images in part by exploiting the sound of words.[48] This appeal to multiple senses, as much as the mood of majestic nostalgia, draws Wright's catalogue into a cohesive riff.

This passage follows Wright's account of being beaten by his mother after he burns down the house. As he writes, "For a long time I was chastened whenever I remembered that my mother had come close to killing me. Each event spoke with a cryptic tongue. And the moments of living slowly revealed their coded meanings."[49] By the formal logic of this passage, Wright's near severance from his mother and family—and, indeed, from life itself—inaugurates a heightened sensitivity to his own powers, as a writer, to re-create the world through language. Returned from the brink of death, Wright describes the natural world as if he were seeing it for the first time (or the last). *Black Boy* thus dramatizes the process Wright outlines in "Memories": forced exclusion (here, from family) produces an "oblique vision" through which the ordinary (a wooden shack, a sunset) appears extraordinary.

Again, at a literary historical moment when such descriptive expressionism is coded as "feminine," Wright decouples the notion of "feminine" writing from the notion of apolitical, "art for art's sake" decadence.

His "feminine" prose style at once protests and flouts the author's exclusion from the dominant culture and the domain of the literary. In *Black Boy*, Wright describes his desire to "master words" as "the single aim of [his] living."[50] Insofar as his lyrical writing announces a seizure of the means of literary expression, we might regard it as the stylistic counterpart to his anecdote, in *Black Boy*, about using his white co-worker's library card to check books out of his local library.[51] By announcing its own labor (the fact that it has been worked over, or over-"wrought"), this prose style highlights Wright's hard-won achievement of the literary even as it indicts the society that *makes* black literacy an achievement.

If such moments reveal Wright's occasional tendency toward what is now condemned as "purple prose," they also perform the valuable function of such writing, as Paul West describes it: "The impulse [behind purple prose] is to make everything larger than life, almost to overrespond, maybe because, habituated to life . . . we become inured and have to be awakened with something almost intolerably vivid." For West, purple prose is a sign of "that powerful early-warning system of the sensibilities we call imagination." Echoing Wright's claim that the blues lift everyday things to "a plane of vividness that strikes one with wonderment," West writes that "incandescent" prose renders "the merest thing an inexhaustible object of wonderment." This style calls attention to both the writer and the world his language conjures, giving objects "a more unruly presence," so that "they bristle, they buzz, they come out at you." Wright's visionary language serves to remind the reader, in West's terms, that "it is headily terrifying to be alive, [and] we have no choice in the matter."[52] To specify West's claim, Wright's prose indicates that life may be "headily terrifying" especially when one is alive in the Jim Crow South, and the "aim of one's living" is to remake the world through his own surreptitiously acquired skill.

12 Million Black Voices, which Ellison rightly names Wright's "most lyrical" work, uses this prose style less to flaunt Wright's own hard-won literary achievement than to articulate a collective struggle.[53] The project mobilizes Wright's lyrical writing on behalf of African American workers—Wright's pronoun throughout is not "I" but "we." By utilizing a self-consciously "literary" style for this project, Wright implicitly rejects the notion that the black proletariat's "proper" voice is spare realism. *12 Million* demonstrates his claim in "Blueprint" that "simple literary realism" is insufficient to capture "the complexity, the strangeness, the magic wonder of life." Moreover, to the extent that Wright's vividly lyrical style at once honors and protests segregated black life, Wright's literary politics are more closely aligned with Hurston's than is generally recognized. As June Jordan argues, rather that see Hurston as a figure of affirmation and Wright as a figure of protest, we can see that both authors protest and affirm: to affirm black life, especially "within the American context," is itself "an act of protest," just as to protest white oppression is to "assert[] our need for an alternative, benign environment."[54] Although Wright's and Hurston's treatment of character and plot differ, their vividly lyrical descriptions provide one ground on which to consider them literary allies. Further, the animated tone of their adorned descriptions distances both writers from Jean Toomer's vividly lyrical yet melancholic depictions of the rural South in *Cane* (1923).

As in *Black Boy*, Wright produces stunning descriptions of the natural world in *12 Million*: "The land we till is beautiful. . . . Nights are covered with canopies sometimes blue and sometimes black, canopies that sag low with ripe and nervous stars. The throaty boast of frogs momentarily drowns out the call and counter-call of crickets" (*12M*, 32). Immediately after this feminized depiction of the land, Wright invokes the "charming, idyllic, romantic" portrait of rural black life "they have painted" (*12M*, 35). It may seem that this line ironizes the language he has just used, framing it as speciously "idyllic" or "romantic" and pitting it against the harder following truth: "time slips past us remorselessly, and it is hard to tell of the iron that lies beneath the surface of our quiet, dull days" (*12M*, 34). Rather than reject his own vividly lyrical writing in favor of a spare, severe style, however, this iambic line, ending as it does with three evocative stresses ("quiet, dull days"), serves to *authorize* it. That is, in *12 Million*, Wright's lyrical language becomes an instrument with which to say not only that "the land we till is beautiful" but also that "iron . . . lies beneath the surface of our quiet, dull days." Wright's "feminine" prose style capably articulates both the beauty of the land and the dull despair of being chained to it.

12 Million makes sonorous, feminized language the flexible voice of a complex people. It also raises the political potential of female song to a new plane of vividness through its literary and visual representations of the church. Wright frames the church as a feminized space, claiming that "it is to the churches that our black women cling for emotional security and the release of their personalities" and that "because their orbit of life is narrow—from the kitchenette to the white folk's kitchen and back home again—they love the church more than do our men" (*12M*, 131). At the same time, Rosskam's photographs and Wright's other remarks complicate Wright's patronizing claims that black women "cling" to the church "because their orbit of life is narrow." The book features as many images of men as of women in worship, and Wright asserts that feminized sacred spaces are crucial "centers of social and community life" and sites of wholeness required by all of "us," especially after migrating to northern cities:

> Despite our new worldliness . . . , we keep our churches alive. In fact, we have built more of them than ever here on the city pavements, for it is only when we are within the walls of our churches that we are wholly ourselves, that we . . . maintain a quiet and constant communion with all that is deepest in us. Our going to church of a Sunday is like placing one's ear to another's chest to hear the unquenchable murmur of the human heart. In our collective outpourings of song and prayer, the fluid emotions of others make us feel the strength in ourselves. (12M, 130–131)[55]

If Wright's prose verges on sentimentality when invoking "the unquenchable murmur of the human heart," he nonetheless creates a uniquely heartfelt tribute to black rituals of worship, "collective outpourings of song and prayer." Wright's depictions of black sacred song in Native Son lead one to expect Wright will undermine this passage with a problematizing or ironizing turn. On the contrary, when describing a congregation's cathartic response to a preacher's sermon—in a breathless, italicized passage that Robin Kelley calls the text's "most surreal" moment[56]—Wright states, "Some say that, because we possess [the] faculty of keeping alive this spark of happiness under adversity, we are children. No, it is the courage and faith in simple living that enable us to maintain this reservoir of human feeling" (12M, 73). Turning this "no" on those who would dismiss religious worship as "child-like," Wright also appears to turn on *himself*, revising his anxiously ambivalent treatment of the spirituals in Native Son.

One reason why 12 Million features extended sonorous visions as well as new visions of black song is that it is a work of collaboration. While photography obviously relies on manipulation, selection, and framing, one need not imagine that the book's photographs objectively document reality in order to appreciate that Rosskam's images release Wright from the position of sole representative of African American life. As I have said, because these images diminish Wright's own representative role, they also mitigate his anxiety about inviting sentimental misreadings of his work. Yet at the same time that they free Wright from the singular responsibility of making meaning in words, the images seem to demand a new form of authorial labor, which makes the burden of explication a new opportunity. Here Wright's prose must fulfill the potential of the photograph, which is precisely to lift the image of the ordinary to a new plane of vivid significance. Wright's vivid lyricism thus serves two purposes in *12 Million*: to generate vivid descriptions, which in turn vivify the book's photographs. This composition process concretizes Wright's claim about the blues: that each element of a song seems intensified through the "sheer emotional intensity of the participants"—through collaboration.

Wright's focus on the "participants" indicates that expressive intensity arises not just from one's sense of social severance but also from one's membership in an excluded collectivity. Indeed, such alternative musical subcommunities were a constitutive force in the creation of women's blues. Following the work of Daphne Duval Harrison, McClary writes that "many of the performers who came to be celebrated as the blues queens were displaced young women who found they could patch together a living performing in traveling minstrel shows, vaudeville, urban clubs, and (after the industry reluctantly agreed to try black women singers) the new medium of recording. What resulted was an explosion of female creativity that animated the 1920s—one of the few such moments in Western music history."[57] This sense of participation in a specific community is of course central to the blues *performance* as well, and Smith inspired this participation as well as any performer. Among blues women, she reportedly reigned supreme in her ability to draw listeners—through both her singing and her extravagant beauty—into a collective hypnotism. "You just couldn't stop listening to Bessie and looking at her too when she sang," according to cornetist Demus Dean.[58] Guitarist Danny Barker recalled that "she dominated a stage. You didn't turn your head when she went on. You just watched Bessie. . . . She just upset you. . . . She could bring about mass hypnotism. When she was performing, you could hear a pin drop."[59] As I will discuss in more detail, Smith collaborated not only with her audiences but also with other artists. While she did not always enjoy sharing the spotlight with the musicians who accompanied her, she frequently collaborated with artists whose musical sensitivity and technical prowess matched her own.

Obviously writing, unlike live performance, is solitary work. This was especially true for Wright—who, having been framed as the self-made, representative African American writer, quickly became a wary ambassador to white America. This was a role Wright both chose and had thrust on him by the literary marketplace—and one cost of performing it, as "Memories" reveals, was Wright's anxiety about catering to white fantasies of black emotionalism when depicting black music (an anxiety that, as I have suggested, partly explains his generally spare prose style). In *12 Million*, Wright clearly assumes the role of racial representative who might channel so many "black voices." That the text is meant to function as "wake-up call" akin to *Native Son* is evident from the text's very first words, which frame the imagined reader as privileged and white: "Each day when you see us black folk upon the dusty land of the farms or upon the hard pavement of the city streets, you usually take us for granted and think you know us, but our history is far stranger than you suspect, and we are not what we seem" (*12M*, 10). But while Wright positions himself as a representative—speaking from a "we" that is meant to explain to "you" how we live—this collaborative project transforms the burden of authorial representation into a condition of possibility. Unlike *Native Son*, *12 Million* politicizes sonorous, feminized language; unlike most of his prior work, the text also explicitly valorizes black women's religious expression. These departures suggest that, at precisely the moment when Wright's words do not have to tell the whole story, they begin to tell a new one.

Native Son's Re-visionary Songs

Though it may seem counterintuitive, *12 Million Black Voices* indicates that Wright's engagement with black music finds its fullest expression in his collaborative work in *visual* media. This is not to say that collaboration in visual media per se guaranteed that Wright would create enhanced visions of song. In the stage version of *Native Son* (1941), for instance, director Orson Welles excised long passages of dialogue (he wanted fast-paced, dramatic action), as well as the novel's songs. If playwright Paul Green's diary entries on the subject are to be trusted, Welles's position was "No Negro singing. . . . Too much spiritual stuff in all Negro plays."[60] Wright apparently agreed, or at least approved.

Wright's collaboration with Chenal on the screen version of the novel looked and sounded very different, partly due to the site of the film's production in Argentina. *Sangre Negra*—its Spanish title well suited to an era of widespread anticolonial revolts—was a collaboration of exiles. Wright himself had left the States for France in 1947, while Jewish director Chenal (born Cohen) had left Nazi-occupied Paris for Argentina in 1942. Although Wright publicly assumed complete responsibility for the film, telling interviewers that "if the film is bad, it's all my fault," film is necessarily a collaborative medium, and *Native Son* was necessarily an extranational product;[61] in Chenal's memoir, he tells how the producer speculated that the film would never be made in America—at least not for another ten or twenty years.[62]

Native Son's creation outside the United States was crucial to Wright and Chenal's vision. Unlike many other American writers who had left the States to work in Europe, such as Ernest Hemingway, Chester Himes, and James Baldwin, Wright collaborated with other artists while abroad. His collaboration with Chenal and the rest of the film's cast—along with his attempt to escape the repressive gaze which turns black American celebrities into racial representatives—enabled Wright to improvise on his own earlier work. He did so especially by investing feminized songs with new authority. Like *12 Million*, the film lifts the power of song from the level of prose style to the level of representation. Yet in the film, black women singers themselves voice the outsider's insight that Wright's vividly lyrical prose serves to dramatize.

Even if Bigger does not fully apprehend these women's understanding of and resistance to his condition, Bessie's and Hannah's insights are available to the viewer and do not depend on Bigger's recognition. The medium of film grants Bessie and Hannah autonomy by freeing the story from Bigger's consciousness. To recall and elaborate Wright's comments in "How 'Bigger' Was Born," "Throughout [the novel] there is but one point of view: Bigger's. . . . Because I had limited myself to rendering only what Bigger saw and felt, I gave no more reality to the other characters than that which Bigger himself saw."[63] Bigger, in other words, is the camera in the novel. But the film opens our field of vision. While the viewer loses the intense confrontation with Bigger's interiority that is so important to the novel, she gains the ability to see what Bigger himself does not—including scenes at which he is not present. The most important of these, I suggest, is a church scene featuring Hannah that works quite differently when detached from Bigger's point of view.

While Bessie and Hannah are no longer tethered to Bigger's consciousness, Wright's embodiment of his protagonist aligns these female characters more closely with the author. Here, when Bessie sings to Bigger in a nightclub, we see her singing to Wright himself; when Hannah worships on behalf of her son, she is intimately linked with the author who embodies him. Both women's scenes of song highlight their possession of knowledge that is, as I will show, relevant not only to Bigger but also to Wright himself. As the film aligns Wright with these women, it unsettles his carefully constructed persona of the stoic black male exile. This stance is apparent in *Black Boy*, which narrates Wright's apparently singular ambition to exile himself from the Jim Crow South, and it continues well into his travel writings, where he describes himself as a "rootless man" who seems "not to need as many emotional attachments, sustaining roots, or idealistic allegiances as most people."[64] By drawing Wright into alignment with *Native Son*'s singers, the film revises Wright's own performance of black masculinity.

For Wright, who had wished to work in film for years, the chance to make *Native Son* was a long-awaited opportunity.[65] A number of directors had wanted to adapt the novel. Most promising was the offer from Orson Welles and John Houseman, although they lost their financial backing when the stage version of *Native Son* that they had directed generated less revenue than anticipated.[66] Harold Hecht had offered to direct the screen version in 1947, but with the minor adjustment of making Bigger Thomas white—upon hearing this, Wright reportedly laughed until he cried—and all other offers had fallen through until Wright met Chenal.[67] Wright's collaboration with Chenal was especially fortuitous. First, Chenal was greatly admired by Wright's other collaborator, Welles; further, Chenal's most well-known film was his 1935 adaptation of Dostoevsky's *Crime and Punishment*, a novel that had been formative to Wright's development as a writer of fiction.[68]

Chenal suspended work on three films-in-progress in order to start making the movie immediately. It was decided, in an exchange that Wright would relate with a mixture of bemusement and satisfaction, that Wright himself would play Bigger. Chenal was graver about how this transpired; he tells of discussing the film with Wright and seeing him transform into Bigger before his eyes: suddenly, "the hero was speaking through the mouth of his creator."[69] As press releases of the time never fail to mention, Wright lost thirty-five pounds in preparation for the role. While Wright's transformation clearly attests to his enthusiasm for the project, it is tempting to read his recovery of a younger physique as a reflection of the youthful spirit that surrounded the entire enterprise. Short on funds from the start, Wright and Chenal hired a mainly amateur cast and crew. They found sound engineers and cameramen at the Communist Party workers' union in Chicago. Willa Pearl Curtiss (Hannah) and Jean Wallace (Mary) were the cast's only professional Hollywood actors. Jan was played by an American tourist named Gene Michael. The role of Bessie went to an archaeology student at the University of Chicago, Gloria Madison. Chenal was delighted with Madison; he later claimed that "she entered the role as if Richard Wright had written it just for her."[70]

It was a role that, more than any other, Wright had dramatically revised from the novel. There, Bessie is broke and driven to drink; as Bigger's unloved but convenient girlfriend, she compounds the novel's bleakness. If she recalls Bessie Smith at all, she evokes Smith's appearance in the film *St. Louis Blues* (1929). In this film, Smith plays a woman who, having been thrown down and cast out by her cheating lover, spends the night drowning her sorrows in a glass at the bar (though, of course, also singing with a power that carries her voice above a full chorus and orchestra). However, perhaps because Wright understood the difference between writing and filmmaking—"You can write a book for a minority, but you can't produce a film for a minority"—the film transforms Bessie into a beautiful diva.[71] It is fitting that the film's opening credits "introduce" Gloria Madison "in the part of Bessie Mears" directly after naming the film's two established stars, Wright and Wallace, because the film is really the story of Bigger and Bessie, as a pair.[72] For instance, they *both* start risky new jobs as the film begins: Bigger's first, ill-fated day as the Daltons' chauffeur is the day Bessie exchanges her waitress's uniform for an evening gown to headline at Ernie's.

Yet Bessie's importance to the narrative is most evident in the film's treatment of her death. Whereas the novel narrates Bigger's murder of Bessie in linear sequence, the film, following the nonlinear form of the blues, defers the representation of that murder to a closing flashback. Bessie's absence thus becomes the last plot point to be resolved, after which the film speeds to a close. In a sense, *Native Son* needs to end here, when Bessie becomes *too* much like Bigger; her murder scene makes her the film's most profound victim of false accusation and thereby displaces Bigger's story—the film's primary motivation. After Bigger confesses to killing Bessie, the film segues into a flashback and dream sequence in which Bigger is hiding out in an abandoned building awaiting Bessie's return from an errand when he falls asleep and dreams he is carrying Mary's head in a white-wrapped bundle. Bessie appears in the dream and directs him to a cotton field; he can dispose of his burden there, she tells him, "where it's *all* white." At the far end of the field is Bigger's father, who was lynched in the South when Bigger was a child. Bigger goes to him and falls to his knees: "I was so happy I was crying," Bigger's voiceover explains. "I knew that nothing bad was ever going to happen to me anymore." He is mistaken. Bigger's father soon morphs into a grotesque, laughing Mr. Britten, the white detective on his case.

Now it appears that Bessie has "turned Bigger/Wright in" to his father, in two senses of the phrase: she has turned Bigger over to the paternalistic authority who seals his fate—and, in so doing, has transformed him into the defeated black man on the plantation. Bigger wakes up, realizes the police are after him, assumes Bessie has "snitched on him," and, in the words of the screenplay, "[strangles] Bessie as the siren wails."[73] This dream sequence "explains" Bigger's murder of Bessie. However, it also frames that murder as the product of groundless paranoia, making it clear that Bigger accuses Bessie of a crime she does not commit. In "Memories of My Grandmother," Wright argues that false accusation is the definitive condition of the black American, and while his work (including "The Man Who Lived Underground" and the novel *Native Son*) generally figures criminalization as the specific condition of black *men*, in the film it is *Bessie*, more than Bigger, who represents that plight. Her forced alienation, moreover, endows her with the outsider's insight that Wright finds in the blues.

In a nightclub performance, Bessie sings what we might call Bigger's blues (as well as her own), and thus becomes the film's most cogent internal critic.[74] Bigger has reluctantly brought Mary and Jan to the club where Bessie is performing. She sings a song called "The Dreaming Kind," which the film credits to Lilian Walker Charles.[75] The first verse is as follows:

Love me 'cause I'm lonely
Love me 'cause I'm wild
Love me 'cause I'm only
A dreaming kind of child

This song recalls Smith's "Reckless Blues" (1925):

My mama says I'm reckless
My daddy says I'm wild
I ain't good lookin'
But I'm somebody's angel child.

Despite the lyrical resonance with Smith's song, Wright's designation of the female lover as "only a dreaming kind of child" seems to accord with his dismissive treatment of female characters. Yet Wright himself warned against taking the "bald, literal words" of a blues song at face value and insisted that "the meaning is . . . in the mood and interpretation that Bessie Smith brings to the verses."[76] And indeed the meaning of Bessie's song is only fulfilled in performance, as it is filmed and edited. As she glides around the table where Bigger is seated with Jan and Mary, Bessie embodies the position of "enforced severance" that Wright describes in "Memories," and her performance reflects blueswomen's "oblique vision." In this scene, Bessie steps into the role of knowing outsider that Wright claimed for Bessie Smith and for himself.

The camera structures Bessie's performance as a counterpoint to Bigger's conversation with Mary and Jan. Bessie sings, "Love me because . . . I'm only a dreamin' kind of child," and the camera cuts to Mary, the "dreaming child" extraordinaire, as she raves about Bessie's performance: "All colored people are so gifted!" Bessie later glowers down at Bigger and his companions and sings, "Please don't be forsaken." Where a conventional blues would have delivered this line as a romantic plea ("Don't leave me"), Bessie's song introduces New Testament language that levels a prophetic imperative: as if foreseeing the trouble this association will bring, Bessie implores Bigger not to be forsaken by his new "friends." Mary is right when she exclaims of Bessie, "She knows you, Bigger!" And, she might have added, she seems to know what will happen to you. Bessie's uncanny knowledge becomes apparent when she sings, "Put me here on trial." At this moment, the camera cuts to Jan, who assures Bigger that "one day you'll be able to express yourself any way you want to." This particular juxtaposition of song and image foregrounds the irony of Jan's statement, for *Native Son* is about the *limits* of Bigger's self-expression—and these limits become painfully apparent precisely when Bigger is put on trial. That is, the murder trial exposes Bigger's *in*ability to express himself any way he wants to.[77] In the film, as in the novel, Bigger's lawyer Max speaks for him; Bigger does not speak for himself. Finally, "The Dreaming Kind," insofar as it alludes to Bigger's fatal dream, foreshadows not only Bigger's silencing but also Bessie's own death. Especially due to Chenal's camerawork and editing, then, Gloria Madison's performance of "The Dreaming Kind" acquires a meaning that exceeds its lyrics.

That Bessie demonstrates this prescience through song accords with the Homeric trope of the all-knowing sirens, those seductive goddesses who know everything and threaten to steer Odysseus from his course. But there is nothing mystical or dangerous about Bessie's knowledge; she has gleaned it from living attentively in the world.[78] For instance, when Bigger later tells her he has killed Mary, she instantly replies, "They'll say you raped her" (*NS*, 262).[79] She is right, but this is social observation, not prophecy. In the nightclub scene, the cuts between Bessie's performance and Bigger, Mary, and Jan's dialogue at the table figure Bessie as

Wright's alter ego: her gestures toward Mary's childish dreaming and Bigger's silencing express knowingness about the dual threats of sentimentalization and manipulation of which Wright himself, as I have suggested, was well aware. Because Bessie's insight transcends Bigger's, she is aligned less with him than with his complex creator, to whom she is singing. Her song becomes the medium of alliance between Bessie and Wright; it establishes a knowledge that they share. Bessie thus becomes the answer to Ellison's famous critique of (the novel) *Native Son*. Ellison had criticized Wright for creating a protagonist whose limited consciousness did not admit the possibility of transcending desperate social circumstance—even though Wright himself exemplified that possibility: "Wright could imagine Bigger, but Bigger could not possibly imagine Richard Wright," Ellison declared: "Wright saw to that."[80] Rather than grant *Bigger* the awareness that would allow him to "imagine Richard Wright," the film gives that awareness to Bessie. She is the one who expresses Wright's superior insight into Bigger.

Whereas Wright's early analyses of Smith's blues in a sense prefigure his later treatment of Bessie's role as a singer, his fictional representations of black women's hymns make the film's portrayal of Hannah even more surprising. A key scene of prayer and song that features Hannah revises Wright's earlier fictional depictions of women and sacred song by granting both an unsentimental authority. The scene in question is prefaced by an important moment that is absent from the novel: after Bigger's crime is discovered, police officers and detectives come to the Thomases' home in search of Bigger and inform Hannah that if she knows where her son is and doesn't tell them, she will be "guilty of murder too"—to which Hannah replies, "If I knew where he was I'd never tell the likes of you." When Bigger's sister, Vera, starts to tell them where Bessie lives, Hannah says, "Shut yo mouth, Vera. These men are no friends of ours." Hannah's resistance in this moment extends to her following scene, set in church. In the novelistic version of the church scene, the Thomases all unite in Bigger's cell, along with a preacher, and Bigger begrudgingly tells Hannah that he will pray for forgiveness so that they might be reunited in heaven. (He does not plan to do this and does not believe in the power of prayer but lies to appease his mother.) Hannah, "so happy that all she could do was cry," embraces all her children and "mumble[s] a prayer" along with the preacher's chant. This is a devastating moment, especially because of the contrast between the Thomases' pain and Bigger's willed detachment: "Bigger held his face stiff, hating them and himself, feeling the white people along the wall watching" (*NS*, 346–347). This scene

FIGURE 2. Gloria Madison (Bessie) sings to Richard Wright (Bigger), Gene Michael (Jan), and Jean Wallace (Mary). From the film *Native Son* (1951).

plays out very differently in the film once it is detached from Bigger's consciousness. Indeed, Bigger is not present in the cinematic scene. Moreover, Hannah's prayer is supported by a congregational hymn that is uncannily sounded but unseen.

The sequence begins with an establishing shot of the church and the sound of a hymn, "Leaning On the Everlasting Arms." Once inside, the camera focuses on the pastor as he sings, "What a fellowship, what a joy divine..." The police enter the church, and the camera follows one of the white men as he crawls along the wall, seeking out Bigger's family. The congregation now joins in the pastor's song, and one hears a fully orchestrated choral sound that is all the more striking for being obviously non-diagetic. We do not actually see the congregation singing—the people in the pews are barely opening their mouths—and the disjuncture between image and sound makes the song seem otherworldly; because the source of the hymn does not seem to be the church itself, it appears to issue from "beyond" the people gathered inside it. If the technique creates an alienation effect vis-à-vis the viewer, it also alienates the detective who creeps along the wall: this unplaceable sound renders *him* distinctly out of place. As he moves toward the head of the church, the worshippers kneel, black-clad figures advancing alongside him like a wave.

At this point, the camera resists the detective's invasion, shutting him out of the scene and zeroing in on Hannah. This is the only shot in the film that frames Willa Pearl Curtiss as a powerful, authoritative figure—she is backed by the whole congregation and visually "crowned" by the light fixture above her head. Because the camera focuses on Hannah as the song ends, the hymn seems like a preface to her prayer, which the other congregants supportively witness: "Our heavenly father, I'm calling on your holy name this evening, pleading for help. My son's in deep trouble, Lord. Here on bended knees I'm begging you to look down. Have mercy, and help me save my first-born child, who's strayed so far from the fold." Whereas in *12 Million*, Wright had described black Americans' "wailing blue melodies" as "our banner of hope flung desperately up in the face of a world that has pushed us to the wall" (*12M*, 130), here the otherworldly or implausible sound of the worshippers pushes the white invaders to the wall. We might also recall that, in *12 Million*, Wright asserts that "it is only when we are within the walls of our churches that we are wholly ourselves." In *Native Son*, the church walls circumscribe a space that is not only sacred but potentially threatening. We are a far cry from *The Green Pastures*, as well as the novel from which this scene is translated.

This cinematic scene of worship reveals Wright's gradual sense that the spirituals about which he had previously expressed such ambivalence were united, in their defiant improvisations on the condition of exclusion, with the blues he so admired. This understanding accorded with that of writers like Sterling Brown and Ralph Ellison, both of whom had drawn links between sacred and secular song in the decade between Wright's novel and film. As Wright would tell an interviewer in 1960, "Jazz is linked intimately with the blues and the blues with the spirituals. Jazz comes out of a religious place, very long ago, but it begins on the plantations with the spirituals."[81] Indeed, *Native Son* links religious song with what Wright often called the *wail* of the blues—and even, perhaps, with the sirens which Wright also habitually figures as wailing. Again, *12 Million* invokes "our . . . wailing blue melodies." And Wright's 1949 liner notes to Josh White's "Southern Exposure" (1940) bring black songs and sirens together by insisting that black music can wail the sound of alarm: "These are the blues, the wailing blues, the moaning blues, the laughing-crying blues, the sad-happy blues. But they are also the fighting blues. . . . Under each long drawn out moan is mocking laughter, under each melancholy wail a deepening consciousness."[82] Whether the songs console or confront is a question of audience and of positioning. In *Native Son*, the congregation sustains the "quiet and constant communion" that Wright describes in *12 Million* to produce a softly wailing "fighting blues." The film ends with another such song of resistance. Based on the traditional spiritual "Another Man Done Gone" and performed by a male baritone, this song accompanies an overhead shot of Bigger lying face down on his jail bed, awaiting death in the gathering dusk. The final view of the Chicago skyline evokes the broader resonance of Bigger's story and asks the viewer to consider how many "other men" we are losing.[83]

Not-Belongingness

I have argued that the film's scenes of song matter because they shift the locus of authority to *Native Son*'s female characters. But I do not want to overstate this case. Neither Hannah nor Bessie alters the course of the narrative. Bessie is still murdered. In noting that Hannah defies the state's intrusion into the church and that Bessie expresses outsider's insight, it is not my intention to idealize these characters as unshakable pillars of community or bearers of truth. Nor am I trying to clear Wright of charges of sexism. I want rather to point out that Hannah's quiet indignation and Bessie's prescience—as well as both characters' limited horizons of possibility—resonate with Wright's work and career.

Thus far I have contended that Wright's collaborative work in the medium of film, as well as his literal and figurative distance from his role as representative black American writer, allowed him to explore new ways of representing black men and women in shared struggle through song. The film drew Wright and Chenal into alignment with those female blues singers whom Wright describes in "Memories of My Grandmother"—artists who take dispossession *as a matter of course*, as a fact on which to improvise new visions of the world. Literally created from a position of severance, *Native Son* advanced this new vision by making Wright and Bessie allies, as the insights of Bessie Mears came to mirror Wright's own.

Yet the story of *Native Son* is about the peril of exile as well as its promise. I want to turn to the perilous side of the story in order to qualify the concept of outsider's insight that Wright, Gilroy, and I deploy. Without such qualification, the concept threatens to exalt oppression by citing the incisive vision it can produce: "as if the blues were worth it," in Fred Moten's memorable phrase.[84] So while the invocation of outsider's insight has been a key feature of the African American rhetorical tradition at least since 1892, when black feminist Anna Julia Cooper claimed that "it may be woman's privilege from her peculiar coigne of vantage as a quiet observer to whisper just the needed suggestion or the almost forgotten truth," it is crucial to say that, as Gilroy claims with regard to Wright, "this special condition is neither simply a disability nor a constant privilege."[85] "Outsider's insight" describes a representational trope and a real potential. But the expression of this insight also carries the risks that always attend speaking truth to power: one may be further marginalized, blatantly ignored, or, as Bigger's murder of Bessie reminds us, forcibly silenced.

Indeed, if exile and collaboration allowed Wright the freedom to improvise on his earlier work, he was not free to bring his creations back home; instead, his film was checked and cut at what we might think of as a Cold War customs stop between national lines. Due to the film's racial, sexual, and leftist politics, the New York State Board of Censors only agreed to show the film in the States if it were substantially edited. What was lost in the film's transit from Buenos Aires to New York was about thirty minutes—most of which was the trial scene in which Bigger's lawyer defends him.[86] In currently available VHS versions of the film, where one should hear acute social analysis of the conditions that engendered Bigger's crime—a major set piece in the novel—one instead sees a rapid silent montage of a courtroom scene. While much of the film's new power derives from its artful marriage of sound and vision, the censors divorced sound from vision at the critical moment, leaving only a string of odd images that paradoxically announced their own silencing. In a letter to his agent, Wright wrote that "[what] did the greatest damage was cutting the trial. . . . The trial is shown with arms waving and mouths moving but nothing is heard."[87] Chenal offered his own unflappable response to the cuts in a letter to Wright: "As you must know, they were obliged to make them, otherwise the picture never would have been released in Democracy No. 1."[88]

Film preservationists at the Library of Congress have recently restored what is known as the "uncut international version" of *Native Son* and have converted the reels into digital files.[89] Amounting to 118 minutes, these files constitute the longest publicly available version of the film. While this restored version contains nothing like the novel's extensive courtroom scene, it does reveal an important testimony by Jan. Here is part of Jan's dialogue, which was cut by the censors:

> I was trying to help that boy to be free, to be a man. To me, there are no black or white people. And I offered Bigger my friendship. I made a mistake. . . . And that mistake was thinking that after treating people wrong for three hundred years, I could walk up to the first black man on the street, shake his hand, and make him feel everything's all right. I know now how deep this race hate goes. I wish to God I'd have known it then. . . . If Mary were alive here today, she'd agree with me. For her sake, I sit here and say I blundered trying to follow the noblest impulse of my heart. I am for Bigger Thomas; he doesn't have to be for me. I was for him then, and I'm for him now.[90]

One can see why Jan's statement that good white liberal intentions would be nullified in the face of three hundred years of "race hate" might have been rejected, as it was in Ohio, for "present[ing] racial frictions at a time when all groups should be united against everything that is subversive."[91] But there is a subtler critique at work in this moment, too—in the fact that Bigger's most sympathetic legal witness is still calling him "boy" and is leaving uninterrogated the notion that Bigger would need his "help" to "be a man." Further, although Wright claimed that the cuts to this trial scene "did the most damage," the Library of Congress version indicates that the film's greatest loss was the collective omission of smaller details: the risky ambiguity of the scene in which Bigger lays Mary down on her bed while the camera insinuatingly cuts away to the blind Mrs. Dalton entering the bedroom; Bessie's quick insight, upon learning that Bigger has murdered Mary, that "they'll say you raped her," and Bigger's equally quick reply that "they say all black men do that, so it don't make no difference if I did or I didn't"; the way the detective, Britten, confirms the foregoing remark when he scoffs at Jan for leaving Mary in Bigger's care the night she was killed: "Well there is a pretty story. I can just picture you telling that to a jury: how you left a drunken white girl alone with a nigger."[92] Indeed, what is most dramatically excised from the film is the trope of rape, which applies not only to the idealized white woman but also to Bessie. The possibility that sex with the club owner, Ernie, will be the cost of Bessie's new singing career lurks throughout the film; this subtext surfaces most clearly when

Bessie's co-worker Lola advises her to "get wise and throw in the body" to advance her career.[93] The uncensored version of the film both foregrounds the brutality of raced and gendered sexual myths *and* makes Lola, Bigger, Ernie, and Bessie sexual characters—a feat that may have been fostered by the filmmakers' distance from U.S. notions of respectability, though one that would not survive U.S. translation.

Three months after the film's successful South American premiere, the amputated form of *Native Son* (Chenal called it *"massacrée par la censure"*) opened in New York.[94] The critics were unforgiving. According to a reviewer for the *New York Times,* "Don Dean, who plays Bigger's lawyer [Max], is never clearly revealed in court as the liberal he was in the book and play. . . . The stature of *Native Son* has been reduced with this exposure of film."[95] One reason why Max's liberal politics were not apparent was that his speech, like Jan's testimony, had been silenced.[96] Yet even those who realized the film had been cut could not endorse it. Alton Cook, who reviewed it in the *New York World-Telegram,* ended his critique with a meek disclaimer: "I am told that the picture has been marred by some cuts made in deference to censors. If that is so I deeply regret the annoyance this review may cause but the report is based entirely on what the audiences at the Criterion may expect to see."[97] Cook was justified in reviewing the film based on what audiences would see, and I am not attributing the film's failure exclusively to its censorship. What I am suggesting is that *Native Son*'s fate compels us to qualify the notion that exiled or socially marginalized artists like Wright and Smith enjoy enhanced artistic autonomy. Again, outsider's insight is not a "constant privilege" but a potentiality and a risk.

According to Raymond Williams, the exile must perform his choice, or difference, while envisioning a hypothetical return home.[98] In 1951, the year *Native Son* was released, Wright submitted an essay to *Ebony* magazine titled "I Choose Exile." Here, he declared that he had found there to be "more freedom in one square block of Paris than there is in the entire United States!"[99] Indeed, Baldwin alleged that Wright "was fond of referring to Paris as the 'City of Refuge.'"[100] Yet black Americans in France lived under considerable constraint amid the escalating Algerian war for independence. Threatening to deport African Americans who spoke out on the issue, the French government effectively barred them from participation in the most important political debate of the time.[101] (Under these circumstances, Wright's decision to criticize French colonial rule in Africa in *Black Power* [1954] was a bold one.) While "I Choose Exile" sets French liberty against American oppression, however, it is not, significantly, titled "I Choose France." The essay seems to constitute not only Wright's denunciation of his homeland but also his furious appeal to it.

To note that this essay was not published during Wright's lifetime is not only to say that history ironically confirmed Wright's critique of America's suppression of civil liberties.[102] It is also to indicate that Wright's choice of exile, which needed an audience, clearly jeopardized his claim to one. According to Wright, *Black Power* was "remaindered [in the States] for a few cents" just three weeks after its publication; *The Color Curtain* (1956) did not sell well either.[103] Given Wright's diminishing U.S. readership, the lectures he presented to European audiences in these years, collected in the volume *White Man, Listen!*, seem somewhat mournfully misdirected, as if those whom he needed to listen were now beyond range.

In another sense, however, they were too close, and we might say Wright was singing the blues about their proximity all the way to Buenos Aires. On his way there, he composed a poem called the "FB Eye Blues":

That old FB eye
Tied a bell to my bed stall
Said old FB eye
Tied a bell to my bed stall
Each time I love my baby, gover'ment knows it all.

. . . .

Everywhere I look, Lord
I see FB eyes
Said everywhere I look, Lord
I find FB eyes
I'm getting sick and tired of gover'ment spies.[104]

This comical piece seems especially poignant now that we know Wright's suspicions were justified. The FBI file on Wright, which has since been made public, reveals that the agency had begun to track him in 1944, when he publicly criticized the Communist Party's failure to respond militantly enough to the "Negro question" and refused to serve in World War II. When he moved to Paris in 1947, the newly founded CIA followed. The extent of its influence was striking. As Wright was to learn shortly before his death, the CIA had secretly funded and directed the Congress for Cultural Freedom, an organization founded in 1950 to protect dissenting artists and intellectuals; the organization had published excerpts from *Black Power* in several European magazines and had funded Wright's trip to the 1955 Bandung conference, which produced *The Color Curtain*.[105] In this context, the "FB Eye Blues" reads as a bravely light-hearted response to a desperate situation.

Contrary to what "I Choose Exile" declares, exile did not grant Wright the freedom to speak without censure. He crystallizes the problem when, in his liner notes to a Big Bill Broonzy album, he describes the blues singer's paradoxical "freedom." One of Wright's last projects, the notes contain some of his most candid and sardonic writing. He critiques American sociologists who valorize the putative freedom of the poor when in fact "these learned academic men" mean that "if you are not a respected member of society . . . , you are so declassed that nobody is going to listen to you or judge what you do."[106] Wright's own freedom was ultimately limited not by material poverty but by the state's determination of what he could say and do, particularly as an internationally known figure. Yet if his social position was not like Broonzy's, he could hope that his legacy would be, as his notes for Broonzy's posthumously released album suggest. As Wright elegizes Broonzy and celebrates his life and work, he ascribes the "advantages" of disenfranchisement that the sociologists invoke less to the disenfranchised themselves than to their interlocutors: "This not-belongingness was the strange and dubious wealth of men like Big Bill Broonzy," he writes. If Broonzy's outsider status allowed him to be "daringly truthful" in his music, the real profit is that of his listeners: "we who never knew him . . . are the richer for it."[107]

This sense of the futurity of justice was, ironically, the "dubious wealth" of Wright's Adventist grandmother as well as of the blues singers Wright so admired. These singers insist on remembrance, if not redemption. In the words of the classic blues coda (with which Ellison heads his review of Wright's *Black Boy*), "If anyone asks who sang this song, tell them X been here and gone." It is precisely this survival-by-leave-taking that Wright underscores in his foreword to Paul Oliver's *Blues Fell This Morning* (1960). Blues songs testify, he writes, to the passage of "Blacks, torn from their tribal moorings in Africa, transported across the Atlantic." They record "confused wanderings over the American southland and . . . intrusion into the northern American industrial cities." And, in a statement that recalls the international resonance of *Native Son*'s Spanish title, *Sangre Negra*, Wright points out that they extend far beyond U.S. borders: "In Buenos Aires, Stockholm, Copenhagen, London, Berlin, Paris, Rome, in fact, in every large city of the earth where lonely, disinherited men congregate for pleasure or amusement, the orgiastic wail of the blues, and their strident offspring, jazz, can be heard."[108] Here Wright articulates the promise of a music born of original theft and determined thereafter to wander. This music expresses the knowledge that tomorrow really might not be any better, but it will arrive. When it does, someone will ask who sang this song, and when they do, someone will answer.

Smith's Vivid Lyricism

Wright offers a rather different vision of the blues during his European lecture tours of the late 1950s. About ten years after his expatriation from the States, he seeks to explain to his audiences the various modalities of African American vernacular culture—what he calls "the Forms of Things Unknown"[109]—and he uses Smith's "Backwater Blues" to illustrate them:

> The impulses that prodded so many millions of southern Negroes to leave the plantations for the cities of the South, and the dissatisfaction that drove so many other millions from the cities of the South to the industrial centers of the North are summed up in the "Backwater Blues" as sung by Bessie Smith:
>
> > *Then I went an' stood up on some high ol' lonesome hill*
> > *I went an' stood up on some high ol' lonesome hill*
> > *An' looked down on the house where I used to live*
> >
> > *Backwater blues done cause me to pack mah things and go*
> > *Backwater blues done cause me to pack mah things and go*
> > *'Cause mah house fell down an' I cain' live there no mo'*
>
> Many of them knew that their hope was hopeless, and it was out of this that the blues was born, the apex of sensual despair.[110]

Reading this passage, I have often wondered whether Wright stood before his European listeners and *sang* them Bessie Smith's blues. Limited archives and access may render this question unanswerable. Yet this chapter constitutes my effort to ask, in a different way, what it means to picture Wright singing, and in what specific ways his work might be thought to resonate with Smith's music. I have suggested that Wright's vivid lyricism represents his own form of singing, and that his collaborative work in visual media lifts the political valence of black women's songs to a new "plane of vividness."

In light of those moments in his work when Wright accents the subversive potential of black women's songs, it is hard to know what to make of his claim that the "Backwater Blues" spoke for a people who "knew that their hope was hopeless." But it is important to note, first, that this is a statement shaped by hindsight. By the late 1950s, Wright had seen many black men and women of his generation disillusioned by false promises of democracy, in the North as well as the South, in Europe as well as the States. At the time of the Migration, however, those who made the journey north must have believed anything would be better than the lawless terror and poverty of the South. As if to remind his listeners that he himself had once been with them, Wright concludes this lecture by reading perhaps the most optimistic moment in his oeuvre: the entire last passage of *12 Million Black Voices*.[111] His discussion of African American literature thus draws to a close with these words: "We are with the new tide. We stand at the crossroads. We watch each new procession. The hot wires carry urgent appeals. Print compels us. Voices are speaking. Men are moving! And we shall be with them . . ." (*12M*, 147).

The juxtaposition of Wright's rather grim reading of "Backwater Blues" and his re-citation of the end of *12 Million* itself dramatizes "the apex of sensual despair" that Wright describes with regard to the blues—a palpable severance from one's own possibility, whether real or only imagined. This sense of loss is best captured by Bessie when, just before Bigger kills her, she tells him, "I never thought I'd be like this" (*NS*, 269). I have suggested that Wright's vividly lyrical work both revels in and critiques its own unlikelihood: *I never thought I'd write like this, and neither did you.* But I have also sought to show that Wright's career embodies the very real consequences of claiming literal and figurative alienation. His experiences with the CIA and U.S. censors indicate that his ability to exploit his own displacement was limited; these experiences justify Wright's claim that, if the blues singer's "not-belongingness" is a form of "wealth," this wealth is "strange and dubious."

Certainly Smith's career reveals a similar set of limitations, for her fall from stardom was nearly as dramatic as her rise to it. The Empress's reputation suffered throughout the 1930s, when her record sales sharply decreased due to the Depression as well as the advent of radio and film and the declining popularity of her classic blues style. Columbia Records dropped her from its roster in 1931. Still, in the mid-1930s, she modernized her costuming and started to "swing" Tin Pan Alley material, and it was in the midst of this apparent comeback that she was killed in a car accident on a Mississippi highway in 1937, at age forty-three.[112]

Which brings us to the question, why Smith? Smith had been dead for nearly four years when Wright wrote about her last great hit, "Empty

Bed Blues," in "Memories of My Grandmother." By 1941, Wright might instead have cited any number of the southern bluesmen who then dominated the market for blues recordings, such as Leadbelly, Leroy Carr, or Big Bill Broonzy, and by the mid-1950s, he might have cited (or sung) several other classic blues songs in his discussion of "the Forms of Things Unknown." How then might we account for Wright's decision to invoke Smith until the end of his life?

No doubt part of what drew Wright to Smith was their shared geographical and economic origins, as well as their eventual, if temporary, position as the most successful black artists in their respective fields. Born in the rural South (Smith in Tennessee in 1894, Wright in Mississippi in 1908), both experienced limited formal education and a journey from the extreme depths of poverty to international renown. These similarities may explain why Wright would have taken a particular interest in Smith, even aligned himself with her. They may explain, moreover, why there is a note among his papers claiming that Wright himself had planned to write Smith's biography.[113] Still, these connections do not fully explain why Wright would return to Smith, especially given his relative silence about black artists in general and black female artists in particular.[114]

I have suggested that Wright's "lyrical" prose grants a new valence to a writing style that had by then been marked as problematically feminine. One reason why I believe Smith was important to Wright was that she herself, like Mamie Smith, Ma Rainey, and other blueswomen, developed and popularized new ways of performing black femininity. As many commentators have pointed out, Smith disrupted conventional performances of race, gender, and sexuality through her bisexuality, tough yet vulnerable persona, and raunchy lyrics.[115] Wright seems to have valued the alternative versions of femininity that Smith and other blueswomen represented in contrast to the religious black matriarch about which his fiction expresses ambivalence. Indeed, "Memories" itself stages a contest between Smith and Wright's blues-barring grandmother, Margaret Wilson. Wright suggests that the intensity of both Smith's and his grandmother's vision is produced by systematic severance from mainstream American society. According to Wright, Wilson's rigid Adventism marks her oppressive, if somewhat impressive, determination to reject a world that has rejected her. But what separates Smith's blues from Wilson's spirituals, in Wright's assessment, is that the blues expresses the artistic *license* that social alienation might afford. If Smith was among the *only* black female artists for whom Wright would express uncomplicated respect (his relationship with Margaret Walker was more personal and certainly more fraught), this is partly because of her difference from what Wright considered "the wrong kind of woman."[116] This phenomenon is clearly both problematic and productive. Without condoning this bias, I want to suggest that Wright's engagement with Smith is valuable, not only for what it reveals about Wright's work but also for what it tells us about Smith's own.

The comparison helps us see, for instance, that Smith's own defiance of sentimentality predated and accorded with Wright's. The inventive precision of her singing kept even her most sorrowful songs from sounding morose and her most comedic songs from sounding funny. Thus, Gunther Schuller suggests that on a song like "You've Been a Good Ole Wagon" (1925), Smith "strips [the] vaudeville standard of its intended folksy, 'back home' humor, and turns it into a serious, poignant blues"— one that, moreover, sounds "genuinely sad, yet somehow objective."[117] Such a balance is evident in Smith's buoyantly mournful performance of "Empty Bed Blues" as well. The song is a tour de force of double entendres in which Smith bemoans the loss of an extraordinary lover, a man who could "grind my coffee, 'cause he had a brand new grind," "a deep sea diver with a stroke that can't go wrong."[118] For all the song's comedic appeal, the broad, clarion cry of Smith's voice probes the wound of abandonment. As singer Alberta Hunter described it, "Even though she was raucous and loud, she had a sort of a tear—no, not a tear, but there was a *misery* in what she did."[119] Smith creates this effect by singing most songs near the edge of her vocal break, or what is known in classical music as the *passagio*—the point in the vocal register between the deeper chest voice and the higher head voice. Unlike later soul singers who belt in this range, Smith rarely sounds as if she is straining to reach any notes. But by singing in this part of her range, she produces a sound on the verge of a sonic break—hence Hunter's evocation of the cry or "tear." Smith's sensitive approach to dynamics and intonation also enhances the emotional effect of her music. She belts out some words, like "woke up" in "Empty Bed Blues," delivering them straight ahead with strong vibrato; she gently rounds each verse down—less dejected (or "miserable," in Hunter's terms) than careful to tell each part of her story with feeling.

Ultimately, Smith is important to the conception of vivid lyricism that I have theorized less because of her groundbreaking lyrical performances of black femininity than because of the way she sings. Wright in fact offers an incisive description of her musical practice when he claims that expressive "over-emphasis" lifts "each detail" in a blues song to a new "plane of vividness." The statement attunes us to something important—something more than Wright seems to have intended—about Smith's artistry. Certainly it highlights the fact that a song like "Empty Bed Blues" isolates and amplifies everyday objects—an empty bed, a euphemistic coffee grinder. But when Wright suggests that the blues "over-emphasi[ze]" "each detail," he also hints at the way that the dramatic precision of Smith's singing serves to vivify not just the objects she sings about but *musical* details themselves. Smith's singing generates intensified visions not only of familiar objects but also of the structural components of the blues.

According to Schuller, who remains one of Smith's most incisive listeners, what made Smith "[technically perfect]" was her "remarkable ear for and control of intonation, in all its subtlest functions; a perfectly centered, naturally produced voice (in her prime); an extreme sensitivity to word meaning and the sensory, almost physical, feeling of a word; and, related to this, superb diction and what singers call projection."[120] We hear Smith's vivid lyricism in the way she uses these skills to make the architecture of a song itself vivid: spinning simple quarter notes into bold announcements by projecting a clarion tone and making notes in the deeper register palpable with subtle growls; altering the rhythm of a repeated phrase and breaking it up by breathing in an unexpected place; carving musical phrases into distinct shapes by scooping them up with brief slides or easing them down with a slightly flattened fall-off that sounds like a sigh. This is *lyricism*, not lyrics, made vivid.

We might listen, for instance, to "Empty Bed Blues," which Smith recorded in two parts on March 20, 1928, with Porter Grainger on piano and Charlie Green on trombone. Grainger was Smith's musical director at the time, and Green was one of her favorite accompanists.[121] In this recording, Smith makes her lyrics *and* her lyricism vivid by "word painting," performing the song text in a way that enforces its meaning. The "Part 1" version of the song begins with a laconic introduction by Grainger and Green, after which Smith sings, "I woke up this morning with an awful aching head." Her sharp delivery of "I woke up" arouses the song, but she characteristically lets the first part of the phrase fall, loosely sliding down to "morning." When she repeats the line, she starts it on the beat rather than before to effect a laid-back swing, and, as if to indicate that the word "awful" requires extra effort to sing, she breaks it up by breathing right in the middle of it. As she closes the verse, she pauses and breathes between the clauses "My new man had left me" and "just a room and a empty bed," to isolate the now-empty room and bed. She then catalogues the sexual pleasures she enjoyed with this man, describing them in the present tense as if he were still there; she paints these lyrics through harmonic choices and through her tonal coloring, or the sound she produces. For example, when she repeats the phrase "he thrills me night and day," she leaps a major fourth from "thrills" to "me." When she describes her lover as a "deep sea diver with a stroke that can't go wrong," she projects a deeper tone on "stroke" and brightens the "can't" into a smile.

Parts 1 and 2 of "Empty Bed Blues" also highlight the importance of what Wright calls the "emotional intensity of the participants" in a blues song—or, more useful for our purposes, the musical intensity that the singer and accompanists perform. Both Grainger and Green fill in and enhance the song's precise contours and amplify Smith's delivery of the lyrics. Grainger's winsome though unostentatious piano accompaniment takes backstage to Green's big "talking approach" to the horn, which works in close, comical counterpoint to Smith's singing. Green amps up his growling on the word "coffee grinder" (Smith leaves most of the gravelly sound to him, projecting a clearer tone throughout), and performs a marching ascending flourish in response to Smith's major-fourth leap on "thrills me." Part 2 is a less successful collaboration. Grainger plays a wrong chord on the first verse, Green's trumpet seems to drag, and it's tempting to interpret Smith's frequent singing ahead of the beat as an attempt to speed her accompanists' tempo up. The swing of Part 2 is also hampered by awkward lyrics; Smith delivers mouthfuls of phrases like "I bought him a blanket, pillow for his head at night" with less assurance than the more economical statements of Part 1. Yet when Smith and her accompanists "click," as they do in the first part, they work together to make the textual and musical details of the song vivid.

Wright suggests that this collaborative process gives coherence to verses that otherwise appear, on the page, to be "a series of incidents of domestic discord and defeated love thrown seemingly carelessly together." Yet this assessment seems to ignore the fact that the verses are already "stitched together" by an obvious logic: that of the double entendre. While Wright could not have failed to realize this, he seems to want to cloak Smith's song in more respectable garb, in the prim language of "domestic discord." What I have termed Wright's "reception anxiety" may explain his own misreading of the song; if he feared that the spirituals pandered to white fantasies of black servility, "Empty Bed Blues" was perhaps more of a challenge to bourgeois propriety than he himself could face. At the same time, however, to compare the first and second versions of the song is to hear a certain justice in Wright's claim that the verses appear to be "thrown . . . carelessly together."

As Smith's niece Ruby Walker told Smith's biographer Chris Albertson, the song "was a very long narrative when Bessie performed it on stage."[122] Even Smith's abridged version of the song took up both sides of the record, resulting in a Part 1 and Part 2. In Part 1, Smith sings five verses. The first explains that her lover has left her, the next three describe his sexual prowess, and the final one fulfills the first by suggesting that the speaker's "girlfriend Lou" is now enjoying the sexual favors about which the speaker has mistakenly informed her. Due to the limited time of the record, Smith ends Part 2 more abruptly. She cuts four bars from the last chorus, concluding with two verses that do seem stitched together at random:

> He boiled my fresh cabbage and he made it awful hot
> He boiled my fresh cabbage and he made it awful hot
> When he put in the bacon, it overflowed the pot
>
> When you get good lovin', never go and spread the news
> Yes, he'll double-cross you, and leave you with them empty bed
> blues.

Absent the detail that she has told her girlfriend about her lover, it is not clear why the speaker's outrageous innuendo in the penultimate verse would lead to her cautionary lament about the danger of "spreading the news" in the last. Yet when Wright deems the song's verses "stitched together," he fails to appreciate the conditions of the recording's production. In this sense, his analysis of the song resonates with his U.S. viewers' limited understanding of his own truncated film. While Wright and Chenal operated in the spirit of the blues, as Wright described them, by collaboratively creating a work that improvised on familiar tropes from Wright's oeuvre (women and song) and lifted them to "a new plane of vividness," the film's cuts also ironically aligned it with the blues in the formal sense, enhancing its non-narrative quality.

The abrupt ending to "Empty Bed Blues" was not, of course, an effect of censorship, although censorship did inform Smith's career as well as Wright's. Indeed, "Empty Bed Blues" was allegedly banned in Boston—though its censorship (or rumors thereof) may have served Smith well. In fact, Albertson suggests that Columbia may have invented or amplified this story as a "promotional ploy" designed to boost record sales.[123] If this is so, then the ploy is one Wright would have appreciated, for it exemplifies the phenomenon he frequently celebrated with regard to the blues and his own work: the practice of turning exclusion to one's own advantage, thus making a mockery of exclusion itself.

Ultimately, what separates Smith's vivid lyricism from Wright's is that, whereas Wright's vividly lyrical prose exposes the labor of its own production, a central facet of Smith's class-act aesthetic was to make her musicality sound effortless. For this reason and others, Wright himself may not have considered Smith an artist in her own right. He would not have been alone. As we shall see, Baldwin would later neglect Smith's artistry even as he featured "Empty Bed Blues" in his novel *Another Country* (1962) and cited Smith's centrality to his own artistic development more explicitly than Wright ever did. In light of this oversight, Schuller's attention to Smith's own creative process is crucial. As he explains, "Successive takes of her recordings frequently show that she had a well-defined idea of what she was going to do on each tune. Like a great actress, she created the illusion of total improvisation, even though every move may have been in some manner prepared and studied."[124] Smith and her collaborators may have sought to mask their own musical labor, but the vivid lyricism of their work represented a seizure of the means of artistic production as surely as did Wright's—even as these artists' claims to audience proved as tenuous as they were fierce.

2 / The Timbre of Sincerity: Mahalia Jackson's Gospel Sound and Ralph Ellison's *Invisible Man*

Thanks to Ralph Ellison's writings on music, eloquent style, and self-mythology designed to promote this view, literary critics have often seen Ellison's writing, like Zora Neale Hurston's, as an expansive lyrical answer to Richard Wright's hardboiled naturalism.[1] I hope the previous chapter has shown that dichotomy to be misleading, if not false. A more appropriate distinction between Wright and Ellison is that, whereas Wright often anticipates a readership that will misread his use of black music—and thus needs to leave the States and even the medium of fiction to bring his engagement with Bessie Smith's blues to fruition—Ellison anticipates a readership that will corroborate his complex vision. This faith in the writer's powers of inventive persuasion helps explain why Ellison represents black women's sacred songs in a more celebratory, less anxious manner than does Wright. Like Wright's account of Smith's blues, Ellison's account of women's sacred music illuminates his own literary style.

Ellison's nonfiction music writings mainly concern the male blues and jazz artists who were his heroes—Louis Armstrong, Duke Ellington, Charlie Christian, Jimmy Rushing. As is well known, Ellison figures these artists as custodians of the unrealized promise of pluralistic democracy. Yet this chapter aims to correct the critical bias that Ellison's own bias produces, of reading his work only through his writings on secular male musicians.[2] Instead, I use Ellison's essay on gospel singer Mahalia Jackson to theorize Ellison's creation of a complex yet non-duplicitous narrative voice in his classic black bildungsroman, *Invisible*

Man (1952). When we read Ellison's novel for the "timbre of sincerity" he ascribes to Jackson, we can see that Ellison's faith in fiction matches his faith in black music, and not only on the grounds that both art forms offer templates for social pluralism but more specifically because they both represent this expressive potential: that the black writer and the singer might drop the ironic mask often associated with "crossing over" toward a white audience—or, in Ellison's case, "integrating" the (white) American literary tradition—and instead centralize a sincere black expressive ambivalence. By linking Ellison's and Jackson's work through the concept of sincere ambivalence, I offer a more sincere vision of Ellison's modernist novel than is common, and a more complex vision of Jackson's music. Highlighting both artists' non-duplicitous double vocality, moreover, allows us to theorize forms of audience-performer relations that do not privilege the white gaze.

Given Ellison's brilliant writings on jazz, it is no surprise that the organizers of the 1958 Newport Jazz Festival invited him, along with Sterling Brown and Langston Hughes, to appear on a panel discussion of "Jazz and American Life." What is more surprising is that Ellison's literary beat that year was not jazz but gospel music. His trip to Newport would produce his only article on a female (sacred) singer, "As the Spirit Moves Mahalia" (1958). On the Newport stage that summer, Jackson performed "Come Sunday" with the Duke Ellington Orchestra and, later, a solo set of gospel songs. (This was the second year the jazz festival had featured gospel music, billing it as the music at "the roots of jazz.") Apart from her festival performances, Jackson also sang at Newport's Mount Zion AME Church that weekend, on Sunday morning. In the midst of this busy schedule, she additionally made time to attend Ellison's panel. This, according to one reporter, was Jackson's response to the panel discussion: "There's been too much analyzing here and not enough heart."[3] Granted, the reporter's citation of this remark enforces the troubling binary by which female artists feel things while their male counterparts think about them.[4] Ellison's article on Jackson constructs a version of this binary as well: while his appreciation of Jackson's art verges on reverence, he does not consider Jackson his peer in the expression of ambivalence. I see this as a mistake. Against these artists' mutual misrecognition—whereby Jackson frames Ellison as lacking heart and Ellison frames Jackson as lacking complexity—I show that affective ambivalence is a critical effect of both Ellison's and Jackson's intellectual labor. Hence, I take Jackson's exchange with the cultural critics at Newport, skeptical though it is, as an invitation to draw Jackson and Ellison together.

The concept of Jackson's "timbre of sincerity" was so central to Ellison's article that his working title was "Mahalia, the Timbre of Sincerity."[5] Timbre refers to the distinct sound of a voice—what Nina Eidsheim calls its "color, texture, and weight" and what Roland Barthes terms its "grain."[6] An elusive concept in musical analysis, timbre is often described through physical terms such as "heavy," "dark," "light," and "bright."[7] By associating Jackson's timbre not with a physical property but with a character trait, Ellison implies that Jackson's distinctive vocal sound serves an ethical function. He seems to characterize her timbre as "sincere" to denote her earnest religious purpose. However, he also offers a careful typology of Jackson's myriad singing styles that strains against that interpretive frame. Ellison often stresses that artistic form *is* its meaning.[8] With regard to vocal art specifically, he claims that singer Jimmy Rushing's fusion of expressive styles creates ambiguity.[9] Thus, while sincerity etymologically denotes purity, moments in Ellison's commentary collectively allow us to redefine sincerity as an integrative expressive practice that conveys ambiguities with clarity.

I broadly define this integrative practice as the performance of stylistic variation and citational range. I am thinking here of what Ellison describes as Jackson's use of gospel moans, flamenco cries, and operatic glissandi[10]—and of Ellison's alternate deployment of vivid lyricism;[11] deadpan cadences that recall Hemingway's early work; and allusions to Poe, Dante, Melville, and Louis Armstrong (among others), in the prologue to *Invisible Man* alone. The effect of this integrative practice is to convey conflicting ideas or emotions—what I term *ambivalence*. Like Barbara Johnson, I see ambivalence as a productive force. Rejecting the usual view of ambivalence as "a temporary, unfortunate, and remediable state of feeling," Johnson invests power in "claiming the right to ambivalence," especially insofar as "there may be something deadening about having to renounce one's ambivalence too soon, on someone else's terms."[12] "If resistance is always the sign of a counter-story," she writes, "ambivalence is perhaps the state of holding on to more than one story at a time."[13]

To read for sincerity, as I have defined it, is to view these two stories or meanings as *coexisting without competing*. What I am proposing, then, is a mode of reading double-voiced expression that does not privilege one meaning over the other but instead foregrounds simultaneity and indeterminacy—the unresolved suspension of two (or more) conflicting meanings.[14] This interpretive approach departs from treatments of double vocality in African American Studies, most of which prioritize the Western classical (and etymological) definition of irony as *dissimulation*—saying one thing and meaning another—and privilege latent or coded meanings over manifest ones.[15] Such critical approaches utilize concepts like masking, laughing-to-keep-from-crying blues humor, trickster figures, subversion, and what Henry Louis Gates Jr. terms "motivated Signifyin(g)" or parody.[16] These concepts are especially helpful in capturing and affirming the duplicitous ironic mode in which, for instance, Invisible Man's grandfather suggests he has lived his entire life. On his deathbed, the grandfather tells his family, "Our life is a war and I have been a traitor all my born days, a spy in the enemy's country," and he advises his survivors to face "the enemy" as he has done: to "overcome 'em with yeses, undermine 'em with grins, agree 'em to death and destruction" (*IM*, 16). The dominant critical paradigm I am describing would take the insurrectionary intent of Invisible Man's grandfather to be more important than (if inseparable from) the grinning mask he presents to the world; what matters is the joke he perpetrates on those who would mistake the mask for the man.[17]

Such a reading is appropriate to this particular case—as it is relevant to many others. I myself privileged the "hidden" meaning of the spirituals over the manifest meaning when, in the previous chapter, I highlighted the impulse to escape that "Steal Away" and "Swing Low" encode. But I am proposing an additional hermeneutic here, one which Ellison's narrator seems to invite when he ultimately declares his own form of (non-duplicitous) doubleness, as distinct from his grandfather's: "So I denounce and defend . . . condemn and affirm, say no and say yes . . . I hate and I love" (*IM*, 579–580). This particular doubleness is closer to romantic irony than to classical irony; it entails, in Friedrich Schlegel's terms, a "consistent alternation of affirmation and negation . . . of enthusiasm and skepticism."[18] Yet the timbre of sincerity goes one step further in describing double meanings that do not alternate but instead coexist, as Ellison's use of "and" implies: "I denounce and defend" is substantively different from "denounce *then* defend." Thus, reading for sincerity would mean interpreting "Steal Away" as a song that expresses a longing for divine redemption as much as a gesture toward literal escape. It means considering that, when Ray Charles sings "America the Beautiful" (1972) or when John Coltrane plays "My Favorite Things" (1960), these artists are signifying on or critiquing their source material while also earnestly engaging it—both "meaning it" and not meaning it, to put it bluntly. Finally, as I will explain in more detail, reading for sincerity means understanding Jackson and Ellison to engage at once subversively and affirmatively with the prior texts they cite and refashion.

To explain the gender and racial politics of this intervention, it will be helpful to elaborate on the difference between sincerity and masking. Masking is a key term in Ellison studies and a concept that Ellison genders male. In the 1896 poem that popularized the term, Paul Laurence Dunbar writes,

> We wear the mask that grins and lies,
> It hides our cheeks and shades our eyes,—
>
> . . . .
>
> We smile, but, O great Christ, our cries
> To thee from tortured souls arise.
>
> . . . .
>
> But let the world dream otherwise,
>   We wear the mask![19]

Ellison extends Dunbar's image of the mask by claiming that both white and black men wear the mask, and that they do so not only to hide the sorrow of Dunbar's "tortured souls" but also to cover their true skill and intelligence. In short, theirs is the mask of the con man. In a 1957 letter to Albert Murray, Ellison argues that masking is constitutive of the (male) American character. He finds the "archetypal figure" of the "smart-man-playing-dumb" in "Hemingway when he pretends to be a sportsman, or *only* a sportsman; Faulkner when he pretends to be a farmer; Benjamin Franklin when he pretended to be a 'child of nature,' instead of the hipped operator that he was; even Lincoln when he pretended to be a simple country lawyer."[20] For Ellison, the quintessential agent of this "near tragic debunking of the self" is Louis Armstrong: "Hare *and* bear [are] the ticket; man and mask, sophistication and taste hiding behind clowning and crude manners—the American joke, man."[21] Because American men partake in the "American joke" of debunking themselves in order to advance their prospects, "the 'darky' act makes brothers of us all."[22]

Ellison does not include women in this masking brotherhood. For Ellison, men are the maskers, whereas Jackson and other renowned female singers are "the sincere ones" (*A*, 88).[23] While this chapter will destabilize that gendered binary by theorizing Ellison's sincerity, we could just as well pursue the opposite tack and show Jackson herself to be an adept wearer of the mask. She had been touring the world for years, and had clearly achieved star status, when she offered the Newport audience of 1958 the charmingly disingenuous remark, "You make me feel like I'm a star."[24] Whatever her intention, it is easy to read this comment as an instance when Jackson, like Ellison's maskers, debunks herself to increase her advantage. When she performs the role of the unassuming ingénue, Jackson flatters the Newport crowd into imagining that their appreciation of her prodigious skill is unique, and that illusion encourages the crowd to perform more of their own "goodwill" by maintaining their fervent applause.

Ellison explains the utility of such theatrical social practices in "Change the Joke and Slip the Yoke," an essay published the same year as "As the Spirit": "We wear the mask for purposes of aggression as well as for defense; when we are projecting the future [performing a role we wish to have] and preserving the past [maintaining a role we wish to keep]. In short, the motives hidden behind the mask are as numerous as the ambiguities the mask conceals."[25] The timbre of sincerity, on the other hand, *conveys* the ambiguities that the mask seeks to conceal. This concept therefore allows us to imagine different forms of performer-audience relations than masking posits. Contemporary critical usage sees black performative masking as a process of concealing illicit or aggressive meanings from an audience. This paradigm tends to privilege an oppositional relationship between performer and spectator, the most common scenario being one in which a black artist faces a white audience (notwithstanding Ellison's own comments on white masking). In reading for sincerity rather than masking, I do not question the latter's importance as a theoretical tool; we need it to account for the ways in which African Americans have historically veiled subversive messages as a means of survival. My point is that we additionally need to account for those moments when the obligation to wear the mask diminishes— as it might in safe spaces that are located, in Sondra O'Neale's words, "beyond the mask."[26] These are spaces of sincerity.

In light of the gendered connotations of masking and sincerity I have described, it should not surprise us to note that the black feminist critics who theorized safe spaces coded them as black *female* spaces. By theorizing these spaces, critics such as Patricia Hill Collins and bell hooks not only underscore black women's resistance but also privilege black communities' own internal dynamics over oppositional interracial relations. Though I complicate the assumption that sincerity is a female domain, I follow these critics in using the concept of the safe space to theorize performance that does *not* primarily respond to the white gaze. If "doubleness is constitutive of black performance," then we need to understand that doubleness not only as the practice of conveying different messages to different groups of listeners—or over different frequencies—but also as the practice of telling multiple truths at once, to an audience that might be trusted with them.[27] There are ways of reading *Invisible Man* itself as this kind of discursive space.

"As the Spirit" prompts us to visualize the African American artist's creation of this space through what I term a *reverse crossover* effect. At the very moment that Jackson and other gospel singers are crossing over to a white secular audience (a move their appearance at the Newport festival represents), Ellison insists that Jackson's fans at Newport, most of whom were white, hear Jackson's timbre of sincerity "most distinctly" when they "venture into . . . [Mount Zion] Afro-American Episcopal Church" to hear her sing on Sunday morning (*A*, 92, 93). In short, he calls for the dominant culture to come meet the black artist on her own terms. Toni Morrison's claims about her own work help us visualize this process. In 1998, Morrison responds with exasperation to an interviewer's question about why her fiction does not feature more white characters, a question that would only be directed at a minoritized writer. Stating that "it is inconceivable that where I already am *is* the mainstream," Morrison proceeds to give what is surely among the most incisive accounts of her project as well as, in a certain reading, that of African American literature more generally: "I stood at the border, I stood at the edge, and *claimed* it as central, . . . and [I] let the rest of the world move over to where *I* was."[28] This is precisely the process that Ellison describes when he states that, although Jackson came to perform for white fans on the (secular) Newport stage, they did well to move over to where she was on Sunday morning.

Ellison's own work attempts to effect such reversal as well. In 1963, he asserted, "One concept that I wish we would get rid of is the concept of a main stream of American culture—which is an exact mirroring of segregation and second-class citizenship. . . . I wish that we would dispense with this idea that we Negroes are begging to get in somewhere."[29] Hence, while Alan Nadel reads *Invisible Man*'s formalistic integration of distinct prose styles and allusions as reflecting the "moral imperative" of social integration, I argue that Ellison's integrative practice would figuratively *reverse* integration's conventional course.[30] In my reading, as I have said, Ellison's and Jackson's integrative practice conveys a candid ambivalence. To read for the timbre of sincerity is to read formal hybridity as producing this multiple effect. And to privilege expressive multiplicity over duplicity is to destabilize the paradigm by which the black artist must mask one meaning behind another in order to navigate (or "integrate") the white world (*Invisible Man*'s grandfather's model) and to instead accent the sense in which black doubleness demands to be met on its own complex terms.

In this chapter, I offer a brief biographical sketch of Jackson, show how "As the Spirit" helps us recode sincerity as sincere ambivalence, and explain how the concept of sincerity elucidates Jackson's vocal art as well as Ellison's *Invisible Man*.[31] Rather than offer yet another comprehensive reading of Ellison's novel, I show that "As the Spirit" attunes us to the expressive complexity of the novel's singing women—for instance, the narrator's caretaker, Mary, sings Bessie Smith's "Backwater Blues" (1927) and alludes to Jackson's own "Move On Up a Little Higher" (1947)—and I identify a similar complexity in the non-evasive registers of Ellison's narrative voice.[32]

Mahalia Moves the Spirit

Born in New Orleans in 1911, three years before Ellison, Mahalia Jackson was an ambitious musical genius whose career in many ways anticipates and resonates with Ellison's own. In an account published shortly before Jackson's death in 1972, Anthony Heilbut wrote that Jackson "is not merely one of the supreme gospel singers, . . . [but] she has easily broadcast gospel's appeal more widely than anyone else in history. Not necessarily in the church, where she's only one of many pioneers. But in Europe and white America, Mahalia is the single most important gospel singer."[33] Her unpredictable approach to timing, phrasing, and melody and her extraordinary vocal power and range are key facets of Jackson's art. More broadly, she is known for merging religious music with the sounds and stylings of the blues. Though raised in a Baptist church, she was influenced by the beat-driven music she heard in the Sanctified church next to her home—as well as by Bessie Smith and Ma Rainey, whose recordings she studied religiously in an attempt to "capture their nuances and volume."[34] She moved to Chicago in 1927, the same year Richard Wright arrived there, and soon met Thomas Dorsey, the composer whose Baptist hymns she would transform. According to Horace Clarence Boyer, Jackson's style of "bending a note here, chopping off a note there, singing through rest spots and ornamenting the melodic line at will" not only befuddled several would-be piano accompanists but also made Dorsey "legitimately concerned with what she would do to his songs."[35] However, Jackson's liberal interpretations of Dorsey's compositions, along with Mildred Falls's brilliant piano accompaniment, would establish Dorsey as the "Father of Gospel" and Jackson as the genre's "Queen." Although Jackson originally scandalized parishioners in New Orleans and Chicago with her rocking beat and tendency to lift her dress and roll her hips, she eventually acquired a tremendous following among black listeners.[36] In 1947, five years before Ellison published *Invisible Man*, Jackson's recording of "Move On Up a Little Higher" sold an unprecedented two million copies—leading Malcolm X to salute her as "the first Negro that Negroes ever made famous."[37]

She debuted at Carnegie Hall in 1950.[38] George Avakian signed her to Columbia Records in 1954, certain that she could be a crossover success. Columbia billed her as "the World's Greatest Gospel Singer" and began to promote her with the same publicity and resources they gave their "popular" artists. It worked. Jackson appeared on the *Ed Sullivan Show* in 1956; she appeared at the Newport Jazz Festival in the late 1950s ("before it got to be a beer festival," as she notes in her memoir);[39] she was featured in Douglas Sirk's *Imitation of Life* in 1959; she performed at John F. Kennedy's inaugural ball in 1961; she sang at the March on Washington in 1963. (According to an apocryphal story, it was she who encouraged King, when he paused, to "tell them about the dream.")[40] While Jackson was more engaged in the spectacle of national politics than was Ellison, she additionally assumed a custodial role with regard to gospel music, which was akin to the role Ellison assumed with regard to American literature and culture. In her memoir, *Movin' On Up* (1966) she sets the record straight regarding the transmission of gospel: "A lot of folks don't know that gospel songs have not been handed down like spirituals" but rather "written by Negro musicians like Professor Dorsey" (*M*, 62). And she argues (as Ellison did) that gospel is "not supposed to be just an entertainment" (*M*, 109).

That conviction made Jackson wary of performing at a secular venue like the Newport Jazz Festival, to which the organizers first invited her in 1957. While she was known for bringing "the blues [style] into gospel," she maintained control over the material she recorded with Columbia, and she refused to sing the blues.[41] (She studied Bessie Smith's sound while growing up, she told Studs Terkel, but that was *before* she was saved.)[42] Moreover, she generally refused to sing gospel music in secular venues where blues or jazz were played (*M*, 159). According to Newport impresario George Wein, Jackson agreed to sing at Newport in '57 only because she was also invited to appear at Newport's Trinity Episcopal Church for Sunday mass that weekend.[43] (The gospel program that year included the Drinkard Singers and Clara Ward and the Ward Singers, among others. Cissy Houston later explained that her group, the Drinkard Singers, was nervous to perform at Newport, since "they had never performed for a white, nonchurch audience before.")[44] In 1958, Jackson returned to

Newport to sing with Duke Ellington's band on Thursday and to present her own set on Saturday at midnight (Sunday morning). Later that
Sunday morning, she sang at Mount Zion AME Church, whose pastor
was then A. J. Simmons. Originally founded in 1845, Mount Zion was
the largest church of color in Newport by the mid-twentieth century and
a center of black religious and cultural life. Among the church's distinctions was its possession of the only pipe organ in a church of color in New
England at that time and its establishment, in the 1960s, of the first Black
History Museum in Rhode Island. Mahalia Jackson and Count Basie
were among several prominent artists who attended Mount Zion while
performing at the Newport Jazz Festival. According to current church
member John Sommerville, black artists not welcome in local hotels
would stay at the home of Nellie Brown. In 1974, the church was burned
in a suspicious fire whose cause was never determined; the church was
rebuilt and is now located at the corner of Tilley and Van Zandt Avenues
in Newport.[45] Although Ellison does not name the church, he clearly
acknowledges its significance when he describes Jackson's performance
there—a point to which I will return.

Part album review, part concert review, part essay on American music
and culture, "As the Spirit" briefly addresses the Jackson-Ellington performance before moving on to Jackson's appearance at the church—
which, according to notes among Ellison's papers, was the seed of this
article. Early drafts show Ellison emphasizing the contrast between these
performances in terms of their relative publicity and effectiveness: "Last
July Mahalia Jackson's most publicized appearance in Newport was that
[which] she made with the Duke Ellington orchestra on a Thursday evening, [yet] her most moving appearance came hardly announced, when,
on Sunday morning, she took part in the morning services in the A.M.E.
church."[46]

When discussing the Ellington-Jackson performance, Ellison
expresses dismay at the "banal" lyrics Ellington composed for Jackson
and aristocratically concludes that Ellington and Jackson's "Come Sunday" was "a most unfortunate marriage and an error of taste" (A, 92).[47]
This was a relatively mild critique compared with that of Melvin Tapley,
who had reviewed the festival for the New York Amsterdam News the
previous year. Tapley candidly stated that the inclusion of gospel music
on the Newport program of '57 "desecrate[d] music born of our religious
beliefs." "Why whites will continue to insist on dragging our religious
music in with jazz because it has a rhythm they are intrigued by, and
why dedicated artists consent to help them 'lump' the two together . . . is

an interesting question," he wrote.[48] In contrast, Ellison does not blame white promoters for arranging the "unfortunate marriage" between Jackson and Ellington. Nor does he lament what he describes as the passage of gospel music from "the comparative obscurity of the Negro community" to the mainstream of "our national song style" (A, 90)—a movement that Jackson's gospel set at Newport signifies. Yet Ellison implicitly pushes back against gospel's crossover movement by focusing his article on Jackson's appearance at Mount Zion. By privileging Jackson's performance at church, and the fans that cross over to see her there, Ellison centralizes what happens on Newport's margins. He rhetorically redefines the mainstream.

Ellison's desire to position Jackson squarely within the black church, his essay's mainstream, explains why he limits the meaning of Jackson's art, even as he carefully catalogues her diverse vocal resources. Ellison explains that Jackson's singing "is most eclectic in its use of other musical idioms; indeed, it borrows any effect which will aid in the arousing and control of emotion," so that "it is an art which depends upon the employment of the full expressive resources of the human voice" (A, 91, 90). Among the expressive resources Jackson exploits, Ellison identifies

> the rough growls employed by blues singers, the . . . half-cry, half-recitative [sounds] which are common to Eastern music, the shouts and hollers of American Negro folk cries, the rough-edged tones and broad vibratos, the high, shrill and grating tones which rasp one's ears like the agonized flourishes of flamenco . . . , the gut tones, which remind us of where the jazz trombone found its human source. . . . [Jackson's singing] utilizes half-tones, glissandi, blue notes, humming and moaning. . . . Its diction ranges from the most precise to the near liquidation of word-meaning in the sound: a pronunciation which is almost of the academy one instant and of the broadest cotton-field dialect the next. (A, 90–91)

I will discuss these techniques in what follows, but here it will suffice to illustrate some of Ellison's claims with reference to Jackson's medley "Summertime / Sometimes I Feel Like a Motherless Child."[49] In this song, which appears on one of the albums Ellison reviews in this piece, *Bless This House* (1956), Jackson juxtaposes a traditional Negro spiritual with a song from George Gershwin's 1935 musical *Porgy and Bess*. Throughout "Motherless Child," Jackson deploys nonstandard pronunciation by singing "sometime" instead of "sometimes": "Sometime I feel like a motherless child, a long way from my home." She "liquidates" the word "feel" into a near operatic melisma, shifting from her deep contralto register into what

Heilbut calls a "disembodied soprano." This characteristic move, which creates a "weird, ethereal sound,"[50] is one effect that Jackson uses to "aid in the arousing and control of emotion." Her moaned reprise of "Motherless Child" is another. Jackson's moaning paradoxically *intensifies* the lyrics it mutes: not only does it require more strength and control to repeat the intricate manipulation of "feel" as a moan, but here Jackson does not even breathe before executing the line. (The audible deep breath she takes afterward retroactively dramatizes that choice.) Finally, Jackson performs some of her most intricately bluesy glissandi on the word "home," which may indicate either an expansive desire for home or its infinite recession.

Despite Ellison's attention to Jackson's range of expressive techniques, he works hard to delimit the meaning—or, more precisely, the purpose— of her music. He argues that, whether Jackson is singing across a "jazz beat . . . , rumba, waltz [or] two-step," she "is nonetheless [singing] religious music" (*A*, 93–94). Even albums like *In the Upper Room* (1957), on which "she reminds us most poignantly of Bessie Smith, and [most clearly uses] the common singing techniques of the spirituals and the blues . . . , are directed toward the afterlife and thus are intensely religious" (*A*, 94). This is a curious claim for a writer who argued that form was inseparable from meaning. It seems especially odd when compared with the essay on Jimmy Rushing that Ellison had published about ten weeks before his piece on Jackson. In that essay, "Remembering Jimmy" (1958), Ellison praises Rushing's "sincerity," but he suggests that Rushing's flexible singing techniques create "an art of ambiguity."[51] Rushing brings to ballads "a sincerity and a feeling for dramatizing the lyrics," and this feelingful delivery activates "the mysterious potentiality of meaning which haunts the blues."[52] In a particularly compelling and relevant moment, Ellison writes,

> perhaps because he . . . came from a family already well on its rise into what is called the "Negro middle class," Jimmy has always shown a concern for the correctness of language, and out of the tension between the traditional folk pronunciation and his training in school, he has worked out a flexibility of enunciation and a rhythmical agility with words which make us constantly aware of the meanings which shimmer just beyond the limits of the lyrics.[53]

Ellison would clearly echo this claim about Rushing's pronunciation as he described Jackson's work just weeks later. Jackson's diction, too, "ranges from the most precise to the near liquidation of word-meaning in the sound: a pronunciation which is almost of the academy one instant and of the broadest cotton-field dialect the next." So why not follow his observations about Jackson to the same conclusion and state that Jackson's vocal practice likewise hints at "the meanings which shimmer just beyond the limits of the lyrics"?

We see how justified such a claim might be when we listen closely to Jackson's pronunciative choices in "Summertime / Motherless Child." Indeed, Ellison's astute assessment of Jackson's academy-to-the-cotton-field variations is especially valuable for how it treats her pronunciation *as* a choice. Jackson sings "Summertime," moves directly into "Motherless Child," and then sings "Summertime" again. This medley excavates the Negro spiritual on which Gershwin based "Summertime." (While Gershwin claimed he "wrote [his] own spirituals and folk songs" for the opera, musicologist Samuel Floyd Jr. has traced the deep similarities between the intervallic structures, melodies, and rhythms of "Summertime" and "Motherless Child.")[54] According to Jackson's biographer Laurraine Goreau, this medley was Jackson's way of "moving ["Summertime"] into its source, to her way of thinking."[55] By singing "Motherless Child" between two iterations of "Summertime," Jackson sets the spiritual at the center or core of Gershwin's song. Her decision to pronounce "*sometime* I feel like a motherless child" itself highlights the consonance between the title of Gershwin's song and the language of the spiritual on which it is based.

As Jackson closes her first iteration of "Summertime," she sings, "Till that morning, nothing can harm you, with daddy and mammy . . . standing by." Jackson's invocation of the child's "mammy" alongside the daddy creates the possibility that the child being addressed is, in fact, "motherless." By the end of *Porgy and Bess*, this is indeed the condition of the child to whom "Summertime" is sung. According to Jeffrey Melnick, Gershwin "portentously" gestures toward "the future 'motherless' condition of the child" by "stitch[ing] a whisper of an African American sorrow song into 'Summertime.'"[56] Only a whisper within "Summertime," "Motherless Child" is "the baby's unacknowledged theme in the opera."[57] Jackson makes the child's loss explicit by singing the spiritual. Her pronunciation also destabilizes the fantasy of wealth that the lullaby conjures for the impoverished child. As Kalamu ya Salaam points out, instead of singing, "your daddy's rich / and your mama's good looking," Jackson seems to sing "your daddy *ain't* rich / and your ma is good looking."[58] It is unclear whether she merely blurs the word "is" or substitutes it with "ain't," and this ambiguity is generated by the fact that she liquidates several lyrics in this passage—including "rich" itself, from which she drops the ending consonants. Yet the ambiguity itself is significant, because it indicates the supreme subtlety with which Jackson hints at the reality behind the lullaby's lyrics—and, indeed, behind the opera's pastoral depiction of southern black life. Still, the vision Jackson creates is not entirely bleak. The new story she weaves around and through "Summertime" is both starker *and* more optimistic than the opera's narrative. When she repeats "Summertime" after the "Motherless Child" interlude, she sings, "Daddy and mommy, they'll be standing by." By singing "mommy" in the final verse, Jackson ultimately "restores" the child's mother. As I have suggested, her medley also subversively restores "Summertime" *itself* to its "mother"—its musical source in the African American folk material from which Gershwin drew. Hence, Jackson's performance of this medley sustains both affirmative and subversive attitudes toward "Summertime."

There are several possible explanations for why Ellison resists locating such ambiguity in Jackson's art, including gender and genre biases. With regard to the first, it should be said that Ellison clearly romanticizes Jackson in gendered terms; in an especially unfortunate passage, he writes that Jackson and other singers "enchant the eye as they caress the ear, and in their presence we sense the full, moony glory of womanhood in all its mystery—maid, matron and matriarch" (*A*, 88). In one sense, his depiction of these women resonates with his creation of stock female characters in his fiction. (Adam Bradley cites a working note Ellison wrote on a draft of *Invisible Man*: "Old [M]ary must embody a myth . . . she is the guardian of value.")[59] However, "As the Spirit" also offers a complex vision of female song. Ellison rejects the vocal myths I have discussed in the introduction, which code black female song as pure embodied emotion. (These myths are compounded when it comes to black sacred music, in which the worshipper is thought to directly channel the spirit.) Rather than reproduce such myths of unconscious expression, Ellison stresses that Jackson strategically *projects* sincerity.

Granted, this notion of artful projection is complicated by generic convention, insofar as gospel ostensibly depends on harmonizing the private individual and the public performer. Leaders of the religious ritual often establish their authority by professing to unite their message with their lives; in the words of Dorsey's gospel classic, "I've got to live the life I sing about in my song." Jackson's remarks about her work occasionally advance a similar conception of song as a natural, unmediated extension of life. In an interview with Studs Terkel, she stressed her attempt to make personal, "from-the-heart" music. Yet she also spoke of her practical, musical efforts to do so. She told Terkel, "Sometimes I hear how music is supposed to be sung; there are certain notes I want to make.

I get to my pianist, Mildred Falls. We put it down. So in this way I'm able to capture the voice within me."[60] This practice of searching for the notes, the voice, she wanted to capture reminds us that singing straight from the heart was not as straightforward as Jackson's remarks sometimes made it seem.[61] Ellison seems well aware of this. He is emphatic that readers and listeners not assume that Jackson's singing "is simply the expression of the Negro's 'natural' ability as is held by the stereotype (would that it were only true!). For although its techniques are not taught formally, Miss Jackson is the master of an art of singing which is as complex and of an even older origin than that of jazz" (A, 90). As Cheryl Wall has noted, at least in this moment, Ellison stresses that more than the spirit moves Mahalia.[62]

Again, the most salient reason why Ellison figures Jackson's sincerity as singular in expressive purpose is to consolidate his argument that the "proper setting" for Jackson's art is the black church—and that those who wish to hear her sing should go there. He writes, "I insist upon the church and not the concert hall, because for all her concert appearances about the world she is not primarily a concert singer but a high priestess in the religious ceremony of her church. . . . And it is in the setting of the church that the full timbre of her sincerity sounds most distinctly" (A, 92). The context of this claim is crucial: as I have said, Ellison makes his argument for the church at the moment when gospel is moving out of black sacred spaces and into the popular mainstream. This is the era Heilbut has termed "the golden age of gospel,"[63] when a number of gospel artists were achieving national recognition through recordings and touring and, as Ellison puts it, the music was becoming "a big business, both within the Negro community and without" (A, 91). In this context, Ellison wants to celebrate gospel music's national popularity, but without deracinating it. Thus, while his claim about Jackson's "proper setting" appears to shift the burden of authenticity from race to religion, it matters that the church in which Jackson appears at Newport is an Afro-American Episcopal one.

It is possible to respect the racial and religious politics of Ellison's insistence that this church is Jackson's "proper setting" while also recognizing that Jackson's art is, like Rushing's, an art of ambiguity. We can reconcile these two concepts if we understand the black church to figure a space in which it is relatively safe to express ambivalence. Since slavery, black churches have often functioned as uniquely sanctioned sites of both political and religious expression; they have sometimes been the only social spaces where it was safe to announce desires for freedom. For

FIGURE 3. Mahalia Jackson at Mount Zion AME Church, Newport, Rhode Island, 1958. Photo by Michael Ochs / Michael Ochs Archives / Getty Images.

this reason, churches are commonly figured as "safe spaces" in African American culture. Writing specifically about black women's cultures of resistance, Patricia Hill Collins describes the concept of the safe space by asserting that "while domination may be inevitable as a social fact, it is unlikely to be hegemonic as an ideology within social spaces where Black women speak freely."[64] This concept illuminates Ellison's writings about performance because, although men and women of various cultural identifications may participate in the safe spaces Ellison describes, the purpose of these spaces is to affirm the complexity of black humanity. In theorizing the timbre of sincerity, which resonates most clearly in such spaces, Ellison asks us to attend to forms of black expression which are directed inward, toward what Ellison calls a "shared community of experience" (*A*, 93), rather than focused outward, toward a dominant culture or repressive white gaze.

The fact that Ellison is not advancing black separatism brings us to the reverse crossover effect. He asserts that "only the fortunate few who braved the Sunday-morning rain to attend the Afro-American Episcopal Church services heard Mahalia at her best at Newport. Many had doubtless been absent from church or synagogue for years, but here they saw her in her proper setting and the venture into the strangeness of the Negro church was worth the visit" (*A*, 93). Ellison is concerned with preserving black sacred space, as the site where sincere ambivalence might be especially resonant. But he is also concerned with challenging people unfamiliar with these spaces to enter into them. In asking Jackson's white fans at Newport to step inside the veil, to enter the sacred center of the black community, he is asking them to face the fact of places they do not own and may not understand. He thus aims to destabilize the status of whiteness as privileged belonging. The outsiders who venture into Mount Zion AME do not jeopardize the integrity of the religious ritual for those whose custom it is; here, as in the scene of worship in the film of *Native Son*, the venturers-in lose even the power to impinge. Rather than objectify Jackson as a distant performer on a concert-hall stage, viewers/congregants in the church are challenged to partake in a dynamic communal exchange. So Ellison's article, published four years after the *Brown v. the Board of Education* decision and one year after black students' attempts to make good on that decision resulted in the shameful disaster of Little Rock, offers a different vision of what the nation's efforts to integrate might demand. In "As the Spirit," Ellison complicates reductive notions of black expression *and* marks black space, while sustaining a fluid sense of who the congregation is.

Invisible Man's Timbre of Sincerity

There are moments in *Invisible Man* that show Ellison imagining his novel as a space in which sincerity might be as possible as the evasions of masking. There is no doubt that the novel opens in a wryly defiant mode: "I am an invisible man. No, I am not a spook like those who haunted Edgar Allan Poe; nor am I one of your Hollywood-movie ectoplasms. I am a man of substance, of flesh and bone, fiber and liquids—and I might even be said to possess a mind. I am invisible, understand, simply because people refuse to see me" (*IM*, 3). The narrator could also be said to end in this defensive register: "'Ah,' I can hear you say, 'so it was all a build-up to bore us with his buggy jiving. He only wanted us to listen to him rave!'" Yet the next line—"But only partially true" (*IM*, 581)— reminds us that this agonistic trickster stance is but one of Ellison's narrative modes. The timbre of sincerity names another.

In the prologue to the novel, Ellison stages the narrator's own challenging encounter with the timbre of sincerity, as expressed by a female sacred singer. In this famous opening scene, the narrator smokes marijuana while listening to a phonograph recording of Louis Armstrong's "What Did I Do to Be So Black and Blue?" He "slip[s] into the breaks" of the song and hallucinates a descent "into its depths," where he encounters a church congregation and a moaning "singer of spirituals" (*IM*, 8–10). The narrator inadvertently enters the woman's space and must meet her on her own confounding terms. The moaning woman utilizes various expressive resources—the moan and the laugh—to express what the narrator names "ambivalence." I follow Claudia Tate in seeing this singer of spirituals as one of the narrator's key guides.[65] I suggest this is so because the singer models the timbre of sincerity with which the narrator will go on to challenge his own listeners—especially as he eulogizes his black friend Tod Clifton, who has been killed by a white police officer.

When the narrator asks the woman why she moans, she tells him that it is because her master—whom she both loved and hated—is dead. She has killed him, because while she loved him, she loved her freedom more:

> *"I dearly loved my master, son," she said.*
>
> *"You should have hated him," I said.*
>
> *"He gave me several sons," she said, "and because I loved my sons I learned to love their father though I hated him too."*
>
> *"I too have become acquainted with ambivalence," I said* ... *"Why do you moan?"*
>
> *"I moan this way 'cause he's dead," she said* ... *"I laughs too, but I moans too. He promised to set us free but he never could bring hisself to do it. Still I loved him ..."*
>
> *"Loved him? You mean ...?"*
>
> *"Oh yes, but I loved something else even more."*
>
> *"What more?"*
>
> *"Freedom." (IM, 10–11)*

The singer's expressive practice is complex but not duplicitous. She moans as much as she laughs, and hates as much as she loves. She doesn't laugh in order to hide the moan, or pretend to love in order to mask her hate. We might say that hers is the sincere ambivalence of gospel music, broadly understood, as a testimony to "good news and bad times."[66] According to Craig Werner, the spiritual "Nobody Knows the Trouble I've Seen" succinctly conveys this doubleness: we witness gospel paradox "when 'glory hallelujah' is the line that follows 'Nobody knows the trouble I see,' and no one finds that confusing."[67] As the exchange continues, Invisible Man asks the woman, *"What is this freedom you love so well?"* She answers, *"I done forgot, son. It's all mixed up. First I think it's one thing, then I think it's another. . . . I guess now it ain't nothing but knowing how to say what I got up in my head"* (*IM*, 11). By defining freedom itself as the capacity to express her own conflicting thoughts ("what I got up in my head"), the singer of spirituals revalues expressive ambivalence. In Barbara Johnson's words, she "claim[s] the right" to "[hold] on to more than one story at a time." She also, in my view, attunes us to the sincerely ambivalent registers of Ellison's own narrative voice.

We might look more closely, for instance, at the first lines of the novel I have cited. Here, Ellison draws on oral and literary traditions to eloquently convey ambivalence: "I am an invisible man. No, I am not a spook like those who haunted Edgar Allan Poe" (*IM*, 3). The allusion both establishes the narrator's familiarity with American literature and signifies on Poe through the use of the word "spook." According to Clarence Major, slaves first used this term to refer to ghosts, then to signify white people (as in pale as a ghost). White people appropriated the term and used it to signify black people, who then countered by spoofing on that white usage and referring to *one another* as "spooks."[68] So while Invisible Man appears to simply assert that he is not a ghost like those that populate Poe's ghost stories, he also uses the vernacular meaning of the word "spook" to "call Poe out" for being haunted by the presence of black people in America. Indeed, in "Twentieth-Century Fiction and the Black Mask of Humanity" (1953), Ellison reads Poe's dehumanizing depictions of slaves as attempts to manage this hauntedness.[69]

Here, we could privilege the "hidden," latent meaning (the critical protocol I described earlier) and imagine that Ellison is winking at readers who get the joke through a subversive citation of Poe. We could also privilege the second meaning and claim that Ellison is conceding that a racist writer can still be a useful literary resource. As Robert O'Meally suggests, Ellison draws on Poe's technique in creating his own "elaborated detective story."[70] Reading for sincerity, however, means seeing both meanings as simultaneously operative and equally valid. Insofar as we hear Ellison's own voice inflecting his narrator's, we might conclude *both* that he resents Poe's depictions of black people *and* that Poe's ghost stories (nonetheless) represent a literary legacy he finds useful; he both derides Poe and derives from him. As Ellison writes in "Twentieth-Century Fiction and the Black Mask of Humanity," "the essence of the word is its ambivalence."[71] His use of the word "spook" engages exactly this ambivalence, reminding us that linguistic meaning is a product of historical contestation over the power to represent, to define oneself and others. His project as an American writer is to claim his right to such complexity, to signal it rather than simplify it.

One recording of Mahalia Jackson's especially resonates with Ellison's attempt to exploit the multiple meanings of the fundamentally ambivalent word. In 1949, Jackson recorded a song called "Mahalia Moans."[72] Though she refused to sing the blues, the form of this song—a moaned version of the gospel standard "Walk with Me, Lord"—is a sixteen-bar blues. The song's upbeat swing proves that the moan has a fuller range of meaning than we may suspect. As Heilbut notes, "The holy laugh is from that diaphragmatic root where moans originate."[73] Jackson's blue notes, her slides between major and minor tones, also reflect this emotional flexibility. Peter Antelyes explains the effect of the blue note well: "by slipping between major and minor, the blue note challenges the conventional meanings of those polarities, signifying not positive or negative, not happiness or sadness, longing or contempt, but both at once and neither."[74] Perhaps due to the brevity of this track, it was merged with another song, a chant recorded in 1969. Here Jackson sings a line from the 59th Psalm: "Weeping may endure for a night, but joy, joy, joy's gonna come in the morning." We hear the intended word to be "morning," but Jackson pronounces it as "moaning." Again, this pronunciation was not simply an unconscious byproduct of Jackson's southern accent; in a song I will go on to discuss, her 1947 recording of "Move On Up a Little Higher," she pronounces the r in "morning." By pronouncing "moaning" here, Jackson partly evokes the pathos of the gospel moan; she brings a sense of "mourning" into the morning, the conventional time of renewal. (The way Jackson growls the word "joy" similarly complicates the meaning of that word.) Yet the notion that joy might come in the morning *and* through the act of moaning also reminds us that people moan to express not only grief but also pleasure. The moan which precedes the chant makes this second meaning especially audible. In this performance, then, Jackson's stylistic or generic hybridity yields multiple meanings, from moaning to mourning, which Fred Moten gathers into print as "mo(ur)nin(g)."[75]

Invisible Man's eulogy for Tod Clifton is perhaps the most dramatic instance in which the narrator likewise activates multiple resources to clearly express such ambivalence. As the narrator speaks to a diverse audience that has gathered to mourn Clifton, he conveys the resourcefulness necessary to project his ambivalence about Tod's death and the memorial service itself. I suggest that this moment also hints at the possibility that the text might not just represent but also *enact* the timbre of sincerity that the funeral oration conveys, because the post-oratory text keeps "speaking" in the same style and tone that characterizes the narrator's oration. By implicating the reader as a witness to the ritual represented in the text, the passage briefly makes the novel itself a space in which readers might reckon with the timbre of sincerity.

The funeral begins as an old man begins to sing "Many a Thousand Gone." (This itself is a song of ambivalence. The speaker announces his freedom—"No more auction block for me, no more, no more"—while also refusing to forget those who have not been able to seize theirs: "Many thousands gone.") In a vision that recalls Ellison's depiction of Jackson's mixed congregation, even "white brothers and sisters" and people "born in other lands" join in with the old man's song (*IM*, 453), and the singing assembly helps the narrator begin and then continue to labor through his speech. Invisible Man opens with confrontation, accusing the crowd of wanting mere entertainment. "What are you waiting for me to tell you?" he shouts at them. "What good will it do? What if I say that this isn't a funeral, that it's a holiday celebration, that if you stick around the band will end up playing 'Damit-the-Hell the Fun's All Over'?" (*IM*, 454). Since the people do not leave, he delivers a mournful eulogy that also becomes a call to arms. Ellison draws on myriad resources here: Invisible Man's voice recalls both the steady cadence of a black preacher preparing for emotional escalation as well as the deadpan, continuous "ands" of Hemingway's early fiction:[76]

> "Such was the short bitter life of Brother Tod Clifton. Now he's in this box with the bolts tightened down. He's in the box and we're in there with him, and when I've told you this you can go. It's dark in this box and it's crowded. It has a cracked ceiling and a clogged-up toilet in the hall. It has rats and roaches, and it's far, far too expensive a dwelling. . . . Tod Clifton is crowded and he needs the room. 'Tell them to get out of the box,' that's what he would say if you could hear him. 'Tell them to get out of the box and go teach the cops to forget that rhyme. Tell them to teach them that when they call you *nigger* to make a rhyme with *trigger* it makes the gun backfire.'" (*IM*, 458)

Invisible Man begins with a wry allusion to Hemingway's "Short Happy Life of Francis Macomber" (1936). As if taking leave of the realist tradition Hemingway represents, he conjures an image that may have been inspired by Kafka's "Metamorphosis" (1915): Clifton's casket expands, incredibly, to accommodate not just Clifton but also the assembled crowd. Finally, in a ghostly ventriloquization that recalls Ellison's opening allusion to

Poe, Invisible Man activates Clifton's voice from within the casket: "Tell them to get out of the box." Invisible Man's speech resounds with the timbre of sincerity because it reveals the integrative work required to express ambivalent ideas that are equally true. He wants the crowd to hear him and wishes they did not have to be there, assembled for the funeral of his friend. He wants them to be safer than Tod was but also to fight for that safety by confronting the police, an obviously dangerous move. Invisible Man's expressive labor peaks in an act of prosopopoeia, the granting of voice to one who is absent or deceased. As if indicating that his own voice is insufficient to complete his statement, he reaches for another—and it is Tod's imagined voice, brought back from the grave, that completes the narrator's rhyme and turns the gun back around on the cops: "When they call you *nigger* to make a rhyme with *trigger* it makes the gun backfire." We may recall the collaborative work Jackson describes when she speaks of needing Mildred Falls to help her "capture" her own voice.

What is most remarkable about this scene, however, is how it momentarily addresses the style of the funeral oration to the reader by extending the language and syntax of the oration into the following narrative. It is not that Ellison figuratively includes the reader in the congregational ritual he represents, but that he positions the reader as witness to its trace or aftermath. Invisible Man tells the crowd, "'His name was Clifton and he was young and he was a leader and when he fell there was a hole in the heel of his sock and when he stretched forward he seemed not as tall as when he stood'" (*IM*, 456). As if stunned into suspension, the narrative keeps "speaking" in the same deadpan rhythm: "We drove away and when the cars stopped moving there was a grave and we placed him in it. The gravediggers sweated heavily and knew their business and their brogue was Irish. They filled the grave quickly and we left. Tod Clifton was underground" (*IM*, 459–460). Ellison himself called the funeral scene a peripeteia, or turning point, in the novel, because it emboldens the narrator to break with the exploitative Brotherhood with which he has been working to organize the community.[77] But the scene also marks a shift in the timbre of the narrator's address. When Ellison extends the narrator's oration into free indirect discourse, he brings the timbre of sincerity that shapes that oration one step closer to readers, or turns up the volume on it. For a moment, he makes the novel itself a space in which sincerity seems as viable as masking.

The narrator's lastingly unresolved final question, however, seems skeptical of this prospect. While Ellison's essay on Jackson celebrates the dynamic whereby Jackson "sings in [the congregation's] own voice of faith" (*A*, 93)," his narrator expresses skepticism about the possibility of "speaking for" whoever the text's "you" might be:

> And it is this which frightens me:
>   Who knows but that, on the lower frequencies, I speak for you?
> (*IM*, 581)

As Lesley Larkin points out, the narrator's *fear* that he might be "speaking for you" "undermines the identificatory claim the narrator appears to make." Larkin rightly locates this fear in the double meaning of the phrase "speaking for," which can suggest active "representation" of readers but also "a more passive ventriloquism" of dominant ideologies, as one's words are conscripted into preexisting views. In Larkin's reading, the text shifts the responsibility for deciding the result onto Ellison's readers.[78] The difference between speaking on behalf of and at the behest of readers depends on who the "you" is, and on how they are reading.

The difficulty of knowing for whom one is speaking, particularly when one is asked to "uplift" or "represent" a racially defined group, makes Mary's role in this novel complex. I agree with Laura Doyle that, insofar as Mary tries to fashion the narrator into a "race man," she is "at once a subversive and conservative voice."[79] As the narrator says, "Mary reminded me constantly that something was expected of me, some act of leadership, . . . and I was torn between resenting her for it and loving her for the nebulous hope she kept alive" (*IM*, 258). Yet if Mary's view of black male leadership inspires the narrator's ambivalence, Mary's songs express her own. The way she sings hints at this complexity: "I could hear Mary singing, her voice clear and untroubled, though she sang a troubled song. It was the 'Back Water Blues'" (*IM*, 297). In addition to Smith's "Backwater Blues," Mary also alludes, as I've noted, to Jackson's "Move On Up." Soon after Invisible Man comes to stay with her, Mary tells him she hopes he will be "a credit to the race" and relates a theory of racial uplift that moves forward by looking back. This means "fight[ing]" for "the ones on the bottom" of the national caste system despite personal success—a task for which young blacks from the South like the narrator are especially well suited, in Mary's view:

> "It's you young folks what's going to make the changes. . . . Y'all's the ones. You got to lead and you got to fight and move us all on up a little higher. And I tell you something else, it's the ones from the South that's got to do it, them what knows the fire and ain't forgot

how it burns. Up here too many forgits. They finds a place for they-selves and forgits the ones on the bottom. Oh, heap of them *talks* about doing things, but they done really forgot. No, it's you young ones what has to remember and take the lead." (*IM*, 255)

On one level, Mary's allusions to both Smith's and Jackson's signature songs indicate that she maintains and extends the line that connects these women, blues mother and gospel daughter. She thus embodies the cultural memory she urges Invisible Man to sustain. Yet we might also hear a challenging ambivalence in Mary's songs—especially in her allusion to Jackson's "Move On Up"—that links Mary with the singer of spirituals in the prologue. To closely read Jackson's performance of "Move On Up" is to hear that the song itself expresses the ambivalence that Mary inspires in the narrator. Jackson generates multiple possibilities as to what "taking the lead" might actually mean.

As Ellison writes in his essay on Jackson, "Move On Up" was the song that "brought [Jackson] to national attention" (*A*, 89). This was ten years after Jackson had released commercially unsuccessful records with Ma Rainey's label, Decca. A song composed (but not yet copyrighted) by Memphis-based minister William Brewster and sung by his soloist, Queen C. Anderson, "Move On Up" was "surreptitiously secured" for Jackson in 1947.[80] (Jackson's description of the song as "an old spiritual I had known since I was a little child" is disingenuous [*M*, 86].) Laurraine Goreau tells the story of the recording as a last-minute, last-chance affair in which Jackson and her accompanists, James "Blind" Francis (organ) and Reverend James Lee (piano), rehearsed Jackson's singing arrangement all day and recorded the song in two sides just before dawn on September 13.[81] According to Boyer, one thing that makes their recording unique is that it features a Hammond organ, which had not been used on gospel recordings before; this was Jackson's innovation.[82] Another thing that makes this recording unusual is the extraordinarily slow tempo at which Jackson sings it. ("Mahalia sang it slower than anybody else," James Lee noted.)[83] From the song's first words, it is clear that Jackson will *take her time*—a choice that is striking especially when one compares this first version with her later up-tempo recording of the song from 1954.[84]

The song charts a movement up to heaven, through a pantheon of biblical figures and loved ones: "Gonna move up a little higher, gonna meet old man Daniel / Gonna move up a little higher, gonna meet the Hebrew children . . . / I'm gonna feast with the Rose of Sharon!" The ascent the lyrics announce is also, according to Brewster, a call for black upward mobility. As Brewster said, "The fight for rights here in Memphis was pretty rough on the Black church, . . . and I wrote that song. . . . We'll have to move in the field of education. Move into the professions and move into politics. Move into anything that any other race has to have to survive. That was a protest idea and inspiration. I was trying to inspire Black people to move up higher."[85] While it is crucial to appreciate Brewster's political intent, it would be a mistake to suppose that "Move On Up" smuggled a message about black upward mobility to listeners *in the guise of* a message about heavenward progress. Rather, it sustained the apparent ambivalence of desiring *both*, in equal measure. In her memoir, Jackson stresses the double meanings of the spirituals that I have noted in the previous chapter: "When the colored slaves on the plantations sang, 'Steal away to Jesus, I ain't got long to stay here,' they weren't talking just about Heaven; they were expressing their secret hope that they, too, would have their chance to escape up North to freedom" (*M*, 181). Jackson does not substitute the "secret hope" of worldly escape for the stated hope of heavenly redemption. Instead, Jackson's language—"weren't talking *just* about Heaven"—augments or doubles the meanings in the spirituals. This is the kind of complexity without duplicity that masking does not account for.

Further, the way Jackson *performs* the song calls the "social message" itself into question, raising the question of what exactly is being moved into. Though Brewster did not write the song for Jackson, he reportedly acknowledged that Jackson "knew what to do with it. She could throw the verse out there."[86] Jackson powerfully projects the verses in part through the technique of word painting discussed in the previous chapter: she starts in the lower part of her register and moves upward on each consecutive verse, musically dramatizing the ascent that the lyrics describe. She also speeds up the tempo a bit as she goes. Because the song's lyrics are quite repetitive, however, it takes an audible amount of labor to keep "throwing" the verses "out there." I reproduce one verse here to illustrate the way in which, as Guthrie Ramsey notes, the lyrics tend to "pile on one another":[87]

> [I'm gonna] move on up a little higher, Lord, meet with old man
>   Daniel
> Move on up a little higher, Lord, meet with the Hebrew children
> Move on up a little higher, Lord, meet with Paul and Silas

Move on up a little higher, Lord, meet my lovin mother
Move on up a little higher, Lord, meet that Lily of the Valley,
    feast with the Rose of Sharon!

The music of this verse, which mainly consists of what Ramsey calls a "nonteleological vamp," is as static as the lyrics themselves.[88] Boyer writes, "Since each one of the statements melodically travels a short distance and turns on itself to be repeated, the melodic action is held in place for several phrases, while the element of repetition serves its function to get the message across."[89] Again, because the repetitive lines could just as easily sound plodding, I would stress the vocal work it takes to *make* repetition a compelling force that might help "get the message across." Because each "move on up a little higher" stays in place, Jackson must create the illusion of movement by constantly embellishing the melody in different ways. For example, before the "ascent" section, Jackson ends several lines with intricate descending glissandi. When she sings, "I'm going home, live on high," she sings "home" in a swift eight-note cascade. In contrast to the relatively unembellished "Summertime / Motherless Child," this performance affirms the words of congregants who said Jackson could "add more flowers and feathers than anybody," all of which were "exactly right."[90] Jackson's rendition of the song revels in "moving on *in*" to the structure of the song as much as the hope of moving up through it. In this sense, her performance codes upward mobility as a turn inward. It is precisely by moving more deeply and virtuosically into the texture of the song that she manages to move up through it.

Jackson's interpretation of "Move On Up" therefore invites us to consider that moving further into a self-sustaining community might be imperative for, if not preferable to, moving into whatever, in Brewster's words, "any other race has to have to survive." If the song conveys Brewster's integrative aspiration to move "into the professions and . . . into politics," then Jackson's rendition of it also imagines empowered, even sacred, black consolidation. Her performance envisions an audience that would reckon with the simultaneous expression of desire for integration, self-determination, and communal transcendence.

We might hear the final address of the narrator in *Invisible Man* as voicing a similar order of ambivalence with regard to what it means for him to move on up into the world "above ground"; what it means to integrate; and what it means to represent, or "speak for," an indeterminate "you." These are, in some ways, questions of what it means to cross over. While these questions inspire ambivalence, the narrator figures ambivalence as productive rather than paralyzing. He seems to recognize, as bell hooks writes, that contradictions may be embraced and even "celebrate[d] . . . because they mean we are in a process of change and transformation."[91] In a closing moment of the epilogue (part of which I have cited), the narrator echoes the insights of the moaning woman beneath the music who tells him that she both loves and hates, and that freedom lies in loving: "I sell you no phony forgiveness, I'm a desperate man—but too much of your life will be lost, its meaning lost, unless you approach it as much through love as through hate. . . . So I denounce and I defend and I hate and I love" (*IM*, 580).

In a draft that, once divided, became the prologue and the epilogue of *Invisible Man*, Ellison links this resolution to denounce and defend and hate and love to a vision of race represented by Mary. As he resolves to reject the propagandizing of Ras the Destroyer, Invisible Man determines to

> let Ras run that race, he was a race man; I had graduated. Now I
> would watch the others. . . . So let them run, let them ramble and
> gamble on the outcome, I was retiring. And there was Mary, yes.
> Yes she had tried to run me too, but that was the obligatory race,
> the contest to which I was born, and if you won you were loved
> and if you lost you were loved and the only demand was simply
> that you tried, that you ran your best wearing the simple colors
> of hope and endurance for what she thought of as "the race," the
> group "we" that were bound together by common hope and expe-
> riences, but which she lived out in far richer, warmer, more human
> terms. . . . That race was still to run and still to be won.[92]

Here, the race is "the group." It is also an action. Both meanings are operative at once because for Ellison, a constitutive feature of black iden-tity is the act of expanding the definition of what blackness can be—what this identity might encompass and enable. Thus, the "race" is constituted by a continuous gesture toward individual possibility and community that one "live[s] out"—and it must be "lived out in . . . richer, warmer, more human terms" than limiting categorical identities allow. Jackson herself displays this dual process of claiming "her people" and redefining the "race" when she speaks of contemporary struggles for racial justice: "Sometimes when there has been trouble in the streets, I say to myself, 'This is not my people. My people have been so patient!' But Jesus was patient, too, until they provoked him, and he got angry and went into the temple" (*M*, 215).

FIGURE 4. Ralph Ellison at the American Academy in Rome, 1957. Photo by James Whitmore / Time & Life Pictures / Getty Images.

I have theorized the timbre of sincerity not to deny the very real tensions between black artists and white (and black) audiences but to propose that Ellison's expansive vision of blackness includes an insistence that the black artist is free to imagine—and to seek to engender—an audience that is more generous than the one he or she may actually find. The concept of sincerity helps us see that Ellison not only responds to but also, as Hortense Spillers puts it, "creates his audience."[93] Indeed, when Ellison describes his novel as "a mere game of 'as if'" that represents "a thrust toward a human ideal"—when he calls *Invisible Man* "a raft of hope"—he seems to imagine audience in the way that director and performance theorist Herbert Blau describes: as "a figure of speech."[94] Such statements remind us that "the future has no constituency"—or, at least, only "a very shadowy one."[95]

If the sincere registers of Ellison's fictional voice imagine an audience before whom the need to mask might diminish, because it would not be ironic to centralize black consciousness in "American literature," then Ellison's later statements about his work represent attempts to cultivate precisely that readership. His essays consistently posit black literature as complex mainstream rather than margin. In "What America Would Be Like Without Blacks" (1970), for example, Ellison writes that the American language itself is forged "by merging the sounds of many tongues, brought together in the struggle of diverse regions. . . . So there is a *de'z* and *do'z* of slave speech sounding beneath our most polished Harvard accents, and if there is such a thing as a Yale accent, there is a Negro wail in it—doubtless introduced there by Old Yalie John C. Calhoun, who probably got it from his mammy."[96] If "the black man [is] a co-creator of the language that Mark Twain raised to the level of literary eloquence" in *The Adventures of Huckleberry Finn* (1884), then so too is he (or she) co-creator of Hemingway's language, insofar as Hemingway considered *Huck Finn* the novel from which "all modern American writing springs."[97] With these claims in mind, we can see that when Ellison appointed Twain and Hemingway as his ancestors, he was not performing a subversive seizure of white power so much as he was asserting common ground. To put this in analogous terms: Ellison's rhetorical construction of his place in the American literary tradition is less like his narrator's shrewd hijacking of the local electric company's energy supply to illuminate his underground hole and more a reminder that an African American inventor is at the source of electric light technology itself. For Ellison, becoming an African American writer is not a matter of invading—or evading—a "white" literary tradition or marketplace; it is a matter of sincerely asserting that he already belongs there.

Coda: "Precious Lord"

"What we know is that which was then becoming," Ellison writes of be-bop in "The Golden Age, Time Past" (1959).[98] Ellison's essay on Jackson, written during "the golden age of gospel," documents a moment in which gospel music itself was still becoming—or gaining widespread recognition as—a major force in American cultural and political life. Kalamu ya Salaam reminds us that, although Jackson's decision to sing "popular music and jazz [though not the blues], even going so far as to perform at the Newport Jazz Festival," may not seem "particularly noteworthy" today, at the time it was "considered one short step from blasphemy."[99] Partly due to timing, Ellison fails to anticipate the implications of Jackson's intrepid boundary crossing. Specifically, he fails to see how Jackson, like the singing man at Tod's funeral and like Invisible Man, in his eulogy, could generate a spiritual experience of community in a secular space. By crossing established musical and cultural lines, Jackson was not profaning the sacred but aiming to sacralize the supposedly secular. She describes a performance at the Royal Albert Hall in London, for instance, as follows: "There may have been more than religious people out there in the audience—jazz fans and rock-and-roll people.... But when I sang the songs of God,... the reception they gave me was like a religious revival audience" (*M*, 149). Such remarks reveal that when Ellison insisted the church was Jackson's "proper setting," he underestimated her ability to "make church" wherever she was. Eleven years after *Invisible Man*'s publication, Jackson would sing at the March on Washington, alongside Martin Luther King Jr. In light of this spectacular appearance, Kenneth Warren is right to point out, Ellison's insistence that Jackson's "proper setting" is the church does acquire a "rearguard aspect."[100]

Then again, it is possible that Ellison did witness Jackson's sacralization of secular space and simply failed to write about what he saw, because this process was evident in Jackson's performance at Newport in 1958. As I have noted, Jackson performed a solo set on Saturday night/Sunday morning—presumably, just hours before she went to sing at Mount Zion Church. While Ellison supports his own point that the church is Jackson's true setting by citing Jackson's "complain[t]" about the limited time of recording—"I'm used to singing in church, where they don't stop me until the Lord comes" (*A*, 93)—Jackson was certainly capable of expanding the temporal parameters of her nonchurch performances. She does this at Newport by generating a false ending or unexpected reprise. As we can see in Bert Stern's documentary *Jazz on a Summer's Day*, Jackson appears to finish the song "Didn't It Rain" (in the midst of a rainstorm); she is about to exit the stage when she starts the song up again. A common tactic in gospel performance, the reprise does not signal Jackson's pure spontaneous response to the spirit, unless we imagine it is divine providence that leads her to pause just in front of the microphone at stage right. But the reprise does move Jackson's performance closer to a congregational rite, thereby transforming the audience's sense of what they are witnessing/participating in.[101] The effect of this moment is therefore akin to what happens when Ellison extends his narrator's oratorical style into the narrative fabric of *Invisible Man*.

As with the novel's final address, however, the racial dynamics of this moment remain an open question. According to Ellison's argument in "As the Spirit," even the act of witnessing/participating in Jackson's performance at Newport could not match the transformative experience of leaving the festival to attend Sunday service at Mount Zion. On the Newport stage, Jackson may simply have served as the messianic black mother who redeemed instead of challenged the listeners who "made her feel like a star." But one implicit point of this chapter has been to stress that the possibility one reads in these moments depends as much on how one imagines the audience as it does on how one imagines the performer. In this case, we might say that to read this moment skeptically is to privilege (and simplify) a white gaze. This point helps us appreciate one of James Baldwin's major interventions in the discourse on black female singers, which is to centralize not only black performers but also black listeners—a turn I discuss in the following chapter.

According to Heilbut, by the mid-1950s, Jackson had "priced herself out of the black church" and "almost all her appearances were before white audiences."[102] Still, she worked to preserve an unalienated "down-home" persona. "Ever since I began singing in the big concert halls, people have been trying to teach me to be grand, but I just can't do it" is the first line of her 1966 memoir (*M*, 11). Whether or not Heilbut is right that her "regal status had obviously isolated her," Jackson's public role was complex.[103] Her critics were less vehement than the young artists and intellectuals who accused Ellison of being a sellout and a race traitor. But she was not immune to such charges. In her memoir, she relates a young black woman's tearful challenge in the late 1950s: "Miss Jackson, how can you sing 'My country, 'tis of thee, sweet land of liberty,' as if you believed it when you know the white people in America don't want us here? It's not our country." Jackson writes, "She felt that I was being a hypocrite and that I had let my race down." Like Ellison's, Jackson's claims to U.S. citizenship could sound either conservative or idealistic: in response to this woman, Jackson insists that "it *is* our country," and there are "better days ahead" (*M*, 128–129). At other moments, Jackson was more nationalist than patriot, more black feminist race woman than darling gospel saint. She stresses in her memoir that "if a colored man wants to marry a woman he can be proud of, there's no need for him to seek out a white woman" (*M*, 102), and she passionately defends black women in an appearance with Jesse Jackson: "Don't you knock the black woman. She gave up the greatest thing she had, her *body*, for her man.... And you know who brought Martin Luther King to Chicago when all the *Negro* ministers were too scared? It was a *black* woman, *me*."[104]

Despite these contradictions—or better, in keeping with them—Jackson came to be known by many people as the musical voice of the Civil Rights Movement. Harry Belafonte called her "the single most powerful black woman in the United States."[105] If Ellison did not see this coming, neither could Jackson have foreseen the price of such a position. She "retired from politics" (or, in any case, from overtly political public appearances) after King's death. But she was there to sing at his funeral.[106] As King had requested, she sang his favorite hymn, "Precious Lord." Her performance would have evoked not only the song's particular significance to King but also the legendary story of its composition, according to which Thomas Dorsey wrote it just after the death of his own wife and child. Aretha Franklin would extend the song's associative matrix of loss and survival when she sang it at Jackson's own funeral four years later.

Ellison would tie *Invisible Man*'s funeral scene to King's memorial service upon submitting the funeral episode—of which he remained especially proud—to the 1970 anthology *This Is My Best*. In his preface to the scene in that volume, Ellison explains that he sought to evoke "those ritual and ceremonial forms . . . which Negro Americans had begun to structure to their own religious and cultural needs as far back as the early days of enslavement, and which recently were to be observed most movingly during the funeral ceremony for Martin Luther King."[107] I have argued that, as he renders Tod's funeral, Ellison not only depicts sacred black ritual but also expresses the timbre of sincerity that he associates with sacred black space and even briefly moves that timbre into the fabric of the novel itself. It is Ellison's perhaps audacious faith that the African American novelist might express a complex voice akin to that of a sacred musician that makes his work so compelling. If he does not fully credit Jackson herself with this complex expression—a mistake this chapter aims to remedy—neither does he frame her as his muse. Jackson's singing is therefore not a model for but rather an analogue to Ellison's writing. This is so even when Jackson, like the singer of spirituals in the prologue to *Invisible Man*, shifts from words (the basic unit of the writer's craft) into moans. Of the practice of moaning in gospel, Heilbut writes, "The essence of the gospel style is a wordless moan. . . . Always these sounds render the indescribable, implying, 'Words can't begin to tell you, but maybe moaning will.'"[108] From an Ellisonian perspective, however, it is not that the moan *transcends* language or expresses what "words can't begin to tell you." Rather, if, as Ellison claims, "the essence of the word is its ambivalence," then the desire of the singer of spirituals to express both love and hate through the moan *parallels* Ellison's attempt to maximize the ambivalence of the American language through his work on the page. The timbre of sincerity names this effort. We hear this timbre in Ellison's novel when we grant him the technical and imaginative freedom not only to mask meanings but also to multiply them, in advance of an inchoate audience that shimmers on the horizon of his text.

3 / Understatement: James Baldwin, Bessie Smith, and Billie Holiday

Thus far I have argued that Richard Wright's and Bessie Smith's shared expressive techniques both protest and embrace social exclusion and that Ralph Ellison's and Mahalia Jackson's techniques ask us to conceive complex black expressive acts as central rather than marginal insurgencies. James Baldwin takes his place in this musical-literary tradition at a moment when black music is assuming center stage in American culture. As the nation moves fitfully toward integration in the 1960s, Baldwin pushes back against the national embrace of black music by reasserting the music's marginal status and privileging black listeners. His writings about Bessie Smith and Billie Holiday are instrumental to this process. Here I theorize Baldwin's relationship with these singers less by highlighting shared literary and musical technique than by examining Baldwin's alternately conservative and radical modes of listening to these artists.

Baldwin not only writes about Smith and Holiday more often than does any other writer in this book, but he is also the only author in this study to say he wants to write like a female vocalist (Bessie Smith) sings. That statement anticipates theories of "the Black Aesthetic" that privilege music as a model for black writing—theories which, as I note in the introduction, still shape literary criticism today—while also re-gendering the Black Aesthetic vision of music by foregrounding female singers. Still, Baldwin's invocations of Smith and Holiday are as instructive for their conservative gender politics as for their innovative racial politics. While Baldwin claims Smith's and Holiday's music as a culturally specific resource, he figures Smith and Holiday not as artists but as tragic, natural muses whose work he must translate to the general public and mediate through the "high art" forms of his own fiction and essays. That balance of power productively shifts over the course of his career, however, as Baldwin moves from representing black musical meaning as an object to staging it as a collaborative process. Although Baldwin, like Wright and Ellison, never quite recognizes female singers as intentional artists on par with writers, it is when he acknowledges his own role as a co-creator of musical meaning, rather than a mere translator of it, that he establishes closer kinship with black women singers and forges a more intimate rhetorical connection between black music and writing. Baldwin's music writings thus offer an alternative critical trajectory out of the Black Arts Movement, inviting a vision of the Black Aesthetic that does not idealize music as a stable muse to which writers stake their claims—a paradigm that becomes especially unsatisfying when the musicians in question are women—but instead asks how writers reshape the music through ongoing literary performances of listening. Baldwin's later work signals an internally dynamic musical-literary tradition through which writers perform responsibility to, rather than responsibility for, black musical meaning.[1]

Baldwin's early music writings figure Smith's and Holiday's songs as models of black expressive "understatement." Understatement is quite distinct from the technique of word painting discussed in chapter 1, because whereas word painting *enhances* lyrical content through performative choices, understatement describes a contrast between the tragic lyrics a vocalist sings and the resiliency her performance conveys. As Ellison writes in *Invisible Man* of Mary's performance of "Backwater Blues," "Her voice [was] clear and untroubled, though she sang a troubled song."[2] For Baldwin, this contrast between vocal delivery and lyrical content signals the singer's heroic assertion of emotional distance from her own painful experience (represented by the lyrics). She can now understate that experience, which means she can move on. To recall a phrase from the previous chapter, Baldwin privileges the concept of "laughing to keep from crying"—of encoding the cry within the laugh—instead of the candid double meanings I have stressed in Jackson's and Ellison's art. Like Ellison's writings on sincerity, though, Baldwin's theory of understatement carries its own significant gender and racial politics. First, understatement, like masking, is an expressive practice that is generally gendered male; yet Baldwin disrupts that binary by applying the concept to Smith's and Holiday's work. Further, on the brink of the early

1960s transatlantic "blues revival," Baldwin resists the white embrace of black music more forcefully than Ellison does by claiming black musical understatement as a form of expression that is uniquely legible to, and useful for, black people. Hence, whereas Ellison applauds the mixed congregation that follows Mahalia Jackson to a local Newport church, Baldwin closes his 1962 novel *Another Country* with a scene of his black female singer-protagonist, Ida, listening to Jackson's album *In the Upper Room* (1957) in isolation, removed from her white lover.[3] Through his writings on black female singers, Baldwin resists white appropriation of black music and establishes himself as an authoritative spokesman for an imagined black community defined primarily through shared resilience.

The authority Baldwin claims to interpret Smith's and Holiday's "understated" songs is not only racialized, however, but also gendered. In making this point, I take a different approach from other scholarly discussions of Baldwin's engagement with music, which uniformly celebrate this dimension of his work. But I also show how Baldwin's music writings engender a new understanding of musical understatement—and, by extension, of the relationship between black music and literature. Baldwin encourages us to apprehend understatement not only as a function of Smith's terse lyrics or Holiday's minimalist vocal style (as other commentators have done) but also as a product of these singers' collaborations with accompanists. Reading understatement as an effect of accompaniment, moreover, allows us to appreciate the role that Baldwin plays, as a writer or "literary accompanist," in helping us to hear musicians' work as understated. Indeed, in *Another Country*, Baldwin refigures understatement as a function of interpretation—as an effect one creates through attentive, inventive listening instead of a static quality one detects or observes. Like sincerity, then, understatement becomes a subjective concept that one reads for. We can view this shift from detection to interpretation through Jean-Luc Nancy's distinction between hearing and listening. Nancy associates hearing with "understanding" or "decod[ing]" the meaning of a sound, "as if 'hearing' were above all 'hearing say.'" One listens, on the other hand, by "straining toward a possible meaning, and consequently one that is not immediately accessible."[4] Listening is a self-reflexively creative act. By refiguring understatement as a product of listening, *Another Country* serves as a hinge between Baldwin's earlier and later representations of black music: while he initially uses black women's music to exercise masculine power in an interracial struggle for cultural authority, he ultimately uses writing to collaborate in the creation of musical meaning. This development establishes greater artistic parity between Baldwin, Smith, and

Holiday: instead of bearing witness *on behalf of* female singers, Baldwin begins to bear witness *to* them.

Three years after Ellison's encounter with Jackson at Newport, in a radio interview occasioned by Baldwin's publication of *Nobody Knows My Name* (1961) and anticipating his forthcoming *Another Country*, Studs Terkel played Baldwin Bessie Smith's "Backwater Blues" (1927). Baldwin's response is as follows:

> What struck me was the fact that [Bessie Smith] was sing-ing . . . about a disaster, which had almost killed her, and she ac-cepted it and was going beyond it. The *fantastic* understatement in it. It is the way I want to write, you know. When she says, "My house fell down, and I can't live there no mo'"—it is a great . . . a great sentence. A great achievement.[5]

Baldwin first points out that Smith "was singing . . . about a disas-ter, which had almost killed her," and then stresses the "understate-ment" of her song. The progression of these statements is important. If listeners did not appreciate the magnitude of the disaster to which "Backwater Blues" testified, then they would not hear Smith's song as understated; "my house fell down, and I can't live there no mo'" might instead sound like a mild account of an imaginary scenario. Baldwin, as his response suggested, could identify Smith's line *as* understated because he understood its objective correlative. When Ellison states in a 1953 speech that "understatement depends . . . on commonly held assumptions," he implies that an artist's understatement only registers as such if one's listeners possess the kind of prior knowledge that Bald-win performs here.[6]

Baldwin racializes this knowledge by grounding the ability to per-form and hear understatement in a particular narrative about black life. Describing "the experience of generations of Negroes" in *The Fire Next Time* (1963), he writes, "If one is continually surviving the worst that life can bring, one eventually ceases to be controlled by a fear of what life can bring; whatever it brings must be borne."[7] For Baldwin, this habit of resilience enables Smith's matter-of-fact, economical expression of experiential "disaster" in "Backwater Blues." It also allows some listen-ers to hear Smith's line as a "great achievement"—as an expression of undaunted morale—whereas others will mistake it for fantasy or trag-edy. As Baldwin asserts, "In all jazz, and especially in the blues, there is something tart and ironic, authoritative and double-edged. White Americans seem to feel that happy songs are *happy* and sad songs are *sad*. . . . Only people who have been 'down the line' . . . know what this music is about."[8] While Baldwin shrewdly avoids the essentializing claim that all *black* Americans understand jazz and the blues, his language indicates that the "people who have been 'down the line'" and thus know "what this music is about" are probably not white.

The point of this move is not to wholly alienate the white readership that Baldwin in fact solicited throughout his career.[9] His music writings themselves often construct a nonblack reader: "Maybe I should explain this to you—a Negro has his difficult days . . ."[10] But Baldwin's aim is to counter self-serving conceptions of white advantage and demoralizing conceptions of black disadvantage by refashioning black suffering into black privilege. Even more than Wright, who hails Smith's (and his own) "outsider's insight," Baldwin consistently stresses the superior insight of the marginalized. (He extends the legacy of his early mentor, in this regard, even as his essays seem to reject Wright's influence.)[11] In a 1971 conversation with Nikki Giovanni, Baldwin claims, "We have an edge over the people who think of themselves as white. We have never been deluded into believing what they believe."[12] The 1989 documentary *The Price of the Ticket* includes an interview in which Baldwin is asked by a white British interviewer, "Now when you were starting out as a writer, you were black, impoverished, homosexual. You must have said to yourself, 'Gee, how disadvantaged can I get?'" Baldwin responds, laughing, "No, I thought I'd hit the jackpot. . . . It was so outrageous you could not go any *further*, you know. So you had to find a way to use it."[13] This "use" of social marginalization is not appropriable by white people, Norman Mailer's conception of the "White Negro" to the contrary (about which, more later). As Douglas Taylor insightfully states, for Baldwin, "Blackness involves making a space out of no space, and valorizing one's abjection within white supremacist discourses with such finesse that whites begin to feel the privation is theirs."[14] One way Baldwin "valoriz[es] . . . abjection" with "finesse" is by insisting that, if suffering can redeem, it can just as easily embitter or destroy.[15] His declaration in *The Fire Next Time* is a common refrain: "I do not mean to be sentimental about suffering—enough is certainly as good as a feast—but people who cannot suffer can never grow up, can never discover who they are."[16] Suffering is not a guarantee of but a prerequisite for such maturity. With regard to music, then, it is not that everyone who has suffered can effect understatement, but that one cannot express it or hear it without having suffered. In this sense, the white "privation" Taylor speaks of is experiential, epistemological, and expressive.

Hence, in his remarkable 1964 essay "The Uses of the Blues," Baldwin claims that Smith's and Holiday's music is a product of their painful experiences, and that his ability to authenticate that music is a product of his. Smith's and Holiday's songs are not a matter of "fantasy" but are "very accurate, very concrete," he writes. "I know, I watched, I was there" (*U*, 59). In statements such as this one, however, Baldwin figures black female musicians in particular as embodying a material, extratextual reality that his writing must validate. The effect is to cast Smith and Holiday as embodied "others" to and enabling forces for the more "cerebral" art of black men. Baldwin's essays and fiction consistently repeat this structural logic: in several works, the telos of black female singers' testimonies to suffering is a male artist's creative breakthrough. We find this logic in Baldwin's account of Smith in "The Discovery of What It Means to Be an American" (1959), his depiction of black women singers in "Sonny's Blues" (1957), and his portrayal of Ida in *Another Country*. As Valerie Smith writes, such logic recalls an "association of black women with reembodiment [that] resembles rather closely the association, in classic Western philosophy and in nineteenth-century cultural constructions of womanhood, of women of color with the body and therefore with animal passions and slave labor."[17] Insofar as Baldwin's representations of Smith and Holiday are not only self-authorizing but also protective, we might also link them to figurations of Africa as the "motherland" which black men must protect from colonial "conquest."

What is fascinating about *Another Country*, though, is that it thematizes and, I believe, points a way out of this very problem. In this sense, it contains the arc of Baldwin's writings about music. Because Ida's singing career is sacrificed to a sexual contest between black and white men—Ida speaks of feeling that she is treated like a whore by "white men, and black men, too"—the novel highlights violent attempts to "protect" a feminized black music from white appropriation.[18] Yet Baldwin also offers an antidote to his own problematic treatment of black music by reconceptualizing understatement as a collaborative process instead of an object. Ida's brother, a jazz drummer named Rufus, has something Ida does not: a musical community of accompanists who will sympathetically *interpret* another player's solo as understated. As I suggest through close readings of Smith's and Holiday's work with instrumentalists, accompaniment is interpretation that co-creates musical meaning. Insofar as *Another Country* turns understatement into a matter of collaborative creation, it highlights the shift in Baldwin's work, as he starts to co-create black musical understatement through what we might call interpretive literary accompaniment. Indeed, his early interpretation of Bessie Smith's music as "fantastically understated" points us in this direction, insofar as "understated" does not seem to be an apt stylistic or sonic descriptor of what Langston Hughes called "the bellowing voice of Bessie Smith."[19] Baldwin's later writing fulfills the gesture by raising the possibility that *any* form of black expression, however elaborate or passionate, might accurately be thought to understate the origin of its production in "one of the most obscene adventures in the history of mankind."[20] In one of his last essays on music, "Of the Sorrow Songs: The Cross of Redemption" (1979), understatement becomes not something "out there" that Baldwin authoritatively identifies but a condition that he co-creates by naming it as such. Baldwin thus uses his later nonfiction to become the kind of accompanist that Ida lacks.

Baldwin's Uses of the Blues

Baldwin first credits Bessie Smith with enabling his work as a black novelist in 1959, and female singers remain central to his rhetoric of racial self-authorization for years. In "The Discovery of What It Means to Be an American," Baldwin tells of suffering a nervous breakdown and retreating to Switzerland to recover and to finish *Go Tell It on the Mountain* (1953). "There," he writes, "in that absolutely alabaster landscape, armed with two Bessie Smith records and a typewriter, I began to try to re-create the life that I had first known as a child and from which I had spent so many years in flight." He continues, "It was Bessie Smith, through her tone and her cadence, who helped me dig back to the way I myself must have spoken when I was a pickaninny, and to remember the things I had heard and seen and felt. . . . I had never listened to Bessie Smith in America (in the same way that, for years, I would not touch watermelon), but in Europe she helped to reconcile me to being a 'nigger.'"[21] Baldwin explains that Smith's singing reattunes him to the world of his childhood, and he somewhat cryptically implies that she helps him reclaim his maligned social role. Both processes enable him to write his highly autobiographical first novel.[22] By this logic, Smith becomes symbolic mother to Baldwin's "pickaninny," and midwife to his first book.[23]

From "Discovery" on, Smith becomes a talisman and a touchstone in Baldwin's work. He will soon claim Smith's understated music as characteristic of black expression in general, invoking "Backwater Blues" as an ur-text of understated black realism and setting the work of Smith and also of Holiday against the fantasies of security that, for Baldwin, define American whiteness. For instance, in a review of Richard Wright's posthumously published *Eight Men* (1961), he calls one of Wright's stories "as spare and moving an account as that delivered by Bessie Smith in 'Backwater Blues'"—thus using their shared admiration of Smith to make peace with Wright and perhaps assert racial kinship with him, after Wright's death.[24] In "The Black Boy Looks at the White Boy" (1961), an essay on Norman Mailer that critiqued, among other things, Mailer's respect for the Beat writers, Baldwin contrasts Smith's realism with Jack Kerouac's black imaginary. This essay marks an important turning point in Baldwin's writing on Smith: here he cites her work to establish a dichotomy between black and white responses to suffering.

Baldwin quotes the now-infamous passage in *On the Road* (1957) in which Kerouac's narrator, Sal Paradise, wanders the streets of Denver "wishing [he] were a Negro, feeling that the best the white world had offered was not enough ecstasy for [him], not enough life, joy, kicks, darkness, music, not enough night . . ."[25] Baldwin calls this "absolute nonsense, . . . and offensive nonsense at that," and he contends that while there is "real pain" in this passage, the pain is "thin, because it does not refer to reality, but to a dream." He encourages the reader to "compare it, at random, with any old blues":

> Backwater blues done caused me
> To pack my things and go.
> 'Cause my house fell down
> And I can't live there no mo'.[26]

By now, it should be clear that, far from being "any old blues" selected at random, "Backwater Blues" is Baldwin's blues of choice. Here he uses it to figure a culturally specific style of expressing a culturally specific reality. He sets a verse of the song against Kerouac's work to establish a contrast between black realism and white fantasy. While, according to Baldwin, the white man expects the world to help him "in the achievement of [his] identity," the black man knows "the world does not do this—for anyone."[27] The black man's survival depends on knowing this: "One had to make oneself up as one went along. This had to be done in the not-at-all-metaphorical teeth of the world's determination to destroy you. The world had prepared no place for you, and if the world had its way, no place would ever exist."[28] Indeed, Smith's "Backwater Blues" articulates an African American subject accustomed to making herself up as she goes along ("Backwater blues done caused me to pack my things and go"); displacement dismays but does not surprise her ("My house fell down and I can't live there no mo'").

It is fitting that Baldwin should set "Backwater Blues" against *On the Road* to attack the "dream" of the Beats and white hipsters like Mailer.

The white male protagonists of Kerouac's novel have the luxury of displacing themselves, and as they roam the country in pursuit of the relentless spirit they hear in bop music, these men—"Holy flowers floating in the air . . . , all these tired faces in the dawn of Jazz America"—idealize jazz musicians and black men in general as "the happy, truehearted ecstatic Negroes of America."[29] Notwithstanding the question of whether Kerouac himself critiques or affirms these moments of what Kobena Mercer would call "racial romanticism,"[30] Baldwin seeks to correct such misreadings of black music and black life by claiming Smith's blues as understated accounts of suffering that are decipherable only to black Americans well acquainted with "the world's determination to destroy" them.

Baldwin's article was partly responding to Mailer's 1957 essay "The White Negro," in which Mailer had described white hipsters' romanticization of black jazz musicians as renegade culture heroes. But Baldwin did not challenge Mailer's depiction of black *life* so much as his depiction of black *expression* (and white comprehension thereof), by stressing laconic opacity where Mailer waxed poetic about black ecstatic transparency. According to Mailer, the black man was the prototype for white nonconformists disillusioned by World War II and the atom bomb because he had already grown accustomed to the threat of senseless death that these developments represented. The black man already knew "in the cells of his existence that life was war, nothing but war," and thus "he kept for his survival the art of the primitive, he lived in the enormous present, he subsisted for his Saturday night kicks, relinquishing the pleasures of the mind for the more obligatory pleasures of the body, and in his music he gave voice to the character and quality of his existence, to his rage and the infinite variations of joy, lust, languor, growl, cramp, pinch, scream and despair of his orgasm."[31] Famously, for Mailer, that orgasm was synonymous with jazz—a music that communicated effortlessly to its listeners, regardless of their life experience, "because it said, 'I feel this, and now you do too.'"[32]

Baldwin issued his most powerful challenge to that presumption of instantaneous communication in an article published in *Playboy* magazine in 1964. "The Uses of the Blues" continued Baldwin's work of recovering Smith's legacy,[33] while also offering readers his views on Holiday, who had died five years earlier. This essay focuses on Smith's "Backwater Blues" and Holiday's "Billie's Blues" (1936), two songs that are central to *Another Country* as well. Baldwin begins by claiming, "The title 'The Uses of the Blues' does not refer to music; I don't know anything about music. It does refer to the experience of life, or the state of being, out of which the blues come" (*U*, 57).[34] Baldwin soon makes it clear that he knows a good deal about this state, and he uses Smith to assert this knowledge. As he writes,

> Bessie Smith, who is dead now, came out of somewhere in the
> Deep South. I guess she was born around 1898, a great blues singer;
> died in Mississippi after a very long, hard—not *very* long, but very
> *hard*—life: pigs' feet and gin, many disastrous lovers, and a career
> that first went up, then went down; died on the road on the way
> from one hospital to another. . . .[35] Well, Bessie saw a great many
> things, and among those things was a flood. And she talked about
> it and she said, "It rained five days and the skies turned dark as
> night." . . .
> Well, you know, that is all very accurate, all very concrete. I
> know, I watched, I was there. . . . I have seen it all . . . What the
> blues are describing comes out of all this. (*U*, 57–59)[36]

Thus did Baldwin describe the blues and their Empress for a readership which might not know, which would have to be told, that Smith was "dead now." The presumed ignorance of Baldwin's audience gave him considerable license to fashion his own image of the singer. Assuming the folksy gravitas of a seasoned storyteller, Baldwin describes Smith rising from the mists of an obscure place and time ("somewhere in the Deep South," "around 1898") to sing what she lived; her classic songs "Gimme a Pigfoot and a Bottle of Beer" and "Gin House Blues" become testimonies to a life of "pigs' feet and gin." Smith expresses herself in such a natural, pedestrian manner that she does not even sing. Rather, she "s[ees]" a flood and, in Baldwin's vernacular, "talks[s] about it"; she "sa[ys]" the first line of her song.

Baldwin similarly portrays Holiday as singing the truth of her life—a life which, in his telling, rivals Smith's in its bleakness:

> Billie Holiday came along a little later and she had quite a story,
> too, a story which *Life* magazine would never print except as a
> tough, bittersweet sob-story obituary—in which, however help-
> lessly, the dominant note would be relief. She was a little girl from
> the South, and she had quite a time with gin, whiskey, and dope.
> She died in New York in a narcotics ward under the most terrify-
> ing and—in terms of crimes of the city and the country against
> her—disgraceful circumstances, and she had something she called

"Billie's Blues": "My man wouldn't give me no dinner / Wouldn't give me no supper / Squawked about my supper and turned me out-doors / And had the nerve to lay a padlock on my clothes / I didn't have so many, but I had a long, long way to go." (*U*, 58)

Although Baldwin critiques *Life* magazine's "tough, bittersweet sob-story obituary" for Holiday, he too portrays Holiday as a victim of "crimes of the city and the country against her." Baldwin frames "Billie's Blues" (a Holiday composition and her most recorded song) as something she "had"; a disposition as much as a song, "Billie's Blues" becomes Holiday's testimony to her difficult life. Like Smith's, Holiday's music is both simple—it is a direct expression of lived experience—and in need of translation by Baldwin. It is necessary that he tell readers, "'Gin House Blues' is a real gin house," "'Backwater Flood' [*sic*] is a real flood," and "when Billie says, 'My man don't love me,' she is not making a fantasy out of it. This is what happened, this is where it is. This is what it is" (*U*, 59).

Baldwin's authentication of Smith's and Holiday's work is proprietary. Not just anyone can know that their understated songs testify to disastrous reality. How, then, does Baldwin know this? When he writes, "I know, I watched, I was there," he does not mean that he was present at Smith's performances (he was only thirteen years old when she died in Mississippi); nor does he imply that he was present at the Mississippi River flood of 1927, which Smith's "Backwater Blues" was thought to detail (he was three at the time and living in New York).[37] When he calls "Backwater Blues" "very accurate, very concrete," he is not measuring its accuracy against the real-life flood but suggesting that the song accurately testifies to a collective history of unnatural displacements. Like the speaker of Langston Hughes's "The Negro Speaks of Rivers" (1921), who attests to having "known" rivers from the Nile to the Mississippi, from the dawn of civilization to the present, Baldwin establishes himself as a witness to this collective history. Just as Hughes ascribes this deep knowledge to a nameless, generalized "Negro," Baldwin racializes his ability to apprehend Smith's and Holiday's songs and suggests that black Americans have a special purchase on the interpretation—and also the execution—of understated expression. He wryly asks readers to imagine Doris Day singing "God Bless the Child" (1941), another song written and popularized by Holiday (*U*, 60). The implication is that a Doris Day rendition of the song would be untenable, since Day, like Kerouac, trades in the perpetuation of fantasy, not the truth telling of Smith and Holiday.

Although Baldwin generally neglects Smith's and Holiday's artistry by asserting that their songs are direct expressions of lived struggle, he goes furthest toward crediting them with creating *art* out of experience when he praises their achievement of a critical distance from the stories they tell. As they sing about painful experience, they are "commenting on it, a little bit outside it." The ideal effect of this critical distance is to train listeners to stand outside their own suffering and therefore to bear it:

> When Billie or Bessie or Leadbelly stood up and sang about it, they were commenting on it, a little bit outside it: they were accepting it. And there's something funny—there's always something a little funny in all our disasters, if one can face the disaster. So that it's this passionate detachment, this inwardness coupled with outwardness, this ability to know that, All right, it's a mess, and you can't do anything about it . . . so, well, you have to do something about it, . . . but all right, OK, as Bessie said, "Picked up my bag, baby, and I tried it again."[38] This made life, however horrible that life was, bearable for her. It's what makes life bearable for any person, because every person, from the time he's found out about people until the whole thing is over, is certain of one thing: he is going to suffer. There is no way not to suffer. (*U*, 59)[39]

Baldwin would continue to praise Smith and Holiday for their "inwardness coupled with outwardness," their ability to recognize the "disaster" and also to laugh at the apparent impossibility, and the absolute necessity, of going on nonetheless. As he told an interviewer in 1973, "Billie Holiday . . . gave you back your experience. She refined it, and you recognized it for the first time because she was in and out of it and she made it possible for you to bear it. And if you could bear it, then you could begin to change it."[40] He made a similar claim about his friend Nina Simone.[41] The proper "use" of these artists' blues, then, is as a tool for survival and change. This usage depends on listeners' ability to apprehend the disastrous reality that Smith's and Holiday's songs encode and to appreciate the singers' capacity to manage that disaster with style.

Taken together, Baldwin's essays perform the important cultural work of claiming Smith's and Holiday's blues as part of a usable past for black Americans—of celebrating black women's blues as, to use Kenneth Burke's phrase, "equipment for living."[42] This was an act of reclamation, for while Smith had once been (accurately) billed as "The Greatest and Highest Salaried Race Star in the World," her image had not aged well. When Baldwin writes of never listening to Smith in America, "in the same way that, for years, [he] would not touch watermelon," he is describing a broader generational trend—by the 1950s, Smith had been recast as an entertainer who enforced racist stereotypes of black emotionality and promiscuity.[43] (Wright's ambivalent citation of Smith's blues in his 1950s lectures, discussed in chapter 1, may reflect that shift.) Yet Baldwin's recuperation of Smith was also part of a collective effort. As the Civil Rights Movement sparked widespread interest in recovering black history and culture, several African American writers would reevaluate the blues and other folk music, taking up the work that Wright and Ellison had begun. So when Baldwin says that his stay in Switzerland allowed him to listen to Smith without shame and even to take her as his muse, he is participating in a more widespread effort to reconstruct an African American heritage—even as he stages his own "rediscovery" of Smith's work abroad, apart from the site where white Americans are themselves increasingly embracing or first "discovering" Smith's work.

Baldwin's recuperation of the blues prefigured and resonated with that of other Black Arts writers, particularly LeRoi Jones (later Amiri Baraka), who published the landmark *Blues People* in 1963. The first popular full-length study about black music written by a black critic,[44] *Blues People* was a deeply influential socioanthropological examination of the music as a direct index of African American life—a perspective on the music that Baldwin's "Uses of the Blues" clearly shares. Following Wright, both Baraka and Baldwin forged deep bonds between black music and black history, even as the blues-based (white) British invasion and the U.S. blues revival threatened to pry them apart. (The majority-white Newport Folk Festival first featured black blues musicians in 1963, six years after the Newport Jazz Festival had first featured gospel singers like Mahalia Jackson.) While theorists such as Frantz Fanon, Ron Karenga, Sonia Sanchez, and Haki Madhubuti at times disavowed the blues as regressive music that appealed to white people because it expressed black resignation, Baldwin and Baraka claimed the music with a vengeance, pushing back against white attempts to appropriate music that "belonged" to black "blues people." Indeed, the uneasy interracial sounding of Smith's recordings that Baldwin stages in *Another Country* (which I will discuss shortly) constituted the tragic, same-sex counterpart to the climax of Baraka's play *Dutchman*, produced two years later; in *Dutchman*, a black man lashes out at his would-be white seductress by lambasting white people who claim to "love" Bessie Smith while failing to realize that Smith is in fact telling them, "and very plainly, 'Kiss my black ass.'"[45]

Affirming the energy, if not the militancy, of Baraka's vision of black music, Black Arts theorist Larry Neal argued that the blues modeled "defiant" "survival on the meanest, most gut level of human existence."[46] Jazz singer and cultural critic Abbey Lincoln set black female singers—the three vocalists Baldwin cites in *Another Country*—at the center of this argument. In her 1966 essay "The Negro Woman in American Literature," Lincoln herself used the Burkean phrase "equipment for living" to describe the work of "the compassionate trailblazer" Bessie Smith, as well as "the great stylist and innovator" Billie Holiday and "the revered and beloved Mahalia Jackson."[47] Lincoln writes that these artists' "portrayals of life's experiences are functional and act as 'equipment for living,'" in that they "are preparations for what to expect in the business of living in the U.S.A."[48] This affirmative view of the blues fostered by Wright, Ellison, Baldwin, Lincoln, and others still dominates Black Studies today. As Adam Gussow glosses it, "[The] blues are not sorrow songs (or not *only* sorrow songs), but *survivor* songs: the soundtrack of a spiritual warriorship that refuses to die—and . . . wrests far more than its share of swaggering lyric joy out of an evil world, inscribing personhood and sustaining the tribe in the process."[49]

Baldwin's writings on Smith and Holiday, however, also reveal potential limitations of this idealized view, for while Baldwin claims these singers as representative survivors, he also naturalizes and simplifies their work. By implying that the critical distance he associates with understatement comes naturally to them and by narrowly defining their lives through suffering—"not *very* long, but very *hard*"—he suggests that Smith and Holiday naturally and exclusively understate the pain that determines their lives. That these representations sustain a gendered imbalance of power becomes apparent when we see that in Baldwin's fiction, as much as his nonfiction, black women's expressions of suffering foster male authorization. For example, in "Sonny's Blues," black male communion is facilitated by black women singers, who, as in "Uses of the Blues," express the pain of their lives through song. The female singers of "Sonny's Blues" are religious worshippers, and, although their song is not *stylistically* understated, it does require (male) decipherment. In a pivotal scene, Sonny and the narrator witness a minirevival on the street in Harlem; three black women and one man testify and sing. Sonny is particularly drawn to a woman singer with a "warm voice," and he can read what lies behind her singing, "how much suffering she must have had to go through to sing like that."[50] Sharing this recognition with his brother helps Sonny talk about his own struggles with heroin addiction, so the telos of women's sung testimony to suffering is fraternal understanding. This understanding in turn enables the narrator to appreciate the story's culminating moment of male communion: Sonny and his jazz band's performance.

In the sexually charged and racially integrated landscape of *Another Country*, Bessie Smith does not facilitate such communion, but Ida does. In an early scene, Ida's brother Rufus listens to Smith's "Backwater Blues" with his white friend, Vivaldo, an aspiring novelist (and Ida's future lover). Rufus is in despair. Baldwin writes, *"There's thousands of people*, Bessie now sang, *ain't got no place to go*, and for the first time Rufus began to hear, in the severely understated monotony of this blues, something which spoke to his troubled mind" (*AC*, 49). The blues are not consolation enough, though. Rufus needs Vivaldo to hear the song as he does, to detect the desperation its "severely understated monotony" encodes. As Peter Szendy insightfully states, "what summons us to listen . . . is our desire for someone, always one more person, to hear us hearing. I want you to listen to me listening."[51] Yet Vivaldo can't do this for Rufus, can't hear what he hears in the music, primarily because he does not share Rufus's experience of being made to suffer because of his race.[52] The scene comports with Baldwin's claim that blues understatement is distinctly legible to black listeners, while revealing the disastrous consequence of Rufus's and Vivaldo's failure to realize this. Had Vivaldo recognized this difference, he might have asked Rufus what he heard in the song, and Rufus might have attempted to make his own listening, in Szendy's terms, *"transmissible"* to his friend.[53] Shortly after this failed encounter, Rufus leaps to his death off the George Washington Bridge—the striking finale of the novel's first section.

As the novel concludes, however, Ida does what Smith's voice failed to do: she ushers Vivaldo into an understanding of Rufus's pain. As Ida tells Vivaldo, "[Because] I'm black . . . , *I know* more about what happened to my brother than you can ever know. *I watched* it happen—from the beginning. *I was there*. He shouldn't have ended up the way he did" (*AC*, 415, my italics). Ida uses the same language Baldwin employs to establish his understanding of Smith's work in "Uses of the Blues": "I know, I watched, I was there." However, Ida's understanding serves Vivaldo's art rather than Ida's. Now, "a detail that [Vivaldo] needed for his novel, which he had been searching for for months, fell, neatly and vividly, like the tumblers of a lock, into place in his mind" (*AC*, 427). As Smith did for Baldwin, Ida enables Vivaldo to write his first novel. Again, the black female singer becomes the vehicle for the male artist's work. As Ida and

Vivaldo embrace, "it was she who was comforting him. Her long fingers stroked his back, and he began, slowly, with a horrible, strangling sound, to weep, for she was stroking his innocence out of him" (*AC*, 431). Here, Ida disabuses Vivaldo of the juvenile fantasies of race, and thus of life, that Baldwin accuses Kerouac and Mailer of harboring; she helps him accept the stark reality represented by Smith's "Backwater Blues," and this acceptance is the key to his art.

The Uses of Understatement: Smith's and Holiday's Accompanied Blues

I will return to the novel shortly. Here, I want to take a cue from Rufus's attention to Bessie Smith's interaction with James P. Johnson to theorize the relationship between accompaniment and understatement in Smith's and Holiday's own work. When Vivaldo plays the recording of "James Pete Johnson and Bessie Smith batting out *Backwater Blues*," Baldwin brings the song's lyrics to bear on Rufus's predicament; but he has Rufus, with the ear of an instrumentalist, pick up on Johnson's accompaniment: "The piano bore the singer witness, stoic, ironic" (*AC*, 49). I want to suggest that Johnson's act of "witnessing" Smith helps to *create* the "severely understated monotony of this blues," and that we might therefore apprehend Smith's and Holiday's understatement partly as a product of their musical accompaniment. To see accompaniment as a key force in creating understatement is one way to shift our attention from singers' biographies to their music, as Hortense Spillers invites us to do;[54] instead of imagining that Smith and Holiday stand outside their own experience and comment on it, I focus on the ways their accompanists stand outside these singers' delivery of the lyrics and musically "comment" on that. This vocal-instrumental interaction generates an ironic contrast between what is sung and how it sounds: musical understatement. With regard to "Backwater Blues," for example, the line "my house fell down and I can't live there no mo'" might be considered *rhetorically* understated because it is a matter-of-fact and economical expression of experiential "disaster." What makes Smith's song *sonically* understated, however, is the setting of the lyrics within an upbeat musical arrangement. Smith's tersely expressed grievance *swings*, and this is largely due to her collaboration with Johnson. It is Johnson who establishes the song's rolling-rocking movement in his piano introduction, laying the foundation for Smith's pitch-perfect entrance into the song and seemingly effortless roll up the fifth on the first key word, "rained": "Well it rained five days and the sky turned dark as night." As I discuss in more detail, Johnson plays near-comedic flourishes, or musical commentaries, on Smith's concise lyrics throughout the song. Hence, even in those moments when Smith deploys word painting to augment her lyrical message, it is possible to hear her songs as understated because of Johnson's piano work. These artists create understatement together.

Locating Smith and Holiday in their respective milieus, despite Baldwin's tendency to treat them interchangeably, also reveals the different gendered and sexualized meanings of their understated work. Although producer John Hammond recorded Smith's last studio session and Holiday's first session within two days of each other in November of 1933—a feat of U.S. recording history—the singers inhabited quite distinct performance cultures. Smith began her career in vaudeville shows before recording as a blues singer; Holiday recorded blues (Smith's among them), but she was mainly known as a jazz singer who moved from swing into the bop era. These different contexts meant that Smith and Holiday activated understatement differently and to different ends. Although I start with Smith, I focus on Holiday in the following discussion, as I believe that she is Baldwin's model for Ida in *Another Country*—indeed, Baldwin extracts Ida's very name from Holiday's surname—and Holiday's collaborative understatement therefore highlights Ida's lack thereof.

This is the last verse of "Backwater Blues," one Baldwin never cites: "Mmmm, I can't move no more. . . . There ain't no place for a poor ol' girl to go."[55] As Farah Jasmine Griffin has pointed out, Smith's last lines speak to the "gendered dimension of displacement," reminding us that "gendered and raced subjects are the most dislocated" people in America.[56] The effect of omitting this verse is to enforce Baldwin's claim that the blues are understated accounts of black suffering; to acknowledge that this is a song partly "about" black womanhood, a doubly marked subject position, would presumably have undermined the generalizing thrust of his argument. Yet Smith's understatement carried its own gender politics, in its refusal to elicit pity for gendered suffering or to respect prohibitions on female desire. Smith's and Johnson's collaborative understatement authorizes songs that make suffering and sexual desire at once comic and sacred.

As Jackie Kay writes, "The fascinating thing about the voice of Bessie Smith, for all its blueness, is its total lack of sentimentality. She can sing unnerving, sad songs without a note of self-pity. It is the very flatness of her voice, singing about tragedies, that so moves us. It is not in any way the voice of the victim."[57] The "flat" sound Kay describes is not a matter of intonation but of the evenness with which Smith stresses each word of a song such as "Backwater Blues." This practice gives each lyrical line a heavy, relentlessly matter-of-fact momentum. Yet the little flourishes or commentaries Johnson plays at the end of each line temper the gravity. After Smith sings, "They rowed a little boat about five miles 'cross the pond," Johnson performs a skipping trill in the upper range of the piano; the trill evokes chase scenes from early silent films in which a piano scores accelerated moving images. Indeed, since the piano sounds "as if [it] [is not] taking any of this so seriously," we might envision a sped-up cinematic scene of people rowing across the water with comically pitiful speed.[58] So while Smith's *persona* is that of a woman alone, perhaps abandoned by community and social institutions that could help her, Johnson's accompaniment buoys the lyrics and belies the speaker's claim to isolation. These artists work together to depict a tragedy without casting Smith in the role of the victim. It is fitting that Smith sings, "Backwater blues done caused me to pack my things and go"; rather than lament that the *flood* drives her away, she indicates that the song, the blues, keeps her moving.[59]

Smith's understatement was perhaps most radical when she used religious metaphor to sing about sexual desire in songs like "Preachin' the Blues" (1927). While such songs defy white and black bourgeois norms, they might also specifically challenge the patriarchal culture of the black church. As I have noted in the previous chapter, the church has long been figured as a uniquely safe space for African American expression. However, blueswomen rose to popularity at a time when the church, according to Angela Davis, was becoming an increasingly male-dominated sphere.[60] As "women like Gertrude ["Ma"] Rainey and Bessie Smith helped to carve out new space in which black working people could gather and experience themselves as a community," Davis writes, these women were not only affirming black working-class culture but also creating a space of female agency in which it was safe to express sexual desire.[61] In this alternative space, Smith became, in Ellison's words, a "priestess" of her own ceremony.[62] She comically utilized religious rhetoric in order to position herself as an irreverent match for church authorities.

In "Preachin' the Blues" (the song form of which is less a blues than a vaudeville tune), Smith uses sermonic language to impress on her audience, which she figures as female, the virtues of sexual selectivity: "I will learn you something if you listen to this song / I ain't here to try to save your soul, just want to teach you how to save your good jelly roll."[63] The word "just" downplays the significance of Smith's sexual advice, relative to "soul-saving" evangelism. And yet Johnson's work on this piece contains fewer comical flourishes than his accompaniment to "Backwater Blues," recorded the same year. His upbeat yet spare piano work "stays out of Smith's way" and thus affirms the importance, if not the gravity, of her words. Here, Johnson plays it straight, while Smith uses a comically provocative metaphor, and this ironic contrast between musical accompaniment and lyrical content generates musical understatement. In "Preachin' the Blues," Johnson helps Smith assert her expressive authority in nonreligious spaces and thus contest the male authority of the church. The song implies that if sex is not as serious as religion, neither can religion be as grave a matter as religious authorities claim.

Holiday generated musical understatement partly by developing a subtler performance style and mode of lyrical interpretation than Smith's. I want to highlight the racial and gender politics of these aspects of her work, while also showing that Holiday's musical understatement was, like Smith's, largely an effect of accompaniment. First, Holiday's understated style enabled her entry into a male-dominated jazz scene. In a discussion of the rise of the "cool" aesthetic in jazz culture, Scott Saul writes that "a key, if often unnoticed, baseline for all speculations about the meaning of 'hip'" was that "the hipster was male."[64] So while Holiday's early training (like Mahalia Jackson's) consisted of listening to Smith's records and trying to develop Smith's "big sound," her era was a good time not to.[65] Robert O'Meally describes the difference between Smith's and Holiday's performance cultures: whereas Smith "came up shouting above bands under huge outdoor tents to crowds sometimes numbering in the thousands and then projecting with great force into the dull ear of early recording machines," "Holiday was a microphone singer. She had come of age, artistically, at a time and in places where she was not expected to shout above a band or a roomful of noise, but instead almost to whisper her lyrics as she moved from table to table in speakeasies."[66] Unlike Smith, Holiday did not dance, tell jokes, or wear flamboyant costumes. As O'Meally writes, "She came out onto the stage, she sang, and then she left, sometimes with the house going dark while she made her invisible disappearance."[67] Producing her own form of theatricality, Holiday both participated in and helped to create a new aesthetic of musical cool.

In a rather remarkable turn, Holiday used this "male" aesthetic to sing about gendered oppression.[68] She managed to address this oppression despite being accompanied by all-male bands and managed by men in part because her testimony was so understated as to be unthreatening to—and, indeed, relatable to—male listeners. Thus, while Leon Forrest describes Holiday as sharing painful truths with her listening "sisterhood of women" by expressing "the double victimization of the Black female: slavery and sexual de-basement," he also stresses that Holiday's understatement fostered *cross-gender* identification: "Because [Holiday] was so understated, you were allowed to think about your own heartbreak, in a much more cool, reflective manner." She consoled both male and female listeners in part by giving them the sense that "your agony was special—as you really suspected all along—if not remarkable."[69] Further, the sensuality of Holiday's performances may have moved listeners to imagine themselves as her would-be saviors, in contrast with the lovers who had mistreated her in the past. Her understated lyrics and performance helped her to signify such injustice in a manner that was less accusatory than inviting.

Moreover, the emotional range of Holiday's music, like Smith's, covered far more than pain, a point for which Baldwin's selective citation of "Billie's Blues" does not account. Baldwin cites the verse in which Holiday sings of her man's crimes against her—"My man wouldn't give me no [breakfast], wouldn't give me no dinner, squawked about my supper [then he put] me outdoors"—but leaves out the hip, assertive verses which compose most of the song and express a sassy self-assurance. Holiday soon shifts to focus on her own attributes, ending the song with this verse:

> Some men like me 'cause I'm happy, some 'cause I'm snappy,
> Some call me honey, others think I've got money.
> Some say, "Billie, baby, you're built for speed."
> Now if you put that all together, makes me everything a good man
> needs.[70]

Holiday's humor is subtle. Where she might have emphasized the "built for speed" innuendo—a phrase first used for cars and a sexual metaphor for the body that contrasts with "built for comfort"—she instead folds the line casually into the rest of the verse.[71] But she conveys a spirited elegance throughout the song, not least when detailing rejection.

For instance, in the 1944 Commodore recording of the song, when Holiday sings the line "squawked about my supper then he put me outdoors," she sings every word but "outdoors" on the same note, an A-flat. She thus evokes the monotonous nagging, or squawking, which the lyrics describe. Further, since A-flat is the fifth note of the D-flat scale in which "Billie's Blues" is set, it produces an unstable sound that wants to resolve. When the note does resolve to an E-flat, on "outdoors," Holiday elicits

FIGURE 5. Billie Holiday jam session, 1942. Photo by Gjon Mili / Time & Life Pictures / Getty Images.

the listener's sense of relief. Musically, the harmonic movement brings appealing resolution; semantically, it indicates that getting "outdoors" may prove more liberating than the lyrics themselves suggest. Likewise, when Holiday sings, "I didn't have so many, but I had a long, long ways to go," she lilts her inflection on "didn't" as if to match her signature head tilt, that quick and vaguely conspiratorial shrug.

Holiday's interactions with her small swing ensemble play a crucial role in making this 1944 performance understated. Maya Gibson explains that small ensembles, as opposed to larger swing bands, were attractive for musicians because they "offered them the rare opportunity to play with some of the best musicians around."[72] According to jazz pianist Teddy Wilson, who often arranged these sessions, "In their own bands [these players] were the number one soloist . . . , but at my recording sessions they themselves were one of seven top soloists."[73] Holiday was uniformly respected in these settings, "an equal among equals."[74] On this session, her accompanists are pianist Eddie Heywood, bassist John Simmons, and drummer Sid Catlett. One way in which they support and foster Holiday's understated sound is by punctuating her lyrics in stop-time form—halting after each line in the verse where she details her lover's wrongdoings ("My man wouldn't give me no dinner . . ."). The rhythmic hits during this section generate the listener's expectation that something new is about to happen, preparing for the movement that the end of the verse delivers: "put me outdoors." At this point, the trio supports Holiday's vocal line with a crescendo that tells us that getting outdoors is less an indignity than a welcome change. Heywood even enhances the song's humor, as Johnson does for Smith. After Holiday sings, "I ain't good lookin'," he traipses down the keyboard with ironic indulgence, as if to ask, *Did you catch that?* Together, Holiday and her accompanists generate musical understatement by playing on this story of "tragic" loss.

The understatement of "Billie's Blues" demonstrates Holiday's mastery, in a male realm, of a supposedly male aesthetic. Appropriating this aesthetic enables Holiday to assert her belonging among male musicians and to address and defy gendered violence. Holiday's persona in this song is neither a stoic loner nor a victim at the mercy of her lover or an unjust society. She is not a long-suffering survivor who "had a long, long ways to go." Instead, she is a woman for whom it is not only a necessity but a *pleasure* to survive. If this notion is at odds with what we think we know about Holiday's life—her struggle to record what she wanted, and to perform where she wanted, her well-founded paranoia about the police, her betrayal by lovers, and the relentlessness of her addiction— it's important to realize that her singing was informed by but never reducible to her personal problems. Like Smith's, Holiday's music was a medium through which to imagine new ways of being and becoming. "Billie's Blues" highlights the role of community in this becoming, both lyrically and sonically defining a self in relation to others. The last verse in particular ("some men like me 'cause I'm happy, some 'cause I'm snappy . . .") indicates that other people's comments might help us on our way, perhaps toward new love—especially if one can creatively "put [them] all together." The trick is to decide whom to listen to. Deciding what to take in order to move on, Holiday's speaker asserts emotional and sexual autonomy. Her performance of "Billie's Blues" imagines an audience before whom it will be safe to do so, because it dramatizes the fact that Holiday already has such listeners, in the form of her accompanists.

"Do You Love Me?": Understatement in Another Country

The supportive accompaniment that Holiday gets from her band is what Rufus has and what Ida lacks in Another Country. The difference is gendered and sexualized. Ida does not have the male support that fosters Smith's and Holiday's understatement and helps them express sexual autonomy. On the contrary, Ida's very career is compromised by interracial male competition. In staging this violence, Another Country exposes the troubling gender politics of Baldwin's own efforts to claim black music and to resist white appropriation thereof. But the novel also posits an alternative to Baldwin's gendered practice of racial self-authorization: it opens up the possibility of collaboratively co-creating music through interpretation rather than translating its message and legitimating its experiential veracity. I turn to Rufus's listening and performance to show how this is so.

As I have said, when Rufus and Vivaldo listen to "Backwater Blues," Rufus picks up on the dialogue between Smith and Johnson. The song reminds Rufus of his mutually torturous relationship with Leona, a poor white woman recently arrived in New York from the South. Yet Leona is not the only loss of which "Backwater Blues" reminds Rufus. The song also reminds him, I think, of his break with his band. Baldwin's description of Smith and Johnson's interaction recalls his description of Rufus's jazz ensemble in an earlier scene (the night Rufus meets Leona). In this sense, "Backwater Blues" signals the musical-emotional camaraderie Rufus has forfeited. In that earlier scene, set in a Harlem club, Rufus and his bandmates bear witness to a young saxophone player in the "stoic, ironic" way that Johnson bears witness to Smith. But here, Baldwin refigures the relationship between accompaniment and understatement I have described. Rufus's accompaniment does not generate musical understatement in the form of ironic contrast, but Rufus's act of witnessing helps make this musical moment understated in another way: Rufus figures the solo as semantically understated by imagining the layers of meaning it encodes.

Rufus does not know the saxophone player well enough to know where he's from—"he was a kid of about the same age as Rufus, from some insane place like Jersey City or Syracuse"—but Rufus nonetheless sympathetically and inventively interprets his solo as he accompanies it. The sax player

> stood there, wide-legged, humping the air . . . , shivering in the rags
> of his twenty-odd years, and screaming through the horn *Do you
> love me? Do you love me? Do you love me?* . . . This, anyway, was
> the question Rufus heard, the same phrase, unbearably, endlessly,
> and variously repeated, with all of the force the boy had. . . . The
> boy was blowing with his lungs and guts out of his own short past;
> somewhere in that past, in the gutters or gang fights or gang shags;
> in the acrid room, on the sperm-stiffened blanket, behind mari-
> juana or the needle, under the smell of piss in the precinct base-
> ment, he had received the blow from which he never would recover
> and this no one wanted to believe. (*AC*, 8–9)

The other musicians, at least to Rufus's mind, *do* seem to believe it: "each man knew that the boy was blowing for every one of them" (*AC*, 9). Like Smith's and Holiday's collaborators, the members of the band "stayed with [the soloist], cool and at a little distance, adding and questioning and corroborating, holding it down as well as they could with an ironical self-mockery" (*AC*, 9). However, unlike Smith and Holiday, this soloist is "*screaming* through the horn"; the impassioned force of his perfor-mance threatens to overwhelm his accompanists, who must "[hold] it down as well as they could." For this reason, the other players' "ironical self-mockery" cannot make the player's solo *sound* understated, in any conventional stylistic sense. But Rufus's interpretation of the solo pushes us to define understatement in a new way: as the product of a creative act of interpretation.

In an incisive reading of this scene, Marisa Parham stresses that "*Do you love me?*" is *Rufus's* creation: "this, anyway, was the question Rufus heard."[75] And Rufus's interpretation of the music figures it as understating or encoding a great deal, in terms of the player's lived experience ("gang fights or gang shags," "the acrid room," "the sperm-stiffened blanket"). Here, Rufus models the practice of listening, as Nancy defines it. Because the listening ear is attuned not only to sense but also to sound, "to be listening is always to be at the edge of meaning"; it is to experience "an intensification and a concern, a curiosity or an anxiety."[76] Through this act of listening, Rufus creatively decodes the sax player's solo and guesses what it means to the other musicians. Whether or not Rufus reads the solo or his bandmates' understanding thereof "correctly" is beside the point. In foregrounding Rufus's effort to interpret the music, Baldwin figures the sax player's solo as understated to the extent that Rufus works to decipher it: it is *only* Rufus's effort to translate the instrumental solo into words, to imagine what lies "somewhere in [the] past" of the song, that suggests this solo understates anything. Of course, Rufus's act of interpretation is simultaneously an act of accompaniment; as he "reads" the player's solo, he is giving the soloist the space and support he needs to make his musical statement. Like Smith's and Holiday's collaborators, then, Rufus helps create musical meaning through interpretative accompaniment.

No one in the novel works to decipher Ida's songs, to read them as understated expressions of pain. Ida's lack of interpretive accompaniment is all the more ironic because, as I have suggested, she is modeled after Billie Holiday, who died in 1959, as Baldwin was writing *Another Country*. In one scene, Ida dances with Vivaldo to a record by Holiday; she later listens to "Billie's Blues"; and one of her listeners remarks (as if Baldwin wanted to ensure that readers did not miss the connection) that she "reminds [him] of the young Billie Holiday" (*AC*, 158, 398, 358). The women share similar biographies as well. Both are raised in northern cities (Baltimore and New York); both work as prostitutes from a young age; and both seek to escape this work by pursuing careers as singers, although the economics of prostitution haunt their new careers. Ida explains to Vivaldo that she started singing after Rufus died, primarily to redeem herself in his eyes: "I decided I ought to try to sing, I'd do it for Rufus, and then all the rest wouldn't matter. I would have settled the score. But I thought I needed somebody to help me" (*AC*, 419). The somebody she turns to is Steve Ellis, a "famous" and "powerful" white TV producer, with whom she has an affair (*AC*, 164). Not unlike Holiday's career, which was complicated by her abusive relationship with manager-lover Louis McKay, Ida's singing threatens to become an extension of, rather than an escape from, the work of selling her body—a problem that Richard Wright and Pierre Chenal also address through their representation of Bessie's singing job in the film of *Native Son*.[77] By including this aspect of Ida's story in *Another Country*, Baldwin reveals how difficult it is for a woman to work in the male-dominated musical culture that Holiday entered and that Baldwin dramatizes in "Sonny's Blues." Alienated from her own sexuality and bereft of a supportive community—whether in the form of the church, friends, or fellow musicians—Ida has no listener-accompanists to attentively interpret what she says or sings.

Ida gives her first public performance, and the only one the novel dramatizes, in a bar in Greenwich Village. Her set begins well. She and the instrumentalists soon warm to each other, so that "the musicians played for her as though she were an old friend come home and their pride in her restored their pride in themselves" (AC, 255). Although this moment recalls Sonny's triumphant reunion with his band in "Sonny's Blues," the instrumentalists' "pride" in Ida is a heavy burden to bear; as Baldwin's syntax indicates, their pride in themselves depends on it. After this performance, "the musicians were now both jubilant and watchful, as though Ida had abruptly become their property" (AC, 256). In a draft of this scene, Baldwin uses the term "responsibility" instead of "property"; his revision clarifies the gendered power dynamics here.[78]

For an encore, Ida sings "Precious Lord," which she dedicates to Rufus's memory. Neither the audience nor the band quite know what to do with this decision: "There was a brief spatter of applause, presumably for the dead Rufus; and the drummer bowed his head and did an oddly irreverent riff on the rim of his drum: *klook-a-klook, klook-klook, klook-klook!*" (AC, 255–256). Ida is deeply serious, though. Indeed, Baldwin's description of her face recalls William Gottlieb's famous 1947 photograph of Holiday (see fig. 8), which captures her in the agonizing ecstasy of performance: "Her eyes were closed and the dark head on the long dark neck was thrown back. Something appeared in her face which had not been there before, a kind of passionate, triumphant rage and agony" (AC, 256). This scene is focalized through the perspective of Eric, a white character who has loved Rufus but has just met Ida. Eric thinks that

> Ida did not know how great a performer she would have to become before she could dare expose her audience, as she did now, to her private fears and pain. After all, her brother had meant nothing to them, or had never meant to them what he had meant to her. They did not wish to witness her mourning, especially as they dimly suspected that this mourning contained an accusation of themselves—an accusation which their uneasiness justified. (AC, 256)

When Ida completes her performance, Eric muses, "the applause was odd—not quite unwilling, not quite free; wary, rather, in recognition of a force not quite to be trusted but certainly to be watched" (AC, 256).

The audience's reaction here is not so different from the one Baldwin describes with regard to Rufus's performance. There, too, when confronted with the sax player's solo, "a curious, wary light appeared" in "all of the [listeners'] faces" (*AC*, 8). What is different about Ida's performance is that the spectators' response is the *only* response we see. Instead of Ida's or her bandmates' perspectives, we get Eric's outside view. And Eric does not decode this performance as Rufus decodes the sax player's. Instead, he abstracts Ida's performance and figures it as overstated: "What she lacked in vocal power and, at the moment, in skill, she compensated for by a quality so mysteriously and implacably egocentric that no one has ever been able to name it. This quality involves a sense of the self so profound and so powerful that it does not so much leap barriers as reduce them to atoms. . . . It transforms and lays waste and gives life, and kills" (*AC*, 253–254). Eric models failed reading in this moment.

Ida's band does not read or foster her understatement either, and it is this that dramatically separates Ida's experience from Holiday's: regardless of audience, Holiday typically had a supportive community on the bandstand itself. Though it may seem paradoxical, the collaborative support of male musicians enabled Holiday to express an understated yet powerful form of sexual autonomy—or, at least, to create personae that did so. That Ida lacks this community of sympathetic interpreter-accompanists becomes clearer as the novel unfolds. Her relationships with white men (Steve Ellis and Vivaldo) soon make her the object of interracial male competition. This competition, moreover, affects her singing. When Vivaldo accompanies her to an out-of-town gig, he feels that "the atmosphere was deadly; the musicians had not wanted him along . . . and Ida had sung only two songs, which did not seem much after such a long trip, and she had not sung them well. He felt that this had something to do with the attitude of the musicians, who seemed to want to punish her, and with the uneasy defiance with which she forced herself to face their judgment" (*AC*, 319–320).

The musicians' judgment becomes painfully evident in a later scene that Ida retroactively narrates to Vivaldo, as she finally confesses her affair with Ellis to him. As Ida tells it, Ellis commands her to go up and sing with the band one night, though she has not been scheduled to do so. After her performance, the bass player accuses her of being a "black white man's whore" and banishes her from their musical community:

> "When it was over, and the people were clapping, the bass player
> whispered to me, he said, 'You black white man's whore, don't you

never let me catch you on Seventh Avenue, you hear? I'll tear your little black pussy *up.*' And the other musicians could hear him, and they were grinning. 'I'm going to do it twice, once for every black man you castrate every time you walk, and once for your poor brother, because I loved that stud. And he going to thank me for it, too, you can bet on that, black girl.' And he slapped me on the ass, hard, everybody could see it." (*AC*, 425)

The bass player accuses Ida of aiding in white supremacist culture's "castration" of black men by sleeping with Ellis, and his response is to threaten her with rape. His logic anticipates Eldridge Cleaver's description, in *Soul on Ice* (1968), of turning to sexual violence in an effort to restore his wounded masculinity. Cleaver explains that he raped white women to avenge white men's violations of black women. Rather than seek to redeem black women, however, Cleaver made them collateral damage in his project to redeem black men: he assaulted black women to "practice" assaulting white women.[79] Through Ida's scene of subjection, Baldwin shows how black women suffer when struggles for racial justice are coded "in terms of redeeming black masculinity"—a masculinity which, as bell hooks writes, is narrowly defined through (hetero)sexuality.[80] Here, the jazz community in *Another Country* proves to be as homosocial a sphere as it is in "Sonny's Blues," but exclusively, violently so.

Due to Ida's raced and gendered displacement, the lyrics to "Backwater Blues" ultimately resonate more with her experience than they do with Rufus's. Ida's humiliation on the bandstand is especially painful for how it exiles her from even the memory of her closest kin. The bass player invokes Rufus as justification for and approving witness to the sexual violence with which he threatens her. As he banishes her from Seventh Avenue (here a metonym for Harlem's jazz community), he claims his love for Rufus as the reason for doing so. In a single gesture, then, the man discursively alienates Ida from a community of male musicians and affirms his affective bonds with the men, including Rufus, on whose behalf he threatens her. Thus, Ida, like the singers in "Sonny's Blues," serves to catalyze communion between men. As I have noted, she performs this function again when she helps Vivaldo understand Rufus's pain; in the later scene, she fulfills the abortive promise of the scene in which the two men have listened to "Backwater Blues."

As the only major character in *Another Country* with whose point of view the narrative never aligns itself, Ida is primarily a vehicle for others' enlightenment. This is not to say that she lacks agency—she chooses to have the affair with Steve Ellis—but that Baldwin obscures that agency by veiling the intellectual and emotional processes that inform Ida's choices.[81] It is possible that Baldwin's narrative strategy reflects Ida's sense of her own powerlessness, her clearest expression of which ironically takes the form of a statement about her inability to communicate it. In a key scene, Ida rides in a cab through Central Park with Cass, a white friend of Rufus's. Ida tells her,

> "*You* don't know, and there's no way in the world for you to find out, what it's like to be a black girl in this world, and the way white men, and black men, too, baby, treat you. You've never decided that the whole world was just one big whorehouse and so the only way for you to make it was to decide to be the biggest, coolest, hardest whore around, and make the world pay you back that way. . . . You don't know that behind all them damn dainty trees and shit, people are screwing and sucking and fixing and dying. Dying, baby, right now while we move through this darkness in this man's taxicab. And you don't know it, even when you're told; you don't know it, even when you see it." (*AC*, 347–348)

Here Ida appears to serve her role as the character who must enlighten white characters about the nature of black suffering in America. As David Leeming writes, Ida, like Baldwin, must "carr[y] the message of Rufus's tragedy to the 'white liberal' world."[82] More specifically, Ida must enlighten white characters about the intersection of race, class, gender, and sexuality by explaining "what it's like to be a black girl in this world." However, Ida begins and ends this heated disclosure by underscoring its ineffectuality: "You don't know, and there's no way in the world for you to find out. . . . You don't know it, even when you're told; you don't know it, even when you see it." While I have framed Ida's dilemma in musical terms, suggesting that she is a soloist without collaborators to read and foster her understatement, we can extend that concept to her exchange with Cass if we see that Ida's "confession," however explicit and passionate its tenor, would only serve its purpose if Cass could read it as an understatement.

What would it take for Cass to do this? Perhaps, as Baldwin writes of black moviegoers' responses to Sidney Poitier, it would require that Cass "supply the sub-text—the unspoken [meaning]" of Ida's statements with information "out of [her] own [life]."[83] That subtext would be Cass's own suffering but also her complicity in compounding Ida's, if only through inattention. Further, Cass would have to decipher Ida's expression while also apprehending her limited capacity to do so. This is what Peter Szendy implies when he describes the ethics of listening, or the "*responsibility of listening,*" as self-reflexive: one must "*listen to oneself listening.*"[84] No one in the novel reads Ida this way, because they cannot read themselves.

Baldwin ends *Another Country* without explaining what becomes of Ida's art. Whereas the detail for Vivaldo's novel comes into his mind with mysterious ease, all that is clear about Ida's singing career is that recovering and advancing it will require a great deal of social and artistic labor. Baldwin opens a window of possibility, however, when he has Ida listen to Mahalia Jackson's album *In the Upper Room* in a final scene. Baldwin's citation of this album extends the matrilineage of female vocalists the novel has charted: from Smith to her admirers and self-appointed apprentices, Holiday and then Jackson. Indeed, we might recall from chapter 2 that this is the album on which Ellison claims that Jackson "reminds us most poignantly of Bessie Smith."[85] Further, this is the only moment in the novel when a character plays an album by one of Baldwin's still-living contemporaries. If Smith and Holiday both represent a history of black artists' tragically early deaths, Baldwin may have Ida listen to Jackson to indicate Ida's potential to reclaim her art and survive.[86] This final turn toward sacred music also hints that Ida may do so by returning to the church, her ties to which she signals when she sings "Precious Lord"—even though Smith and Holiday both represent the possibility of achieving expressive autonomy beyond it.

These possibilities are simply conjectural, however, because, unlike the scene in which Rufus and Vivaldo listen to Smith's music, Baldwin does not transcribe the lyrics to Jackson's songs or relate Ida's response to them. Instead, he withholds Ida's experience of listening from Vivaldo and from the reader:

> [Vivaldo] rose, and went to the bathroom and washed his face, and then sat down at his work table. She put on a record by Mahalia Jackson, *In the Upper Room*, and sat at the window, her hands in her lap, looking out over the sparkling streets. Much, much later, while he was still working and she slept, she turned in her sleep, and she called his name. He paused, waiting, staring at her, but she did not move again, or speak again. (*AC*, 431)

Music here becomes a way of forging a private sanctuary akin to Jackson's heavenly "upper room."[87] Vivaldo is as removed from Ida's listening to Jackson as he was from Rufus's listening to Smith, but instead of lamenting the distance this time, the novel accepts it like a truce.

FIGURE 6. James Baldwin and Nina Simone, c. 1960s. Schomburg Center for Research in Black Culture, New York Public Library, Astor, Lenox and Tilden Foundations.

Baldwin marks the lovers' psychic separation as Ida calls out to Vivaldo in her sleep from a space beyond answering—but it's still Vivaldo's name she is calling; it could be worse. Ida's expressive power is ultimately a product not of understatement but of precisely such unanswered calls and silences ("she did not . . . speak again"). In this regard, her interiority constitutes the novel's most haunting other country. Yet Ida's opacity also creates an opportunity to revise and expand Baldwin's representation of black female vocal performance, as Gayl Jones does in *Corregidora* (1975), the subject of the next chapter. Like *Another Country*, Jones's novel also begins with a fall—this time that of a female singer, who will live to tell her own tale.

"No Way for You to Find Out": "Of the Sorrow Songs"

Another Country sold over a million copies, making it, along with *The Fire Next Time*, one of Baldwin's two best-selling books. According to Scott Saul, these works established Baldwin as "*the* American black intellectual celebrity."[88] In Larry Neal's grim assessment, "the civil rights movement . . . was the new 'in' for the white liberals. James Baldwin was also 'in,' pleading for a new morality to people who saw him as another form of entertainment."[89] In this context, Ida's speech to Cass—"There's no way in the world for you to find out . . . You don't know it, even when you're told"—seems to reflect Baldwin's own anxiety about addressing a white liberal readership. Indeed, Baldwin seems to confirm Neal's claim and to echo Ida's in his final interview with Quincy Troupe. Here, he offers the rather dire verdict that "whites want black writers to mostly deliver something as if it were an official version of the black experience. But the vocabulary won't hold it, simply. No true account . . . of black life can be held, can be contained, in the American vocabulary. As it is, the only way that you can deal with it is by doing great violence to the assumptions on which the vocabulary is based. But they won't let you do that."[90] Baldwin's understanding of a white publishing industry and readership that "won't let you" tell the truth about black life resonates with Ida's sense of expressive impossibility and with his depiction of Ida's audience, which does not wish to accept the "accusation of themselves" signified through her performance of "Precious Lord." In these moments, Baldwin suggests that the very sign of blackness elicits "hearing"—a mode of reading through a preestablished "system of signifying references"—instead of listening.[91] Baldwin's role as a black writer would only get harder in the aftermath of Civil Rights and Black Power, insofar as the dominant culture could seem to have decided on willful inattention or presumptive hearing in place of embattled listening.

As with Ida, however, Baldwin's problem of address was not solely interracial. His reception was also marked by intraracial tensions, as his relationship with a younger generation of black (male) writers grew increasingly complex. According to James Smethurst, Black Arts activists continued to regard Baldwin with "tremendous respect."[92] David Leeming, however, states that as Baldwin "grew . . . more radical in his views," he was also increasingly "criticized as irrelevant by the very young men to whom he so much wanted to give support."[93] He was rejected by the younger generation somewhat as he himself had rejected Richard Wright, but on rather different grounds. As Douglas Field has shown, Baldwin's sexuality rendered him a pariah to black nationalist groups that "aligned liberation with an aggressive and heterosexual masculinity."[94] Younger black activists dubbed him "Martin Luther Queen," and King's own supporters looked askance at him; Baldwin was conspicuously not invited to speak at the March on Washington.[95] Having "once defined the cutting edge," Baldwin himself "was now a favorite target for the *new* cutting edge," including Ishmael Reed and Eldridge Cleaver.[96] According to Henry Louis Gates Jr., "a new generation . . . was determined to define itself as everything Baldwin was not," so that "by the late sixties, Baldwin-bashing was almost a rite of initiation."[97] Cleaver delivered the most well-known, but by no means the only, assault on Baldwin and his work when he decried the fact that Rufus and Eric have sex in *Another Country*; the act of sleeping with a white man made Rufus, in Cleaver's view, "the epitome of a black eunuch who has completely submitted to a white man."[98] The accusation did not destroy Baldwin or his career, but it did signal one of many displacements that Baldwin would suffer as a gay black American writer.

Baldwin's later figuration of understatement as a fundamental condition of black expression could be read as an exasperated response to such alienation. Yet what is most important is that *in spite of* such displacement, Baldwin would use his music writings to ardently align himself with an imagined black community. He would continue to invoke Smith and Holiday as well as younger artists like Nina Simone and Aretha Franklin.[99] Through these invocations, as noted in the introduction, Baldwin implicitly participated in a tradition of black gay men's celebrations of (sacred and secular) female singers. At the same time, passionate engagement with black music was what Baldwin continued to hold in common with the writers who shunned him—as well as with those who, like Nikki Giovanni, regarded him with unabated admiration.[100] Seventeen years after *Another Country*, Baldwin published his most heated and potentially confounding essay on black music, "Of the Sorrow Songs: The Cross of Redemption." This piece shows Baldwin working in the tradition of younger writers who, as Larry Neal described them, were not so much protesting white oppression as they were "turn[ing] [their] attention inward to the internal problems of the group" and "recognizing the beauty and love within Black America itself."[101] (In this sense, they were answering Wright's 1937 injunction to prioritize black readers over white approval.)[102] Here Baldwin rejects his role as "the new 'in' for the white liberals," while also navigating—or, better, embracing—the readerly obstinacy he lamented to Troupe. Rather than aim to enlighten readers as to the messages music encodes, Baldwin acts as co-creator of black musical meaning, performing creative interpretations akin to Rufus's that model a self-reflexive *"responsibility of listening."*

Commissioned by Baldwin's future biographer James Campbell for the *Edinburgh Review*, "Of the Sorrow Songs" concerns the publication of James Lincoln Collier's *The Making of Jazz* (1979). Baldwin critiques Collier, a white jazz critic, for writing a purportedly "'comprehensive' history" of the music without comprehending the life circumstances or history of the people who create it. The specific provocation for the essay seems to be Collier's claim that Louis Armstrong and Charlie Parker were the only "two authentic geniuses in jazz" and that Parker "was a sociopath . . . who managed . . . to destroy his career—and finally himself" (*SS*, 119). Baldwin contends that it is absurd to limit the number of jazz's "authentic geniuses" to two and unjust to call Parker a self-destructive "sociopath." In a sense, one might say that Baldwin, confronted with his own real-life Vivaldo in the person of the well-meaning yet myopic Collier, assumes a role akin to Ida's. Like Ida, who strives to correct assumptions about the pathology of the black male jazz musician—as she tells Vivaldo, Rufus "shouldn't have ended up the way he did" (*AC*, 415)—Baldwin argues that American hostility toward the jazz artist is what causes his downfall.

However, Baldwin also revises Ida's role, because the function of his essay is less to enlighten the white jazz critic by decoding the music than it is to fashion black music as intrinsically understated. The metaphorical turns, structural gaps, and elisions that pervade this putative exegetical account of black music figure the music as resistant to decoding, or as necessarily understated. As in *Another Country*, then, Baldwin makes understatement less a laconic or dispassionate stylistic mode to be identified than a condition one interpretively creates. In so doing, he confronts the problem with U.S. racial discourse more generally: understate the conditions of black life in America, and you're at risk of being unheard or misunderstood; state the truth, and you're accused of exaggeration, paranoia, bitterness. Baldwin addresses the possibility that one's candid confession might be distorted as overstated—a problem faced by black writers since the slave narrative—by proposing that it may just as well be read as *understated*. He suggests that one finds understatement where one looks or listens for it, and he models this hermeneutic approach—an approach which, as I have said, we might call interpretive accompaniment, and which Baldwin would call the act of bearing witness to another.

"Of the Sorrow Songs" energetically constellates Baldwin's characteristic claims about black music. Baldwin hails the music as muted yet necessary equipment for living: "this music called 'jazz' came into existence as an exceedingly laconic description of black circumstances, and as a way, by describing these circumstances, of overcoming them" (*SS*,

121). He insists that black music encodes true and disastrous experience: "Music comes out of life. . . . This music begins on the auction block" (SS, 121, 124). And he argues that it remains unheard: "There is a very great deal in the world which Europe does not, or cannot, see: in the very same way that the European musical scale cannot transcribe—cannot write down, does not understand—the notes, or the price, of this music" (SS, 120). Unsurprisingly, Baldwin also figures Smith's and Holiday's songs as understated, authoritative accounts of black life in America.

What is most compelling about the last move, however, is that even as Baldwin appears to offer his most explicit decoding of Smith's "Backwater Blues," his interpretation is another ruse; it is not really any clearer than his remarks about Smith's "disaster" in his interview with Terkel eighteen years earlier. He writes, "By the time of 'Farewell to Storyville,' and long before that time, the demolition of black quarters . . . was an irreducible truth of black life. This is what Bessie Smith is telling us, in 'Back Water Blues.' This song has as much to do with a flood as 'Didn't It Rain' has to do with Noah, or as 'If I Had My Way' has to do with Samson and Delilah, and poor Samson's excess of hair" (SS, 121).[103] In a sweeping gesture, Baldwin purports to decode Smith's blues, a gospel song recorded by Jackson, and a blues recorded by Blind Willie Johnson, in order to insist that these singers are not telling biblical stories but rather asserting the fact of black Americans' continued displacement and dispossession. Yet this explication is slippery: Baldwin reveals "what Bessie Smith is telling us" by invoking "the demolition of black quarters" as well as by alluding to what other songs are *not* telling us. He turns to metaphor, negative simile, allusions that depend on insider knowledge when he states that "Backwater Blues" "has as much to do with a flood as 'Didn't It Rain' has to do with Noah." It thus makes sense for Baldwin to claim that black music still "has not been 'decoded,'" as he himself has not decoded it. Such evasions may be read as a flaw of this essay, but they are also its point: "If you think I am leaping, you are entirely right" (SS, 121).

"Of the Sorrow Songs" extravagantly enacts Baldwin's decision not to *explicate* black musical understatement but instead to help *make* black music understated, to discursively frame it as a necessarily understated response to "one of the most obscene adventures in the history of mankind" (SS, 122). By assuming the role of interpretive accompanist to this music (a role akin to that of James P. Johnson and Rufus), Baldwin bears witness *to* Smith, Holiday, and other artists, instead of bearing witness on their behalf. His extraordinary roll call dramatizes this practice, while also implicitly scorning Collier's claim that Armstrong and Parker are the only names worth knowing: "How did King Oliver, Ma Rainey, Bessie, Armstrong, . . . Bird, Dolphy, Powell, Pettiford, Coltrane, Jelly Roll Morton, the Duke, . . . Miss Nina Simone, Mme Mary Lou Williams, Carmen McRae, the Count, Ray, Miles, Max—forgive me, children, for all the names I cannot call. How did they, and how *do* they . . . make of [their] captivity a song?" (*SS*, 123). Syntactically, the list of names short-circuits the statement that begins as a question, which makes the line an anacoluthon, a sentence that begins in one form and ends in another. This anacoluthon performs in miniature the work of the essay as a whole: it signals a turn whereby, rather than offer an explanation of the music that would challenge Collier's apparent dismissal of it, Baldwin turns his rhetorical energy toward honoring the musicians themselves—here, in a long list of names. Put differently, Baldwin's elusive, figurative language in this essay is not designed to win arguments against an opponent but instead to creatively accompany the musicians themselves and to align Baldwin with imagined readers who already cherish them. So although Baldwin does restart his question after the roll call derails it, the point of this passage is much less to answer the question—"how did they, and how *do* they . . . make of [their] captivity a song?"—than it is to name these names.

Baldwin's move from informant to witness-accompanist means that even his invocation of his favorite Smith and Holiday songs works differently here. In the following passage, Baldwin figures African American women as the authoritative spokeswomen for a black American experience Collier has missed:

> Collier has had to "hang" in many places—he has "been there," as someone predating jazz might put it: but he has not, as one of my more relentless sisters might put it, "been there and back."
>
> My more relentless sister is merely, in actuality, paraphrasing, or bearing witness to, Bessie Smith: "picked up my bag, baby, and I tried it again." And so is Billie Holiday, proclaiming—not complaining—that "my man wouldn't [give] me no breakfast / wouldn't give me no dinner / squawked about my supper / and threw me outdoors / had the nerve to lay / a matchbox on my clothes."
>
> "I didn't," Billie tells us, "have so many. But I had a long, long ways to go." (*SS*, 120)

Baldwin suggests that these women express a racialized understanding of what it means to have "been there and back," an experience of life that Collier fails to grasp. But he does not only assemble these women as witnesses against Collier. He also stages an internal community by having them bear witness to each other: "My more relentless sister is merely . . . bearing witness to Bessie Smith. . . . And so is Billie Holiday." Here, the interpretation of black music becomes an unapologetically creative process in which Baldwin is an intimate collaborator or orchestrator, bringing black musicians and everyday people into a dialogue with one another.

This is not to say that Baldwin closes the circle or decides to preach to the choir. He works to bridge the "interpretive divide" between black nationalists and white liberals, as Vaughn Rasberry writes, by declaring both "the impossibility and the inevitability of integration" throughout his career.[104] But his writings on music engage this tension in different ways at different times, by privileging hearing and then listening, in Nancy's terms. While Baldwin initially constructs a stable meaning that only black people might hear (despite integration), he later performs a dynamic, mutually constitutive relationship between black musicians and listeners (which may become all the more imperative because of integration). Rather than claim that black women singers speak the truth—"'Backwater [Blues]' is a real flood"—Baldwin ultimately implies that this truth is created and renewed through repeated acts of listening "at the edge of meaning": *Do you love me? . . .* This, anyway, was the question Rufus heard."

I have not used the term "unspeakable" in this discussion because, although Baldwin clearly prized the term (along with "unutterable"), it is not a useful concept for the literary analysis I undertake here. In my view, Baldwin's writing on black music is important not because Baldwin *reveals* the "unspeakable" or "unutterable" aspect of the music but because he *creates* it. He does so in order to prompt listening. The notion that black music indexes the "unspeakable" or that which "words can't begin to tell you"[105] should signal a beginning, "an intensification and a concern," not an answer or an end point to discussions of black music. We might revisit one of Baldwin's best-known statements here: "It is only in his music, which Americans are able to admire because a protective sentimentality limits their understanding of it, that the Negro in America has been able to tell his story."[106] How is it that Baldwin—a writer as committed to "telling the story" of black life in America as any twentieth-century artist—might be moved to claim that "it is only in his *music* . . . that the Negro in America has been able to tell his story"? I hope to have elucidated such rhetorical gestures by showing that music holds a privileged place in Baldwin's attempts to align himself with an imagined black community in the mid-twentieth century. To rewrite Baldwin's line, it is only—or, rather, especially—in his writings on black music that Baldwin is able to corroborate the black artists he loves, instead of translating their stories to others.

The collective function of these writings is not to frame music as a superior medium that expresses what language cannot but to use literary language to shape how music might be heard. Thus, in response to the apparently impossible problem that "you don't know it, even when you're told," Baldwin performs an answer akin to his interpretation of Smith's blues: "All right, it's a mess, and you can't do anything about it . . . so, well, you have to do something about it, . . . but all right, OK, as Bessie said, 'Picked up my bag, baby, and I tried it again.'" Baldwin's career represents a series of such "tryings again" as he continues to seek, as he writes in "Sonny's Blues," "new ways to make us listen."[107] Indeed, his writerly project may be best understood through a remarkable moment of musical interpretation in that story. The narrator listens to his brother play and muses, "A piano is just a piano. It's made out of so much wood and wires and little hammers and big ones, and ivory. While there's only so much you can do with it, the only way to find this out is to try; to try and make it do everything."[108]

4 / Haunting: Gayl Jones's *Corregidora* and Billie Holiday's "Strange Fruit"

By claiming in the previous chapter that James Baldwin's writings not only transmit but also create musical meaning, I have proposed a reciprocal relationship between black music and literature. In this view, black music is not a stable authenticating source of inspiration for black writers; instead, it is a force that writers such as Baldwin use their own literature to re-create. Indeed, this may be precisely what it means to say that writers are inspired by music: that they are moved or instigated to use their literary art to shape how music is heard. I want to turn now to Gayl Jones's 1975 tour de force *Corregidora* to elaborate the implications of this view. Jones calls *Corregidora* a "blues novel," and the designation works on several grounds. Not only is Jones's narrator, Ursa, a blues singer, but blueslike repetition, ambiguity (such as Ralph Ellison hears in Jimmy Rushing's blues), and themes of love and trouble are key components of this text.[1] Blues-oriented interpretations of the novel focus on these elements, which are stable structural and thematic elements of the blues genre. Critics suggest that the blues is a healing, affirmative expressive medium for Ursa and, indeed, that the blues are an enabling force for Jones as a writer. Jones herself has fostered these ideas about her work, as I explain. What would it mean, however, to reverse the formulation and ask not what the music "does for" *Corregidora* but what the text does with or for the music? Here, rather than read Jones's "blues novel" through predetermined and abstracted ideas about the blues, I reverse and specify the methodology by using the novel to reexamine Billie Holiday's changing performances of her signature song, "Strange

Fruit" (1939–1959). In this reading, black literature is not authenticated by a stable image of black music but instead serves to make music newly, productively, strange.

One reason to pair Jones with Holiday in particular is that Jones cites the singer in her novel. As Baldwin does with Ida in *Another Country*, Jones has characters compare her narrator, Ursa, with Holiday. Critics have followed that lead. Toni Morrison, for instance, describes Ursa as "a kind of combination Billie Holiday and Fannie Lou Hamer."[2] But here I compare Jones, rather than her narrator, with Holiday, and I do so on the basis of the discourse that surrounds both artists: both Jones's novel and Holiday's music are consistently called "haunting." I ask what listeners and readers might be describing when they use this term, I theorize haunting as a formal strategy that both Jones and Holiday deploy, and I use Jones's "haunting" narrative performance to reread Holiday's "haunting" vocal art. In my view, *Corregidora* invites us to untether Holiday's music from the mythos of her painful life and thus reveals new facets of Holiday's power and mysteries about her work. What I am saying, more broadly, is this: that the point of questioning idealized conceptions of black music and its relation to African American literature is to invite new readings of the literature that in turn *enhance* our apprehension of black music's power.

Every arena of national culture has mythologies that are repeated so often as to become clichés. Fans of black popular music, for instance, will tell you that you could hear Billie Holiday's tragic life through the audible wear in her voice. They will say that you could hear Miles Davis's sullen personality in his playing; that gospel-turned-pop artists like Sam Cooke and Aretha Franklin "took the church with them"; that Luther Vandross sang better at a heavier weight; and that Bobby Brown destroyed Whitney Houston. (Such narratives are common enough in the realm of literature, too: Richard Wright's work suffered when he left the States, James Baldwin's did the same when he overextended himself as an activist.) In addition to revealing certain truths, these stories fulfill important functions—for instance, they help create community and serve as cautionary tales. Yet *Corregidora* asks what additional stories such commonplaces about Holiday obscure. Jones raises this question in the twilight of Black Arts but on the brink of a lasting Holiday revival. She publishes *Corregidora* just three years after the 1972 Holiday biopic (and Diana Ross vehicle) *Lady Sings the Blues* appears and just as Holiday's recordings are reissued to coincide with that film. As Farah Jasmine Griffin writes, *Lady Sings the Blues* "shot Diana Ross into superstardom,

sparked interest in Holiday and raised the price of the Holiday com-
modity. It also spawned two decades' worth of articles, essays and books
claiming to reveal the 'real Holiday.'"[3] With this Holiday revival in mind,
we can see that *Corregidora* not only stages a daughter's process of coming to know her mother's past but also asks how we might "know" the
previous generation of black female artists. By reminding us how much
remains *un*known about Holiday, Jones invites us to be haunted by Holiday again and to reanimate our limited archive of cultural knowledge by
telling new stories about her vocal art.

In an effort to explain what made Holiday such a "memorable" vocalist,
singer Finis Henderson told novelist Leon Forrest that, although Holiday
"didn't have a powerful voice" and "couldn't blow you off the stage," she
had "a haunting voice."[4] Perhaps no other term is so consistently applied
to Holiday's vocal timbre, style, and signature song—what Angela Davis
calls Holiday's "haunting antilynching appeal."[5] *Corregidora*, too, is per-
sistently described as a novel that not only thematizes black women's
transgenerational haunting by slavery but is itself a haunting work[6]—so
much so that Bruce Simon asks, "Why have most readers of *Corregidora*
compulsively returned, as it were, to images of haunting and possession?"[7] Unlike Simon, I answer this question not through a psychoanalytic reading of traumatic repetition but through a study of expressive
practice, of what Jones (like Holiday) *does* to create haunting effects. Put
differently, I am less interested in the psycho-subjective experience of
being haunted than I am in theorizing the strategies listeners and readers
are responding to when they call Jones's and Holiday's work haunting.
To explore this matter, I stage commentators (myself included) as a chorus of listeners, all of us providing our own imperfect accounts, or renditions, of what we "hear" in *Corregidora* and "Strange Fruit," and I read
these responses as an effect of Jones's and Holiday's formalistic choices.
I suggest that "Strange Fruit" is considered the most haunting song in
Holiday's repertoire not only because of the racial and sexual terrorism
it describes but also and especially because of how Holiday sings it. Likewise, Jones's novel about transgenerational traumas of enslavement and
sexual terror is haunting because of how Jones shapes this material.

My understanding of Holiday's and Jones's haunting strategies is
informed by Avery Gordon's seminal work on social haunting. According to Gordon, haunting is a "sociopolitical-psychological state" "in
which a repressed or unresolved social violence is making itself known";
it "describe[s] those singular yet repetitive instances" in which "the over-
and-done-with comes alive."[8] Since, as I've said, I treat haunting as a

practice instead of a state, I show how Jones and Holiday *make* "the over-and-done-with" come alive. They do so by repeating familiar texts, tropes, or patterns with an unsettling difference, in a process akin to what playwright Suzan-Lori Parks calls "incremental refrain," or "Rep & Rev" (repetition and revision).[9] Clearly, the term "unsettling" is subjective, and the practice of "rep and rev" might unsettle on many different grounds. We might think of a quiet vocal performance that suddenly turns to a scream, or even a stunning interpolation of a familiar song. Here I analyze haunting practice by identifying some of the many forms that repetition with a disturbing difference can take. For instance, I suggest that we are reading a haunting practice when Jones perverts key words as her novel progresses and that we are hearing such practice when Holiday "pounce[s] on" the lyrics to "Strange Fruit," a song she sang for twenty years, "like they had never been hit before."[10] These unpredictable, unaccountable, or "out of character" moments disrupt the illusion of intimate knowledge that Jones's and Holiday's work often generates. These artists generate intimacy by performing painful material, and they disrupt it by repeating that material with a significant difference. This is why I describe their haunting work as a combination of subject matter and technique.

The illusion of intimacy seems to be central to the practice of haunting when we consider that the other major axis of Holiday commentary, in addition to the language of haunting, is the language of intimate connection.[11] As I noted in the previous chapter, Holiday was a "microphone singer." This new technology facilitated Holiday's relatively "small" sound, allowing her to sing in a manner previously reserved for intimate (literally close) company and still be heard by everyone in a club or a theater. This is one reason why people commonly say that Holiday could make "each member of her audience feel as though she were singing directly to them."[12] But the discourse of intimacy takes another form as well: when listeners compare Holiday's early recordings from the 1930s with her later recordings of the 1950s, they figure Holiday's *voice itself* as expressing something "directly to them." Describing Holiday's late-career voice, jazz critic Whitney Balliett writes that it "took on a subtly dismaying hue. . . . Her undertones and low notes began to sound almost burnt; they took on an acrid quality."[13] Critics narrativize this change through reference to Holiday's biography, meaning her much-publicized "personal life." So the question becomes, how is it possible for Holiday's listeners to represent her as both radically "available" to them and also as haunting them? We can reconcile these discursive strains if we see that Holiday's vocal practices haunt precisely by *thwarting* listeners' assumptions of intimate knowledge. Accordingly, Forrest compares Holiday's "haunting" voice with a "small incandescent lyrical light," suggesting that Holiday's voice haunts by granting listeners an unexpectedly partial confession, a revelation only as bright as "a small . . . lyrical light" in the dark.[14] Indeed, as I will suggest, even the infamous change in Holiday's voice does not confess what it seems to. Rather than hear Holiday's timbre as a window that can't help but express her tragic life, I hear Holiday herself as a "timbral virtuoso" who continues to *use* her different vocal colors and textures.[15] By tracing this process through Holiday's changing renditions of "Strange Fruit," I exploit a commonplace that is worth holding on to—and, indeed, concretizing: that Holiday "never sang a song the same way twice."

It is on the basis of this concept that Jones links her creative process with Holiday's in an interview with poet Michael S. Harper:

> I always like everything to be different . . . , to work itself out differently. If I've done something, I don't like to do it again. Why do something again when you've already done it? Why say something the same way again? Why sing something the same way twice? I'm thinking about Billie Holiday here, of course. That's the tradition. I like to change a tune.[16]

While Jones is referring to her practice of approaching each of her literary works differently, we can see her "changing the tune" within *Corregidora* itself. She performs "rep and rev" throughout the novel, making "over-and-done-with" words, scenes, and even generic conventions "come alive," in Gordon's terms. As I have said, this practice disrupts the illusion of intimacy Jones's work otherwise generates. It signals an interior complexity that the narrative (or, indeed, singing) voice will not transmit.[17] Because Jones links epistemological claims about the singer's private life with sexual claims to her body, what is at stake here is not only an insistence on intentioned, imaginative female artistry that dispels the myth of black women's transparent expression but also a claim to sexual autonomy that counters the black female singer's subjection to the sexual male gaze. Haunting is thus in part a defensive strategy through which both Holiday and Jones deny the myth of the transparent black female voice (written and sung) and related claims to the black female body. In this sense, both artists' insistence on not "saying" or "singing" something the same way twice is an aggressive refusal.

But haunting is also a productive instigation: as these artists disrupt the illusion of total access to the stories they tell and signal their own inaccessible complexity, they raise questions about the subjects of their work (Ursa's story, lynching) and also about the reified mythologies that surround their own careers. Because these questions can usually only be answered imaginatively, haunting expression encourages people to tell what Gordon calls "ghost stories," stories that fill otherwise irreparable gaps in our cultural memory or archive of collective knowledge.[18] When Gordon writes that haunting provokes a sense of "something-to-be-done," or *something you have to try for yourself,* this "something" is precisely the listener's or reader's imaginative attempt to supplement the archive of collective knowledge whose gaps haunting highlights.[19] Here I demonstrate this process by showing how *Corregidora* instigates new stories about Holiday's life and work. Thematically and formally, Jones works to disentangle the black female voice from the publicly "known" self. Her novel compels us to consider that even Holiday's own claim that "she sang what she felt" was less an answer than a candid evasion. What might this possibly explain? Why might listeners think they know what she *felt* or even whether they are to understand this "feeling" in terms of biographical facts or in terms of the emotion generated through the act of singing itself? In reopening such questions about Holiday's life and work, *Corregidora* expands the cultural archive of what can be said about Holiday and her music.

Unfamiliar Rituals I: *Corregidora*

Jones was born in Lexington, Kentucky, in 1949, and has to date published five works of fiction, three collections of poetry, a play, and a scholarly study of African American literature called *Liberating Voices,* written in 1982 but published in 1991.[20] *Corregidora* was her first novel. Like Holiday, who was born a generation before her, Jones has been described as both, in Trudier Harris's words, an "anomaly" and a "phenomenon."[21] According to Harris, Jones is an anomalous figure in African American literary culture in terms of her themes (madness, sex, same-sex desire, etc.), educational pedigree (her PhD from Brown University), and public persona ("Her legendary shyness has perhaps attained a level comparable to her outlandish writings, as some would label them").[22]

Toni Morrison stresses the "phenomenal" aspect of Jones's anomalous status when she describes reading a draft of *Corregidora,* for which she was to become Jones's editor. Jones had written the novel while studying creative writing at Brown with Michael S. Harper in her early twenties (the same age as Holiday when she first sang "Strange Fruit"). In an article published in *Mademoiselle* magazine the same year *Corregidora* appeared, Morrison describes the book and its author as veritable wonders:

> What was uppermost in my mind while I read her manuscript was that no novel about any black woman could ever be the same after this. . . . So deeply impressed was I that I hadn't time to be offended by the fact that she was twenty-four and had no "right" to know so much so well. . . . Even now, almost two years later, I shake my head when I think of her, and the same smile of disbelief I could not hide when I met her, I feel on my mouth still as I write these lines. . . . Ursa Corregidora is not possible. Neither is Gayl Jones. But they exist.[23]

While Morrison's enthusiasm is important (and was designed to be infectious), it is also important to note that Jones represents *Corregidora* in the completely opposite way. As Jones discusses the novel in interviews, she shares very little information about her identity but much more about her process of writing *Corregidora*—a process in which Morrison herself figured instrumentally.[24] If Jones does not represent her novel as quite the lightning bolt that Morrison describes, she does remystify *Corregidora* by representing it as a work that, despite being published, is *still* in process, still in flux. Her interviews thus distance her work from her identity and destabilize the identity of the work itself. This procedure describes *Corregidora* as well, as a novel whose terms keep modulating so that the narrator herself seems changeable and still in process. In this way, the novel offers a template for reading Holiday's ever-changing performances of "Strange Fruit" without recourse to her biography—or of seeing these changing performances as Holiday's mode of reauthoring herself, of finding new ways of being and becoming, as the previous chapter suggests.

While Harris is right that Jones eventually acquired a reputation for "legendary shyness," she was very candid about her writing process in the decade following *Corregidora*'s publication. In fact, no other artist in this study seems to have been asked as much or to have shared as much about the creative process. (Wright, Ellison, and Baldwin often discussed the aims and themes of their work but did not discuss the material processes of composition to the extent that Jones did.) This interest in literary craft, and Jones's willingness to speak about it, are partly attributable to a contemporary development: university creative writing programs, one of which Jones attended. Still, Jones's use of this discourse is important. First, she shares information about her writing process *in lieu of*

FIGURE 7. Gayl Jones, c. 1976. Bentley Historical Library, University of Michigan, Faculty and Staff Files, Box 66.

information about her life. Claudia Tate prefaces an interview with Jones by explaining that "she will not discuss her private life."[25] Beyond the fact that she was born in Kentucky, attended Connecticut College and Brown, and was at that time an assistant professor of English at the University of Michigan, "she refuses to divulge additional biographical information, contending that her work must live independently of its creator, that it must sustain its own character and artistic autonomy."[26]

Jones's other comments explain why she maintains that position. She speaks to Tate of critics who "can't separate or don't want to separate . . . the character's neurosis/psychosis from the author's psychological autonomy" and tells Charles Rowell that she began to write about Afro-Brazilian slavery partly in an effort to evade that interpretive mistake. Writing about a time and place obviously distant from her own was "a way of getting away from things that some readers consider 'autobiographical' or 'private obsessions' rather than literary inventions—that they don't accept as imagination from a black woman writing about black female characters in a certain American world."[27] Peter Manso displays this hermeneutic limitation in a 1998 *New York Times Magazine* profile of Jones when he writes that, instead of publicly unleashing the "bottled-up black rage" that a (white) professor believed Jones harbored, Jones "let her anger run through the pages of *Corregidora*."[28] Here, Manso not only gives someone else the power to describe Jones's inner life but also simplistically figures her work as a direct channel of her (allegedly) suppressed emotion; according to his language and syntax, Jones does not write the novel but passively "let[s] her anger run through" it—a natural force like water or fire.

In her interviews, Jones works to resist such interpretations by withdrawing her biography as a frame of reference for her work. Instead, she indicates that her texts should be read on their own terms because they have a logic and life of their own. She stresses what Tate calls the "artistic autonomy" of her work when she depicts *Corregidora* as unstable and subject to change—as a palimpsest script and as a score on which to improvise. She likens her first draft, which she "never did type or show . . . to anyone," to "a prose poem or a song."[29] She explains that the published novel contains traces of this version: italicized exchanges between Ursa and her estranged husband, Mutt, that she calls "ritualized dialogue." And she expresses interest in writing "a sequel to *Corregidora*" that would return to her earlier conception of the text "as a 'song' rather than a 'story.'"[30] Indeed, Jones concludes her discussion of the novel by saying she wants "to go back and study" her first draft of it.[31]

Hence, even as she "explains" her work, she destabilizes the very status of her novel as a finished product. In this sense, she repeats and revises the genre of the interview itself—a genre designed to reveal the person behind a stable body of work—in order to disrupt the illusion of intimacy that this genre otherwise generates. As I've said, this process is central to *Corregidora* as well.

Throughout the novel, Ursa's foremothers tell her of the sexual and psychic violence inflicted on them by Corregidora, the Portuguese slave owner whose name they still bear, in an effort to make her a living witness to slavery. However, when Mutt throws Ursa down a flight of stairs, she loses her unborn child and her capacity to bear other children. She thus needs to find a way to sustain her foremothers' memories without being able to pass them on through another generation—and without becoming enslaved to the past herself. Blues-oriented readings of the novel see Ursa's singing as performing this regenerative function for her, particularly due to Ursa's statement that the blues help her to "explain what [she] can't explain."[32] Jones herself, as I have noted and will discuss at more length, has supported this reading. Psychoanalytic readings that foreground repetition compulsion, on the other hand, if they somewhat schematically read the novel as a case study of traumatic behavior, nonetheless remind us that repetition with a difference—understood in blues terminology as "worrying the line"—might signal paralysis instead of progress.[33] So whereas blues-oriented approaches offer a positive reading of the novel's repetition by linking it with blues repetition, psychoanalytic approaches treat recursion as a problem. We can unite these (musical and psychoanalytic) critical strands by seeing that Jones's "blues repetition with a difference" makes the novel productively unsettling. Ultimately, the novel may unsettle the very expectation that the blues, as a concept, might tell us something coherent about this book—even as Jones instigates new stories about the blues and especially about Holiday's work.

As I have noted, Jones makes the "over-and-done-with" "come alive" by repeating and revising specific words, scenes, and generic conventions. This technique makes the familiar strange and complicates the reader's ostensible "connection" with Ursa, the teller of this tale. We might note, for example, how Jones repeats the word "piece" with an unsettling difference to subtly link the very concept of narrative revelation with sexual submission to an interlocutor or reader. Reflecting on the stories she has told Mutt about the Corregidora women's past, Ursa thinks, "I never really told him. I gave him only pieces." "Your pussy's

a little gold piece, ain't it, Urs?" she remembers or imagines Mutt saying, "My little gold piece" (C, 60).[34] To constellate these moments is
to wonder about one's own position of (sexual) power as the reader of
this text. Jones's use of repetition to defamiliarize or complicate textual
information explains why critics use the dual discourse of intimacy and
alienation to describe their experiences of reading *Corregidora*. Tate tells
Jones, "I had the sense that I was hearing a very private story, and that
Ursa had especially selected me to hear her story," but also "felt as if I
were placed in a puzzle, and there were no directions."[35] In a more recent
article on Jones's use of the "rhetoric of silence," Jennifer Cognard-Black
rightly points out that "the 'I' [of the narrative] is . . . consistently and
insistently held back in the same instant it is extended."[36]

Jones courts and thwarts intimacy especially in moments of "ritualized dialogue" in which Ursa addresses Mutt or an undefined witness.
These passages may alienate readers even while appearing to draw them
into Ursa's private life. See, for instance, the warning that Ursa delivers
to her potential assaulters: "*I am Ursa Corregidora. I have tears for eyes. I
was made to touch my past at an early age. I found it on my mother's tid-
dies. In her milk. Let no one pollute my music. I will dig out their temples.
I will pluck out their eyes*" (C, 77).[37] Here Jones repeats the intimate structure of address she has established in earlier ritualized passages while
revising tone and language to reveal a more violent side to Ursa's character than the reader has previously seen. Although Jones mitigates the
second-person threat that appears in a handwritten draft—"I will dig out
your temples. I will pluck out *your* eyes"—the lines still haunt.[38] One's
sense of estrangement here is related to—it is produced by—imagined
intimacy: who *is* this character who seems to be disclosing so much?

Jones generates an interplay between intimacy and estrangement in
these passages not only through tonal changes but also through structural ones. She gradually removes the "he said / she said" cues that would
stage lines for the reader and even shears quotation marks from certain
lines; indeed, an early draft shows Jones crossing out quotation marks
as a dialogue proceeds.[39] By thus withdrawing the narrative framework,
she puts the reader in the uncomfortable position of being a witness to,
but not the intended *audience for*, these encounters, which now seem
composed of a private, even unspoken language:

> "*Where did you get those songs? That's devil's music.*"
> "*I got them from you.*"
> "*I didn't hear the words.*"

> *Then let me give witness the only way I can. I'll make a fetus out of grounds of coffee to rub inside my eyes. When it's time to give witness, I'll make a fetus out of grounds of coffee. I'll stain their hands.*
> (C, 54)

Jones's image of the coffee fetus underscores the human means at the heart of production, reminding us that enslaved women gave birth, as Hazel Carby puts it, "to capital itself in the form of slaves."[40] But the fetus made of coffee grounds aborts the system, because it *is* the product that it should have lived to cultivate. In this sense, the coffee fetus reads as a final offering, as Ursa's attempt to abolish her foremothers' traumatic past and thus restart history. Indeed, the next line is this: "*Everything said in the beginning must be said better than in the beginning*" (C, 54). At the same time, this "beginning" relies on prior language for effect. The image of the fetus made of coffee grounds recalls and transmutes two earlier elements in the novel: Ursa's great-grandmother, who was known as "the coffee-bean woman" (C, 60), and Ursa's own aborted child. The image is haunting—familiar because located in prior moments in the novel but alien because it perverts them, too. As Jones intensifies and concentrates images we have already seen, we find the same stimulant painfully deployed, like coffee rubbed directly in the eyes. The violence and unpredictability of this moment, paired with the sense that Ursa is not actually addressing the reader, indicates Ursa's inaccessible interior complexity. In this way, Jones dispels the illusion of the transparently expressive voice.

In the novel's final scene, Jones offers the reader a privileged view of Ursa and Mutt's reconciliation but without providing, as Tate puts it, "directions" as to how to read it. She repeats and revises Ursa's earlier exchanges with Mutt by staging a reconciliatory dialogue in the present, while also repeating and revising general narrative conventions regarding romantic reunions by playing with timing and character development. First, in what Melvin Dixon calls "the narrative's only strain on credibility," Jones stages the final scene twenty-two years after the novel's main action.[41] Further, she does not present Mutt as a reformed or "different man" from the one who pushed Ursa down the stairs; the only thing that separates the Mutt we see at the end from the one we see at the beginning is a patently artificial passage of time. Because she does not justify the lovers' reunion by establishing both characters' emotional growth, Jones disrupts conventional ideas about how conclusions are (to utilize the language of creative writing workshops) "earned." To leave the reader unconvinced that Mutt "deserves" Ursa's forgiveness is to leave the final reunion undefended, and this is a critical move for a novel thoroughly concerned with questions of judgment, with bearing witness and sustaining evidence of crimes—a book whose very title translates as "female judge." Rather than entreat understanding ("Please don't talk about me when I'm gone"), the conclusion silences imminent judgment ("Ain't nobody's business if I do," to quote Holiday again, and Bessie Smith before her). The productive effect of this silencing, however, may be to "speak back to" a history throughout which black men's and women's sexual intimacy has been policed.

Ursa marks her reconciliation with Mutt by giving him oral sex, and the novel ends as they trade lines in the manner of blues musicians:

"I don't want a kind of woman that hurt you," he said.
    "Then you don't want me."
    "I don't want a kind of woman that hurt you."
    "Then you don't want me."
    "I don't want a kind of woman that hurt you."
    "Then you don't want me."
    He shook me till I fell against him crying. "I don't want a kind of man that'll hurt me neither," I said.
    He held me tight. (C, 185)

This ending has inspired several contrasting interpretations—whether readers believe it disempowers Ursa, heals her, or (in my view) insists on not quite doing either. Positive readings stress that Mutt and Ursa's closing exchange mimics the form of a sixteen-bar blues stanza; in this view, their balanced "song" signifies rehabilitation and peace.[42] However, due to the disruptions of narrative convention I have described, it seems to me that the closing scene doesn't ask us to believe that either Mutt or Ursa is through hurting the other person or even that they will stay together. What is ultimately haunting about this ending is that, despite its intimate setting and tone, it doesn't ask us to believe anything.

Still, the indeterminacy of the conclusion itself reveals an important aspect of the blues and its legacies, one that we miss if we expect that song will signal healing or empowerment for Ursa. I think Mutt and Ursa's exchange alerts us to the real uncertainty that adheres in the blues proposition itself. "If you treat me right baby, I'll stay home every day," Holiday sings, with a wry glint in her eye.[43] The blues barely conceals its suspicion that the terms of agreement it proposes will not hold. As opposed to the American popular song tradition, Davis writes, "romantic love is seldom romanticized in the blues"—mainly because popular songs' celebrations of marriage and female domesticity were not relevant to economic conditions that compelled black men to travel and black women to work outside the home.[44] For an extreme but nonetheless useful illustration of this point, we might consider the song "My Blue Heaven," a hit for the white crooner Gene Austin in 1927: "Just Molly and me / and the baby makes three, / we're so happy in my blue heaven." Bessie Smith released "Backwater Blues" the same year: "Backwater Blues done caused me to pack my things and go, 'cause my house fell down and I can't live there no mo'." In the face of such displacements, the blues often express ambivalence about the prospect of sustaining romantic relationships.

We might think here, too, of how often the lyrics of soul songs insist on love and commitment while hinting at loss or betrayal. "I don't want nobody else"—the definitive statement of a subgenre we might call the "reassurance song"—always works as an acknowledgment that such desire is possible. As Jones's contemporary Donny Hathaway sings, "No, I ain't got nobody else in mind. . . . I know it's you."[45] To the extent that this *does not go without saying* in a blues tradition, such songs are direct extensions of the blues. Esther Phillips takes up this tradition from a woman's perspective in "Baby, I'm for Real" (1971), a song that consists entirely of restatements of the title sentiment to a skeptical party and ends with an insistent riff: "I would never, never, never let you go . . . 'cause I love you so!"[46] Again, it's necessary to say this because, as Phillips's interlocutor seems all too aware, one can't take it for granted. The reassurance song expresses a sense of choice and contingency instead of romanticized fate. One chooses to "never let you go" and could choose otherwise; this makes love a risk in the blues tradition. Insofar as Ursa and Mutt decide to try anyway, Jones may suggest that Ursa's vulnerability, her willingness to risk being hurt, is resolution enough for the novel. What I am suggesting is that the novel tells us as much about the blues and its legacies as the blues tells us about the novel.[47]

Further, as I have said, Jones tells and invites new stories about the female singer's art. She clears new space for these stories by troubling the narrative of the blueswoman's transparent singing voice. After Ursa's "fall" down the stairs, her friend Cat compares the change in her voice to Ma Rainey's. She claims that Rainey's voice improved "after all the alcohol and men . . . because you could tell what she'd been through. You could hear what she'd been through" (C, 44). On one hand, the narrative appears to endorse Cat's idea that Ursa's voice itself expresses her traumatic experience. But through this exchange Jones also, more subtly, interrogates listeners' claims to hear a singer's life in her voice. Note that Cat uses the words "tell" and "hear" interchangeably. The conflation is significant because it implies that what one "hears" in the voice has a lot to do with the story one "tells"—with, in other words, oneself. Further, Jones marks the limitations of Cat's particular story when she juxtaposes Cat's comments with Ursa's own private reflections. Ursa understands the "strain" in her voice to index not only her publicly witnessed tragedy (her fall) but also an untold past of transgenerational suffering: "Stained with another's past as well as our own. Their past in my blood" (C, 45). This unvoiced meditation suggests that whatever Cat hears in Ursa's voice is not the whole story. By analogy, the passage troubles the public's presumptions to discern private histories in legendary voices like Holiday's.

The stakes of this gesture become clearer as Jones explicitly cites Holiday and brings her legacy to bear on Ursa's experience. In these moments, Jones critiques listeners' claims to deep knowledge of iconic singers by linking such claims with (sexual) ownership. *Corregidora* thus challenges the mythology of the transparently expressive black female singing voice by revealing the racialized, gendered, and sexualized power relations this mythology supports. There are two scenes in which Ursa's male listeners use Holiday and other popular female singers as vehicles through which to make sexual advances toward Ursa. The first is a "courtship scene" between Ursa and Mutt that takes place in 1947:

"I like you," he said. "I got some Della Reese records. She's my woman. I like you though. I mean, I don't just like your singing, I like you too."

I said nothing.

After a while, he said very quietly, "You got somebody?"

I said, "No."

He smiled a little. "Yeah, she's my woman. Her and Ella. The rest of em can't do nothing for me. Now the Lady Billie she . . ." (C, 150)

Mutt invokes famous singers in a tentative effort to establish common ground with Ursa, to flirt with her. He makes a vernacular claim to kinship with Della Reese and Ella Fitzgerald when he says, "She's my woman. Her and Ella." Yet the following line also hints at his sense of sexual power over these singers: "The rest of em can't do nothing for me."[48] This moment echoes popular discourse on Holiday. For instance, when British jazz musician and critic Spike Hughes writes of seeing a young Holiday perform in the 1930s, he describes her as a "quite irresistible" "tall, self-assured girl with rich golden-brown skin, exquisitely shown off by the pale blue of her full-skirted and low-cut evening frock, her black, swept-up hair."[49] "She was not the sort you could fail to notice in a crowd at any time," he writes, but "in the crampt low-ceilinged quarters of a Harlem speak-easy she not only registered, but like a Gypsy fiddler in a Budapest cafe she came over to your table and sang to you personally"; indeed, Hughes suggests, the eighteen-year-old Holiday "was the first of the coloured girls to exploit a bedside manner of singing."[50] That remark is Hughes's segue into his belated discussion of Holiday's vocal art.

Mutt establishes a subtler erotic claim to his favorite female singers when speaking with Ursa in the passage cited above. He continues, "Now the Lady Billie she . . ." At this point, Jones's typescript draft includes a handwritten extension to the sentence, "she's a fine woman," which Jones then crosses out in favor of maintaining the original ellipsis. This punctuation mark is apt because it presages the complex, elliptical story that will unfold for Holiday over the coming decades.[51] Indeed, the next time a character in the novel mentions Holiday it is 1969, ten years after her death. Here a male speaker manifests proprietorship of Holiday by claiming to know her private story, or presuming that he can fill the temporal and epistemological space marked by the earlier ellipsis. Jones sexualizes the man's claim to knowledge by juxtaposing his discussion of Holiday with an invasive conjecture about Ursa's body. After Ursa's performance, the man tells her,

> "You know the onliest other time I felt this good was when I was in the Apollo Theater. That was a long time ago. . . . The Lady was singing. Billie Holiday. She sang for two solid hours. And then when she finished, there was a full minute of silence, just silence. And then there was applauding and crying. She came out and was nervous for a full thirty-two seconds. And then she sang. And you see what they done to her, don't you?"
>
> I said, "Yes."
>
> "If you listen to those early records and then listen to that last one, you see what they done to her voice. They say she destroyed herself, but she didn't destroy herself. They destroyed her."
>
> . . . He took another drink. He was drinking T-bird. Then he sat looking at me.
>
> "I bet you got some good pussy."

I said nothing. I really hadn't expected that. I just looked back at
him. (*C*, 170–171)

This is a repetition with a truly sobering difference: it underscores the
distance between Ursa's initial encounter with Mutt, her future husband, and her encounter with this man—who, if he comes across as more
pathetic than threatening, still brings a stinging verbal violation of Ursa
into the text.

Jones is not only repeating and revising her own earlier scene. She is
also, as with Ursa and Mutt's courtship scene, repeating and revising a
prior social script. This script represents Holiday's voice as an index of
her personal suffering. In one of Amiri Baraka's Holiday prose poems,
for instance, the speaker claims that Holiday's voice records her private
history of sorrow and injustice: "Billie's voice was once light bouncy,
a swing-band banner popping in the wind of syncopation. Life here
changed that. As she lived it, grew heavy inside her a steel mystery murdering of feeling with feeling. By the end of her life Billie's songs were
genuinely frightening. You not only hear the song but the pain."⁵² Like
Ursa's anonymous interlocutor, who claims that "if you listen to those
early records and then listen to that last one, you see what they done to
her voice," Baraka's speaker claims a special insight into Holiday's life
based on the change in her voice. Like the man in the novel, who speaks
vaguely (as insiders do) of "what they done to her voice"—"They say she
destroyed herself, but she didn't destroy herself. They destroyed her"—
Baraka figures Holiday's voice as carefree until "life here changed that." I
am not suggesting that Baraka himself sexualizes Holiday or her victim-
hood. I am pointing out that, in *Corregidora*, such claims to knowledge
are claims to power, and that Jones codes that power as sexual. Particularly through the scene between Ursa and the Billie Holiday fan, she links
listeners' protective "love" of black women singers with sexual claims to
their bodies ("I bet you got some good pussy").

These moments offer a lens through which to read even accounts
by Holiday's most earnest protectors. At the start of the essay "A Solo
Long-Song for Lady Day" (1993), for instance, Leon Forrest establishes
his credentials for writing about Holiday by stating that, in addition to
writing a scene inspired by "Strange Fruit" in his novel *There Is a Tree
More Ancient than Eden* (1973), he has also "gotten into [his] share of
arguments concerning the meaning of [Holiday's] art." Somewhat like
Baldwin in his early nonfiction, Forrest expresses a defensive authority
over Holiday's work. Yet Forrest goes further than Baldwin by using this

authority to elaborate the sexual trauma he thinks is the root of Holiday's art:

> *Must I go back to the imperatives of miserable men in her life, as the materiality, fish and bone of her art. . . . Couldn't marry the President [Lester Young], he was gay. Problem for that kind of gal, how does a sexually vibrant woman marry a homosexual who understands her? Talk to Virginia Woolf? Most probably Billie didn't know of her; Lady Day had the President, whom she had named, but she couldn't fuck him; she could only love him. . . . Both Billie and Virginia driven mad over their art? Each wrote diaries. Billie wrote diaries into her songs. Both divine ladies were molested as children. How can you be molested as a girl, and trust men?*[53]

As misleading as I find Forrest's suggestions that Holiday's art depended on "the imperatives of miserable men in her life" and that she "wrote diaries into her songs," I am somehow most troubled by the disingenuous rhetorical question, "Talk to Virginia Woolf?" Forrest's subtly condescending answer—"most probably Billie didn't know of her"—registers the power differential between the male writer and his muse. Holiday's singing is forged only by pain, whereas Forrest's writing is influenced by artists like Holiday and Woolf. While Holiday may inspire him, he holds the power to excavate her secrets and bring them to light. Again, whereas this power dynamic is present in Baldwin's early writings on Smith and Holiday, the sexual intrusiveness of Forrest's reflections is new.[54]

In her book on Holiday, Griffin highlights Rita Dove's Holiday poem, "Canary" (1989), in which Dove writes, "Fact is, the invention of women under siege / has been to sharpen love in the service of myth."[55] Women under siege are invented when others define them primarily through their pain. This is how the listeners I have cited define Holiday. Such representations allow listeners to imagine that they are special custodians of Holiday's memory or protectors of the myth they have created. *Corregidora* explores the dangerous side of such protectiveness, the point where protection becomes violent possession. Mutt worries that Ursa is arousing other men's desire by performing. He urges her to stop singing, and when Ursa refuses, he throws her down a flight of stairs, displaying a painful version of his own sharpened love.

I have suggested that Jones's haunting narrative strategy responds to this threat of intimate ownership. Her most dramatic, brilliant move in this regard may be one I have already described: to instantiate twenty years of Ursa's life to which the reader has very little access. (The one scene the reader witnesses within these twenty years is Ursa's visit to her mother to learn "her private memory" [*C*, 104]—an addition prompted by Morrison's editorial comments.)[56] Twenty years is approximately the amount of time between the early and late stages of Holiday's career, between her first and last performances of "Strange Fruit." I have discussed the common view that a comparison between Holiday's early and later recordings reveals "what they done to her" (just as Cat suggests that Ursa's and Ma Rainey's voices convey what they've "been through"). Jones rejects this assumption when she moves her novel ahead twenty years; here it's as if the record skips, alerting readers to the fact that they don't know *what* they've missed. Yet twenty years is also the approximate space of a generation, which invites us to ask what the time leap yields in addition to what it retracts. Precisely because Jones challenges the idea that the female singer's voice itself "records" a discernable history, her novel encourages new stories about the connection between Holiday's life and her art.

Unfamiliar Rituals II: "Strange Fruit"

Where does one begin to tell the story of Holiday's decision to sing "Strange Fruit"? We might start by noting, simply, that it *was* a decision, and one that significantly altered her career. As Maya Gibson writes, if "Strange Fruit" was "simply the most politically charged song she sang," it was also a "career-changing event" for Holiday as a musician.[57] (In this regard, Holiday anticipated the "political" turns taken by soul artists like Nina Simone, Stevie Wonder, and Marvin Gaye three decades later.) Several music historians and critics have noted that the song marked Holiday's transition from "girl singer" in a swing ensemble (the role that the previous chapter stressed) to a principal performer, a recitalist. Producer John Hammond called "Strange Fruit" "artistically the worst thing that ever happened" to her: "The beginning of the end for Billie was 'Strange Fruit,'" he declared.[58] Hammond claimed that becoming "the darling of the [white] left-wing intellectuals" made Holiday "mannered" and self-conscious, so that she lost her earlier spark.[59] For her part, Holiday pegged Hammond as a "square" who, she said, "wants to run my life [and] tries to tell me and everybody else what to do," and she continued to perform "Strange Fruit."[60] Although she spoke of feeling nauseous after singing it, she often insisted on doing so: when some New York club owners tried to ban the song, she had her contracts stipulate that she could sing it if she chose.[61] The song's importance to Holiday is also clear when we consider that she hoped to title her memoir "Bitter Crop," after the song's last two lyrics.[62]

Notwithstanding the link that Holiday's preferred title indicates between "Strange Fruit" and her life story, and despite what the film *Lady Sings the Blues* would have us believe, Holiday did not witness a lynching firsthand. The eponymous 1956 memoir on which the film is based tells a more convincing, if more elusive, story about the song's meaning to Holiday: "When [composer Lewis Allan] showed me that poem, I dug it right off. It seemed to spell out all the things that had killed Pop" (*LS*, 94). At this point I should note that, while Holiday's memoir was based on interviews and conversations between Holiday and journalist William Dufty, it is generally regarded as Dufty's invention. Yet I agree with Robert O'Meally that *Lady Sings the Blues* "is best considered a dream book, a collection of Holiday's wishes and lies," which is telling even in its deceptions.[63] Here, in a memoir that is not really a memoir, Holiday tells the story of a father who may not have been her father and who was not, properly speaking, the victim of a lynching such as that which "Strange Fruit" describes.[64] Clarence Holiday, a guitarist with big bands like the Fletcher Henderson Orchestra, had died while on tour in Texas in 1937. The segregated hospitals in that state prevented him from receiving treatment for an illness until he reached Dallas, by which time he had developed pneumonia; he died in the Jim Crow ward of the Veterans' Hospital.

Clarence Holiday's death recalls the myth of Bessie Smith's death that still lingers in the popular imagination—a myth Baldwin repeats when he writes that Smith "died on the road on the way from one hospital to another"—and it explains why the myth has such staying power. As noted in chapter 1, Smith died from a car accident on a Mississippi road in 1937, but it is unlikely that she died en route from a white hospital that turned her away to a black hospital that would treat her; her biographer Chris Albertson rejected that story in 1972, arguing that Smith's rescuers would never have brought her to a white hospital in the first place. Yet the story of Smith's death is a cautionary tale like those I cited at the start of this chapter. It tells a truth about what happened, what could have happened, and what still happens to the many black people killed in a racist society that, as Ruth Wilson Gilmore defines it, "produc[es] and exploit[s] . . . group-differentiated vulnerability to premature death."[65] Holiday evoked myriad forms of racial violence when singing "Strange Fruit." It was not necessary that she directly witness the specific form of racial terrorism the song describes in order to sing it.

Hence, I distinguish "Strange Fruit" from Holiday's biography not only because conflating them undermines her artistry but also because it demeans her complex political commitments. Holiday committed to singing "Strange Fruit" *in spite of* the fact that she, like many of her listeners, had not witnessed a lynching per se. When Holiday began to perform the song in 1939, the number of lynchings had declined, yet technological developments in communication and photojournalism meant that public consciousness about lynching was at its height. The widely publicized case of the Scottsboro Nine, though it did not involve a lynching (narrowly understood), "came to symbolize the pressing need to resist the racist ideology that so easily justified lynching."[66] This was a moment when many white Americans, moved by that trial and newly sensitized to economic and social disenfranchisement by the Great Depression, joined black people in protest. By 1936, for instance, the Association of Southern Women for the Prevention of Lynching had "been endorsed by over 35,000 white southern women."[67] It was in the spirit of such interracial alliance that a Jewish schoolteacher from the Bronx named Abel Meeropol (pen name Lewis Allan) would compose the song "Strange Fruit" and that a white jazz fan named Barney Josephson would found Café Society, the first integrated nightclub in New York and the place where Holiday first performed the song. By singing "Strange Fruit" in this venue, Holiday aimed to expand the category of people who would understand lynchings to be their "proper" concern: chic New Yorkers, black and white, who were not in the South.

Rules about the staging of the song were strict at Café Society. Josephson insisted that service would stop, everyone in the house would be silent, and the club would be dark except for a spotlight on Holiday's face while she sang "Strange Fruit." She would leave the stage (this was always her last number) in the midst of applause. But Holiday could not rely on theatrical staging alone to make her performance effective. Nor could she rely on the song's lyrics, haunting though they were. A brief analysis will demonstrate that Allan's lyrics enact the repetition with an unsettling difference I have traced through Jones's novel. This poetic structure, rather than subject matter alone, is what makes the lyrics haunting:

Southern trees bear a strange fruit
Blood on the leaves, blood at the root
Black bodies swinging in the southern breeze
Strange fruit hanging on the poplar trees.

While the "strange fruit" of the first line is initially a mystery, by the time the word "fruit" reappears in the fourth line, we understand that it refers to a human body; the southern trees are trees of death, not life. Allan's use of incremental repetition to pervert the word "fruit" corresponds with Jones's use of incremental repetition to pervert the word "coffee" as she invokes the "coffee fetus," her novel's own "strange and bitter crop." By figuring the body as food, both Allan and Jones link lynching and slavery, respectively, with acts of cannibalism. In addition to the level of the word, Allan effects haunting poetics at the level of line and stanza variation. He evokes the conventional "pastoral scene of the gallant South," which the next line ironically turns into the image of the hanged person's "bulging eyes and the twisted mouth." The lynched person's body springs into detail here, but the next and final stanza describes the body with a difference: visual detail now recedes, as if the "sudden smell of burning flesh" has burned it away: "Here is a fruit for the crows to pluck / for the rain to gather, for the wind to suck."

The way Holiday performs the song brings the haunting effect of the lyrics to life. As I note in the introduction, vocal performance or realization of a score is a form of authorship, which is why a great poem on the page will suffer from a bad live reading, and why the lyrics of "Strange Fruit" were not sufficient to ensure a haunting performance. On the contrary, as Angela Davis writes,

> "Strange Fruit" is a song that poses serious problems for its singer. Its metaphors are so forceful that an overly dramatic rendition might have transformed its powerful emotional content into histrionics. . . . This kind of art sometimes misses its aim and occasions pity instead [of solidarity]. If those who were touched by "Strange Fruit" were left feeling pity for black victims of racism instead of compassion and solidarity, this pity would have recapitulated rather than contested the dynamics of racism. It would have affirmed rather than disputed the superior position of whiteness.[68]

The threat of evoking pity rather than compassion is one of which Holiday seemed well aware. It is precisely the problem of controlling the song's reception, rather than her own painful or purgative experiences of singing it, on which she focuses in Lady Sings the Blues: "I worked like the devil on it because I was never sure I could put it across or that I could get across to a plush night-club audience the things that it meant to me" (LS, 94). One way Holiday worked to "put it across" was by forcefully articulating specific words in counterpoint with her accompanist.

As *Lady Sings* describes one performance, "When I said, '. . . for the sun to rot,' and then a piano punctuation, '. . . for the wind to suck,' I pounced on those words like they had never been hit before" (*LS*, 96). The language of attack here is striking. By staking a claim to language that could be experienced as originary ("like they had never been hit before"), Holiday aimed to confront listeners with a statement that was familiar in form yet alien in execution. Again, it is this mixture of the recognizable and unpredictable that makes for a haunting performance. So even as this protest song was becoming a *standard*—the song that audiences would come to Café Society expressly to hear Holiday sing— her haunting performances marked a refusal to standardize it. In what follows, I analyze some of these performances to show how they are haunting individually and especially collectively, as part of a narrative about Holiday's career. Her performative revisions to the song—and in particular, her strategic modulation of her changing vocal timbre— haunt by signaling just how much remains unknown about her life as a singer.

Holiday first recorded "Strange Fruit" for Commodore Records in 1939, a few weeks after her twenty-fourth birthday.[69] (The B-side of the album was "Fine and Mellow.") This first recording is dispassionate; in fact, Holiday sings the song almost briskly and only subtly dramatizes the lyrics. For instance, when she sings the line "Black bodies swinging in the southern breeze," she elongates the last two words and swings them, eerily, back and forth. In general, however, the lyrics sound terrifying because of how sweetly Holiday sings them, gently pronouncing the word "pluck" ("here is a fruit for the crows to pluck") and pushing the word "bulging" ("bulging eyes") out softly. She begins the last word, "crop," in her deeper register and gracefully shifts into her head tone, closing with a brief vibrato. Holiday's gentle performance here generates the form of understatement I described in the previous chapter, in which the sound of the music ironically contrasts with the lyrical content of a song. Here we can see how the understated performance can be haunting: Holiday's unpredictably restrained delivery of the graphic lyrics signals a discomfiting distance between singer and song; this distance invites the listener to fill in the gap by supplying or experiencing some of the emotion that Holiday herself withholds. This is why Gunther Schuller contends that "it is Billie's pure, un-self-pitying . . . approach to [the song] that haunts our memories."[70] While I do not posit a strict correspondence between Holiday's experience and "Strange Fruit" and thus would not call this performance "un-*self*-pitying," Schuller is right that

Holiday's decision to sing the song prettily instead of theatricalizing its lyrics makes this a haunting performance.

A live performance recorded at the Los Angeles Philharmonic in 1945 shows Holiday revising her own prior version of the song.[71] She begins by thanking the audience and telling them, "And now I'd like to sing a tune. It was written especially for me. And it's titled 'Strange Fruit.'" (Although the song was not written especially for her, it became part of Holiday's personal mythology to state that it was—somewhat as Mahalia Jackson would claim she had known "Move On Up a Little Higher" since childhood.) Holiday closes her brief introduction with the somewhat incongruous "I do hope you like it," then clears her throat and begins. She starts this rendition more slowly, gravely elongating the word "southern," and she sings "swinging in the southern breeze" higher than she does in the first version, enhancing the eerie delivery of these rolling notes. While her performance is more dramatic here, what is most compelling is the fact that her accompanist, Ken Kersey, sounds unable to anticipate her phrasing. "And the twisted mouth," "scent of magnolia," "here is a fruit," "for the rain to gather"—Holiday begins each of these phrases before Kersey can complete the figures that make up his interludes. This interplay between vocal and piano lines is not ironic and affirmative, as in collaborative understatement; instead, it is uneven and tense. It enhances the song's drama by setting the listener in the role of the accompanist: neither of us can keep up with Holiday. As she destandardizes, denaturalizes, and revitalizes the song, she raises perhaps unanswerable questions about these different versions of it. For instance, was the tension between Kersey's piano and Holiday's vocals improvised or planned?

Holiday's voice has changed by the time of her 1956 studio recording of "Strange Fruit," which begins with an extravagantly beautiful trumpet introduction.[72] In addition to the new arrangement, the most striking repetition with a difference here is Holiday's manipulation of what Balliett calls her "acrid" tone. The term describes the way Holiday's throat now seems to catch on the words she sings, especially in her lower register. While this sound may reflect the new condition of her voice, close listening reveals that Holiday is using it as a new tool. For instance, as she sings the phrase "southern breeze," she drops the pitch of the second syllable of "southern" and shaves it with her voice so that the word grates against itself. It is important to stress that this is the first time Holiday has dropped this particular word. If she wished to avoid the abrasive sound her lower register produces, she could certainly have sung the word higher, as she does in both of the prior versions I have discussed. Instead she pronounces the friction, bringing the edge in her voice to bear on the phrase "for the wind [to suck]," as well as on the final word, "crop," before a drumbeat falls to cut off the word and the song. To consider that Holiday is exploiting the new shades in her timbral palette to enhance her music is to perceive another gap between standard stories about her life and the performance we hear. This gap engenders new questions: Does she prefer this grating sound, and if so, why?

In 1959, five months before her death, Holiday sang "Strange Fruit" on a British television show called *Chelsea at Nine*.[73] This performance brings together several of the haunting strategies I have noted—lyrical attack, restrained performance, unexpected intonation—and raises questions about the stories behind these techniques. First, it is this performance that resonates most clearly with the description of "Strange Fruit" in *Lady Sings*, published three years earlier. To repeat and elaborate that passage, "When I came to the final phrase of the lyrics I was in the angriest and strongest voice I had been in for months. My piano player was in the same kind of form. When I said, '... for the sun to rot,' and then a piano punctuation, '... for the wind to suck,' I pounced on those words like they had never been hit before" (*LS*, 96). These statements seem to capture or predict Holiday's attack of the lyrics; in the footage of this performance, she appears disgusted as she sings the words "bulging" and "burning." Thus, we might see her "dream book" as a place where Holiday *planned* future performances like this one, in addition to recording past ones.

Baraka writes in his Holiday poem, "The Dark Lady of the Sonnets" (1962), "At the point where what she did left singing, you were on your own."[74] Here, instead of representing Holiday's voice as an index and symbol of suffering, Baraka engages Holiday's effect on her listeners. Though I don't know what he has in mind, I think of this *Chelsea at Nine* performance. If by leaving singing, Baraka means ceasing to "perform" in the sense of engaging an audience, then Holiday seems to do that here; she neither confides in nor confronts her audience. Instead, she lets her viewers witness the song, somewhat as Jones lets readers witness her ritualized passages. As was typical of her performance style, "She came out onto the stage, she sang, and then she left."[75] Here we see that what Shane Vogel might call Holiday's "despectacularizing" style could mark a subtle yet steely refusal to entertain that made its own demands: *I will not entertain you, and you will pay attention.*[76] In this 1959 performance, her composure is arresting.

FIGURE 8. Billie Holiday at Carnegie Hall, 1947. Photo by William Gottlieb / Redferns / Getty Images.

However, there is another sense in which Holiday "leaves singing" in this performance. In the last lines of the song, she emits the word "drop" seemingly without preparation. She starts the word on a G, and does not so much descend down a fourth to the E as stretch the note out and down over the interval. Musically, the stretch is uncanny; it is also alarming in that it conjures, through word painting, the hanging body the lyrics describe. On the final word, "crop," Holiday opens the note so far that the center drops out before oscillating down a half step and back up to the E. In this brief void, her voice threatens not to resolve, and when the song ends, one senses that she has dropped *us*. While the moment itself is striking, what is especially haunting to me—because it is so at odds with the image of Holiday as a natural who sang the song without premeditation (who "dug it right off")—is my sense that Holiday intentionally developed that effect. In the live 1945 performance, one can hear her striving for the effect she achieves here; in the earlier recording, however, she executes both the descent on "drop" and the oscillation on "crop" in a safer, less dramatic manner.

The increased flexibility and control Holiday displays in this *Chelsea at Nine* performance help us see why critics such as O'Meally dispute claims that her voice was "destroyed," in the words of the man in Jones's novel, and instead contend that, toward the end of her career, "when she was at her very best, . . . she was an even greater artist than she had ever been before."[77] Here, too, *Lady Sings* rings truthful: "Anybody who knows anything about singing says I'm for sure singing better than I ever have in my life. If you don't think so, just listen to some of my old sides like 'Lover Come Back' or 'Yesterdays,' and then listen to the same tunes as I have recorded them again in recent years. Listen and trust your own ears. For God's sake don't listen to the tired old columnists who are still writing about the good old days twenty years ago" (*LS*, 210–211).

My purpose in analyzing these performances, however, is not only to revise the standard narrative that Holiday's work declined as her career progressed. Many listeners and commentators have done this (Holiday herself included) by arguing for the superiority of the album *Lady in Satin* (Columbia, 1958) to Holiday's earlier works. My point is simply that we should not ascribe whatever improvement we might hear to magic or accident. I have cited Balliett's comment that Holiday's voice "took on a subtly dismaying hue. . . . Her undertones and low notes began to sound almost burnt; they took on an acrid quality." Balliett continues, "She refused to let on that anything had changed, and this bravery gave her a confusing majesty."[78] Yet Holiday's "majesty" may have been less a matter of bravery than of hard-won pride, because her later sound was the product not only of age and substance abuse but also of work. As if playing on this fusion of incident and intention, in *Corregidora* Cat tells Ursa, "You got a talent. A talent or a craft" (*C*, 29–30). To ignore the latter is to misunderstand the ongoing training that defines a professional singer's career. Insofar as Holiday continued to work, and to find ways to exploit her changing vocal timbre, we can see that even the change in her vocal tone—the element of her art that seems to grant listeners a window into her life—does not "betray" what it is assumed to. This is not to call the rust a ruse, but it is to say that Holiday's altered vocal sound does not tell or confess one simple story.

We might recall that when Cat describes Ma Rainey's voice, she tells Ursa that "you could tell what she'd been through. You could hear what she'd been through." Comparing Holiday's earlier and later recordings of "Strange Fruit" sets that statement in a different key, so to speak, revealing that part of what Holiday had "been through" was an ongoing process of training. One *knows* this, and yet it must be conceded that this aspect of her career marks a profound chasm in the public memory of her. This is what is largely unrecorded, the day-to-day practice of practicing. It is here that one strains to imagine . . . Holiday singing along with Bessie Smith's and Louis Armstrong's records, not getting the phrasing quite right, starting over . . . Alongside such "behind-the-scenes" visions, we may also consider that Holiday practiced just as often in plain view. As Geoff Dyer states of jazz history generally, "One of the reasons jazz has evolved so fast is that musicians have been obliged, if for no other reason than to earn decent money, to play night after night, two or three shows a night, six or seven nights a week"—and "not just to play but to improvise, to invent as they play."[79] In this regard, every performance is also a rehearsal for the next one.

Despite the intentionality and effort I am describing, though, there remains the fact that *Lady Sings* consistently privileges the discourse of "feeling." Passages such as the following seem to contradict the view of Holiday's work I have advanced:

> With me, it's got nothing to do with working or arranging or rehearsing. Give me a song I can feel, and it's never work. There are a few songs I feel so much I can't stand to sing them, but that's something else again.
>
> If I had to sing "Doggie in the Window," that would actually be work. But singing songs like "The Man I Love" or "Porgy" is no more work than sitting down and eating Chinese roast duck, and I love roast duck. I've lived songs like that. When I sing them I live them again and I love them. (*LS*, 43–44)[80]

In response to this passage, we might reject the notion that "it's got nothing to do with arranging or rehearsing" by citing testimonies to the contrary. We might consider Holiday's close work with pianist Teddy Wilson to prepare and arrange her songs, or Josephson's account of Holiday's strict and "meticulous" rehearsal practice: "If the pianist was one note behind, or too fast, she would pick it up. If she wasn't satisfied she'd let them know, and they'd be scared to death of her. . . . They always treated her as a star, as a princess."[81] We might also note that the passage in fact qualifies the link between feeling and singing by implying that feeling can be disabling as well as enabling: there are some songs Holiday feels *too* much, so that she "can't stand to sing them."[82] However, I would like to highlight the closing statements and ask what exactly is being felt and lived. The lines "I've lived songs like that. When I sing them I live them again and I love them" indicate not that Holiday is singing her life but that she is living her songs. It seems that her songs are the medium, the frame of reference, through which she apprehends other experiences: *what is happening now is like that song*, not *this song is like what happened to me*. The distinction matters because it suggests a life in which song is as "real" as anything that happens when one is not singing. This value system may simply describe the life of a professional musician— not least a musician who was one of the best jazz singers of her time. As O'Meally reminds us, Holiday "was trading choruses with some of the greatest jazz players in the world" by age eighteen, "had sung with Duke Ellington's orchestra in a movie and was a headliner with Count Basie" by age twenty-one.[83] The "life" we hear in Holiday's voice, then, is largely a life of singing. This is not to say she had no identity outside of her career; it is instead to point out that it is hard to tell where one ends and the other begins, especially if we take seriously the claim in *Lady Sings* that Holiday's singing might—at least, at times—have felt less like "work" than pleasure, like "sitting down and eating Chinese roast duck."

Even in Holiday's later period, according to Schuller, she "could still conjure up much of her former magic," and in such moments her singing "passed . . . into a realm that is not only beyond criticism but in the deepest sense inexplicable."[84] This language recalls Morrison's statement that "Ursa Corregidora is not possible. Neither is Gayl Jones. But they exist." Insofar as these artists may pierce the horizons of our rational expectations, one's encounter with them may be felt as spiritual. Yet we can say this without relegating Holiday and Jones to the realm of the ghostly or ideal. I do not think it is especially useful to hear Holiday as "haunting" in the sense of, in Forrest's phrase, "speaking from another world." This description follows a tradition of supernaturalizing black female vocalists that we can trace back to the colonial period. Eileen Southern's *Music of Black Americans* (1971), for instance, documents early representations of black women singers as "spellb[inding]," "almost otherworldly" creatures.[85] While such descriptions reductively idealize black women themselves, they can also efface or misrepresent singers' impact on their listeners, because to supernaturalize the voice is to foreclose response to it. When Forrest writes that "there was something eerie and haunting about [Holiday's voice], and its capacity to hold you in a fixation, as if she was speaking from another world," he suggests a voice that is *so* "other" as to mute and immobilize listeners.[86] Yet the haunting voice also exacts response, through which one pays respect to what one cannot grasp or release. This is the condition of terror as well as of love; the former draws us toward the limits of comprehensibility, as love familiarizes us with the limits of intimacy. What is challenging about Holiday and Jones is that they ask listeners and readers to engage these limits by performing their own responses to them.

To "Listen and Make Your Own Promises"

One of my aims here has been to show, though it sounds counterintuitive, that literary analysis can recover the power and mystery of music that idealized accounts of music obscure.[87] In the case of *Corregidora*, this is so because Jones's complication of vocal transparency and haunting revisionary techniques remind us of Holiday's real obliquity while prompting attention to her own revisionary performances. At least with regard to "Strange Fruit," Holiday's oft-noted refusal to sing a song the same way twice was the sign not just of a hip ethos or supreme skill but also of a haunting strategy. Yet I want to return to my point that Jones herself creates a romantic or idealized concept of black music, especially in her valuable and comprehensive literary critical study *Liberating Voices*. Reconsidering this work will help clarify the cultural significance of the haunting literary music Jones creates in *Corregidora*.

Jones's own commentary has been instrumental to analyses of *Corregidora* that valorize Ursa's singing as healing, if not fully curative. Indeed, Jones offered what would continue to be a standard critical interpretation of the novel when she told Charles Rowell that "[Ursa's] story is connected to [her ancestors' stories], but she also wants her own choices and acts of imagination and will—most of which come through singing her own songs."[88] One premise of *Liberating Voices* is that music is a similarly empowering medium for African American writers who aim to "[free] the African American character and voice in literature."[89] In Jones's analysis, black writers from Dunbar to Morrison integrate elements of black oral and musical forms into their work in order to revise restrictive Western literary conventions and to create "self-authenticating" works that "restore a sense of wholeness to African American character in literature."[90]

The seminal moment in Jones's account of this turn toward oral forms is the Black Arts Movement, during which she came of age. The next chapter will address this turn, and the way Nikki Giovanni's work complicates it, but for now I will note that, when Jones privileges music as the "authentic" form of black expression to which literature should aspire, she follows key Black Arts writers. In 1966, Baraka asserted that African American artists' most "profound contribution" was their music, not their writing, and that writers' liberation depended on following the musical vanguard.[91] Larry Neal made a similar point:

> Listen to James Brown scream. Ask yourself, then: Have you ever heard a Negro poet sing like that? Of course not, because we have been tied to the texts, like most white poets. The text could be destroyed and no one would be hurt in the least by it. The key is in the music. Our music has always been far ahead of our literature. . . .
> . . . Our music has always been the most dominant manifestation of what we are and feel, literature was just an afterthought, the step taken by the Negro bourgeoisie who desired acceptance on the white man's terms.[92]

While Jones does not frame black literature as a dispensable "afterthought" to music, she too contends that "our music has always been far ahead of our literature" and that it has been "the most dominant manifestation of what we are and feel." For these reasons, "the key" to black literature's evolution "is in the music." As she writes,

> Many African American fiction writers and poets acknowledge the superiority of the black musician as artist, and from their early efforts to reshape literature to their own cultural dynamics these writers have made thematic and stylistic references to African American music as a guide, with the recognition that the music possesses a greater capacity for complexity and scope. Of course, much of the music's refinement is due to its remaining, as an art form and ritual, an unbroken though modified continuum of oral tradition, whereas the "writers" (griots) had to readjust to written literature in an environment that discouraged or banned such efforts as criminal.[93]

Jones sees black music as the "superior" African American art form because it has retained its ties to "the oral traditions of Africa" and to living realities of black community.[94] The music has maintained its integrity by escaping the comprehension, and thus the prohibition, of white listeners (as Baldwin would put it, it was not "decoded"). Because music was not "discouraged or banned" as print literacy was, black musicians have developed a "greater capacity for complexity and scope" than writers have. Music continues to be "the highest artistic standard developed within the African American culture," Jones concludes, "so it is important to continue to discover ways in which it can be translated into words and literature."[95]

Jones's vision of history and artistic evolution may be dubious: as she herself acknowledges, music was never completely free from prohibition, since slaves were prevented from playing the "talking drums" in America; moreover, it is not clear why sustaining a connection to African oral traditions would make black music especially "refine[d]." But what is important to me is the nature of this gesture. I have argued that Ralph Ellison utilizes a vision of the church as a historically safe space for African American expression in order to make particular claims about Mahalia Jackson's art and its reception. Similarly, Jones advances a particular version of African American history in order to call for a culturally specific literary practice. By figuring black music as what Baraka would call a "changing same" in African American expressive culture— one that black people have created on their own philosophical, social, and aesthetic terms—Jones makes it a force that can link black people to a discrete tradition and to each other.[96] She wants African American literature to do the same. So if *Corregidora*, in my reading, interrogates precisely such stories as Jones tells about the development of black music in *Liberating Voices*, *Liberating Voices* reminds us that the point of interrogating these stories is to establish a sense of kinship, hard-won though it may be.

Indeed, the Black Arts musical bias may haunt literature and criticism precisely because it was geared toward building a community that still seems elusive. As Amy Ongiri argues, the Black Arts Movement did not so much ride a glorious wave of black solidarity as it tried to manage and reverse the felt erosion of black communities. Black Arts leaders aimed to "provide a model for African American advancement that would avoid the pitfalls of mainstream institutional inclusion, including the disintegration of African American culture and community that was believed to have been produced by [the end of legalized segregation and] the Civil Rights Movement."[97] In Ongiri's analysis, then, anxiety about class stratification was a major component and motivation of the Black Arts Movement itself. Black Arts theorists valorized black music in part because music presumably crossed class lines more successfully than literature did (hence Neal's prioritization of music over writing on the basis that the latter was the medium of the "Negro bourgeoisie").

Jones published *Corregidora* at a moment of cultural crisis. She had already witnessed the assassinations of leaders such as Medgar Evers, Malcolm X, and Martin Luther King Jr. The United States was in the midst of a recession and the conservative backlash represented by Daniel Patrick Moynihan's memo to Richard Nixon: "The time may have come when the issue of race could benefit from a period of 'benign neglect.'"[98] These developments created a new set of dislocations for black Americans, which were largely experienced along class lines. As bell hooks notes in an essay published the year before *Liberating Voices*, "Racial integration has . . . altered in a fundamental way the common ground that once served as a foundation for black liberation struggle. Today black people of different classes are victimized by racism in distinctly different ways. Despite racism, privileged black people have available to them a variety of life choices and possibilities."[99] One way black writers and scholars of Jones's generation sought to build connections with their predecessors and with communities fractured along class lines was by sustaining the previous generation's image of music as the form that, as Jones writes, "more easily transcend[s] class boundaries" between black people.[100] Like Baldwin, then, Jones evokes music to gesture toward a complexly conceived community.

What *Corregidora* implies, however, is that these lines of connection remain vital only if one stays curious about them. This is why it matters that the novel figures black music less as a stable metaphor for community or as a vehicle for self-expression than as an instigation. Why music? Why Holiday? Why "haunting"? Why, indeed, does Jones assert in *Liberating Voices* that enslaved "'writers' (*griots*) had to readjust to written literature in an environment that discouraged or banned such efforts as criminal"? Why would the *griots* not become singers, instead of writers? What *is* the value of New World black writing, and why is it, as Jones states, "important . . . to discover ways in which [music] can be translated into words and literature"? One answer I have posed here is that Jones's fiction begets other fictions—about the musical figure of Holiday and the musical form of the blues that Jones putatively "translates." In this way, Jones's "griot" is a writer who keeps the songs of a musical-literary tradition alive.

To elaborate Baraka's statement about Holiday in "Dark Lady of the Sonnets," "At the point where what she was was in her voice, you listen and make your own promises."[101] While this line may seem to support the kinds of presumptions I have critiqued, by which listeners claim to hear "Holiday herself" in her voice, Baraka leaves the question of "what she was" intentionally vague. Unlike the man in *Corregidora* who alludes to "what they done to" Holiday when speaking with Ursa, Baraka's line does not imply shared knowledge. Rather, his ambiguity indicates that one *cannot* know "what she was," but that hearing Holiday "in her voice" should compel response. That is, it should compel listeners (including writers) to put themselves into *their* voices—not merely to repeat the commonplace but to say something new, to remember something new. Moreover, if what haunts is not the experience of identifying with Holiday but the ongoing realization that we can't, then artists like Holiday and Jones ask listeners to keep enacting, in Marisa Parham's words, a "kind of remembering that relies less on one's own personal experience . . . than it does on what one is ready to see, touch, or hear."[102] This conception of haunting is important because it makes receptivity, more than identification, a grounds for response. As Holiday's own decision to sing "Strange Fruit" indicates, the proper scope of one's responsibility includes not only those experiences one shares but also those experiences to which one is receptive. In this view, as in Michael Hardt's reading of Spinoza's work, "every increase in the power to act and think corresponds to an increased power to be affected—the increased autonomy of the subject . . . always corresponds to its increased receptivity."[103]

What exactly, then, are we called to do? The answer is not simply to "never forget" the racial terror that lynchings in the United States represent. It is rather to tell the story of the *incommensurability* between such incidents and the people who have tried to represent them. As Gordon writes of Morrison's *Beloved* (1987), "a knot of half-signs weaving a story and marking a limit *is* the story, a story that exists in the profound Everywhere between 'Slavery with a capital S' and a seemingly anonymous slave woman who killed her child."[104] There are so many stories between lynching and Holiday's "haunting antilynching appeal," between New World slavery and Jones's first novel. It is precisely because there is so much these artists' voices will never tell that we may be moved to keep telling their stories. This response to haunting practice is what Cathy Caruth calls "transmission," relaying "the address of another . . . that remains enigmatic yet demands a listening and a response"; it is what Joseph Roach terms "surrogation," what Jacques Derrida calls "being-with specters," what Avery Gordon calls "writing ghost stories," and what Gayatri Spivak means when she defines the "untranslatable" not as that which can't be translated but as that which one "*never stop[s] (not) translating*."[105]

Holiday's interpreters continually demonstrate this process, not only by writing about her but also by singing "Strange Fruit." Jazz vocalist Cassandra Wilson, for example, describes "Strange Fruit" as a song that "made [her] skin crawl" but that she "always felt [she] had to get to" and thus decided to record herself, in 1996.[106] Wilson's "transmission" of "Strange Fruit" necessarily prioritizes ancestry over ego; to surrogate Holiday's signature song is to know one can never do it "better" than Holiday did. But one can do something else. Paraphrasing Wilson's own words, David Margolick writes that "one approaches the song . . . not by trying to outdo or enhance Holiday, a fool's errand by any definition. Instead, Wilson stripped the song bare."[107] Wilson's "Strange Fruit" is haunting in its own right, especially insofar as Wilson seems to acknowledge that Holiday never wanted "Strange Fruit" to be a fixed monument: Wilson's subtle vocals evoke Holiday's first recording of the song, while her insistent trumpet accompaniment evokes the 1956 arrangement. While she pays tribute to Holiday's rendition(s) of the song, Wilson also creates her own path through "Strange Fruit," as is signaled by her addition of a wandering acoustic guitar.[108]

Jones describes a similar form of transmission when she stresses the often difficult work of acknowledging and extending the legacy of one's literary predecessors. It may not be worthwhile, in her view, to write another neo-slave narrative "unless the writer can say something different or explore some new dimension of the Afro-American slave experience that hasn't already been done and done finely by Ernest Gaines in *The Autobiography of Miss Jane Pittman* [1971] and Margaret Walker in *Jubilee* [1966]. . . . What are the truths about it that haven't already been told?"[109] Put simply, the point seems to be that one must either add something vital or else leave it alone. We may perceive this haunted labor in Jones's decision to feature a black female singer in her first novel, as Ann Petry does in *The Street* (1946) and Baldwin does in *Another Country*, but to write the novel in the singer's own voice. *Everything said in the beginning—which is never really a beginning—must be said better than in the beginning.*

Of course I am not suggesting that all witnesses or interpreters will "say it right." Far from it. Despite Jones's careful orchestration of revelation and concealment, *Corregidora* would itself fall prey to reductive sensationalism; the first paperback edition features the *New York Times Book Review*'s appraisal that "the sexual writing—and this is a book with virtually no other subject than sex—is a model of grace and taste. And it is sexy!"[110] Reading this review, I am reminded of an anecdote regarding "Strange Fruit": at a show in Miami, one woman reportedly asked Holiday, "Billie, why don't you sing that sexy song you're so famous for? You know, the one about the naked bodies swinging in the trees" (*LS*, 95). (She declined.) These are limit cases, but they highlight the fact that one always risks misreading, misrecognizing, getting it wrong when responding to haunting expression. Admitting as much, finally, allows us to de-idealize inspiration itself—to realize that it doesn't always feel good. Writers like Jones have been moved to write about Holiday, and singers like Wilson have been moved to cover her songs, as much out of worry and pain as pleasure. In a sense, we may always labor under the shadow of a haunting—whether that is an insurmountable precedent or an inescapable past—because what moves us has as much to do with what we are wounded by as it does with what we love. Holiday seems to have known this. As she's reported to have said of a performance of "Strange Fruit," "I was flailing the audience, but the applause was like nothing I'd ever heard" (*LS*, 96).

5 /   Signature Voices: Nikki Giovanni, Aretha Franklin, and the Black Arts Movement

By reading *Corregidora* as a text that instigates new stories about Billie Holiday's music, I have also implicitly offered a new story about the legacy of the Black Arts Movement: that writers like Jones sustain the movement's aesthetic principles (e.g., the power of black music) precisely by questioning its truisms (e.g., "Billie Holiday sang her life"). Here I apply this mode of inquiry to the Black Arts Movement itself in order to tell a new story about this complex moment. I begin by positioning "Queen of Soul" Aretha Franklin and "Princess of Black Poetry" Nikki Giovanni as key participants in the movement.[1] Centralizing Giovanni and Franklin's artistic relationship will revise the dominant image of Black Arts as a family affair between black men, as well as eschew the elevation of black music—and specifically instrumental jazz—as the model for Black Arts poetry. At a moment when many of Giovanni's peers exalted the relatively unpopular avant-garde jazz of Sun Ra, Albert Ayler, John Coltrane, and other male artists as a prototype for black writing, Giovanni would perform a gesture at once more populist and more egocentric: choosing Franklin, a star vocalist, as her artistic counterpart.[2] I link Giovanni and Franklin by showing how both exploit music and (song) text to establish their "signature voices"—singular, authoritative voices that pay tribute to and call out toward others. The phrase "signature voice" itself brings textuality and vocality together, evoking *signature*'s connotation of writing—its etymological root in the Latin *signare*, "to sign" or "to mark"—and I theorize this concept in an effort to equalize and harmonize both expressive forms.[3]

Giovanni writes a poem for Franklin; she discusses her in interviews over the course of her career (once telling an audience at a reading that if reincarnated, she would like to "come back as Aretha Franklin");[4] and she composes a foreword to a book about Franklin's landmark album with Atlantic, *I Never Loved a Man the Way I Love You* (1967). But when we highlight Giovanni's rather beautifully arrogant claim that she possesses "as much of a signature voice [as a poet] as Aretha Franklin has as a singer," we can see that Giovanni does not agree with her contemporaries that music is the premier black expressive medium to which other art forms should aspire.[5] Instead, she asserts her own signature poetic voice as analogous to Franklin's music. She thus invites us to theorize a less parasitical and more supportive role for poetry vis-à-vis music. To take a cue from Giovanni's attention to backup singers in her poem "Dreams" (1968), we might say that Giovanni does not so much frame Franklin as a muse or model for her poetry as she backs *Franklin* up by underscoring the nuance and force of her music. This claim will sound familiar, as I have identified a similar effect in James Baldwin's rhetorical techniques and in Gayl Jones's narrative strategies. Here, however, I locate this effect in Giovanni's poetic form in order to argue that even musically oriented Black Arts poetry needn't be thought to aspire to the condition of song.

While music is clearly, in the words of Stephen Henderson's seminal study of black poetry, a "poetic reference" in Giovanni's work, Giovanni's work is also a *preface to* Franklin's music.[6] Her poetry is equally a record of musical sound and a score for future performances of listening. The title of the collection in which her "Poem for Aretha" appears, *Re:Creation* (1970), itself signals this dual impulse to reenact past phenomena and create new ones. If I stress the latter activity in the following analysis, this is in part because our critical practice is already so strongly inclined toward the former: one starts with ideas about music and asks how poetry and other literary forms bear them out. But my bias toward the poem's status as score is also designed to stress that Giovanni is not merely documenting or confirming a widely accepted view of Franklin's work; instead, like *Corregidora*, her poetry animates the archive of cultural knowledge about a singer who has often been more admired than heard. In short, I emphasize the function of Giovanni's poetry as score to show how it engenders understandings of music that do not preexist it.

For Giovanni, the term "signature voice" names an approach to language that makes an artist's work identifiably hers: *If you hear my poem you'll know it's me.* On one level, this concept refers to expression in general and thus encompasses the unique stories Giovanni uses her poetry to tell. But Giovanni's metaphorical reference to "hear[ing] my poem" also indicates that—whatever her specific syntactical and linguistic habits—her signature poetic voice textualizes oral and musical effects. We can use Giovanni's literary practice to study Franklin's analogous vocal techniques. Franklin enacts her own signature voice—or, in her terms, "Aretha-ize[s]" a song—not only by revising a song's storyline but also by "speechifying" and otherwise vocally manipulating the song text.[7] Through these techniques, Franklin and Giovanni assert their expressive authority while also paying tribute to others and eliciting others' voices. The term "signature voice" describes both operations: the artist's self-assertion and her extension of authority toward others. To reformulate a commonplace about the blues, that the blues singer says "I" but means "we": Giovanni and Franklin say "I" and mean "I" while *also* meaning "we."[8] So their signature voices are singular (a term Giovanni also uses in this chapter's epigraph) without being insular. They are individual but not individualistic.

As I noted in the introduction, and as Gayl Jones states in *Liberating Voices*, Black Arts theorists were the first to collectively privilege black speech and music as models for, in Stephen Henderson's words, the "most distinctly and effectively Black" poetry.[9] Giovanni's work can be (and often has been) read through this lens. Not only does her poetry from this era represent black speech and allude to music, but she has also given public readings from the start of her career and has produced several spoken-word albums—most notably *Truth Is On Its Way* (1971), recorded live with the New York Community Choir, and *The Way I Feel* (1975).[10] While I would certainly not claim that Giovanni is *exclusively* invested in print culture, I do believe her valuation of print sets her apart from the most well-known Black Arts theorizations of orality and textuality, and thus the conceptual framework established by her contemporaries does not fully account for her work. For instance, while Henderson claims that the "distinction between singing Black songs and reading Black poems" is "merely academic" and "not at all very useful," the distinction between printed poetry and oral performance *is* important to Giovanni.[11] In an interview, she stressed the "*difference* between songwriting and poetry" and asserted that "most lyrics do not read well. They sing well." She spoke a line from a Supremes hit to illustrate the point, demonstrating how flat it sounded when spoken, rather than sung: "'Baby, baby, baby, where did our love go.' *What?*"[12]

Just as "most [song] lyrics do not read well," most poems do not sing well—and the fact that Giovanni's poetry is *not* song is, I would argue, precisely the point.[13] Her print-based techniques pay homage to others and elicit others' voices. They also attune us to Franklin's music. So when Amiri Baraka claims that "those of us in the Black Arts Movement . . . wanted our poetry to *be* black music," he does not speak for Giovanni.[14] Though it may sound paradoxical, maintaining a conceptual distinction between song and text allows us to apprehend the dynamic *interplay* between these discrete forms, and between self and other, that Giovanni and Franklin create. This approach allows us to see, for example, that when Giovanni mimics a song's fade-out by ending her "Poem for Aretha" with repeated lines from a Temptations song, she is not only paying tribute to the Temptations but also asserting, through the fade-out form, the ongoing authority of her foregoing claims. Likewise, when Franklin's backup singers revise the song text of Otis Redding's "Respect" (1967) to stress the prefix "Re-," Aretha's nickname, they not only claim the song for Franklin but also democratize it through their participation.

Therefore, my argument that both artists' signature voices rely on music and text is partly meant to disrupt the binary by which music is racialized as black and text is racialized as white. To recall Neal's statement from the previous chapter, "Ask yourself . . . Have you ever heard a Negro poet sing like [James Brown screams]? Of course not, because we have been tied to the texts, like most white poets." But I more specifically mean to challenge the binary association that underwrites Neal's segregation of (black) music from (white) text—that is, the association of music with what Neal terms "collective ritual," and writing with silent isolation or the "cold technology" of the printed page.[15] To quote Neal again, "The poet must become a performer, the way James Brown is a performer—loud, gaudy and racy. . . . Poets must learn to sing, dance and chant their works. . . . We must make literature move people to a deeper understanding of what this thing is all about, be a kind of priest, a black magician, working juju with the word on the world."[16] In my view, Giovanni's printed poetry itself performs a dynamic relationship between music and text, self and other.[17] Both Giovanni and Franklin use music and text to establish signature voices that gesture toward broader imagined communities.

Finally, to set this formal dialogue between women artists at the center of a story about Black Arts is to propose a new vision of the movement's

gender politics. What Phillip Brian Harper calls the "profoundly problematic masculinist ethic" of the movement is well known and is evident
in the work of writers such as Baraka, Neal, and Don L. Lee.[18] At the
same time, Cheryl Clarke points out that "wherever they stood in relation to the Black Arts Movement, most black women writers of that time
wrote *because* of it—and still do."[19] From these observations there follow
two general lines of analysis. One line sees black women poets as self-
degradingly male identified; thus, Harper's selective reading of Giovanni's poetry leads him to conclude that Giovanni conflates blackness with
maleness and that she "so insistently invokes a phallic standard of political engagement . . . as to suggest that no other term was available—not
even to her who . . . explicitly referenced herself as . . . a 'black female
poet.'"[20] Another approach sees black women artists as responding to
the sexist impulses of many male writers by valorizing black womanhood on the level of content.[21] Keeping in mind, however, that "standing
against men, or against patriarchy, might not be structurally so different
from existing *for* it," I depart from both critical paradigms by staging the
Black Arts Movement as a dialogue (sometimes supportive, sometimes
conflicted) between black women artists themselves, and by asserting
that this conversation often takes place on the level of form.[22]

In what follows, I frame both Giovanni and Franklin as Black Arts
participants. I show that Giovanni's "Poem for Aretha" and Franklin's
1967 recording of Sam Cooke's "A Change Is Gonna Come" (1963) establish both artists' signature voices through the act of paying homage, and
I show how "Dreams" and "Respect" also elicit the voices of others. I
end by extending this reciprocal reading of music and poetry toward
other musically oriented Black Arts poems. Overall, this chapter aims
to prompt new connections between black music and writing by showing that the very movement that has engendered our critical bias toward
the former offers several different ways of articulating the links between
them.

Black Arts and Beyond

Beyond Giovanni's continual invocations of Franklin, these artists,
born one year apart, invite comparative study because of their contemporaneous rise to national fame. Franklin was crowned the "Queen of
Soul" in 1968, shortly before Giovanni was deemed the "Princess of Black
Poetry."[23] It is not my intention to account for Giovanni's and Franklin's
ascension to stardom, much less to explain why Giovanni in particular

FIGURE 9. Nikki Giovanni, 1970. Photo by Jack Robinson / Jack Robinson Archive / Condé Nast.

was celebrated at a moment when several other black female poets were publishing first books. (Cheryl Clarke reminds us that, in addition to Giovanni's *Black Feeling, Black Talk*, Audre Lorde's *First Cities*, Carolyn Rodgers's *Paper Soul*, Alice Walker's *Once*, and Sonia Sanchez's *Homecoming* were all published in 1968.)[24] However, I do want to briefly address the past and present constituencies that these artists' iconic voices might be thought to represent.

Giovanni was born and raised in Knoxville, Tennessee. She graduated from Fisk University and briefly attended Columbia University before self-publishing her first collection of poems. She rarely cites influences, although her published conversation with Margaret Walker (1974) reflects the extensive sweep of the young poet's reading—from nineteenth-century

African American writers to contemporary poets, novelists, and literary critics. Far from racializing oral expression as black and literary expression as white, Giovanni seems to view the task of sustaining the African American literary tradition as a black nationalist project in its own right. She is one of the strongest defenders of the black literary tradition among young writers of her generation. In contrast with Amiri Baraka, for instance, who rejected Phillis Wheatley's "pleasant imitations of 18th century English poetry" and Charles Chesnutt's "embarrassing ... paternalism," while setting both writers against "the richness and profundity of the blues,"[25] Giovanni insists that both Wheatley and Chesnutt should be read on their own artistic terms and according to their own historical contexts.[26] Insofar as Giovanni reaffirms writers who do not explicitly engage with black speech and music, her response to Baraka anticipates Harryette Mullen's response to Henry Louis Gates Jr.'s *The Signifying Monkey* (1988) by two decades; in "African Signs and Spirit Writing" (1996), Mullen argues that "any theory of African-American literature that privileges ... the trope of orality to the exclusion of more writerly texts will cost us some impoverishment of the tradition."[27]

Despite Giovanni's respect for her literary "elders," however, she did see her generation of black writers as doing something new: as "chang[ing] our focus of address" and thus correcting the problem Richard Wright had highlighted thirty years earlier, that "Negro writing has been addressed in the main to a small white audience rather than to a Negro one."[28] Priding herself on being "a poet of the people" who primarily addressed black readers, Giovanni rejected the notion that black people needed her to speak *for* them: "Once we released those voices no one needed to speak for them. They're an elegant people. They're capable of speaking for themselves."[29] What was true for poetry was true for politics: "As a leader, you're only representing the legitimate desires of someone else. No leader created the movement. And that's what everybody seems to miss. Movements create leaders."[30] If Giovanni herself was a creation of the people, she also, as she put it, "released" their voices, in part by presenting herself as a model to support and emulate. Having self-published her early collections, she incessantly toured the country giving talks and readings at the height of her fame—or, as Neal would put it, "working juju with the word on the world."

Franklin's career embodies a similar convergence of extraordinary artistry with receptive social moment. Franklin was the daughter of the famous Reverend C. L. Franklin, who was the leader of the Bethel Baptist Church in Detroit, a key ally of Martin Luther King Jr., and a preacher nationally known as "the man with the million-dollar voice." Her father's position meant Franklin was surrounded by the finest gospel musicians of her time, including Mahalia Jackson. The two influences she would most often cite, however, were gospel star Clara Ward, who, like Franklin, was a pianist whose self-accompaniment shaped her vocals, and Judy Garland, who "offered the example of impeccable diction and a clear voice throbbing with trumpeted emotion."[31] (Anthony Heilbut also cites Billie Holiday as an influence, suggesting that Holiday's *Lady in Satin* [1958] was very popular among gospel singers and that Franklin adopted Holiday's "delicately playful approach to time and phrasing.")[32] The "golden age of gospel" that Ellison captured was waning when, at age eighteen, Franklin followed in the footsteps of Bessie Smith, Billie Holiday, and Mahalia Jackson by signing a contract with Columbia Records executive John Hammond. She explained her decision to cross over from gospel to secular music in a guest column for the *New York Amsterdam News*: "The blues is a music born out of the slavery day sufferings of my people. Every song in the blues vein has a story to tell of love, frustrations and heartaches," Franklin wrote. "I think that because true democracy hasn't overtaken us here that we as a people find the original blues songs still have meaning for us."[33]

She retained strong ties to the church, however—a fact made resoundingly clear by her 1972 cross-back-over album *Amazing Grace*, recorded live at the New Temple Missionary Baptist Church in Watts, Los Angeles. For just one illustration of Franklin's performative power, we might listen to her rendition of "Amazing Grace" on this album, how she lingers over the line "through many dangers, toils, and fears," tarrying over the "through" (working *through* it), slowly bringing the assembled congregation to a fever pitch of excitement. The film of this performance reveals that when Franklin finally hits the high C on "dangers" that listeners are waiting for, a group of men seated behind her simultaneously leap to their feet.[34] Yet Franklin's music was, of course, especially resonant in an era of Civil Rights, Black Power, and feminist movements. If her version of "Respect" became black America's "national anthem" during what David Llorens called the "summer of 'Retha, Revolt and Rap" (1967), this was because black radical leader H. Rap Brown and "Revolt" were already part of the social equation.[35] As Charles Keil notes, Franklin's hits like "Respect" and "Think" "can be made into public discourse in the late 1960s because there's a public arena for [their lyrics] to . . . resonate into."[36] So while Angela Davis argues that blueswomen like Bessie Smith did not have the sociopolitical structures that would allow their critique to become protest, these structures were available to Franklin and were strengthened by her.[37] As she put it, "I'm not a politician or political theorist. I don't make it a practice to put my politics into my music or social commentary. But the fact that 'Respect' naturally became a battle cry and an anthem for a nation shows me something." Or, as Sherley Anne Williams would later recall, "Aretha was right on time."[38]

While Giovanni and Franklin emerged as voices of their generation, both have suffered from "critical neglect."[39] They are therefore also linked, and distinguished from other artists in this study, in terms of their relatively unsung status within the U.S. academy. Scholars of African American culture have not embraced these artists as they have Bessie Smith, Holiday, Wright, Ellison, Baldwin, and Jones. Virginia Fowler states that Giovanni has been popular with readers yet neglected by gatekeepers of culture since her early career:

> Just as black critics equated [Giovanni's] material success with a betrayal of black causes . . . , her white critics equated her widespread popularity with aesthetically inferior writing. To early black critics, poetry should be "for the people," but it should not lead, apparently, to recognition or material gain for the poet. And to white critics, long comfortable with the notion that poetry was actually for an elite few, Giovanni's continuing popularity has itself been evidence of "low" art.[40]

Giovanni's place in the literary canon is clearly signaled by her inclusion in the *Norton Anthology of African American Literature* (1997, 2003)—but even this inclusion is marred by a prefatory statement of ambivalence about her abilities as a writer. In the introduction to her poetry in the volume, Houston Baker not only attributes Giovanni's "instant fame" to her "revolutionary proclamations and the accessibility of her simple nostrums" but also suggests that the shift in her work was motivated solely by her desire to maintain commercial success: "By the early 1970s, Giovanni had realized that what the critic Arthur P. Davis called 'the new poetry of black hate' had exhausted its market, and she produced a surprising collection of love poems called *My House* (1972)."[41]

Franklin's esteem in the world of popular music is unquestioned. When in 2008 *Rolling Stone* magazine asked two hundred musicians and music critics to determine the "100 Greatest Singers of All Time," they ranked Franklin number one.[42] These critics seem to recognize Franklin's status as an "exorbitantly gifted" singer, pianist, arranger, and composer who in some ways "colonized American music for the gospel style."[43] Her enduring cultural legacy was confirmed when she was selected to sing at the inauguration of President Barack Obama in January 2009—an event to which I will return at the end of this book. Yet as of this writing, Franklin has curiously failed to capture the scholarly imagination. Matt Dobkin is right to say that, compared with Smith and Holiday, Franklin "has gotten woefully short shrift in terms of her musical contributions . . . , probably because . . . her hit-making ability has lent her an aura of 'pop' . . . that doesn't often [yield] the kind of canonical enshrinement that Bessie and Billie enjoy as blues and jazz artists."[44] With regard to scholarship on black women's music during this period, Nina Simone has emerged as the more common (and certainly no less worthy) subject of academic work than Franklin.[45] This may be due to authenticating criteria established by Black Arts theorists: Simone's music did not "cross over" to white consumers to the degree that Franklin's did, and Franklin never recorded a protest song as fierce as Simone's "Mississippi Goddam" (1964).

Nevertheless, I underscore Franklin's influential cultural politics here, and not only by framing "Respect" as a black feminist anthem—many others have done this—but also by positioning Franklin as a key voice of the Black Arts Movement. For one, we might recognize that Franklin is, as Guthrie Ramsey writes, "a notable exception to [the] unspoken rule" whereby theorists of "the Black Aesthetic" would use "black male composers and performers to illustrate their rhetorical, musical, and polemical points."[46] For example, in the 1970s, both Stephen Henderson and Sherley Anne Williams invoke Franklin in their rather different theorizations of the Black Aesthetic. Henderson uses a (black male) critic's review of Franklin's gospel album *Amazing Grace* to explicate his concept of "saturation," or the "ultimate experience of Blackness" that art can produce; Williams cites Franklin's version of Redding's "Respect" to show that African American music "reflect[s]" and instigates dialogue about "a wide range of values in the national black community."[47] Giovanni, for her part, simply claims in a recent interview that "Aretha was the black aesthetic."[48] In a slightly different register, we might highlight the fact that Franklin publicly offered money for the bond to bail Angela Davis out of prison in 1971. In this context, it seems fitting that, twenty-seven years later, Davis would theorize black female singers' radical politics in the landmark study to which I have referred several times throughout this book.[49]

"Cause Nobody [Else] Deals with Aretha": Giovanni's Signature Tribute

No single work of this era embraces Franklin as a Black Arts ally as explicitly as Giovanni's "Poem for Aretha."[50] Giovanni opens the poem by framing Franklin as "a mother with four / children having to hit the road" and imagines the day-to-day drudgery of her fame, but she goes on to render her a larger-than-life leader of the late-sixties "revolt": "aretha was the riot was the leader if she had said 'come / let's do it' it would have been done."[51] Giovanni humanizes Franklin in order to lend depth to the tale that follows—to underscore the price of Franklin's service to the movement (or, more accurately, movements) that claimed her as their voice.

Moreover, as I have said, Giovanni's signature poetic techniques illuminate Franklin's analogous musical techniques. As I will show, Giovanni revises conventional stories and inventively textualizes oral and musical effects, while Franklin revises the narrative of a song she is covering and inventively vocalizes a song text through her speechlike intonation, lyrical interpolations, and choral work with backup singers. Thus, for both artists, creating a signature voice is about telling a new story and making the material text of that story sound or look distinct. Again, their signature voices are individual but not individualistic: in "Poem for Aretha," Giovanni creates her signature voice through the act of paying tribute to someone else. This process also describes Franklin's "tribute" performance of Cooke's Civil Rights anthem, "A Change Is Gonna Come."

Giovanni advances her own distinctive version of Franklin's story by revising a long tradition of literary tributes to black female singers. Rather than bemoan Franklin's troubled life (as do many elegies for Holiday) or exalt the effect she has on her fans (as does Sterling Brown's poem for Ma Rainey and Frank O'Hara's poem for Holiday), Giovanni's "Poem for Aretha" hails Franklin's broad aesthetic and political impact on her milieu.[52] The presentism of this poem is an intervention in its own right: unlike other poets, Giovanni writes about Franklin while she is still alive. She thus departs from what Barbara Johnson calls "the long tradition of idealizing dead women in Western poetry." As Johnson asks, "Is it possible for a woman to have authority only on the condition that she be dead?"[53] Giovanni answers no, while additionally asking whether it is possible for an authoritative figure like Franklin to have *sympathy* before death. She implores Franklin's fans to recognize the spectacular gift Franklin gives and (to quote the title of jazz legend Sidney Bechet's memoir) to treat it gently.

The poem opens, as Clarke insightfully notes, as if explaining why Giovanni is writing it: "cause nobody deals with aretha" (*PA*, 17).[54] Giovanni targets the reader's sympathies by figuring Franklin as "you" and evoking the bodily funk that is the unexpected price of fame: "then comes the eighth show on the sixth day the beginning / to smell like the plane or bus the if-you-forget-your-toothbrush- / in-one-spot-you-can't-brush-until-the-second-show the / strangers / pulling at you cause they love you but you having no love / to give back" (*PA*, 17). In Giovanni's account, Franklin's fame isolates her not only from her fans but also from her own family: "and if you read the gossip columns the rumors that your / husband / is only after your fame / the wondering if your children will be glad to see you and / maybe / the not caring if they are" (*PA*, 17). By omitting punctuation or line breaks that distinguish one thought from the next, Giovanni hardly allows the reader herself time to "care" about the feelings of Franklin's children; the poem's relentless enjambment evokes the pace of a hectic touring schedule that might have Franklin "scheming to get out / of just one show and go just one place where some doe-doe-dupaduke / won't say 'just sing one song, please'" (*PA*, 17).

Having established the crisis, Giovanni shifts into the first person to voice precise opinions as to how Franklin should be "dealt with":

and i'm not saying aretha shouldn't have talent and i'm
certainly
not saying she should quit
singing but as much as i love her i'd vote "yes" to her
doing four concerts a year and staying home or doing whatever
she wants and making records cause it's a shame
the way we are killing her (*PA*, 18)

Expanding the scope of her argument to other artists, past and present, she writes,

we eat up artists like there's going to be a famine at the end
of those three minutes when there are in fact an abundance
of talents just waiting . . .
. . . .
aretha doesn't have to relive billie holiday's life doesn't have
to relive dinah washington's death but who will
stop the pattern (*PA*, 18)

SIGNATURE VOICES / 185

I will return to Giovanni's line breaks shortly, but here we might note that she keeps lines moving by breaking them up in odds ways, for instance between verbs ("she should quit / singing"), before prepositions ("an abundance / of talents just waiting"), and on either side of an adverb ("i'm / certainly / not saying"). When Giovanni records a spoken version of this poem for the album *Truth Is On Its Way*, she does not pause to signal these line breaks but instead delivers each complete sentence in a more conventional way: "And I'm certainly not saying she should quit singing."[55] Hence, it is only the sight of the page that reveals Giovanni's unorthodox linear arrangement. I will suggest that this arrangement elucidates Franklin's approach to a song text, for instance, as she interpolates "A Change Is Gonna Come."

For now, however, we might note that Giovanni critiques the popular narrative according to which "the painful experiences and early deaths of [Bessie] Smith, Holiday, and Franklin's most direct predecessor, [Dinah] Washington," suggested "a necessary correlation in the lives of black female royalty between pain and artistry," in Michael Awkward's words.[56] While this tragic representation of Franklin was especially glaring in the 1968 *Time* magazine cover story that depicted Franklin as the sorrowful Queen of Soul, Giovanni also critiques black fans for perpetuating it.[57] The "we" here, as in much of Giovanni's poetry from this period, seems to evoke a specifically black (and hip) audience ("I address my people"). In chapter 3, I discussed Baldwin's focus on Smith's and Holiday's suffering; in chapter 4, I explored literary allusions to "what they done to" Holiday's voice. Here Giovanni asks black readers to reconsider who the "they" is—to take responsibility for female singers' survival. Again, Giovanni departs from earlier elegies to suffering black women vocalists by voicing this intervention at the height of Franklin's career. She seeks to save Franklin from "the way we are killing her" before it is too late.

Announcing that she "need[s] Aretha's music," Giovanni proceeds to list, with amusing candor, the changes Franklin has wrought on the entire cultural landscape of her moment:

the advent

of aretha...

. . . .

forced

dionne to make a choice (she opted for the movies)
and diana ross had to get an afro wig pushed every

Black singer into Blackness and negro entertainers
into negroness . . .

. . . .

the Black songs started coming from the singers on stage
   and the dancers
in the streets
aretha was the riot was the leader if she had said "come
let's do it" it would have been done
temptations say why don't we think about it
              think about it
              think about it (*PA*, 19)

Here Giovanni, working in what Stephen Henderson might call the "hyperbolic" mode, makes Franklin responsible for Dionne Warwick's starring role in the 1969 film *Slaves*; Diana Ross's switch from a bob to an Afro hairstyle; and the Temptations' more overtly political music of this era.[58] With regard to the latter, Giovanni alludes to the Temptations' "Message from a Black Man" (1969). The song opens with Melvin Franklin's deep bass statement, "Yes, my skin is black, but that's no reason to hold me back," which is supported by the other members' falsetto refrain: "Why don't we think about it, think about it, think about it . . ."[59]

Giovanni creatively appropriates the Temptations' song to establish Franklin's leadership as well as the authority of her own account. First, the Temptations' suggestion that we "*think* about it" sounds relatively meek in contrast to Franklin's call to *action* ("come / let's do it"). But further, Giovanni uses the Temptations' lyric self-reflexively, to signal that her poem is what the reader ought to "think about." She takes creative license with the song in order to produce this effect. The Temptations actually end their song with a more commanding counterpoint between the lyric "No matter how hard you try, you can't stop me now" and a revoicing of James Brown's 1969 anthem "Say It Loud (I'm Black and I'm Proud)." But while song and poem end with different lyrics, they conclude with a similar form: Giovanni mimics the repetition and tapering off of the Temptations' recording to create her own poetic fade-out. When utilized in musical recordings, as it is in so many of Franklin's own songs, the fade-out resists the time constraints of radio play by sonically outlasting them.[60] By crafting her own fade-out on the page, Giovanni creates a poem that at once insists on being the final word (what we might call a message from two black women) and refuses to let that word end.

Giovanni's authority in this poem is produced through her use of speakerly effects in addition to musical ones. While on the one hand, of course, her use of "everyday" vernacular speech might make her poem relatable to others, the poem also demonstrates that to use oral effects on the page is not necessarily to issue a democratic call for readerly response. Composed in what Clarke calls Giovanni's "'teachin-rappin' style," "Poem for Aretha" presents the reader who would perform it with enjambed statements that move at a rapid clip and require the quick "catch-breaths" that singers of fast songs must learn to master.[61] Rather than invite conversation, this technically demanding poem challenges the reader to participate in performing Giovanni's version of the story. In this sense, if the poem can be said to seek a reader's response, that response may best be imagined as an affirmative amen. This work unites what Kalamu ya Salaam calls the two "trains of African American aesthetics, the text-oriented and the speech/music-oriented."[62] But it is by exploiting the *distinction* between text and music—the fact that this poem is different from the Temptations' song, and that it is a speechlike performance one can't speak back to—that Giovanni performs her signature voice.

That voice continues to resonate, insofar as critics still take Giovanni's poem as an authoritative record of Franklin's cultural impact. In particular, Giovanni's claim that "Aretha was the riot was the leader if she had said 'come / let's do it' it would have been done" is frequently cited by critics who write about Franklin.[63] Giovanni's compelling past-tense account makes it easy to forget that "Poem for Aretha" was written only three years after the "advent of Aretha" it celebrates: Franklin had just released "Respect" in 1967.[64] Indeed, the poem seems to prematurely memorialize Franklin (a move Giovanni echoes by telling an audience she would like to be reincarnated as Franklin when the singer is still alive). It's important to ask why that is. On one hand, Giovanni's impulse to offer an authoritative version of a moment still in the making may respond to a time when black music was changing rapidly, as Motown ceded its hold on popular music to Atlantic and Stax Records' more "soulful" sound. But the poem's urge to record Franklin's impact ahead of time may also respond to the recent premature deaths of so many black musicians: Billie Holiday (1959), Dinah Washington (1963), Sam Cooke (1964), John Coltrane (1967), Otis Redding (1967). These losses constituted the musical counterpart to other "riot" leaders such as Richard Wright, Medgar Evers, Malcolm X, Martin Luther King Jr. More losses were soon to come: by 1973, "many of the radical/revolutionary shape-shifters had been destroyed or imprisoned: the Black Panthers imploded; George Jackson was framed and murdered in the Soledad Prison yard; Huey P. Newton was jailed; Eldridge Cleaver had long since escaped to Algeria; . . . Stokely Carmichael had expatriated to Africa; H. Rap Brown was in prison; Assata Shakur . . . was jailed."[65] In this light, one can see why Giovanni would seek to "protect" Franklin from "the way we are killing her" but also to have the first word on how she should be remembered. Through her artful textualization of oral and musical effects, Giovanni creates a preemptive and proto-memorial for Franklin and constructs her own early authority.

"Change": Franklin's Signature Tribute

"Poem for Aretha" attunes us not only to the political valence of Franklin's music but also, as I have said, to the processes through which Franklin creates her own signature voice. We hear these processes clearly in her version of "A Change Is Gonna Come." Recorded three years after Sam Cooke's mystifying death in a Los Angeles motel, Franklin's "Change" is an elegy for Cooke, who was one of her idols (as well as a love interest); a political statement that witnesses and affirms Cooke's own; and a story about assuming one's voice through the process of apprenticeship. Michael Awkward notes that Franklin often asserts her own artistic authority, or "regal sonic presence," by covering songs associated with other artists.[66] Her tribute to Cooke is a moving instance of this practice. At a moment when Cooke's song is on the verge of becoming a standard—Otis Redding had recorded it in 1965—Franklin's rendition of "Change" has the effect Shane Vogel describes: "the song takes on another meaning of standard—that of a banner by which one announces her advance."[67] I have suggested that Giovanni both pays tribute to Franklin and authorizes her own poetic account by revising a prior textual tradition and "textualizing" speech and musical effects. Similarly, Franklin both memorializes Cooke and establishes her own authoritative performance of his song by "speechifying" and otherwise interpolating the song text in her own way. Franklin's interpretive strategies, drawn from the gospel tradition, express her belonging in a specific musical community, while also displaying her distinctive use of communal techniques. Like Giovanni's "teachin-rappin" style, these expressive practices render Franklin's performance at once relatable and phenomenal.

Franklin's version of "Change," in which she accompanies herself on piano, begins with a short prelude: "There's an old friend that I once heard say / something that touched my heart, / and it began this way."[68] This setup seems like a corny show-tune convention. But when Franklin launches into the first line of the song, "I was born," with a beautifully dramatic ornamentation around the word "born," we know that a tour de force is on the way. Because of this introduction, as well as the "he saids" which Franklin interjects into the lyrics ("he said, 'it's been a long time coming'"), Matt Dobkin claims that Franklin creates a "meta-song" that depoliticizes Cooke's protest song. According to Dobkin, Franklin's "Change" is a personal tribute that finally allows Franklin to identify with her idol: "In effect, the song is Aretha's artistic opportunity to *become* Sam Cooke, which in a sense had been her crossover goal all along."[69] A comparison of Cooke's and Franklin's recordings makes this interpretation untenable.

While Franklin follows Cooke's lead in omitting the song's most topically political verse—"I go to the movie, and I go downtown, / somebody keep telling me, 'Don't hang around'"[70]—it is not the case that she creates a metaversion of "Change" that renders it a mere personal tribute. Nor is it true that Franklin's framing narrative subordinates her version to Cooke's. On the contrary, Franklin's decision to begin with the pretext of ventriloquizing Cooke dramatizes the process by which she makes the song her own. She performs this "changing of the guard" when she feminizes the narrator: "I went to my brother, / And I asked him, 'Brother, could you help me please?' / He said, 'Good sister, I'd like to but I'm not able . . .'" Franklin's "good sister" is all the more meaningful because the phrase is an addition, not a substitution; Cooke's interlocutor does not say anything in response to the request for help. This new "sister" marks the point where Franklin ingeniously assumes the "I" of the song. This is *not* what Cooke "said," and indeed Franklin ceases to interject "he said" into the lyrics from this point on. It is fitting that Franklin performs this changeover in the bridge of the song, the peak of musical tension and drama before the last verse. This makes the bridge not only a point of musical departure or variation but also a place of passing over and through, from Cooke's song to Franklin's version thereof.

Franklin stakes her claim to "Change" not only by literally revising the lyrics but also by interpreting them in her own style. When Giovanni makes her case for Franklin's "genius," she tells Margaret Walker, "Just listen to what the woman can do with a *line*."[71] One thing Franklin consistently "does with a line" is to sing the song text like it would be spoken.

As Lara Pellegrinelli writes, "Speechifying song is like vernaculariz-ing language: putting one's own stamp on it, making it like one's own speech."[72] This practice bespeaks Franklin's roots in the black Baptist church, the primary source of her vocal art and, as my discussion of black religious music in chapter 2 will have indicated, a rich and complex artis-tic terrain. Franklin herself has called the church "a testing ground for [her] as a singer" and has frequently said she "never left" it: "The church goes with me."[73] Indeed, when ethnomusicologist Pearl Williams-Jones explains that one of the "basic sources from which gospel singing has derived its aesthetic ideals" is "the rhetorical solo style of the black gospel preacher," she cites Franklin as an exemplar of this speech-song con-tinuum.[74] But while Franklin's use of this technique implies, as Dionne Warwick states, that in "everything that [Franklin] does, she still carries forth her gospel training," Franklin's "speechification" of a song text also allows her to advance her own signature voice, to "[put] her own stamp" on a song.[75]

On the broadest level and in virtually all of her songs, Franklin exploits the relationship between speaking and singing through her use of a vocal register known as the chest voice. The chest voice is the deeper register that uses thicker vocal chords and is associated with con-tralto, tenor, and bass ranges. It is distinguished from the head voice, the higher register that engages thinner vocal folds and is associated with soprano and falsetto singing. Especially in gospel and popular music, an impressive range is often determined by the range of upper-octave notes a singer is able to sing (or to "belt") without shifting from the chest to the head voice. One of the most striking things about Franklin's vocal art is the range she displays in this register—one aspect of what Heilbut calls Franklin's "pyrotechnique."[76] Erik Leidal explains it insightfully: "The power in Aretha's voice results from her ability to carry up enough 'weight'—a vocal term that is used to describe the depth of tone in one's chest voice—to a stunning height, where pitches can still be well-sung and sustained. Few other singers have achieved this so well in any genre: it is a feat of nature in itself, a training that requires conditioning and maturity, as well as a certain amount of raw talent."[77] While Franklin's range sets her apart, her use of the chest voice itself unites her with oth-ers, because this is the register in which most people speak. Franklin's singing stays unusually close to speech registers—closer than singers with a less extensive chest voice range, who must shift into their head voices to reach the notes she reaches, and certainly closer than soprano and falsetto singers, who work primarily in their upper range. Her contralto singing thus produces a curious form of what we might call audio-sympathy: we are at home speaking in this range, but very few people can sing in it (well or otherwise).

To track Franklin's speechification of song on a more local, detailed level, we might first listen to the way she sings the line "And I asked him, 'Brother, can you help me please?'" Adding a caesura before the word "brother," she sings the first syllable at the outer limit of her range and then lets the word fall, as if calling to someone. The entire coda, in which Franklin "takes the song to church" against the ostinato pattern of Spooner Oldham's organ, is a heady display of such speechlike effects. Listen, for example, to Franklin's use of melisma to stress and stretch the word "real": "Yeah, it's been an uphill journey! . . . It's been *real* hard, every step of the way!" For another example of this technique, we might listen to the second verse of "I Never Loved a Man" (1967), in which Franklin sings, "The way you treat me is a shame / How could you hurt me so bad?"[78] The first line descends, but the next one jumps the octave to "how could you"—stressing the "could" and bending it upward. Here Franklin mimics a speech pattern in order to express a sudden outrage, as if the force of the insult had just been borne in on her. This speechifying practice acquires special significance in Franklin's cover of Dionne Warwick's "I Say a Little Prayer" (1968). After riffing on the main theme, Franklin ends the song by singing, "This *is* my prayer!" Her bluesy accentuation of the word "is" italicizes the word and works to suggest that the song as a whole has been her prayer.[79] Here we can see Franklin poignantly navigating her crossover from gospel to soul music, implying that this secular love song is its own form of sacred expression. At the same time, technically speaking, the way Franklin strains toward that note on "is" affirms her place in the gospel tradition. As Warwick explains, "We call it 'squalling,' when Aretha reaches for a note to express a feeling—that is very typically gospel."[80]

Finally, we can hear Franklin's speechifying gospel aesthetic in her maximalist approach to a song text. She adds several new lyrics into "Change," using her outstanding musical and poetic sensibility to create the illusion of everyday speech. Giovanni's poetic enjambment, in which the ending of each printed line leads inexorably toward the next, attunes us to Franklin's analogous creation of lyrical flow—a practice that dramatically distinguishes her version of "Change" from Cooke's. Whereas Cooke leaves a notable amount of space around each lyrical statement, Franklin fills in all the gaps; she thus emphasizes the song's rolling 6/8 time signature and makes the song *move* in a way that Cooke's characteristically cool, unhurried version does not. The change is gradual, however. In the first verse, Franklin follows Cooke's version virtually word for word, even pronouncing "I've been running every since" just like Cooke does. But she increasingly interpolates the song text as she proceeds, so that by the time she gets to the bridge, she is singing *twice* as many lyrics as Cooke sings in that part of the song. She manages to fit new words into the song's structure by performing a kind of rhythmic and harmonic enjambment whereby each repeated phrase leads directly to the next. Listen to how differently Cooke and Franklin perform the moment when the brother refuses the speaker aid. In the same amount of musical time, Cooke sings, "But he winds up knocking me / Back down on my knees, Lord!" while Franklin sings, "And when I, when I looked around, I was right back down, / Down on my bended knees, yes I was, Oh Lord!" This additive process escalates until Franklin is ad-libbing whole extra choruses at the end of the song. One of her more extraordinary embellishments in this section begins with a seemingly unmotivated "sometimes." The word seems to come out of nowhere, an isolated adverb akin to Giovanni's "certainly" that Franklin harmonically suspends over Oldham's wheeling organ pattern, before completing the thought:

> Sometimes! . . . I've had to cry all night long, yes I did!
> Sometimes! . . . I had to give up right for what I knew was wrong.
> . . . But I believe, I believe, this evening
> A change has come . . .

Franklin's use of the past tense in this concluding section marks another revision to Cooke's lyrics, as Cooke consistently sings "a change is *gonna* come." The revision makes sense, however, to the extent that Franklin marks the musical changeover she has performed—an ending that resonates with Giovanni's own self-reflexive closing gesture ("why don't we think about it") in "Poem for Aretha."

Ultimately, Franklin's performance of "Change" both elegizes Cooke and extends the political legacy of his song through her own voice. We hear this political legacy not only in the song's lyrics but also in Franklin's introduction, which, theatrical as it may seem, frames her recording as an act of public mourning. In 1967, the very gesture of publicly mourning black life is a political statement. If Giovanni's "Poem for Aretha" responds to the musical and political losses black America had suffered by 1970, Franklin's "Change" emphasizes that these iconic losses were *intimately* experienced. Indeed, Franklin's decision to "surrogate"

by the US men was that I needed to redirect my energies and use them to give my man strength and inspiration so that he might more effectively contribute his talents to the struggle for Black liberation."[84]

Yet "Dreams" both evokes this narrative and also overturns it, for when Giovanni's speaker voices her desire to be "a sweet inspiration," she alludes to another popular female vocal group, the Sweet Inspirations. Though the group's membership changed several times, the most famous Sweet Inspirations lineup featured Sylvia Shemwell, Estelle Brown, Myrna Smith, and Cissy Houston, who formed the group about five years after her 1957 gospel appearance at Newport, noted in chapter 2. Among the stars the Sweet Inspirations backed up were Otis Redding, Solomon Burke, Dusty Springfield, and, when it came time to record her 1975 spoken-word album *The Way I Feel*, Nikki Giovanni.[85] However, the group was perhaps best known for backing up Franklin. Hence, Giovanni's poem implicitly moves from Ray Charles's backup singers to Franklin's, and this movement records the course of popular music history: while Charles was among the first artists to bring the gospel sound into the pop mainstream, Franklin followed his lead. (As Craig Werner writes, "Ray Charles had laid the track; Aretha rolled into the station.")[86] Indeed, in the late 1960s, Franklin herself would record both of the Charles songs that Giovanni cites here ("Drown in My Own Tears" [1967] and "The Right Time" [1968]), and her backup singers for the second would be the Sweet Inspirations. Giovanni's decision to end with singers best known for backing up Franklin, then, fully reroutes the story of women settling down to the task of inspiring men. In its movement from Charles's backup singers to Franklin's, "Dreams" becomes an homage to black women singers who back up *other black women*.[87]

Giovanni candidly subverts conventional narrative here, but she also—and more subtly—eschews expectations regarding transparent transcription of speech and song by foregrounding the materiality of the poetic text. We might note, first, that even her phonetic spelling of the "raelets" and "margery hendricks" relies on the sight of words to activate the aural dimension of language, and thus can only be performed in print. These phonetic representations also create new meanings. For instance, Giovanni's half-right, half-wrong spelling of the word "Raelette" re-genders the word. She subverts the feminine ending "-ette," but without masculinizing the word as she might have had she opted for the more phonetically predictable "ray." Her "transcription" of the singers' lyrics is similarly creative; indeed, it cannot properly be called a transcription. For one, when Giovanni renders Hendricks's interlude on this song, she elongates the "baaaaa" of Hendricks's "baby," suggesting a melisma on the first syllable of that word; in the song itself, however, Hendricks performs her virtuosic shiver of a four-note run on the second syllable, not the first.[88] Giovanni's departure from recorded sound indicates that she is creating what Meta Jones might call a "textually specific resonance" as she spatializes the singers' lyrics on the page.[89] For example, when Giovanni writes the lyrics "drowned" and "talking," she gives us a "dr" in the first lyrical line and a "king" in the last. She thus invites us to consider that this poem, dated six months after Martin Luther King's assassination and following a poem titled "Reflections on April 4, 1968," alludes to King's "I Have a Dream" speech in its evocation of a moment "before I learned black people aren't suppose to dream."[90]

So while it seems that Giovanni is voicing the poet's desire to be a singer here, "Dreams" also displays the poet's ability to create new meanings by rendering musical sounds on the page. To be sure, the poem partly depends on the reader's *"memory of a specific song or passage of a song,"* as Henderson claims of the "New Black poetry."[91] But an interpretive opportunity arises from the *difference* between remembered or recorded musical sound and poetic re-creation. In this sense, it is imperative that what Henry Louis Gates Jr. would call Giovanni's "talking book" does *not* talk. When Giovanni titles her first collection of poetry *Black Feeling, Black Talk*, she signals the "talk" her work represents but also the talk it seeks to elicit—and not only in the literal form of oral performance, as Neal and Henderson would have it, but also in the figurative form of interpretation. Again, the poem is both record and score, tribute and preface. While "Dreams" certainly pays homage to musical figures like the Raelettes and the Sweet Inspirations, it also works to elicit a unique imaginative response on the part of the reader.

For this reason, Giovanni does not display the "obeisance to black music" which Clarke claims is characteristic of Black Arts poets.[92] But nor does Sonia Sanchez, when she writes "—a poem for nina simone to put some music to and blow our nigguh / minds—" (1970).[93] Nor does Sherley Anne Williams, when she writes "I Want Aretha to Set This to Music" (1982), a poem that offers "verses" one has to imagine Franklin singing.[94] We might think, too, of Giovanni's poem "The Way I Feel" (1975), in which the speaker tells her lover, "most time when you're around / i feel like a note / roberta flack is going to sing."[95] These poems and citations are compelling because they make the reader *imagine* what this poetic music might sound like. They make us read more inventively than we'd have to if these called-for songs already existed.

FIGURE 10. Aretha Franklin and singers in Palermo, Italy, 1970. Photo by Jan Persson / Redferns / Getty Images.

Backup: The Musical Text of "Respect"

To highlight the textually specific "trace" of Martin Luther King in "Dreams" is to glean this subtle yet specific political point: that the Civil Rights Movement itself had been driven by ostensibly "supporting" figures ("movements create leaders," in Giovanni's words), and that these figures might therefore sustain the movement even after King's death. Franklin herself, like her father, was one such supporting figure, whose centrality to the movement Dick Gregory expressed by saying that he "could hear Aretha in the sixties three or four times an hour, where [he] never heard [Martin Luther] King except on the news."[96] But by naming the Raelettes and the Sweet Inspirations, Giovanni also turns the spotlight on the artists behind stars like Franklin. She redefines backup singers as leaders in their own right—important enough to change the whole sound of a song and iconic enough to inspire a young girl's dreams. (Her speaker wants to be a Raelette, not Ray Charles.) In this sense, "Dreams" prompts attention to backup singers' own musical power.

We might start with the moment Giovanni centralizes in "Dreams," Hendricks's short interlude in "The Right Time." The surprise of Hendricks's gravelly timbre executing pitch-perfect runs, combined with the sense that her delivery is rather *too* fierce for the rest of the song, makes her solo the track's most striking moment. Charles seems to acknowledge this when, in his 1958 Atlantic recording of the song, he prefaces Hendricks's interlude by saying, "Woah! Sing your song, Margie." (In this moment, Charles, like Giovanni, defies what John Corbett calls the requirement that the background singer remain "nameless.")[97] Charles proceeds to sing backup for Hendricks, and for a few choruses, "The Right Time" *does* become her song. While Franklin's singers do not assume center stage in this way, Giovanni's focus on backup vocalists attunes us to the crucial role they play in Franklin's work. These singers engage listeners by inviting them to join in the dialogue or to back Franklin up along with them. So whereas Giovanni calls for readerly participation through her inventive evocation of musical sound, Franklin calls for participation by modeling the sound of collectivity within a song itself. Her ensembles help her advance a signature voice that is distinctive—*if you hear this song, you'll know it's Franklin*—but not individualistic.

The singers on Franklin's cover of Otis Redding's "Respect" are her sisters, Erma and Carolyn Franklin. Before analyzing their revisions of the song's story line and text, I should point out that Franklin's decision to record "Respect" two years after the "King of Soul" had released it was in some ways a bolder move than her decision to record "Change"—in part because Redding, a formidable genius in his own right, was still alive. (Upon hearing Franklin's version, Redding is famously reported to have said, "I just lost my song. . . . That girl took it away from me."[98] He was kidding, but prescient.) Franklin's "Respect" was more coup than tribute—a means of asserting her identity as the "Queen of Soul" to Redding's king.

Franklin's lyrical revisions were one important part of this procedure. Redding's song essentially establishes a relationship between a sugar daddy and the woman he comes home to: "Oh, your kisses are sweeter than honey, and I'm about to give you all my money." The economics of this trade—the fact that the speaker is giving the woman all these things in *exchange* for sex—is indicated by the couplet form, which rhymes "honey" with "money." The premise of the song, however, is that sweeter-than-honey kisses are not sufficient repayment for the man's material gifts: he also wants respect "when [he] get[s] home." Indeed, his need for it only increases as the song fades out: "Respect is what I want, respect is what I need. . . . Got to, got to have it!"[99] Franklin gives her speaker a new degree of economic and emotional autonomy.[100] While Redding's speaker comes home (ostensibly, from work), Franklin's speaker stays home. But in a turn that her location in the home does not explain, she becomes the one with the money. She sings, "Ooh, your kisses / are sweeter than honey / But guess what? / So is my money!" The "guess what," Franklin's own addition, punctuates her revision of the song's sexual economy, as does her change in rhythm: she stresses all three words of the triplet, "*so is my,*" before landing on "money." Thanks to such revisions, Franklin's cover version was widely embraced as an anthem of black power, and more specifically of black female power, upon its release. As I have noted, Franklin herself was pleased to call "Respect" "a battle cry." As Giovanni recalls, "'Respect' came out, and it was like, 'Oh my God, Aretha's covering Otis.' . . . I could not get to the record store fast enough to get that album. . . . Everybody started to say, 'Did you hear what she *did*?' Everybody started to analyze that album."[101]

Even before assessing Franklin's lyrical revisions, Giovanni's contemporaries would likely have been struck by the fact that Franklin had changed the whole sound of the song. Her version dramatically departs from Redding's in terms of its musical arrangement, not least because Franklin makes backup vocalists a central part of the song. (There is no comparison between her singers' elaborate lines and the muted backing "hey hey heys" on Redding's track.) Franklin announces this particular innovation immediately, as the very first vocal sound we hear on her track is the backup singers' "woo!" Carolyn and Erma's presence on the song creates a productive sonic tension between soloist and group. On the one hand, the singers' tightly composed backup lines—which Franklin wrote herself and on which she "drill[ed] her singers to perfection"— create the musical framework through which Franklin's lead vocals can shine.[102] The backup singers function similarly to the gospel chorus Leidal describes in his reading of "Mary Don't You Weep" (1972): they "create the place out of which Aretha may rise," "a safe place to signify."[103] But in addition to providing the setting for Franklin's stellar lead vocals, Erma and Carolyn Franklin also open "Respect" to other voices—and not only because of their participation in the song but because of the range in which they sing. That is, while Aretha's belting range, as I have said, marks the outer limits of vocal possibility, Erma and Carolyn work in a more conventional range. This in itself makes the song more "available" to others: while listeners may not be able to sing along with Franklin's main line, they are more likely to be able to sing in the backup singers' range—though it should be said that the average listener would be hard-pressed to match the harmonic and rhythmic precision with which these backup singers perform.

I have shown how Giovanni manipulates a sonic text, for instance by spatializing the Raelettes' lyrics on the page, to engender new meanings. She attunes us to the analogous and equally significant work that Franklin and her backup singers perform in this regard. They parse the lyrics of Redding's song into new harmonic segments, such as a rolling "ree-ree" pattern. They also embellish the original song text by adding a revolving "sock it to me" line—an innovation for which Aretha often shares credit with Carolyn.[104] Finally, of course, Franklin breaks down, or re-spatializes, the text of the title itself (another thing Redding does not do) by singing each letter: "R-E-S-P-E-C-T." As Franklin has wryly noted, "I thought I should spell it out."[105] The "ree-ree" pattern the backup singers add is also important, because it affirms Franklin's appropriation of Redding's song. First, if we think of the "re-" as a prefix, we might hear the singers stressing the extent to which they are remaking, or re-creating, this song. But the "ree-ree" lyric makes the song Franklin's own in a more literal way: in the backup singers' hands, "Respect," the name of the song, becomes "Ree," Franklin's nickname (alternately, "Re Re"). Hence, through this "ree" pattern, Erma and Carolyn make the song synonymous with Aretha herself.

However, while the singers may be heard to voice sisterly support of Franklin's self-assertion, they also *complicate* Franklin's own call for "respect" by asking for "just a little bit" of it.[106] As if preparing for the likelihood that the addressee will not be able to deliver the major respect that Franklin herself demands, the backup singers offer to settle for less. Then again, their charming plea for "just a little bit" may be designed to help them get what they want. It's hard to tell whether the phrase signals a moment of antifeminist accommodation or a savvy strategy of male manipulation. But what *is* clear is that the "just a little bit" establishes the song's groove and propels its momentum. In this section, Franklin's vocals accent the first beat of each measure, and the backup singers jump in on the second beat and drive the measure home. In other words, the conciliatory request for "just a little bit" of respect and the big demand for it are both crucial parts of the song's sonic movement. So if "Respect" is a "battle cry," it is a cry voiced by a number of women, who all contribute something different and even contradictory to its advancement.

These women sound like they are getting along, though they are not saying the same thing.

That the song thrives on, is animated by, apparent contradictions, also becomes clear when we raise the common question of what exactly the singers mean by "whip it to me" and "sock it to me." Are they asking for sex or respect?[107] The song refuses to resolve that question, deeming the choice a false one. "Indeterminacy" is not quite the right word here because, like Mahalia Jackson's and Ralph Ellison's sincerely double-voiced utterances, "Respect" constitutes and demands a space in which both sex and respect can be requested without any cognitive dissonance; it creates a space in which "I want you to come home and sock it to me" is fully compatible with "I want your respect." As Atlantic producer Jerry Wexler suggests, for Franklin, "respect" meant what Redding had meant by it—"regard for another's welfare"—and it also meant "sexual attention of the highest order."[108] Collaging and combining these seemingly disparate ideas, the Franklins make "Respect" not a straight-ahead anthem of women's liberation but rather a record of the different positions and tones that make a hybrid movement move.[109]

The Franklins' re-creation of "Respect" thus compels us to ask who is included in the category of "black woman" that Giovanni herself not only celebrates but also discursively purports to represent in this era—for instance, in "My Poem" (1968), in which (as Phillip Brian Harper notes) she calls herself "black female poet."[110] If we take Franklin and her backup singers at their word, this category must include both those who would issue a big demand for respect and those who would request just a little bit of it. For that matter, it must include black men and women seeking same-sex love and respect—a gay community that has long supported and been supported by Franklin.[111] At a moment when, as Clarke notes, many black people felt anxiety about being "outside of the circle," or on its margins—i.e., not black enough to be part of the revolutionary moment— "Respect" may be most radical in spurning standard ideas about who counts as "authentic" members of the group and thus in expanding the "inner circle" that Giovanni's own work from this period imagines.[112]

Having centralized this formal Black Arts conversation "between women," I want to briefly expand the circle of my own analyses to consider some of Franklin's and Giovanni's contemporaries. While statements such as Baraka's claim that Black Arts poets wanted their poetry "to be black music" or Neal's declaration that "the key is in the music" can appear to represent the literary ambitions of a diverse group of writers, it is misleading to regard those statements as fact—or, indeed, as synonymous with the work of poetry. That view obscures other effects of Black Arts poets' engagements with music. Giovanni's work indicates that, in addition to scoring such collective rituals as Neal and Henderson invoke and prompting the reader's oral performance, as Kimberly Benston incisively notes, Black Arts poems also function as signature scores for future listening and writing.[113] When poets creatively translate free jazz (then called "the new thing"), they are striving to *make* this unpopular music a populist form—to make it the sound of a people's revolution. We find this generative literary activity even in those works that seem to most poignantly subordinate poetry to a lost music: elegies to the hero-saint of the Black Arts Movement, John Coltrane.

We might turn, for example, to Michael S. Harper's "Dear John, Dear Coltrane" (1970). As Giovanni does in "Poem for Aretha," Harper creates a deeply humanized image of Coltrane—"So sick / you couldn't play *Naima*, / so flat we ached for song you'd concealed / with your own blood"—and a mythic image of Coltrane as a Christ figure. Harper also advances his own poetic portrayal of Coltrane's music. He makes a refrain of "a love supreme," echoing the chant Coltrane performs in the first movement of his landmark 1965 suite. But Harper also creates a four-part structure that mirrors the four movements of Coltrane's masterpiece. When Harper's third stanza shifts into short lines that stage a quick call-and-response—"*Why you so black? / cause I am / why you so funky? / cause I am*"—this section provides readers and listeners with a linguistic way to apprehend the up-tempo third movement of "A Love Supreme" itself, which is entitled "Pursuance."[114]

Sonia Sanchez similarly reinvents Coltrane's music in "a/coltrane/ poem," also from 1970. Here Sanchez depicts potentially mystifying horn sounds such as Coltrane's "scrEEEccCHHHHH screeeeEEECH-HHHHHH."[115] But she also makes such "out" sounds legible—if more alarming—when she associates them with, among other things, the dying screams of

MAIN/LINE/ASS/RISTOCRATS (ALL
THEM SO-CALLED BEAUTIFUL
PEOPLE)
    WHO HAVE KILLED
WILL CONTINUE TO
        KILL US WITH
THEY CAPITALISM/18% OWNERSHIP
OF THE WORLD.[116]

Through an act of interpretive listening akin to Baldwin's accounts of black music, Sanchez figures Coltrane's music as both call and counter-call, both white shrieks and black songs of redemption. The following passage offers lyrics to accompany the (wordless) melody of Coltrane's version of "My Favorite Things" (1960):

```
(to be     rise up blk/people
sung              de dum da da da da
slowly     move straight in yo/blkness
to tune           da dum da da da da
of my      step over the wite/ness
favorite   that is yesssss terrrrrr day
things.)   weeeeeeee are tooooooooday.117
```

In one sense, as James Smethurst points out, the poem works more effectively as a tribute to Coltrane on the page than it would in performance: the poem's two adjacent columns better represent the simultaneity of Coltrane's quartet and Coltrane's own simultaneous production of different notes (multiphonics) than would any single reader who took the poem as a score to perform.[118] On an even more basic level, we can see that Sanchez uses poetry to re-create Coltrane's "My Favorite Things" in her own image, just as Coltrane himself revised the original show tune. In so doing, she hints at one reason why Giovanni's contemporaries might have preferred wordless jazz to soul music: not only may the former have seemed more resistant to white appropriation, but it also gave writers more room to invent their own literary music, to advance their own signature voices. *If you hear my poem you'll know it's me.* One would not confuse Sanchez's Coltrane with Harper's.

Insofar as these poems supplement or enhance the experience of listening to Coltrane's music, they make the implicit argument *not* that Coltrane's music exceeds poetry but that it is too complex and sacred to go without saying—to go, that is, without literary mediation. Neither of these poets creates the final word on Coltrane's music. Instead, they engender a conversation, in the form of what eventually becomes a subgenre of contemporary African American literature: the Coltrane poem. If Black Arts poets sought to dispel the vision of free jazz as an abstract art form divorced from black people, the continued popularity of the Coltrane poem suggests that, at least as far as the poets are concerned, they succeeded.[119]

Spirits in the Dark

Since the Black Arts era, Franklin has acquired a reputation for public reserve a bit like that of Gayl Jones. She rarely grants interviews and even more rarely discusses her personal life. Her 1999 memoir is "singularly unrevealing."[120] Perhaps we should not be surprised to realize that, as Franklin has receded from the public eye, Giovanni has emerged as a key spokeswoman for her, especially in the past decade. If Franklin does not say much for herself, Giovanni says a great deal on her behalf, contributing comments about Franklin's music and cultural significance (as well as her authoritative imprimatur) to projects such as Dobkin's 2004 book on the making of *I Never Loved a Man*. Giovanni's foreword to that book is especially important because there she writes about one aspect of Franklin's signature sound that descriptions of vocal practices don't quite capture: the *timbre* of her voice. In so doing, Giovanni performs an act similar to those writers who represent Coltrane's supposedly ineffable wordless music. She implicitly rejects the cliché that Franklin's voice "defies description" and refuses to reserve her depiction of Franklin's voice, as is common, for the genre of elegy.[121] Instead of claiming her writing to be overwhelmed by Franklin's voice, she uses her writing to back Franklin up—and, as poet Linda Susan Jackson says of her own tributes to Etta James, to "give her her flowers while she is [still] alive."[122]

We have seen several commentators describe the sounds of other singers in this book. Among those who have memorably described Bessie Smith's vocal quality and style are Alberta Hunter ("there was a kind of tear in her voice") and James Baldwin ("the *fantastic* understatement"). A considerable amount of writerly energy has been channeled toward describing Billie Holiday's voice, of which Rita Dove and Leon Forrest write compelling accounts. Ellison may be the finest recorder of Jackson's singing voice, though Anthony Heilbut also skillfully evokes her techniques—for instance, her tendency to activate a "disembodied soprano" to produce "a weird, ethereal sound."[123] When it comes to writing about Franklin's sound, however, critics whose profession it is to write about music continually profess themselves at a linguistic loss. Robert Christgau writes that the force of Franklin's singing "is so ineffable that no one has ever satisfactorily described it in words."[124] Even as Nelson George admits that "'intangible' is a word that music critics overuse daily," he writes that "Franklin's voice communicated so wide a range of emotion as to truly defy description."[125] Critics frame their own descriptive failure as a sign of respect and even reverence. Hence, musicologists Charles

Keil and Steven Feld title their exchange about why neither of them has yet written about Franklin "Respecting Aretha," and Dobkin asks, "How can one properly put into words something so mystical, so spiritual, as Aretha's voice . . . ?"[126] As noted in chapter 4, one effect of supernaturalizing the female singer's voice is to foreclose response to it. We see that problem here.

But critics will break the silence when it comes time to elegize Franklin. Indeed, most of the descriptions I have cited—of Smith and Holiday, especially—have been written after these singers have passed on. Perhaps writers reserve their portrayals of singers' voices for elegies because these voices change over time. Franklin's sound on recordings of the 1960s is not her sound today, so the question is not only, how does one describe her voice? but also, which voice does one describe? And further, how does one account for its changes? It is generally a singer's death that moves writers to explain such changes, as elegiac accounts of Holiday's voice attest. Yet Giovanni's work is instructive because it does not figure music as a prior power that the poet gestures nostalgically back to; instead, it apprehends music as a force that the poet co-creates in time—and, in "Poem for Aretha," memorializes ahead of time.

Fittingly, given the notion of the singular *and* plural signature voice I have proposed, Giovanni figures Franklin's inimitable vocal quality as the product of women's collective work. Female ancestral care and the domestic rituals of eating are the two main elements to which Giovanni imaginatively attributes Franklin's vocal sound. As she writes,

Maybe [Aretha] caught a cold when she was an infant and her mother or grandmother rubbed her chest with oil of cloves. Something like that must have given her voice that smoldering quality. Maybe it was the jowl bacon in the pinto beans with a side of cold water corn bread, or maybe fried fish with hush puppies. There had to be okra 'cause she lived with Mahalia Jackson, so there must have been stewed okra with tomatoes or just good old collard greens with a splash of hot vinegar. Fried chicken. . . . Try Matty's, she said [in her hit song about the restaurant]. And we all did.[127]

Here Giovanni creates a kind of down-home genesis story in which maternal care and healing produce Franklin's vocal timbre, "that smoldering quality." In the process, she restores maternal presence to the famously "motherless" Franklin. Franklin's mother, Barbara Siggers Franklin, a gifted pianist and singer in her own right, separated from Clarence Franklin when Aretha was young and died of a heart attack shortly thereafter. Giovanni redresses this loss by imagining multiple mothers for Franklin: grandmother, mother, Jackson. While Franklin did not "live with" Mahalia Jackson, Jackson was a frequent visitor to the Franklins' home. She was there because of C. L. Franklin, whom Giovanni strategically absents from the scene in order to create a wholly female space.

In another remarkable move, Giovanni eschews the expectation that Jackson's presence will be significant for what it might teach Franklin about singing. There is no training in this narrative, no mentorship. Instead, Giovanni implies that Franklin's voice is as natural as eating and as culturally specific as choosing to eat foods like jowl bacon and cornbread. In this sense, her account follows the long discursive tradition of naturalizing black women's vocal art that I have challenged throughout this book. While she sustains some myths I have aimed to dispel, however, Giovanni also creates new myths that may be useful: she invites us to hear the black woman's singing voice as a product and force of female nurturance and connection.

Giovanni extends this woman-oriented vision of black music in a particularly beautiful moment of a conversation with Claudia Tate. Here she creates an alternative history of black music in order to underscore black women's voices and to picture them calling for each other. This image of music does not grant it priority over writing, although it can, as Giovanni indicates, inform our understanding of her poetry. Speaking about her 1978 collection, *Cotton Candy on a Rainy Day*, she tells Tate,

> If you look through [this collection], you'll hear a lot of music. 'Cause if you're in trouble, you don't whistle a happy tune and hold your head erect. You hummm. You hum a basic gospel tune. Can you imagine what a slave ship must have sounded like? Imagine what a slave ship must have sounded like to the women. All the slave-ship stories we've heard so far have been from men. All the men heard was the agony of the men. That's valid. But just imagine what a slave ship must have sounded like to a woman. The humming must have been deafening. It had to be there. . . . The men didn't bring it over. I'm not knocking the men. They brought the drums for sure. But they didn't bring the hum. . . . We women were the ones in the fields in Africa. . . . Black men were out hunting in Africa, but in America they were in the fields with the women. [That's where] they learned the [hum,] from [the] women. So what

you're hearing in our music is nothing but the sound of a woman calling another woman.[128]

These comments echo a remark that Baldwin makes in his 1973 conversation with Giovanni. But Giovanni changes that remark in an important way. Baldwin had said, "When you're in trouble—When I'm in trouble I do not sing a Doris Day [song] or a Tin Pan Alley tune. You find yourself humming and moaning something."[129] Like Baldwin, Giovanni racializes the hum (setting it against the upbeat tunes implicitly coded as white), but she claims it specifically for black women. In so doing, she creates a dialogue not only with Baldwin but also with the work of Mari Evans. In "I Am a Black Woman" (1970), Evans writes,

I am a Black woman
the music of my song
some sweet arpeggio of tears
is written in a minor key
and I
can be heard humming in the night
Can be heard
humming
in the night.[130]

Like Evans, Giovanni genders humming as a female practice. But she figures the hum not only as an expression of suffering—"some sweet arpeggio of tears"—but also as a sign of reciprocal female support.

This woman-oriented vision of black song attunes us, finally, to one last aspect of Franklin's work: her performative identity as a woman singing to—and especially with—other women. Citing songs such as "Ladies Only" (1979) and her appearances on shows like *The View* and *Oprah Winfrey*, Heilbut calls Franklin "the greatest example of a woman singing to other women."[131] I would place her more in a *tradition* of women singing to other women that stretches back to the advice songs of Bessie Smith. (To recall "Empty Bed Blues," "When you get good lovin', never go and spread the news . . .") But what makes Franklin unique, among the singers in this book, is her commitment to singing *with* other women. Her contribution to American music is decidedly female in this regard. We hear this not only in songs like "Respect," "The Thrill Is Gone" (1970), and "Didn't I (Blow Your Mind This Time)" (1972), in which female backup singers voice a girl-group-style support of Franklin as she confronts a man. In this era, Franklin also uses women singers on the upbeat love song "You're All I Need to Get By" (1971), which is originally a male-female duet but which Franklin takes as a solo with female backing vocals (while gamely invoking her earlier all-girl coup with a line that is itself a rhythmic feat: "We got our love and some R-E-S-P-E-C-T, oh!"). We may consider Franklin's decision to absent that song's male presence alongside Giovanni's vision of a C. L. Franklin–less household. While Franklin's singers may address a beloved located outside the song who is "all [they] need to get by," they may just as well be heard to serenade each other.

Perhaps even more striking is Franklin's decision to use *only* female singers, rather than a mix of men and women, on non-romantic songs such as her cover of Nina Simone's "Young, Gifted and Black" (1972) and her gospel anthem "Spirit in the Dark" (1970). There is no readily apparent (that is, conventional) reason for this. "Spirit in the Dark," for instance, which Franklin composed, does not gather a group of women against (or for) a male addressee. On the contrary, the song stages a scene of worship in which men are democratically recognized right alongside women: "Tell me Sister, how do you feel? Tell me, my brother, brother, brother, how do you feel?"[132] But women lead the mixed-gender celebration the song conjures. Insofar as the spirit they celebrate also denotes "sexual ecstasy," as E. Patrick Johnson contends, the song's political project is to conceive a holistic black joy.[133] This song joins the contemporary effort to sanctify darkness, hailing an erotic *religious* spirit best experienced "in the dark" alongside the black magic reclaimed by a movement that called itself Black Arts. Giovanni invites us to hear black women supporting each other in this endeavor—not exclusively, but especially. Like Giovanni's hum, and her writings on Franklin, these songs become a way for black women to say to each other, *I am here with you, backing you up.*

Epilogue. "At Last": Etta James, Poetry, Hip Hop

I have focused on the nine artists in this book due to the depth of the writers' engagements with singers; my desire to analyze artists with whom many readers are likely to be familiar and to make some interventions in scholarly conversations about them; my aim to craft a historical narrative that leads up to (and back to) the Black Arts Movement; and, of course, personal preference. However, Nikki Giovanni's attention to the backup singers "behind" the stars also prompts reflection on the many artists behind or beyond the ones this book has featured. As my introductory catalogue of literary allusions to singers will have signaled, there are so many other relationships to explore. What new insights, for example, might Sterling Brown's "Poem for Ma Rainey" (1932) yield about Ma Rainey's music and Brown's own work? How might Sherley Anne Williams's "I Want Aretha to Set This to Music" (1982) attune us to a different aspect of Franklin's aesthetics than does Giovanni, just as Gayl Jones highlights a different aspect of Billie Holiday's art than does James Baldwin?[1] Another study might also have foregrounded the writer who is most obviously present and absent from this one; although Amiri Baraka's poetry or commentary appears in nearly every chapter, I do not perform sustained analyses of Baraka's engagements with women singers such as Sarah Vaughan.[2]

Moreover, as I stated at the outset, I hope this book indicates new directions for analyzing relationships between black musicians and writers even when those musicians are *not* female singers. We might examine book-length collections such as Tyehimba Jess's *leadbelly* (2005) and

Ed Pavlic's *Song for Donny Hathaway* (2008). We might also reverse the equation and analyze musicians' engagements with *writers*. I am thinking, for example, of the fact that Langston Hughes writes the lyrics for Nina Simone's "Backlash Blues" (1967), that Meshell Ndegeocello titles a song after Eldridge Cleaver's 1968 memoir *Soul on Ice* (1993), and that Mos Def and Talib Kweli (Black Star) (re)cite Toni Morrison's extraordinary ending to *The Bluest Eye* (1970) in "Thieves in the Night" (1998).[3] Put simply, beyond the ensemble of artists centralized here, as Giovanni writes in "Poem for Aretha," "there are in fact an abundance / of talents just waiting."[4]

I want to highlight a few such artists here—especially, the brilliant, late Etta James (1938–2012)—while extending the implications of this project to new sites such as the theater of U.S. politics, contemporary African American poetry, and hip hop. Like the writers in this study, black women artists such as poet Linda Susan Jackson and rapper Jean Grae continue to constitute themselves in relation to the classic singers whose legacies they in turn work to revise and revive. This work is always subversive in the context of an amnesiac twenty-first-century culture industry that obscures black antecedents to white neo-soul and R&B artists and privileges young black "postracial" stars over the elders who paved their way—an impulse apparent even in Barack Obama's inaugural ceremonies. Against such amnesiac narratives, contemporary black women artists maintain singers' iconic status in the popular imagination through powerful works that also advance their own signature voices.

Inaugural Songs

As noted in the previous chapter, Aretha Franklin was the featured singer at Obama's 2009 inauguration. While less overtly identified with the Civil Rights Movement than Obama's first choice, the folk singer Odetta, who had passed away earlier that year, Franklin would in retrospect seem like the obvious choice, her appearance reminding anyone who needed reminding that her black feminist anthems and close connection with Martin Luther King Jr. were unshakable Civil Rights credentials that very few living singers could claim. This book's cover image itself reflects that legacy. As noted in the introduction, the photograph captures Franklin's performance at a benefit concert for the Martin Luther King Memorial Fund held at Madison Square Garden in late June 1968. "History would assign her the role of the Last Woman Standing, the most full-throated witness of her parents' generation," Anthony Heilbut writes.[5] And during the week of the inauguration, Franklin would again embrace that representative political role: the night before her appearance at the Capitol building, she interpolated a reference to "the days of Dr. King" into the gospel classic "Precious Memories."[6]

The next day, wearing a coat to keep out the January chill and a gray hat that threatened to steal the show in some viewers' eyes, Franklin sang "My Country 'Tis of Thee."[7] This historic performance is located squarely within the tradition that Farah Jasmine Griffin identifies in her seminal essay "When Malindy Sings" (2004). Here Griffin lists several key moments at which African American women have sung to and for the nation, including Marian Anderson's performance at the Lincoln Memorial in 1939, Mahalia Jackson's performance at the March on Washington in 1963 (and here we might add Jackson's performance of the "Star-Spangled Banner" at John F. Kennedy's inaugural ball in 1961), and Whitney Houston's performance of the "Star-Spangled Banner" at the 1991 Super Bowl during the Gulf War. Griffin contends that such events may foster the illusion that Americans are "one big, unified, biracial family" united under a strong maternal ("mammy") figure—an illusion that is especially desirable in times of national crisis.[8] But in Griffin's view, another potential simultaneously abides in these moments: that the black woman's performance might subvert the dominant narrative and engender transformative understandings of history, community, and collective possibility.

Franklin's performance expressed this subversive potential for several reasons, including her immediate context, historical precedent, and vocal sound. By immediate context, I mean not only the inauguration of America's first black president but more precisely an event that featured other black culture workers like Civil Rights pioneer Reverend James Lowry, who delivered the standout benediction, and poet Elizabeth Alexander, who read her subtle, challenging "Praise Song for the Day." In terms of precedent, Franklin's performance recalled other key occasions at which black women vocalists had sung at the nation's capital: not only Mahalia Jackson's performance at the March on Washington but also Marian Anderson's performance at the Lincoln Memorial, where Anderson appeared after having been barred by the Daughters of the American Revolution from singing at the (integrated) Constitution Hall. Insofar as it evoked these prior moments, Franklin's performance at the U.S. Capitol was the musical analogue to Obama's half-valedictory, half-vindictive statement that the nation was inaugurating "a man whose father less than sixty years ago might not have been served at a local restaurant."⁹ Finally, the *strain* in Franklin's voice told its own subversive story. While still outstanding, her singing voice has been audibly worn by a lifetime of work. What her sound revealed was that, for representatives of the struggle for black liberation and "respect," the journey toward this moment had been long and *laborious*.¹⁰ Franklin's performance did not, then, express the triumphalism or transcendence potentially associated with this event. Instead, her voice itself reminded listeners that, if significant change had come, as she sings at the end of "A Change Is Gonna Come," "It's *sure* been a long way coming! It's been *real* hard, every step of the way!"

Later that evening, however, the spotlight turned to another female singer, Beyoncé Knowles, then age twenty-six. Known by her first (stage) name, as the other singers in this book are called by theirs, Beyoncé is a stellar singer and generally beloved American icon. She was, in some ways, the perfect choice to serenade the president and first lady's first dance at the inaugural ball.¹¹ Wearing a silver satin gown and radiating happiness while singing for the Obamas, Beyoncé performed "At Last," the classic song recorded by Etta James in 1961. In this context, Beyoncé's performance clearly activated the double meanings I have discussed with regard to songs like "Steal Away" and "Move On Up," which express both sacred and social conviction. "At Last" functioned as a love song for the Obamas ("at last, my love has come along, my lonely days are over, and life is like a song"), as well as a paean to Barack Obama, the long-awaited black president, and the Obamas, the long-overdue black first family.

Without diminishing Beyoncé's beautiful performance, I want to highlight what was strange about it: namely, why was Etta James not singing her own song that night?¹² In one respect, the choice of Beyoncé was justified but also made more awkward by the fact that she had recently starred as Etta James in the Chess Records biopic *Cadillac Records* (2008).¹³ Playing a young James on film was one thing; however, singing a song James could have sung herself at this historic event was another—as James's exclusive displeasure with the latter made clear.¹⁴ Quite apart from the film, though, the salient issue was that Beyoncé, as an icon of the post–Civil Rights generation, appeared relatively unfettered by the history of racial segregation that Etta James, like Franklin, embodied. Beyoncé's performance of "At Last" powerfully spoke to the Civil Rights dream of integration and equal opportunity, even as Beyoncé herself, like the Obamas, represented its fulfillment. The sequence of singers that day marked a symbolic transition from the older to the younger guard, from the Queen of Soul for the sober inauguration to Beyoncé for the

FIGURE 11. Etta James rehearses at Fame Studios (Muscle Shoals, Alabama) with Marvell Thomas (piano) and David Hood (bass), 1967. House of Fame LLC / Michael Ochs Archive / Getty Images.

vocal prowess in the entire book: Hines "could sing sweet or gruff. He could growl and he could croon. I mean, [he] had *all* the ammunition; you never knew what he would throw at you. Vocal variety—that's what I learned at the tender age of five—vocal fire. Sing like your life depends upon it. Well, turns out mine did" (*R*, 19).

"Desperate Grace"

In 2007, before *Cadillac Records* and the Obama inauguration respectively absented James from her own story and signature song, Linda

Susan Jackson published a collection of poems that now reads as a counternarrative to such erasures. Jackson is the author of two chapbooks, a fellow of the prestigious Cave Canem writers' workshop for black poets in New York, and a professor at Medgar Evers College/CUNY in Brooklyn. Her extraordinary first book, *What Yellow Sounds Like* (2007), claims Etta James for the African American literary tradition, while challenging the sense in which James's "yellow" or liminal status may have previously excluded her from it. Jackson not only insists on keeping James's music and story alive but she also uses her own poetic craft to re-create James's music and re-mythologize her life. In this way, she does for Etta James what Giovanni did for Franklin, what current R&B and hip hop artists are doing for soul icons, and indeed, what future artists might do for Beyoncé: revitalizing these singers' legacies for a new generation.[20] But Jackson also, like Giovanni, conceived her work as a present-tense tribute to James herself. Explaining her decision to write her poems *before* James's death in 2012, she quoted a saying she often heard while growing up: "Give me my flowers while I'm alive." Her decision to do that for James was not lost on the singer, who, upon receiving the book of poems after a concert, simply noted, "Nobody ever did anything like that for me."[21]

What Yellow Sounds Like models the work my own study has sought to perform, because Jackson herself underscores the reciprocal relationship between music and writing: while the singer inspires the poet, the poet also re-creates the singer, candidly conjuring her muse. This reciprocal dynamic is clearest in the final poem, "The Muse Speaks." But the collection as a whole also accents the role of literature in creating (literature about) music. By weaving several poetic and fictional references throughout the text, Jackson indicates that prior literary works, as much as musical ones, give her a language with which to craft her own portrait of Etta James. On the broadest level, Jackson's meditations on James resonate with Sherley Anne Williams's poetic narrative of coming-of-age through identification with Bessie Smith, in *Some One Sweet Angel Chile* (1982). Jackson also uses the last line of Sterling Brown's "Poem for Ma Rainey" as an epigraph to her poem "Taste of Yellow": "*She jes' gits hold of us dataway.*"[22] And the following passage clearly evokes Morrison's description, in *The Bluest Eye*, of southern black women who deny "the funk": "Grandmother thinks Etta James too randy / for women from Virginia who do not sweat, / women who fear the funk. Pretty women / who cover their sofas with antimacassars . . ." (*Y*, 40).[23] Indeed, Jackson creates resonances between black literary and musical traditions (and asserts her speaker's personal claim to both) when she compares her speaker's Great Aunt Fannie to prostitutes in *The Bluest Eye*, Ursa Corregidora, and Etta James in a single line: "I read about women like her in books, / women with names like *China, Maginot / Line, Ursa*, heard about them in the earthy / grit of Etta James" (*Y*, 65).

Jackson writes with a deep sense of literary tradition, in which her book also pointedly intervenes. In particular, her complex portrait of James rejects the tragic mulatto archetype and gives light-skinned women a literary voice.[24] This means reclaiming and reanimating the concept of "yellow" itself: "Not some color-caste chorine, / Etta nails down defiant mulatto" (*Y*, 38). On one level, Etta James embodies the light-skinned speaker's own complex identity. Yet the speaker's identification with James is not easy or complete. The opening poem, "Dear Miss Etta James," ends with an expression of disapproval mixed with admiration: "Still, the audacity of your baby-blonde hair, / your pear shape, your desperate grace. Well!" (*Y*, 12). The phrase "desperate grace" itself captures the play of emotional contrasts this poem conveys. But further, the phrase aptly describes the expressive contrasts that generally characterize Jackson's poetics, as well as James's vocal art.[25]

We might look, first, at the poetic range Jackson demonstrates as she crafts alternately mythologizing and humanizing versions of the singer. We find a similar thematic impulse in Giovanni's "Poem for Aretha" but not the swift *stylistic* movement between contrasting expressive registers that Jackson's work displays. This poetic variation recalls James's own identity as an artist who could sing anything: doo-wop, blues, gospel, rock, country, jazz. The title poem tells an origin story:

That January day back in '38
somebody picked up a rainbow
and broke the sky in two,
releasing Jamesetta Hawkins
into a two-toned world
that eats up yellow by the dozens,
a yellow so pure it gilds the L.A. sun. (*Y*, 31)

Jackson creates a far more "grounded" James in "Yellow Privilege," in which she surmises that color privilege

to some is always light brown
or butter, but Etta was not on
the high end of that dream. She
was low yellow. Poor, jute thick

braids with frizzy ends, too dark
to pass, too blonde to pass by,
a sock running down in her left shoe. (*Y*, 35)

Jackson effects the play of contrasts these two passages demonstrate not only across the collection but also within each poem—from one line and one word to the next. At the level of poetic line, we see this movement within the first stanza just cited, as the glorious image of James as a mythical bird quickly turns to an evocation of risk: James is descending into a world that "eats up yellow by the dozens." Jackson's unexpected syntactical shift supports this semantic turn: instead of further modifying "world," she modifies "yellow," which is "so pure it gilds the L.A. sun." Here, "yellow" becomes a complex agent, both "pure" and "gilding," glory and glitter. Jackson's syntax creates ambiguity as to whether James possesses this force or is possessed by it.

What James does own, however, is her singing voice. Jackson beautifully evokes the timbre and style of James's singing through the language of contrast—for instance, when she describes "the soft / roughness in her voice, churning / solid into custard" (*Y*, 37).[26] A remarkable passage from the title poem goes further in using such oxymoronic descriptions to poetically justify others:

All the while, Etta stomped
barefoot on stage,
platinum hair authentically blending
with the yolk yellow scream
she hurled from the marrow of her voice
scorched and scared,
jaundiced by the freedom
of surviving a rage
simmering somewhere
between heaven and heat. (*Y*, 32–33)

Here, the notion that "platinum hair" might be "authentic" makes sense because it "authentically blend[s]" with Jackson's equally oxymoronic image of a piercing plasma in "yolk yellow scream." Likewise, it is possible for James, or perhaps her "scream," to be "*jaundiced* by freedom," because this is the complex freedom to choose a life in which one will stay "simmering somewhere / between heaven and heat."

By affirming oxymoron in this way, Jackson's poetics also affirm James's art of vocal oxymoron or contrast, hinting that James's art of contrast is precisely what allows her to survive and perhaps subvert a world that "eats up yellow." When Jackson describes James as "bleeding," "bending," and "blending" notes (*Y*, 38), she suggests that James's vocal ability to shift between opposing forces or sounds enables her to mediate the "two-toned world" that has not made a place for her. In other words, James moves between sonic "tones" to counter the binary limitations of visual ones: "Bending some [notes]. Blending others, / she guts the places / you can't touch" (*Y*, 38). If James's liminal status—between races, classes, sexual cultures, and musical idioms—has excluded her from the black literary tradition, Jackson makes that liminality a source of strength and a sign of James's relentless "rage to survive."

In keeping with the collection's title, *What Yellow Sounds Like* attunes us not only to the politics of James's music but also to the way it sounds, including the very micro-features of James's vocal art. Jackson's own nimble movement between opposed terms—"the soft / roughness in her voice, churning / solid into custard"—illuminates James's protean skill. James demonstrates an unparalleled timbral palette, including a breathy husk, brassy cry, and tight-knit growl. She thus displays the range for which she praises James Earle Hines: like her mentor, she is a singer with "*all* the ammunition." But what Jackson's work also highlights—and what is particularly remarkable about James as a singer—is her ability to move from one mode to the next on a dime. James can switch from a sweet, breathy delivery to a growling belt and back perhaps more dramatically than any other singer in this book. She does this between musical statements as well as within single words, as we can hear in some of her best-known recordings. We might listen, for instance, to the contrast between the last verse of "Trust in Me" (1961) and James's final chorus: "Trust in me, and I'll be worthy of you," she sings, in a relatively sweet, subdued tone, before coming back in a few beats later at nearly full power: "Oh, yeah, yeah! Why don't you trust in me, in all you do . . ."[27] The entirety of "At Last" is a play of such dynamic contrasts. The song begins, "At last, my love has come along." James eases from her chest voice into her head voice, shifts into belting mode for the words "my love," and has segued back into a breathy head tone by the time she sings "along"— "without missing a lick," as she says of the L.A. doo-wop singers.[28] Even more locally, James moves between tones within a single word. Listen, for example, to the way she sings the word "I" in the line "a dream that I can call my own," as well as the word "thrill" in the next line: James begins both words in her full voice and seamlessly eases them into a breathy tone.

I point this out not only because it takes a great deal of skill and control but because I believe it generates what Jackson calls James's sound of "desperate grace." This is especially so when James adds another color to her palette by hollowing out her voice—seeming to open her throat to produce a round, weightless sound. In "All I Could Do Was Cry" (1961), a song in which the speaker describes seeing her beloved marry another woman, James hollows out her voice both times she sings the word "heard" in the first line ("I heard the church bells ringing / I heard a choir singing") and when she sings the word "over" ("And now, the wedding's over").[29] Her dramatic transition between the first verse and the chorus of the song activates the full range of tones and techniques I have described: "I heard them promise, 'till death do us part' / each word was a pain in my heart." James begins the initial "I" strong and clear, eases the word into a higher tone, and then hollows out her voice to suggest that the wind has been knocked out of her. She completes the statement, takes a breath, and blasts the chorus: "All, all I could do, all I could do was cry . . ." When she sings about wedding guests throwing rice at the newlyweds, she sings the word "rice" more fiercely, I would imagine, than anyone has ever done. These swift transitions create a sonic "desperate grace" because they express a voice continually on the edge that never gives way to the edge. In other words, at least in a song like "All I Could Do," James's vocal grace is desperate because it can turn from a whisper to a scream at any moment. The desperation is graceful because it always turns back.

Ultimately, Jackson's own poetic music of contrast and paradox highlights James's art and also co-creates it. That Jackson embraces her poetic role in this creation is clearest in her final poem, "The Muse Speaks." Here Jackson revises the trope of the muse. She depicts not an ethereal angel who sings to the (male) writer but a feisty, opinionated muse who drinks, and she evokes not a one-way channel of inspiration but a symbiotic relationship between creator and created. The mercurial muse needs the poet to give her voice and reassurance: "the tight skin / of your language rescues / me from damp silence" (Y, 75); "Remind me what I give" (Y, 77). Disappointed in the poet's recent ritual offerings, the muse ends by accusing her of "filling me with your flat funk, / your boiled-down blues. Wide / words spread so thin. / You've said everything" (Y, 77). It is fitting, if rather sad, that the collection ends here, as if in acknowledgment that the poet is spent. But what is fascinating is that Jackson reverses the muse-poet dynamic by figuring the *poet* as the one who brings the funk (albeit "flat" now), as well as the blues (albeit "boiled-down"). The muse needs the poet's music, in short, as much as the poet needs the muse.[30] Indeed, it is *only* poetic language that might attune us to James's music in quite this way: by impossibly conjuring the sound of a color, telling us "what yellow sounds like."

"Threats"

On one level, the notion that writers craft their own literary performances to reshape singers' sounds and legacies should be familiar, as this has been a foundational practice of hip hop for decades. Especially since the rise of recognizable samples in the 1980s, hip hop has not only given listeners new ways to hear oft-sampled funk and soul legends like James Brown and George Clinton but has literally *introduced* younger listeners to these artists. I want to focus on one particular song that samples Etta James to extraordinary effect: "Threats," by rapper Jean Grae. This song, like Jackson's poetry—and, indeed, like all the literary works this book has featured—reanimates the singer's legacy. At the same time, in contrast to the writings I have analyzed, the *sound* of the Etta James sample is vital to the black feminist politics of Grae's work. In making this rather basic point about the difference between hip hop and printed poetry, I resist current efforts to bolster hip hop's academic credibility by conflating the two.

Born in Cape Town and based in New York, Grae was still a relatively "underground" talent when "Threats"—a track produced by the equally gifted Ninth Wonder—was released in 2008. The song samples and loops James's church-style introduction to her upbeat love song "Something's Got a Hold on Me" (1963), in which James sings a stretched out "I just gotta tell you" call-and-response with a chorus of women: "I get a feeling that I never never never never had before, no no" ("yeahhhh" from the choir); "I just wanna tell you right now that ah" ("ooooh") "I believe . . . that something's got a hold on me."[31] While this introduction has been sampled by several DJs since the early 1990s, Ninth Wonder's use of it is uniquely brilliant.[32] First, he isolates and loops three moments of this introduction that showcase three different facets of James's vocal palette: the tight growl, the clarion call, and the sensual breath-evacuating tone (on the descending "I wanna tell you right now").[33] He collages these moments, along with the "yeah" and "ooh" of the choir, to create a hard-driving, boom-heavy structure for Grae's rhymes. Further, he makes the backup singers the rhythmic and harmonic base of "Threats," starting the song with the backup singers' "yeah" instead of with James's initial call. Like Giovanni's "Dreams," then, "Threats" amplifies the role of backup singers. Sonically as well as lyrically, this track brings obscured women artists to the foreground: not only by amplifying the backup singers but also by elevating Etta James and, of course, by announcing Grae's own emergence from the shadows into the spotlight.

The decision to start the track not with James's call but with the backup singers' response is a clever move, given that "Threats" itself is a response song—a "cover" version of Jay-Z's "Threat" (2003), also produced by Ninth Wonder.[34] Jay-Z's track samples R. Kelly's "A Woman's Threat" (2000), a song in which Kelly impersonates a woman threatening to replace her lover with another man. Grae appropriates Jay-Z's song (indeed, by working with Ninth Wonder, she creates the effect of also having stolen his producer) to create her own "woman's threat." She begins as if addressing Jay-Z: "I'll jack a beat from ya / take a little bit of heat from ya." The play on "heat" indicates that she will steal some of Jay-Z's fire and also—though this doesn't worry her—catch flack for her decision to "[redesign] the song." Grae makes the feminist politics of this redesigning effort clear as she revises Jay-Z's lyrics. While Jay-Z raps, "This is an unusual musical I'm conductin, / You lookin at the black Warren Buffett so all you critics can duck sic [sic]," Grae reinterprets the line as follows: "This is an unusual musical reconstructed, / You lookin at the new Harriet Tubman, / so all critics can suck this." In place of Jay-Z's claim, "I'm young, black, and rich, so they wanna strip me naked," Grae sings, "Female, black, and young, so they wanna strip me naked." While she adds a nod to Jay-Z by saying she can be found on the New York City subway, "any time of the day / blastin out the headphones the best of Jay," she also declares her power is such that "from here to California niggas will buy me instead." After this powerhouse performance, guest rapper Chen Lo ends the track, as well as the project of "reconstructing" Jay-Z's song; his rap does not riff on the original. While this female-to-male sequence may temper the status of this track as a feminist "takeover," the relative strength of Grae's rhyme also solidifies it.

As Franklin did when covering Otis Redding's "Respect," Grae alters Jay-Z's rhythms and lyrics to her own agenda, while bringing female backup singers (in this case, James *and* her chorus) into the mix. The interplay between foreground and background vocalists is mutually empowering in "Threats." By isolating James's gospel-style introduction, Ninth Wonder not only gives Grae a whole chorus of backing women but also invests her track with the sonic authority that gospel signifies, thus enhancing Grae's self-aggrandizing rhyme. But his recontextualization of

James's song also excavates the meaning of "Something's Got a Hold on Me," recalling James's gospel roots as well as her own secular and feminist compositional "reconstructions." First, James composed "Something's Got a Hold on Me" by secularizing a gospel song by James Cleveland, in which the "something" that's "got a hold on me" is not "love" but "the Holy Ghost." It is therefore unsurprising that James says she wrote her song "with church in mind" (R, 107) and that she would "[work] up the crowd with the holy ghost of 'Something's Got a Hold on Me'" in concert (R, 155). Further, precisely because "Threats" grants James's song a feminist valence that its lyrics do not express, the track recalls the fact that James herself was a feminist force to be reckoned with—a singer whose first teenage hit was a woman's "answer song" akin to Grae's response to Jay-Z (R, 43). Of her decision to reply to a risqué Hank Ballard song by composing equally suggestive lyrics from a woman's point of view, James writes, "Looking back, I . . . see I had feminist leanings before I even knew what a feminist was. If Hank could say, 'Work with Me, Annie,' well, I sure as hell could say, 'Roll with Me, Henry'" (R, 50). Overall then, by asserting Grae's soul-era sonic authority and recovering James's compositional ingenuity and revisionary feminism, the track augments both women's power and thus doubles or pluralizes the "threats" to Jay-Z and Grae's critics that the song represents.

Respect

In arguing that Jean Grae's sample of Etta James matters, I mean to weigh in, as I have said, on a contemporary conversation about the "status" of hip hop. Although I have often spoken about revaluing literature in the wake of Black Arts, current discourse on hip hop reveals a need to revalue music. Because the literary maintains a privileged place within dominant culture, the current trend is to legitimate hip hop as a practice and object of study by calling it poetry. Ralph Ellison scholar and hip hop expert Adam Bradley goes furthest in attempting to "give rap the respect it deserves as poetry" in his recent *Book of Rhymes: The Poetics of Hip Hop* (2009), in which he transcribes rap lyrics and analyzes them as poetic verse.[35] As *New Yorker* critic Kelefa Sanneh points out, Bradley's approach resonates with Jay-Z's own: in *Decoded* (2010), Jay-Z asserts that "hip hop lyrics—not just my lyrics, but those of every great MC—are poetry if you look at them closely enough."[36]

While I understand the cultural politics that motivate this argument, I nonetheless believe that hip hop is best understood as a unique musical form instead of as poetry. I support Sanneh's assertion that what makes Jay-Z's art so compelling "has something to do with his odd, perpetually adolescent-sounding voice, and a lot to do with his sophisticated sense of rhythm. Sure, he's a poet—and, while we're at it, a singer and percussionist, too. But why should any of these titles be more impressive than 'rapper'?"[37] While Sanneh is clearly aware that the answer lies in these titles' differing degrees of artistic respectability, the question productively highlights the biases and limitations of our current analytic lexicon when it comes to music and writing. I hope this book plays a small part in enriching the conversation by approaching black music and literature as distinctive art forms whose practitioners do their own uniquely valuable expressive work, and by offering some new metaphors to describe their connections.

With regard to hip hop, this reevaluation is important not only because treating hip hop as page-oriented poetry simplifies the multifaceted form that artists like Jay-Z and Jean Grae work to master, but also because that approach literally silences the music that hip hop artists sample—much of which is created by women singers. In addition to Grae, several hip hop artists echo the literary tradition this book has traced by collaboratively re-creating the music of female vocalists. Nina Simone's work alone has been featured in songs by Talib Kweli, Kanye West, Timbaland, Common, and Lil Wayne, and in a full-length tribute-style album by the Ghanaian hip hop artist Ohene. Wu-Tang Clan producer the RZA samples Gladys Knight and the Pips' version of "The Way We Were / Try to Remember" (1974), Kanye West samples Aretha Franklin's "Spirit in the Dark" (1970), and jazz musician/producer Mocean Worker samples Mahalia Jackson's "The Lord's Prayer" (1950).[38] To follow the logic of my literary analyses, it is important to consider what these singers themselves do, in addition to what MCs and producers do with them, lest we regard the female singer as object rather than agent. It seems important, for example, to acknowledge that Ninth Wonder's sample works so well in part because it expresses his attunement to James's own unique activation of contrasting timbral textures and shrewd musical reconstructions.

I am sympathetic to Bradley's claim that "the best MCs—like Rakim, Jay-Z, Tupac, and many others—deserve consideration alongside the giants of American poetry."[39] I have made a similar case here, by arguing that singers like Holiday and Jackson "deserve consideration alongside" canonized writers like Wright and Baldwin. Part of what is at stake here is, of course, getting women singers "the respect they deserve." As music reviews continue to frame female singers as natural, unthinking divas, they show there is a great deal of work to be done in this regard. But I would not do this work by claiming that singers *are* writers. Just as I reject the notion that we must authenticate black literature by positing its source in black music, I also resist the notion that hip hop (or, indeed, singing) needs legitimating by association with literature. Instead, I suggest we best appreciate writers' and musicians' respective effects—and their dynamic alliances—when we take them on their own terms. As Nikki Giovanni and Aretha, Erma, and Carolyn Franklin remind us, respect is a two-way street.

Notes

Introduction

1. Angela Davis, *Blues Legacies and Black Feminism: Gertrude "Ma" Rainey, Bessie Smith, and Billie Holiday* (New York: Vintage, 1998), 141.

2. Langston Hughes, "The Negro Artist and the Racial Mountain," *Nation*, June 23, 1926, 694.

3. Langston Hughes, *The Big Sea* (1940; repr., New York: Hill and Wang, 1963), 296; Hughes, *Ask Your Mama: 12 Moods for Jazz* (1961), in *The Collected Poems of Langston Hughes*, ed. Arnold Rampersad (New York: Vintage Classics, 1995), 488–493.

4. Carl Van Vechten, "Negro 'Blues' Singers" (1926), in *"Keep A-Inchin' Along": Selected Writings of Carl Van Vechten about Black Art and Letters*, ed. Bruce Kellner (Westport, CT: Greenwood, 1979), 160–164.

5. Sterling Brown, "Ma Rainey," in *Southern Road* (New York: Harcourt, Brace, 1932), 62–64; Al Young, "A Dance for Ma Rainey" (1969), in *Something about the Blues: An Unlikely Collection of Poetry* (Naperville, IL: Sourcebooks, 2007), 22–24.

6. Jack Kerouac, *On the Road* (1957; repr., New York: Penguin, 1991), 98–99.

7. Edward Albee, *The Death of Bessie Smith*, in *The Zoo Story, The Death of Bessie Smith, The Sandbox* (New York: Coward-McCann, 1960), 63–137.

8. Frank O'Hara, "The Day Lady Died," in *Lunch Poems* (San Francisco: City Lights Books, 1964), 25–26.

9. Amiri Baraka (LeRoi Jones), *Dutchman*, in *Dutchman and The Slave* (New York: Morrow, 1964), 35; Baraka, "Dark Lady of the Sonnets" (1962), in *Black Music* (New York: Quill, 1967), 25; Baraka, "The Lady" and "Billie," in *The Music: Reflections on Jazz and Blues*, ed. Amiri Baraka and Amina Baraka (New York: Morrow, 1987), 117, 285; Baraka, "Sassy Was Definitely Not the Avon Lady" (1999), in *The LeRoi Jones/Amiri Baraka Reader*, ed. William J. Harris (New York: Thunder's Mouth, 1999), 567–570.

10. Malcolm X, *The Autobiography of Malcolm X*, as told to Alex Haley (New York: Ballantine, 1965); Maya Angelou, *I Know Why the Caged Bird Sings* (New York:

Random House, 1969); Alice Adams, *Listening to Billie* (New York: Knopf, 1977); Elizabeth Hardwick, *Sleepless Nights* (New York: Random House, 1979); Ntozake Shange, *Sassafrass, Cypress and Indigo* (New York: Picador, 1982).

11. Sonia Sanchez, "—a poem for nina simone to put some music to and blow our nigguh / minds—," in *We a BaddDDD People* (Detroit: Broadside, 1970), 60.

12. Sherley Anne Williams, *Some One Sweet Angel Chile* (New York: Morrow, 1982), 37–65; Williams, "I Want Aretha to Set This to Music," in ibid., 53–55; August Wilson, *Ma Rainey's Black Bottom* (1982), in *Three Plays* (Pittsburgh: University of Pittsburgh Press, 1991), 1–93.

13. August Wilson, preface to *Three Plays*, viii–x.

14. E. Ethelbert Miller, "Billie Holiday," in *First Light: Selected Poems* (Baltimore: Black Classic, 1994), 179; Fred Moten, "bessie smith," *Callaloo* 27 (Fall 2004): 967–968.

15. Barack Obama, *Dreams from My Father* (1995; repr., New York: Three Rivers, 2004), 92–112.

16. See, for instance, Houston Baker, *Blues, Ideology, and Afro-American Literature: A Vernacular Theory* (Chicago: University of Chicago Press, 1984); Kimberly Benston, *Performing Blackness: Enactments of African-American Modernism* (London: Routledge, 2000); Walton Muyumba, *The Shadow and the Act: Black Intellectual Practice, Jazz Improvisation, and Philosophical Pragmatism* (Chicago: University of Chicago Press, 2009). A notable exception to this rule, Farah Jasmine Griffin's essay "When Malindy Sings: A Meditation on Black Women's Vocality," has been important to my work in this book; see *Uptown Conversation: The New Jazz Studies*, ed. Robert G. O'Meally, Brent Hayes Edwards, and Farah Jasmine Griffin (New York: Columbia University Press, 2004), 102–125.

17. These musical and masculine biases come together with particular clarity in the work of Houston Baker and Henry Louis Gates Jr. since, as Evie Shockley writes, "Baker's version of the blues tradition writes out the woman blues singer in favor of the 'bluesman' and his guitar, and Gates chooses to ground his theory in signifying, typically a men's linguistic practice" (*Renegade Poetics: Black Aesthetics and Formal Innovation in African American Poetry* [Iowa City: University of Iowa Press, 2011], 6–7).

18. See Valerie Smith's characterization of "third-stage" black feminist critics, who analyze the ways in which "the meaning of influence, the meaning of a tradition, the meaning of literary periods, the meaning of literature itself . . . changes once questions of race, class, and gender become central to the process of literary analysis" ("Black Feminist Theory and the Representation of the 'Other,'" in *Changing Our Own Words: Essays on Criticism, Theory, and Writing by Black Women*, ed. Cheryl A. Wall [1989; repr., New Brunswick, NJ: Rutgers University Press, 1991], 46).

19. On a general level, we might say that formal connections are especially "audible" between writers and *singers* (as opposed to instrumentalists) because both writers and singers work with verbal language. However, this book's methodology would equally apply to wordless music, as we could use authors' accounts of that music as interpretive guides to their own writing.

20. Gayl Jones, "Deep Song," in *Chant of Saints: A Gathering of Afro-American Literature, Art, and Scholarship*, ed. Michael S. Harper and Robert B. Stepto (Urbana: University of Illinois Press, 1979), 376.

21. We might think here of the way that Brent Edwards theorizes diaspora through the metaphor of bodily joints, which are both "point[s] of separation" and "point[s] of

linkage." As he writes, "in the body it is *only* difference—the separation between bones or members—that allows movement" (*The Practice of Diaspora: Literature, Translation, and the Rise of Black Internationalism* [Cambridge, MA: Harvard University Press, 2003], 15).

22. Alexander Weheliye's discussion of his decision to read W. E. B. Du Bois's *The Souls of Black Folk* (1903) alongside the practice of DJing—a comparison that works without implying that the two subjects are "congruent" or "symmetrical"—is a useful analogue here (*Phonographies: Grooves in Sonic Afro-Modernity* [Durham, NC: Duke University Press, 2005], 202–203).

23. Ronald Radano, *Lying Up a Nation: Race and Black Music* (Chicago: University of Chicago Press, 2003), xi.

24. Simon Frith, *Performing Rites: On the Value of Popular Music* (Cambridge, MA: Harvard University Press, 1996), 203.

25. In *Phonographies*, Weheliye calls for greater critical attention to the material apparatuses of sound recording and dissemination (CDs, MP3s, and so on). This book does not answer that call, in part because the task of bringing singers' (technologically mediated) vocal practices to light is sufficiently demanding. Still, the subject of recording technology is yielding several important studies—most recently, Jonathan Sterne's *MP3: The Meaning of a Format* (Durham, NC: Duke University Press, 2012)—which may enrich future scholarship on the art of women singers.

26. Baker, *Blues, Ideology, and Afro-American Literature*, 9.

27. I draw these terms from the etymology of "resonance" as detailed in the *Oxford English Dictionary* (2nd ed., 1989). We may envision the resonances I propose through what Ronald Radano terms a "never-ending loop of text and sound" (*Lying Up a Nation*, 12). Like Radano, I find it very helpful to remember that neither music nor writing is the source of the "loop": if black music shapes writing, writing also "discursively constitute[s]" black music (ibid., 11). Still, my aims are different from Radano's. Radano emphasizes the "interracial" nature of black music's discursive creation in order to assert that black music "confess[es] the mulatto truth of a white supremacist nation" (xiii, 12–13), whereas my rather more modest project is less interested in what the loop of text and sound tells us about the formation of black and white identities than in what it tells us about twentieth-century black musical and literary aesthetics.

28. Ralph Ellison, "On Bird, Bird-Watching and Jazz" (1962), in *Living with Music: Ralph Ellison's Jazz Writings*, ed. Robert G. O'Meally (New York: Modern Library, 2001), 69.

29. The Wright-Ellison-Baldwin "triumvirate" is Jodi Melamed's term—see *Represent and Destroy: Rationalizing Violence in the New Racial Capitalism* (Minneapolis: University of Minnesota Press, 2011), 66.

30. Lorenzo Thomas, *Don't Deny My Name: Words and Music and the Black Intellectual Tradition*, ed. Aldon Nielsen (Ann Arbor: University of Michigan Press, 2008), 142; Stephen Henderson, "Introduction: The Forms of Things Unknown," in *Understanding the New Black Poetry: Black Speech and Black Music as Poetic References* (New York: Morrow, 1973), 1–69. For Richard Wright's discussion of "the Forms of Things Unknown," see *White Man, Listen!* (Garden City, NY: Doubleday, 1957), 123–150.

31. Tom Smith, "Public Radio Book Show: Nikki Giovanni" (1990), in *Conversations with Nikki Giovanni*, ed. Virginia Fowler (Jackson: University Press of Mississippi,

1992), 195. Baldwin and Giovanni's conversation is published as *A Dialogue* (New York: Lippincott, 1973).

32. For two of many examples, see Jessica Willis, "Sadly, Mary J. Blige Is Happy at Last," *New York Times*, August 24, 2003, http://www.nytimes.com/2003/08/24/arts/music-sadly-mary-j-blige-is-happy-at-last.html; Gerrick D. Kennedy, "Mary J. Blige Singing a Different Tune These Days," *Los Angeles Times*, November 22, 2011, http://articles.latimes.com/2011/nov/22/entertainment/la-et-mary-j-blige-20111122.

33. Rich Juzwiak, "Beyoncé's Odes to Joy," review of *4*, by Beyoncé, *Village Voice*, June 29, 2011, http://www.villagevoice.com/2011-06-29/music/beyonce-s-odes-to-joy.

34. Lara Pellegrinelli points out that, compared with instrumental music, singing is often undervalued as an art form because of its proximity to speech, which is assumed to be a basic human capacity: hence the Zimbabwean proverb "If you can talk, you can sing" ("The Song Is Who? Locating Singers on the Jazz Scene" [PhD diss., Harvard University, 2005], 108, 126; see also 110).

35. For myths of black expressivity, see Nathaniel Mackey, "Blue Is Green: Black Interiority" (1995), in *Paracritical Hinge: Essays, Talks, Notes, Interviews* (Madison: University of Wisconsin Press, 2005), 199–206. For "myths of vocal gender," see *Embodied Voices: Representing Female Vocality in Western Culture*, ed. Leslie Dunn and Nancy Jones (Cambridge: Cambridge University Press, 1994). In the introduction to that volume, Dunn and Jones explain, "The anchoring of the female voice in the female body confers upon it all the conventional associations of femininity with nature and matter, with emotion and irrationality.... Like the body from which it emanates, the female voice is construed as both a signifier of sexual otherness and a source of sexual power, an object at once of desire and fear" (3).

36. Meta DuEwa Jones, *The Muse Is Music: Jazz Poetry from the Harlem Renaissance to Spoken Word* (Urbana: University of Illinois Press, 2011), 12. Jones points out that "the tendency not to view jazz singers as full-fledged musicians results in part from their limited improvisational roles within jazz bands and ensembles, particularly during the swing era" (130). For an excellent discussion of this phenomenon, see Pellegrinelli, "The Song Is Who?," 60–106.

37. Curtis Wenzel, "Jazz, Scat, and Betty Bebop," *City Pages* (Minneapolis–St. Paul), May 11, 1983, 11, qtd. in William R. Bauer, *Open the Door: The Life and Music of Betty Carter* (Ann Arbor: University of Michigan Press, 2002), ix. (Carter's statement is cited in M. Jones, *The Muse Is Music*, 130.)

38. See Robert G. O'Meally, *Lady Day: The Many Faces of Billie Holiday* (New York: Da Capo, 1991); Farah Jasmine Griffin, *If You Can't Be Free, Be a Mystery: In Search of Billie Holiday* (New York: Ballantine Books, 2001). Albert Murray's *Stomping the Blues* is an important precursor to such studies. Murray stresses that musical models (as well as natural talent) shape a blues singer's work far more than does "personal calamity": "Bessie Smith . . . owes much more to Ma Rainey than to hard luck, and she also owes not a little to the good luck [of] being born with a voice the magnificence of which, like that of Louis Armstrong's trumpet or Duke Ellington's orchestrations, no amount of adversity has yet produced in anybody else" ([1976; repr., New York: Da Capo, 2000], 54).

39. Randall Kenan, "Introduction: Looking for James Baldwin," in *The Cross of Redemption: Uncollected Writings*, by James Baldwin (New York: Pantheon, 2010), xiv.

40. Avery Gordon, *Ghostly Matters: Haunting and the Sociological Imagination* (1997; repr., Minneapolis: University of Minnesota Press, 2008), 203.

41. Billie Holiday with William Dufty, *Lady Sings the Blues* (1956; repr., New York: Harlem Moon, 2006), 96.

42. Aretha Franklin and David Ritz, *Aretha: From These Roots* (New York: Villard, 1999), 109.

43. While Smith's and Holiday's tragically early deaths may partly explain why they (as opposed to, say, Lena Horne or Sarah Vaughan) enjoy a privileged place within the literary tradition—just as such tragedy partly explains John Coltrane's sacred place among black artists—early death is not the primary reason why writers invoke these singers. In fact, of the ensemble of writers gathered here, Baldwin is the only one to highlight singers' tragic lives, and even he stresses their expressive strategies when he describes Smith's and Holiday's understated style.

44. Zora Neale Hurston, "Characteristics of Negro Expression" (1934), in *Zora Neale Hurston: Folklore, Memoirs, and Other Writings*, ed. Cheryl A. Wall (New York: Library of America, 1995), 838.

45. Nikki Giovanni and Margaret Walker, *A Poetic Equation: Conversations Between Nikki Giovanni and Margaret Walker* (Washington, DC: Howard University Press, 1974), 80 (my italics); Ray Charles interview in the documentary *Aretha Franklin: The Queen of Soul*, screenplay by Nelson George, ed. Jody Sheff (A*Vision Entertainment, 1988).

46. Susan Gubar, "'The Blank Page' and the Issues of Female Creativity," in *Writing and Sexual Difference*, ed. Elizabeth Abel (Chicago: University of Chicago Press, 1982), 77, qtd. in Barbara Johnson, *The Feminist Difference: Literature, Psychoanalysis, Race, and Gender* (Cambridge, MA: Harvard University Press, 1998), 114.

47. Deborah McDowell, *"The Changing Same": Black Women's Literature, Criticism, and Theory* (Bloomington: Indiana University Press, 1995), 167.

48. Leslie Dunn and Nancy Jones write that Western literature "testif[ies] to the persistent desire of male artists to control through representation the anxieties aroused by the female voice, even while they license the display, and the enjoyment, of its powers" (introduction to *Embodied Voices*, 3). Farah Griffin presents a more balanced view of male representations of female singers in "When Malindy Sings." According to Griffin, male writers' uses of black female vocality may "reinforce patriarchal constructions of the feminine," as Dunn and Jones put it (ibid.), and replicate exploitative uses of black female song within a broader U.S. national framework—but they may also offer new ways of understanding artistry, community, and potentially transformative politics.

49. Robert Park, "Education in Its Relation to the Conflict and Fusion of Cultures" (1918), in *Race and Culture: The Collected Papers of Robert Ezra Park*, vol. 1, ed. Everett Cherrington Hughes, Charles S. Johnson, Jitsuichi Masuoka, Robert Redfield, and Louis Wirth (Glencoe, IL: Free Press, 1950), 280. Ellison would recount his "humiliation" upon having a black sociology professor relate Park's claim without interrogating it—a formative moment in Ellison's rejection of sociology as a discipline ("Introduction to *Shadow and Act*" [1964], in *Collected Essays of Ralph Ellison*, ed. John F. Callahan [1995; repr., New York: Modern Library, 2003], 57). Park's claim also appears in the "lost" chapter of *Invisible Man* that Roderick Ferguson brings to light

in *Aberrations in Black: Toward a Queer of Color Critique* (Minneapolis: University of Minnesota Press, 2004), 63–64.

50. See, e.g., Josh Kun, *Audiotopia: Music, Race, and America* (Berkeley: University of California Press, 2005), 86–112.

51. Amiri Baraka (then LeRoi Jones), "The Changing Same (R&B and New Black Music)" (1966), in *Black Music*, 180.

52. A. Yemisi Jimoh, *Spiritual, Blues, and Jazz People in African American Fiction: Living in Paradox* (Knoxville: University of Tennessee Press, 2002), 21, 217. Tony Bolden figures music less as a metaphor for black life than as a metaphor for poetry and criticism when he proposes an approach to black poetry that would, like blues music, "reject[] simplistic binary oppositions" (*Afro-Blue: Improvisations in African American Poetry and Culture* [Urbana: University of Illinois Press, 2004], 38).

53. See Sherrie Tucker, *Swing Shift: "All-Girl" Bands of the 1940s* (Durham, NC: Duke University Press, 2000); Gayle Wald, *Shout, Sister, Shout! The Untold Story of Rock-and-Roll Trailblazer Sister Rosetta Tharpe* (Boston: Beacon, 2007); Daphne A. Brooks, *Bodies in Dissent: Spectacular Performances of Race and Freedom, 1850–1910* (Durham, NC: Duke University Press, 2006); Brooks, "'All That You Can't Leave Behind': Black Female Soul Singing and the Politics of Surrogation in the Age of Catastrophe," *Meridians* 8.1 (2008): 180–204; Jayna Brown, *Babylon Girls: Black Women Performers and the Shaping of the Modern* (Durham, NC: Duke University Press, 2008); Alexandra Vazquez, *Listening in Detail* (Durham, NC: Duke University Press, forthcoming). Kimberly Benston also warrants mention for his brilliant readings of John Coltrane's music in his literary critical study *Performing Blackness*. Steven C. Tracy's *Langston Hughes and the Blues* (Urbana: University of Illinois Press, 1988) is another technically expert interdisciplinary analysis.

54. Richard Wright, "Memories of My Grandmother," unpublished typescript (1941), Richard Wright Papers, Beinecke Rare Book and Manuscript Library, Yale University, Box 6, folder 118, 25; Ralph Ellison, "As the Spirit Moves Mahalia" (1958), in *Living with Music*, 92; Studs Terkel, "An Interview with James Baldwin" (1961), in *Conversations with James Baldwin*, ed. Fred L. Stanley and Louis H. Pratt (Jackson: University Press of Mississippi, 1989), 3; Leon Forrest, "A Solo Long-Song for Lady Day," *Callaloo* 16 (Spring 1992): 332–367; Virginia Fowler, "A Conversation with Nikki Giovanni," in *Nikki Giovanni* (New York: Twayne, 1992), 149.

55. See Thomas, *Don't Deny My Name*; Benston, *Performing Blackness*; Cheryl Clarke, *After Mecca: Women Poets and the Black Arts Movement* (New Brunswick, NJ: Rutgers University Press, 2005); James Smethurst, *The Black Arts Movement: Literary Nationalism in the 1960s and 1970s* (Chapel Hill: University of North Carolina Press, 2005); Amy Ongiri, *Spectacular Blackness: The Cultural Politics of the Black Arts Movement and the Search for a Black Aesthetic* (Charlottesville: University of Virginia Press, 2009); Howard Rambsy II, *The Black Arts Enterprise and the Production of African American Poetry* (Ann Arbor: University of Michigan Press, 2011); and Shockley, *Renegade Poetics* (the term "caricature" is Shockley's; 2).

56. Hortense Spillers, "Afterword: Cross-Currents, Discontinuities: Black Women's Fiction," in *Conjuring: Black Women, Fiction, and Literary Tradition*, ed. Marjorie Pryse and Hortense Spillers (Bloomington: Indiana University Press, 1985), 250, qtd. in Farah Jasmine Griffin, "That the Mothers May Soar and the Daughters May Know

Their Names: A Retrospective of Black Feminist Literary Criticism," *Signs* 32.2 (2007): 489.

57. For the notion that vernacular expression draws on printed as well as oral forms, see Brent Edwards, "The Seemingly Eclipsed Window of Form: James Weldon Johnson's Prefaces," in *The Jazz Cadence of American Culture*, ed. Robert O'Meally (New York: Columbia University Press, 1998), 597.

58. Jean Toomer, *Cane* (1923), ed. Darwin T. Turner (New York: Norton, 1988), 142.

59. On Hurston's "speakerly text," see Henry Louis Gates Jr., *The Signifying Monkey: A Theory of African-American Literary Criticism* (New York: Oxford University Press, 1988), 170–216.

60. Henderson, *Understanding the New Black Poetry*, 68, 30–31.

61. Clarke, *After Mecca*, 62.

62. Frederick Douglass, *Narrative of the Life of Frederick Douglass, An American Slave, Written by Himself* (1845), ed. John W. Blassingame et al. (New Haven, CT: Yale University Press, 2001), 20.

63. Shockley, *Renegade Poetics*, 6; Gates, *Signifying Monkey*, xxiv. Harryette Mullen must be cited as a critic who offered an early critique of African American literary criticism's oral bias in "African Signs and Spirit Writing," *Callaloo* 19.3 (Summer 1996): 670–689. Though published a year before the *Norton Anthology of African American Literature* canonized Gates's version of the tradition, Mullen's essay presciently grasped how influential *The Signifying Monkey* and other Black Arts–informed theories of the tradition would be.

64. Toni Morrison, "Unspeakable Things Unspoken: The Afro-American Presence in American Literature," *Michigan Quarterly Review* 28 (1989): 19.

65. See Madhu Dubey, *Signs and Cities: Black Literary Postmodernism* (Chicago: University of Chicago Press, 2004), 43. Shockley makes a similar point in *Renegade Poetics* (8).

66. Baker, *Blues, Ideology, and Afro-American Literature*.

67. Gates, *Signifying Monkey*, 130–131.

68. Cornel West, "Cornel West Interviewed by bell hooks," in *The Cornel West Reader* (New York: Basic Civitas, 1999), 548.

69. Paul Gilroy, *The Black Atlantic: Modernity and Double Consciousness* (Cambridge, MA: Harvard University Press, 1993), 120, 123–124.

70. Weheliye's *Phonographies* is one important study that complicates the sound/text binary while maintaining a bias toward sound. When Weheliye claims that the phonograph itself writes or reproduces sound, he updates Gates's claim that "signifyin(g)" is "the writing implicit in an oral literature" (*Signifying Monkey*, 88) by transposing Gates's oral bias onto a sonic bias. "The sonic remains an important zone from and through which to theorize the fundamentality of Afro-diasporic formations to the currents of Western modernity," Weheliye writes, "since this field remains, to put it bluntly, the principal modality in which Afro-diasporic cultures have been articulated—though clearly it has not been the only one" (*Phonographies*, 5).

71. Gayl Jones, *Liberating Voices: Oral Tradition in African American Literature* (New York: Penguin, 1991), 90.

72. Terkel, "Interview with James Baldwin," 3. In an unpublished letter from 1968, Baldwin writes, "Now, Aretha is singing: I wonder: the way she sounds is the way I want to write. You know, there is something fantastically pure and sad, heart-breaking, and

yet peaceful in all this horror. What a triumph—to be able to sing about it—to give it back to the world" (James Baldwin to David Baldwin and Paula Wayley, 10 March 1968, James Baldwin Collection, the Schomburg Center for Research in Black Culture, New York, folder MG 278 [Correspondence 1961–68]).

73. Amiri Baraka, *The Autobiography of LeRoi Jones/Amiri Baraka* (1984; repr., Chicago: Lawrence Hill, 1997), 337.

74. Toni Cade Bambara, interview with Beverly Guy-Sheftall, in *Sturdy Black Bridges: Visions of Black Women in Literature*, ed. Roseann P. Bell, Bettye J. Parker, and Beverly Guy-Sheftall (New York: Anchor, 1979), 237, qtd. in Jones, *Liberating Voices*, 92.

75. Alice Walker, "From an Interview" (1973), in *In Search of Our Mothers' Gardens: Womanist Prose by Alice Walker* (New York: Harvest, 1984), 264.

76. Paul Gilroy, "Living Memory: A Meeting with Toni Morrison," in *Small Acts: Thoughts on the Politics of Black Cultures* (London: Serpent's Tail, 1993), 182.

77. Amiri Baraka suggests as much when he states that Baldwin's *Blues for Mister Charlie* (1964) "announced the Black Arts Movement" (*Eulogies* [New York: Marsilio, 1996], 105).

78. On gay men's identification with black women vocalists, see, e.g., E. Patrick Johnson, "Feeling the Spirit in the Dark: Expanding Notions of the Sacred in the African-American Gay Community," *Callaloo* 21.2 (Spring 1998): 399–416; Erik Leidal, "Aretha Franklin's 'Mary, Don't You Weep': Signifying the Survivor in Gospel Music," *GLSG Newsletter* 9.2 (October 1999): 3–8; Kun, *Audiotopia*; Michael Montlack, ed., *My Diva: 65 Gay Men on the Women Who Inspire Them* (Madison: University of Wisconsin Press, 2009). While Baldwin expressed ambivalence toward the terms "gay" and "homosexual"—and indeed toward labels of sexual orientation in general (see, e.g., Richard Goldstein, "Go the Way Your Blood Beats: An Interview with James Baldwin," *Village Voice*, June 26, 1984, 13)—I align him with gay men for political purposes and because of his importance to (black) queer theory.

79. See Noliwe Rooks on the Ford Foundation's selective support of Black Studies programs in *White Money/Black Power: The Surprising History of African American Studies and the Crisis of Race in Higher Education* (Boston: Beacon, 2006); and Melamed, *Represent and Destroy*, 32.

80. See Gayatri Chakravorty Spivak, *In Other Worlds: Essays in Cultural Politics* (New York: Routledge, 1987), 205. See also Dwight McBride's excellent discussion of "strategic essentialism" in "Speaking the Unspeakable: On Toni Morrison, African American Intellectuals and the Uses of Essentialist Rhetoric," in *Toni Morrison: Critical and Theoretical Approaches*, ed. Nancy Peterson (Baltimore: Johns Hopkins University Press, 1997), 131–152.

81. Henry Louis Gates Jr., Nellie Y. McKay, et al., eds., *Norton Anthology of African American Literature*, 2nd ed. (New York: Norton, 2003).

82. Henry Louis Gates Jr. and Nellie Y. McKay, preface to ibid., xxxiii.

83. Ibid., xlvi.

84. Ibid., xlvi–xlvii.

85. Ibid., xxxi.

86. Amiri Baraka (then LeRoi Jones), *Blues People: Negro Music in White America* (1963; repr., New York: Perennial, 2002), 102.

87. Diana Taylor distinguishes the "*archive* of supposedly enduring materials (i.e., texts, documents, buildings, bones)" from "the so-called ephemeral *repertoire*

of embodied practice/knowledge (i.e., spoken language, dance, sports, ritual)" (*The Archive and the Repertoire: Performing Cultural Memory in the Americas* [Durham, NC: Duke University Press, 2003], 19). In 1951, Columbia Records producer George Avakian reissued forty-eight of Smith's recordings on four long-playing albums. These albums may be what Baldwin listened to while writing *Go Tell It on the Mountain* (1953), an experience he relates in "The Discovery of What It Means to Be an American" (1959), in *Nobody Knows My Name: More Notes of a Native Son* (1961; repr., New York: Vintage, 1993), 5. Holiday's recordings were reissued to coincide with the 1972 Holiday biopic *Lady Sings the Blues* around the time that Jones was writing *Corregidora*.

88. Baldwin, "Discovery of What It Means," 5.

1 / Vivid Lyricism

1. Kyle Westphal, "*Native Son*—Shot in Buenos Aires, Restored in Dayton," Northwest Chicago Film Society blog, July 2, 2011, http://www.northwestchicagofilmsociety.org/2011/07/02/native-son-shot-in-buenos-aires-restored-in-dayton. As the film's director, Pierre Chenal, reported in a letter to Wright of April 1951, "All the critics are good. Some of them enthusiastic! . . . The cine Gran-Rex has all its seats sold out for three days. A fact which never occur[r]ed till now" (Richard Wright Papers, Beinecke Rare Book and Manuscript Library, Yale University, Box 96, folder 1257; hereafter cited as Wright Papers).

2. Peter Brunette's "Two Wrights, One Wrong" exemplifies the standard critical approach; measuring the film against the novel, Brunette is disappointed by the film's apparently diminished radicalism (*The Modern American Novel and the Movies*, ed. Gerald Peary and Roger Shatzkin [New York: Frederick Ungar, 1978], 131–142). Other works that discuss the film include Page Laws, "Not Everybody's Protest Film, Either: *Native Son* among Controversial Film Adaptations," *Black Scholar* 39 (Spring–Summer 2009): 27–33; John Pyros, "Richard Wright: A Black Novelist's Experience in Film," *Negro American Literature Forum* 9 (Summer 1975): 53–54; and Jerry Ward Jr., "*Native Son*: Six Versions Seeking Interpretation," in *Approaches to Teaching Wright's Native Son*, ed. James A. Miller (New York: MLA, 1997), 16–21. The best source of information on the film is still Michel Fabre's *The Unfinished Quest of Richard Wright*, trans. Isabel Barzun (New York: Morrow, 1973).

3. James Baldwin, "Alas, Poor Richard," in *Nobody Knows My Name: More Notes of a Native Son* (1961; repr., New York: Vintage, 1993), 206.

4. Pyros, "Richard Wright," 53; Laws, "Not Everybody's Protest Film," 32.

5. Richard Wright, *Native Son and "How 'Bigger' Was Born"* (1940; repr., New York: HarperPerennial, 1993), 9. Subsequent citations of the novel refer to this edition and appear in the text as *NS*.

6. Important feminist critiques of Wright's work include Sherley Anne Williams, "Papa Dick and Sister-Woman: Reflections on Women in the Fiction of Richard Wright," in *American Novelists Revisited: Essays in Feminist Criticism*, ed. Fritz Fleischmann (Boston: G. K. Hall, 1982), 394–415; Trudier Harris, "Native Sons and Foreign Daughters," in *New Essays on Native Son*, ed. Keneth Kinnamon (Cambridge: Cambridge University Press, 1990), 63–84; Farah Jasmine Griffin, "On Women, Teaching, and Native Son," in Miller, *Approaches to Teaching Wright's Native Son*, 75–80.

7. For a substantive review of claims that Wright rejects black vernacular culture, which Paul Gilroy contests, see *The Black Atlantic: Modernity and Double Consciousness*

(Cambridge, MA: Harvard University Press, 1993), 156–157, 173. Although several critics have usefully highlighted Wright's engagement with the blues—even rightly noting that Bessie's speeches in the novel *Native Son* resemble blues lyrics—they have treated the blues as a thematic trope or reference in Wright's work. See Edward A. Watson, "Bessie's Blues," *New Letters* 38 (1971): 64–70; Houston A. Baker, "On Knowing Our Place," in *Richard Wright: Critical Perspectives Past and Present*, ed. Henry Louis Gates Jr. and K. A. Appiah (1991; repr., New York: Amistad, 1993), 200–225; Craig Werner, *Playing the Changes: From Afro-Modernism to the Jazz Impulse* (Urbana: University of Illinois Press, 1994), 209–210. Rather than reify the blues as a subject or a set of lyrical statements, I examine the blues as Wright conceived them: as songs, often performed by black women, that structurally and stylistically resonate with Wright's own work.

8. Ralph Ellison, "Richard Wright's Blues" (1945), in *Living with Music: Ralph Ellison's Jazz Writings*, ed. Robert G. O'Meally (New York: Modern Library, 2001), 103.

9. See for instance Ralph Ellison, "Remembering Richard Wright" (1971), in *Collected Essays of Ralph Ellison*, ed. John F. Callahan (1995; repr., New York: Modern Library, 2003): "[Wright] had the kind of confidence that jazzmen have, although I assure you that he knew very little about jazz and didn't even know how to dance. Which is to say that he didn't possess the full range of Afro-American culture" (671). See too Ellison's "The World and the Jug" (1963–1964), in ibid., 186.

10. Richard Wright, "Blueprint for Negro Writing" (1937), in *The Richard Wright Reader*, ed. Ellen Wright and Michel Fabre (New York: Harper and Row, 1978), 43, 44.

11. Henry Louis Gates Jr., *The Signifying Monkey: A Theory of African-American Literary Criticism* (New York: Oxford University Press, 1988), 182.

12. Wright's review of *Their Eyes Were Watching God*, titled "Between Laughter and Tears," originally appeared in the *New Masses* on October 5, 1937. The review, as well as Hurston's "response" in the form of her equally scathing critique of Wright's *Uncle Tom's Children* (1938), appears in *Call and Response: Key Debates in African American Studies*, ed. Henry Louis Gates Jr. and Jennifer Burton (New York: Norton, 2011), 479–481.

13. John Dudley, *A Man's Game: Masculinity and the Anti-Aesthetics of American Literary Naturalism* (Tuscaloosa: University of Alabama Press, 2004), 9.

14. Richard Wright, *Black Boy (American Hunger): A Record of Childhood and Youth* (1945; repr., New York: Perennial Classics, 1998), 9.

15. In "Richard Wright's Blues" (1945), Ellison uses the line from *Black Boy* I have cited, among others in that passage, to illustrate Wright's "lyrical prose" (106, 104). He calls *12 Million Black Voices* Wright's "most lyrical" work in "Remembering Richard Wright," 674. David Bradley, preface to *12 Million Black Voices*, text by Richard Wright, photo direction by Edwin Rosskam (1941; repr., New York: Thunder's Mouth, 1988), xvii. Bradley claims that Wright's work with images is what gives his prose a uniquely "lyrical power" (xvi), a concept I elaborate in what follows. Ellison, "Richard Wright's Blues," 104. Baldwin, "Alas, Poor Richard," 184.

16. Richard Wright, *White Man, Listen!* (Garden City, NY: Doubleday, 1957), 127, 126.

17. Richard Wright, "Memories of My Grandmother," unpublished typescript (1941), Wright Papers, Box 6, folder 118, 25.

18. Ibid.

19. Gilroy, *Black Atlantic*, 111.

20. Although Wright does not seem to have used the term "lyrical" to describe his own writing, he uses it several times when describing "Negro Literature in the United States" in *White Man, Listen!*, where he applies the term to the work of W. E. B. Du Bois (134), Jean Toomer (139), Countee Cullen (140), and Langston Hughes (142).

21. Wright, "Blueprint for Negro Writing," 44.

22. Ibid.

23. Wright, "Memories of My Grandmother," typescript, 23.

24. When speaking with Bigger, Mary also alludes to "We Will Understand It Better By and By": "Isn't there a song like that . . . your people sing?" (*NS*, 74).

25. Wright's interpretation of "Steal Away" and "Swing Low, Sweet Chariot" in *White Man, Listen!* indicates that he may share Bigger's cynical view of these songs. Wright claims that "Steal Away" expresses "a paradoxical note of triumphant defeat" and that "Swing Low" expresses "an unappeasable longing to escape a painful life" (126–127). These claims neglect counterinterpretations of the spirituals advanced by scholars such as Sterling Brown—interpretations that, if they were not widespread when Wright published *Native Son*, were in circulation by the time he gave his European lectures. In "Folk Literature" (1941), for example, Brown pays close attention to former slaves' depictions of spirituals to argue that the songs encoded critiques of slavery (in *A Son's Return: Selected Essays of Sterling A. Brown*, ed. Mark A. Sanders [Boston: Northeastern University Press, 1996], esp. 213–215). On slaves' use of "Steal Away" to signify secret religious meetings, see Gates, *Signifying Monkey*, 68.

26. Wright, "How 'Bigger' Was Born" (1940), in *NS*, 537.

27. Three stories in Wright's *Uncle Tom's Children* also associate sacred song with black women and highlight Wright's ambivalent treatment of both. In "Long Black Song," Sarah's disastrous seduction by a white gramophone-clock salesman is prefigured by her passionate response to the hymn he plays her on his new machine (in *Uncle Tom's Children* [1938/1940; repr., New York: Harper Perennial, 2004], 133). In "Bright and Morning Star," Aunt Sue's spirituals fortify her counterrevolutionary determination to "cling to" "a faith beyond this world" (in ibid., 224). Conversely, in "Fire and Cloud," Wright directly links the spirituals with radical action. Here, a black woman begins to sing the title hymn and is immediately joined in song by an assembled mass of community protestors; together, they embolden the black protagonist, Reverend Taylor, to defy the police and lead his congregation in protest along with white communists (in ibid., 218–220). Yet unlike Sarah and Aunt Sue, who are the protagonists of their respective narratives, the female singer in "Fire and Cloud" is a marginal, if inspirational, character whose subjectivity is not explored. Thus, the religious songs of *Uncle Tom's Children* are at their most politically efficacious when they are divorced from black female subjectivity and used to inspire a revolutionary black male protagonist; the stories that prioritize black female subjectivity also make black women's relationships to religious songs personally or politically problematic.

28. Wright, "Memories of My Grandmother," typescript, 9.

29. Ibid., 3–4 (Wright's emphasis).

30. Wright, "Blueprint for Negro Writing," 40.

31. Wright, "How 'Bigger' Was Born," 531.

32. Gilroy, *Black Atlantic*, 154.

33. Wright, *White Man, Listen!*, 17–18.

34. Richard Wright, *12 Million Black Voices*, photo direction by Edwin Rosskam (1941; repr., New York: Thunder's Mouth, 1988), 128. Subsequent citations of this source refer to this edition and appear in the text as *12M*.

35. Wright, "Memories of My Grandmother," typescript, 25.

36. Lovie Austin qtd. in Chris Albertson, *Bessie* (1972; repr., New Haven, CT: Yale University Press, 2003), 177.

37. Susan McClary, *Conventional Wisdom: The Content of Musical Form* (Berkeley: University of California Press, 2000), 47.

38. Wright, "Memories of My Grandmother," typescript, 23. It should be noted that Wright links this process to surrealism, even as he expresses ambivalence about the term. He insists that the process he is describing "need not be called surrealism at all, if the word is objectionable" (ibid., 22), and that he is "no exponent of Freudian psychology or of the so-called Freudian view of life" with which surrealism is associated ("Memories of My Grandmother," unpublished manuscript [1941], Wright Papers, Box 6, folder 118, 20). There is not space to pursue the surrealist angle here, but it has been extensively addressed by Eugene Miller, in *Voice of a Native Son: The Poetics of Richard Wright* (Jackson: University Press of Mississippi, 1990), and by Robin D. G. Kelley, in *Freedom Dreams: The Black Radical Imagination* (Boston: Beacon, 2002).

39. Wright, "Memories of My Grandmother," typescript, 13 (my italics).

40. Wright, "Memories of My Grandmother," manuscript, 61.

41. Ibid., 41.

42. Ibid., 43 (Wright's emphasis).

43. Wright, "Memories of My Grandmother," typescript, 25.

44. Albert Murray, *The Blue Devils of Nada: A Contemporary American Approach to Aesthetic Statement* (1996; repr., New York: Vintage, 1997), 5.

45. Wright, "How 'Bigger' Was Born," 537.

46. Ellison, "Richard Wright's Blues," 104.

47. Wright, *Black Boy*, 9.

48. Ibid., 8.

49. Ibid., 7.

50. Ibid., 280.

51. Ibid., 244–248.

52. Paul West, "In Defense of Purple Prose," *New York Times*, December 15, 1985, http://www.nytimes.com/1985/12/15/books/in-defense-of-purple-prose.html.

53. Ellison, "Remembering Richard Wright," 674.

54. June Jordan, "On Richard Wright and Zora Neale Hurston: Notes Toward a Balancing of Love and Hatred" (1974), in Gates and Burton, *Call and Response*, 721.

55. To highlight this moment is not to deny the masculine bias of *12 Million*, the last chapter of which hails a new generation of "Men in the Making." Still, this passage calls attention to other moments in the text that privilege black female authority. For instance, the book's only photograph of organized protest shows a line of black women from various states marching past the U.S. Capitol building holding signs in protest of lynching.

56. Kelley, *Freedom Dreams*, 184.

57. McClary, *Conventional Wisdom*, 43–44.

58. Demus Dean qtd. in Albertson, *Bessie*, 165.

59. Danny Barker qtd. in *Hear Me Talkin' to Ya: The Story of Jazz as Told By the Men Who Made It*, ed. Nat Shapiro and Nat Hentoff (New York: Dover, 1955), 243.

60. Paul Green qtd. in Hazel Rowley, *Richard Wright: The Life and Times* (New York: Holt, 2001), 240. For another account of the complex playwriting process, see Margaret Bauer, "'Call Me Paul': The Long, Hot Summer of Paul Green and Richard Wright," *Mississippi Quarterly* 61 (Fall 2008): 517–538.

61. Johannes Skancke Martens, "A Black Writer Becomes a Movie Actor" (1950), in *Conversations with Richard Wright*, ed. Keneth Kinnamon and Michel Fabre (Jackson: University Press of Mississippi, 1993), 149.

62. Pierre Chenal, *Pierre Chenal: Souvenirs du cinéaste, filmographie, témoignages, documents*, ed. Pierrette Matalon, Claude Guiguet, and Jacques Pinturault (Paris: Éditions Dujarric, 1987), 185 (my translation).

63. Wright, "How 'Bigger' Was Born," 537–538.

64. Wright, *White Man, Listen!*, 17.

65. In 1944, Wright had written a film script called "Melody Limited" that dramatized the Fisk Jubilee Singers' voyage to Europe. According to Gilroy, "the Hollywood script editor . . . felt that the script lacked the simplicity and dignity that its theme deserved," and the film was not made (*Black Atlantic*, 238). Wright's journal contains an entry from 1945 in which he writes, "I've been wondering how I can ditch the literary life and start anew at something else. . . . I wish I could make films" (January 21, qtd. in Rowley, *Richard Wright*, 306–307).

66. Rowley, *Richard Wright*, 247.

67. See Brunette, "Two Wrights, One Wrong," 133.

68. According to friend and fellow writer Margaret Walker, Wright considered Dostoevsky—himself a political exile for ten years of his career—"the greatest novelist who ever lived" (qtd. in Rowley, *Richard Wright*, 120; see too 381).

69. "Le héros parlait par la bouche de son créateur" (Chenal, *Pierre Chenal*, 185 [my translation]).

70. "Elle entrait dans son rôle comme si Richard Wright l'avait écrit exprès pour elle" (ibid., 189 [my translation]).

71. Jeanine Delpech, "An Interview with Native Son" (1950), in Kinnamon and Fabre, *Conversations with Richard Wright*, 145.

72. *Native Son*, dir. Pierre Chenal, screenplay Richard Wright and Pierre Chenal, prod. James Prades (Argentina Sono Film S.A.C.I., 1951). Unless otherwise noted, all citations of the film refer to the version released by International Film Forum, 1988.

73. Wright, *Native Son*, screenplay, Wright Papers, Box 84, folder 969.

74. My analysis of Bessie's role in the film is informed by Barbara Johnson's brilliant reading of the novel, in which she argues that Wright's black female characters possess a "dangerous insight" and perform "threatening" readings that "cannot be mastered by the writer," so that "Wright consistently sees the black woman as the reader his writing must face" ("The Re(a)d and the Black: Richard Wright's Blueprint," in *The Feminist Difference: Literature, Psychoanalysis, Race, and Gender* [Cambridge, MA: Harvard University Press, 1998], 73, 69, 70, 73). In what follows, I contend that Bessie functions not only as a reader but also as Wright's alter ego in the film.

75. While the song is credited to Charles, its lyrics are included in Wright's papers—cf. *Native Son* screenplay, Wright Papers, Box 84, folder 969.

76. Wright, "Memories of My Grandmother," manuscript, 21.

77. The film renders Bigger's silence at his trial all the more poignant because it omits the last speech Bigger makes in the novel, when he tells his lawyer, Max, "I didn't want to kill! . . . But what I killed for, I *am*! . . . What I killed for must've been good!" (*NS*, 501). Without this moment of clear, if threatening, self-authorization, Bigger's most "empowered" act in the film is to drop the "Mister" from Jan's name, when he asks Max to "tell Mr. . . . Tell Jan [he] said hello."

78. *The Odyssey of Homer*, trans. Richmond Lattimore (1965; repr., New York: HarperPerennial, 1991), 186, 190 (Book XII, lns. 39-54, 181-191).

79. Bessie's prediction of the rape accusation was cut from the version of the film released in the United States—about which, more shortly.

80. Ellison, "World and the Jug," 162.

81. Georges Charbonnier, "Between Two Worlds" (1960), in Kinnamon and Fabre, *Conversations with Richard Wright*, 222.

82. Richard Wright, "Note on Jim Crow Blues (Southern Exposure)" (1949), typescript, Wright Papers, Box 6, folder 125.

83. This ending, which Page Laws calls "the religious ending" ("Not Everybody's Protest Film," 31) and which appears in the version of the film released by Facets Video (Chicago) in 1996, is the one Wright seemed to have intended. See the *Native Son* screenplay, Wright Papers, Box 68, folder 803, 132, and Box 84, folder 965. The version released by the International Film Forum in 1988 includes a different ending, for reasons that are not clear to me. In this second version, which Laws terms "the existential/agnostic ending" ("Not Everybody's Protest Film," 31), a voiceover from Max's perspective concludes, "I left Bigger feeling that everything, including justice, was still unsettled. And today I feel even less certain of innocence and guilt, crime and punishment, of the nature of man."

84. Fred Moten, *In the Break: The Aesthetics of the Black Radical Tradition* (Minneapolis: University of Minnesota Press, 2003), 197.

85. Anna Julia Cooper, *A Voice from the South* (1892; repr., New York: Oxford University Press, 1990), 138; Gilroy, *Black Atlantic*, 161.

86. See Rowley, *Richard Wright*, 393-394. The cuts to *Native Son* were not Wright's first experience with censorship. Lawrence Jackson details the process by which the Book of the Month Club board—especially judge Dorothy Canfield Fisher—pressured Wright to alter both *Native Son* and *Black Boy* before endorsing them for that program (*The Indignant Generation: A Narrative History of African American Writers and Critics, 1934-1960* [Princeton, NJ: Princeton University Press, 2011], 117, 199-200). In these cases, however, Wright himself made the changes, and his compromise exponentially increased book sales. Jackson explains that by the end of 1945, *Black Boy* had sold 195,000 copies through bookstores and 351,000 through the Book of the Month Club (200).

87. Wright to Reynolds, August 6, 1951, qtd. in Fabre, *Unfinished Quest*, 348. Fabre also explains that, when the producer asked Wright for an official statement of his approval, he said, "I want to tell you how pleased I was that the film followed so closely and faithfully the script." While it made sense for Wright to mask his disapproval in an effort to publicize his film, his double-talk may also indicate that, as dismayed as he was by the cuts, he was not entirely surprised they had been made.

88. Chenal to Wright, April 1, 1951, qtd. in Rowley, *Richard Wright*, 393.

89. For information on the Library of Congress restoration process, see Westphal, "*Native Son*."

90. *Sangre Negra/Native Son*, International Uncensored Version (digitized), Library of Congress (Motion Picture and Television Reading Room), Washington, D.C.

91. Qtd. in Westphal, "*Native Son*."

92. *Sangre Negra/Native Son*, Library of Congress. Of these cinematic moments, only Bessie's remark appears in the novel.

93. Ibid.

94. Chenal, *Pierre Chenal*, 193.

95. A.W., review of *Native Son*, by Richard Wright and Pierre Chenal, *New York Times*, June 18, 1951, Wright Papers, Box 69, folder 827.

96. The Library of Congress's restored film raises as many questions as it answers about Max's courtroom speech. Max claims that the state "has put the Negro people on trial," so that "Bigger Thomas is being denied the right to be judged as an individual." He changes Bigger's plea from guilty to not guilty (the opposite of his strategy in the novel), at which point the sympathetic judge says he must impanel a jury. Against the uproar of the court (many white spectators believe Bigger should be lynched, not tried, as he has already confessed to murder), Max insists that "the world must know what this trial means!" But the jury-trial plot goes nowhere. It is possible that the original film included extra courtroom material that justified this dramatic plot turn and that this material is missing from the Library of Congress version. (According to Westphal, the Library of Congress plans to restore another international version it has found.) What is fascinating, however, is that the search for and discovery of Bessie's body occupies the place where the jury trial should be, and that Bigger's confession that he has killed Bessie unravels the jury plot. Unlike the novel, then, the film frames Bigger's murder of Bessie as an indefensible crime and a betrayal from which the narrative cannot recover.

97. Alton Cook, "Author Plays Lead in *Native Son* Film," review of *Native Son*, by Richard Wright and Pierre Chenal, *New York World-Telegram*, June 18, 1951, Wright Papers, Box 69, folder 827.

98. Raymond Williams, *The Long Revolution* (New York: Columbia University Press, 1961), 90.

99. Wright, "I Choose Exile" (1951), Wright Papers, Box 6, folder 110, 1.

100. Baldwin, "Alas, Poor Richard," 185.

101. Darryl Pinckney, "The Black American Tragedy," review of *Richard Wright: The Life and Times*, by Hazel Rowley, *New York Review of Books*, November 1, 2001, 11. A 1956 article by New York–based reporter Ben Burns indicates that Wright was well aware of his restrictions while abroad. In a statement that Wright considered suing Burns for printing, Wright candidly assesses Americans' precarious positions in France: "You can say or write just about anything you want over here, but don't get started on France's colonies . . . Whoop, the police will be on your neck and out you go in forty-eight hours. There's no explanation—just out you go!'" (Rowley, *Richard Wright*, 473–474).

102. For an account of the essay's rejection, see Rowley, *Richard Wright*, 398–399.

103. Georges Charbonnier, "Richard Wright, For Whom Do You Write?" (1960), in Kinnamon and Fabre, *Conversations with Richard Wright*, 226.

104. Wright, "FB Eye Blues" (1949), in *Richard Wright Reader*, 249. The song contains seven more verses. One copy of the lyrics among Wright's papers has a handwritten note by Wright stating that "Josh White is setting this to music," although there is no record of White having done so (Wright Papers, Box 84, folder 970).

105. See Rowley, *Richard Wright*, 519, 452–453, 459. Buenos Aires itself offered scant refuge from state-sanctioned surveillance at this time. According to David Rock, in the years following the 1948 attempt to assassinate Perón, "the police were . . . regularly set loose against opposition newspapers; opposition politicians were rounded up and imprisoned; rumors of police beatings and torture were widespread" (*Authoritarian Argentina: The Nationalist Movement, Its History and Its Impact* [Berkeley: University of California Press, 1993], 161–162).

106. Richard Wright, "So Long, Big Bill Broonzy," typescript and carbon liner notes (1958?), Wright Papers, Box 8, folder 198, 2–3.

107. Ibid., 3.

108. Richard Wright, foreword to *Blues Fell This Morning: Meaning in the Blues*, by Paul Oliver (1960; repr., Cambridge: Cambridge University Press, 1990), xiii.

109. Wright, *White Man, Listen!*, 123.

110. Ibid., 129.

111. Ibid., 146–147.

112. Cf. Albertson, *Bessie*, 239–241.

113. Wright's papers include twelve pages of scattered and only partially legible notes (not in his hand) on Smith's life and career, as well as a German article about her and its English translation. Attached to these is a note written by his biographer, Constance Webb: "Dick considered doing a biography of Bessie Smith at one time and collected this material to that end. The bio. was not done. He did not write the attached article and the notes are not his" (Wright Papers, Box 79, folder 889). Wright's British friend Paul Oliver—for whose *Blues Fell This Morning* Wright composed the foreword—did write the biography, in 1959.

114. Aside from Gertrude Stein, the literary models Wright would publicly cite over the course of his career were predominantly white American or European men. In *Black Boy*, which includes Wright's fullest account of his formative reading material, Wright famously cites H. L. Mencken as the writer who taught him that "words [could be] weapons." He then proceeds to name thirty-six other male writers to whom he is introduced through Mencken's essays, and singles out Sinclair Lewis, Theodore Dreiser, Stephen Crane, Fyodor Dostoevsky, Stein, and Marcel Proust as important early influences (*Black Boy*, 248–249, 250, 278, 282).

115. See for instance Hazel Carby, "It Jus Be's Dat Way Sometime: The Sexual Politics of Women's Blues" (1986), in *The Jazz Cadence of American Culture*, ed. Robert G. O'Meally (New York: Columbia University Press, 1998), 469–482; Angela Davis, *Blues Legacies and Black Feminism: Gertrude "Ma" Rainey, Bessie Smith, and Billie Holiday* (New York: Vintage, 1998); Jackie Kay, *Bessie Smith* (Bath, UK: Absolute, 1997).

116. For Margaret Walker's candid discussion of her relationship with Wright, including the extensive research she contributed to the novel *Native Son*, see Nikki Giovanni and Margaret Walker, *A Poetic Equation: Conversations Between Nikki Giovanni and Margaret Walker* (Washington, DC: Howard University Press, 1974), 88–101.

117. Gunther Schuller, *Early Jazz: Its Roots and Musical Development* (1968; repr., New York: Oxford University Press, 1986), 236.

118. Bessie Smith, "Empty Bed Blues" (parts 1 and 2) (1928), comp. J. C. Johnson, on *Bessie Smith: The Complete Recordings*, vol. 4 (Columbia, 1993).

119. Alberta Hunter qtd. in Shapiro and Hentoff, *Hear Me Talkin' to Ya*, 247. Hunter seems about to say that Smith has a "tear in her voice." This is a term singers use to describe a catch in the voice that produces brief hollow sounds and can be used to evoke sadness—think of Gladys Knight, Bettye LaVette, or Angie Stone. Hunter's reconsideration makes sense in that Smith does not seem to have such a tear.

120. Schuller, *Early Jazz*, 229.

121. Albertson, *Bessie*, 80.

122. Ibid., 177.

123. Ibid.

124. Schuller, *Early Jazz*, 238.

2 / The Timbre of Sincerity

1. See, for example, Hortense Spillers, "Ellison's 'Usable Past': Toward a Theory of Myth" (1977), in *Black, White, and in Color: Essays on American Literature and Culture* (Chicago: University of Chicago Press, 2003), 65–66.

2. Even Laura Saunders's useful discussion of Ellison's engagement with the black church turns not to gospel but to jazz in order to illustrate Ellison's views on religious expression ("Ellison and the Black Church: The Gospel According to Ralph," in *The Cambridge Companion to Ralph Ellison*, ed. Ross Posnock [Cambridge: Cambridge University Press, 2005], 35–55).

3. Mahalia Jackson qtd. in Sheldon Meyers, "Publishing Jazz Books: The Prospects Are Bright," *Publisher's Weekly*, August 11, 1958, 29. (This source is cited in John Gennari, "Hipsters, Bluebloods, Rebels, and Hooligans: The Cultural Politics of the Newport Jazz Festival, 1954–1960," in *Uptown Conversation: The New Jazz Studies*, ed. Robert G. O'Meally, Brent Hayes Edwards, and Farah Jasmine Griffin [New York: Columbia University Press, 2004], 137.)

4. For a concise account of this convention, especially as it pertains to female singers and male writers, see Leslie Dunn and Nancy Jones, eds., *Embodied Voices: Representing Female Vocality in Western Culture* (Cambridge: Cambridge University Press, 1994), 1–13.

5. Ralph Ellison, "As the Spirit Moves Mahalia," draft, Ralph Ellison Papers, Library of Congress, Washington DC, Box 95 (hereafter cited as Ellison Papers).

6. Nina Eidsheim, "Voice as a Technology of Selfhood: Toward an Analysis of Racialized Timbre and Vocal Performance" (PhD diss., University of California, San Diego, 2008), 200; Roland Barthes, "The Grain of the Voice," in *Image, Music, Text*, trans. Stephen Heath (New York: Hill and Wang, 1977), 179–189.

7. Eidsheim, "Voice as a Technology," 211.

8. "For me, of course, the narrative is the meaning," Ellison writes in his introduction to "Out of the Hospital and Under the Bar," a short story outtake from *Invisible Man* (in *Soon, One Morning: New Writing by American Negroes, 1940–1962*, ed. Herbert Hill [New York: Knopf, 1968], 244).

9. Ralph Ellison, "Remembering Jimmy" (1958), in *Living with Music: Ralph Ellison's Jazz Writings*, ed. Robert G. O'Meally (New York: Modern Library, 2001), 47–48.

10. Ralph Ellison, "As the Spirit Moves Mahalia" (1958), in *Living with Music*, 90–91. Subsequent citations of this version of the essay appear in the text as *A*.

11. As the narrator of *Invisible Man* describes his college in winter, for instance, he remembers, "Over all is a quietness and an ache as though all the world were

loneliness. And I stand and listen beneath the high-hung moon, hearing 'A Mighty Fortress Is Our God,' majestically mellow on four trombones, and then the organ. The sound floats over all, clear like the night, liquid, serene, and lonely" (*Invisible Man* [1952; repr., New York: Vintage, 1995], 35). Subsequent citations of the novel refer to this edition and appear in the text as *IM*.

12. Barbara Johnson, *The Feminist Difference: Literature, Psychoanalysis, Race, and Gender* (Cambridge, MA: Harvard University Press, 1998), 2.

13. Ibid.

14. This reading practice allows us to pursue the concept of indeterminacy that critics such as Henry Louis Gates Jr. and Walton Muyumba invoke but do not utilize as an interpretive principle. For instance, while Gates describes the Yoruba god Esu as "a figure . . . of unreconciled opposites, living in harmony," he uses this concept to signal the indeterminacy of "critical activity as a whole," rather than to inform his discrete literary interpretations (*The Signifying Monkey: A Theory of African-American Literary Criticism* [New York: Oxford University Press, 1988], 30, 35). Muyumba more recently asserts that jazz can be heard to express not only "the tensions of binaries" but also "multiple aesthetic impulses, multiple emotional states, and multiple psychological selves *simultaneously*" (*The Shadow and the Act: Black Intellectual Practice, Jazz Improvisation, and Philosophical Pragmatism* [Chicago: University of Chicago Press, 2009], 21, my italics). While Muyumba does not pursue the point, to take this notion of simultaneity seriously would, I think, mean revising our standard hermeneutics—namely, by suspending the critical discourse of duplicitous irony in favor of sincere ambivalence.

15. "Irony," etym., def. a., *Oxford English Dictionary* (2nd ed., 1989).

16. Gates, *Signifying Monkey*, xxvi. Gates distinguishes between motivated and unmotivated "Signifyin(g)" to denote different effects of revising other texts; the former indicates "negative critique" of an antecedent, the latter, "an act of homage" (xxvi–xxvii). The readings he performs in *The Signifying Monkey* strongly privilege motivated signifyin(g), whereas we might say that to read for sincerity is to read for both motivated and unmotivated forms of signifyin(g), as they appear simultaneously—a point that the following discussion should make clear.

17. Ellison's early, posthumously published short story about a lynching, "A Party Down at the Square" (c. 1940), provides an extreme demonstration of masking in prose. Here Ellison critiques white terrorism by masking as one of its young representatives; his narrator is a fascinated, if nauseated, young white spectator who compares the lynched man's burning body to a "barbecued hog" (in *"Flying Home" and Other Stories*, ed. John F. Callahan [1996; repr., New York: Vintage, 1998], 9).

18. "Irony," in *New Princeton Encyclopedia of Poetry and Poetics*, ed. Alex Preminger, T. V. F. Brogan, et al. (Princeton, NJ: Princeton University Press, 1993), 634.

19. Paul Laurence Dunbar, "We Wear the Mask" (1896), in *The Collected Poetry of Paul Laurence Dunbar*, ed. Joanne M. Braxton (Charlottesville: University Press of Virginia, 1993), 71.

20. Ralph Ellison to Albert Murray, June 2, 1957, in *Living with Music*, 242.

21. Ibid., 243–244.

22. Ralph Ellison, "Change the Joke and Slip the Yoke" (1958), in *Collected Essays of Ralph Ellison*, ed. John F. Callahan (1995; repr., New York: Modern Library, 2003), 109.

23. As it pertains to African American performativity, the division between male masking and female sincerity could be attributed to the gendered history of the mask

itself, which emerges from a tradition of minstrelsy that was dominated by male performers, black and white. This male dominance is succinctly revealed in the title of an early study, *1000 Men of Minstrelsy and 1 Woman* (1909), by Edward LeRoy Rice.

24. See Bert Stern's film *Jazz on a Summer's Day* (USA, 1959), which includes an abridged version of Jackson's performance at Newport.

25. Ellison, "Change the Joke," 109.

26. Sondra O'Neale, "Inhibiting Midwives, Usurping Creators: The Struggling Emergence of Black Women in American Fiction," in *Feminist Studies / Critical Studies*, ed. Teresa de Lauretis (Bloomington: Indiana University Press, 1986), 139, qtd. in Patricia Hill Collins, *Black Feminist Thought: Knowledge, Consciousness, and the Politics of Empowerment* (1990; repr., New York: Routledge, 2000), 101.

27. Jennifer DeVere Brody, *Punctuation: Art, Politics, and Play* (Durham, NC: Duke University Press, 2008), 69.

28. *Toni Morrison Uncensored*, Morrison interview by Jana Wendt, dir. Gary Deans (Princeton, NJ: Films for the Humanities and Sciences, 1998).

29. Granted, Ellison imagines a single mainstream, while Morrison imagines two. As Ellison states, "the main stream of American literature is in me, even though I am a Negro, because I possess more of Mark Twain than many white writers do." However, insofar as Ellison rejects the idea "that we are begging to get in somewhere," his work, like Morrison's, calls readers to where "we" already are ("Transcript of the American Academy Conference on the Negro American, May 14–15, 1965," qtd. in Eric J. Sundquist, "'We Dreamed a Dream': Ralph Ellison, Martin Luther King, Jr., and Barack Obama," *Daedalus* 140.1 [Winter 2011]: 108–109).

30. Alan Nadel, "The Integrated Literary Tradition," in *A Historical Guide to Ralph Ellison*, ed. Steven C. Tracy (Oxford: Oxford University Press, 2004), 145.

31. While I appreciate Barbara Foley's decision to "depart from the circular practice of reading *Invisible Man* through the palimpsest supplied by Ellison's writings after 1952," I agree with Lawrence Jackson that Ellison's post-1952 essays aim to shape the way future readers will understand *Invisible Man* (Foley, *Wrestling with the Left: The Making of Ralph Ellison's Invisible Man* [Durham, NC: Duke University Press, 2010], 6; Jackson, "Ralph Ellison's Politics of Integration," in Tracy, *Historical Guide to Ralph Ellison*, 173). While essays like "As the Spirit" do not tell the whole story about Ellison's work (or about Mahalia Jackson's), they are major contributions by a writer who seems to have imagined that even if he could not finish his second novel, he could at least work to make the first one legible to future readers.

32. Over twenty years ago, Claudia Tate argued that black women crucially foster Invisible Man's development, in "Notes on the Invisible Women in Ralph Ellison's *Invisible Man*" (in *Speaking for You: The Vision of Ralph Ellison*, ed. Kimberly Benston [1987; repr., Washington, DC: Howard University Press, 1990], 163–172). The notion that the novel is musical in its structure or ambition is more commonly rehearsed. Here I bring these two ideas together by framing the significance of Ellison's black female characters in (Ellison's own) musical terms.

33. Anthony Heilbut, *The Gospel Sound: Good News and Bad Times* (1975; repr., New York: Limelight, 1997), 57–58.

34. Horace Clarence Boyer, *The Golden Age of Gospel* (1995; repr., Urbana: University of Illinois Press, 2000), 85.

35. Ibid., 86–87.

36. Heilbut, *Gospel Sound*, 62.

37. Malcolm X, *The Autobiography of Malcolm X*, as told to Alex Haley (1965; repr., New York: Ballantine, 1999), 223.

38. John Hammond reported on gospel's movement into the concert hall in 1952: "The kind of singing that was once confined to the storefront church in Negro ghettos has now become an established institution at Carnegie Hall" ("Gospel Singers' Progress—From Churches to Carnegie," *Down Beat* 19 [November 19, 1952]: 7).

39. Mahalia Jackson with Evan McLeod Wylie, *Movin' On Up* (New York: Hawthorn Books, 1966), 145. Subsequent citations of this source appear in the text as *M*.

40. See, e.g., Craig Werner, *A Change Is Gonna Come: Music, Race & the Soul of America* (1998; repr., Ann Arbor: University of Michigan Press, 2006), 10; Anthony Heilbut, *The Fan Who Knew Too Much: Aretha Franklin, the Rise of the Soap Opera, Children of the Gospel Church, and Other Meditations* (New York: Knopf, 2012), 92.

41. Heilbut, *Gospel Sound*, 59; George Avakian, interview with the author, January 31, 2008.

42. Studs Terkel, "Profile of Mahalia," *Down Beat* 25 (December 11, 1958): 14. Thomas Dorsey had enjoyed a more extended brush with the blues. Before he was saved, he had performed as "Georgia Tom," a blues soloist and accompanist for Ma Rainey.

43. George Wein with Nate Chinen, *Myself Among Others: A Life in Music* (New York: Da Capo, 2003), 182.

44. Cissy Houston qtd. in ibid.

45. The information about Mount Zion's history is drawn from my conversation with John Sommerville, June 9, 2012, as well as from the pamphlet "Mount Zion AME Church: A Historical Background," which I am grateful to Mr. Sommerville for providing me.

46. Ellison, "As the Spirit Moves Mahalia," draft.

47. For a more celebratory discussion of "Come Sunday," as well as a useful sociohistorical contextualization of it, see Stanley Crouch, "Come Sunday: Duke Ellington, Mahalia Jackson," in *Considering Genius* (New York: Basic Books, 2006), 258–270.

48. Melvin Tapley, "Emotional and Musical Fireworks at Newport Jazz," *New York Amsterdam News*, July 13, 1957, 15, qtd. in Gennari, "Hipsters, Bluebloods, Rebels, and Hooligans," 139, 148.

49. Mahalia Jackson, "Summertime / Sometimes I Feel Like a Motherless Child" (1956), on *Mahalia Jackson: Gospels, Spirituals, and Hymns*, vol. 2 (1992; repr., Sony, 1998).

50. Heilbut, *Gospel Sound*, 66.

51. Ellison, "Remembering Jimmy," 48.

52. Ibid., 47.

53. Ibid., 48.

54. George Gershwin qtd. in Jeffrey Melnick, *A Right to Sing the Blues: African Americans, Jews, and American Popular Song* (Cambridge, MA: Harvard University Press, 1999), 130. Samuel Floyd's musicological analysis in *The Power of Black Music* (1995) is glossed by Melnick, who additionally points out that "Motherless Child" ended the 1927 play version of *Porgy* (originally a novel by DuBose Heyward), on which Gershwin based *Porgy and Bess* (ibid.).

55. Laurraine Goreau, *Just Mahalia, Baby* (1975; repr., Gretna, LA: Firebird, 1998), 257. While the musical's depictions of the black southern poor have always been

controversial, Jackson seems to have covered the song on the cusp of a *Porgy* revival. Following Jackson's recording, Miles Davis recorded a big-band version of the opera in 1957; Louis Armstrong and Ella Fitzgerald released their *Porgy and Bess* album in 1958. (Billie Holiday recorded "Summertime" as early as 1936, the year after the opera premiered.) Holiday, Jackson, and Fitzgerald are part of the tradition Daphne Brooks brilliantly theorizes, in which black female vocalists treat the role of Bess as a template for their own acts of sonic insurgency ("One of These Mornings, You're Gonna Rise Up Singing: The Secret Black Feminist History of *Porgy and Bess*," lecture delivered at the University of Massachusetts, Amherst, April 19, 2012).

56. Melnick, *Right to Sing the Blues*, 131, 133.

57. Ibid., 133.

58. Kalamu ya Salaam, "Tok Tok Tok / 'Sometimes I Feel Like a Motherless Child,'" *Breath of Life* (blog), May 14, 2006, http://www.kalamu.com/bol/2006/05/14/tok-tok-tok-"sometimes-i-feel-like-a-motherless-child."

59. Adam Bradley, *Ralph Ellison in Progress: From Invisible Man to Three Days Before the Shooting* . . . (New Haven, CT: Yale University Press, 2010), 195.

60. Terkel, "Profile of Mahalia," 15.

61. See, for instance, this comment by Jackson: "'Lately I've been learning all these terms. You know, I half-moan and bring forth these head tones with a groan . . . the tone is still sustaining. Child—' she gives up—'I don't know how I do it myself'" (qtd. in Heilbut, *Gospel Sound*, 66).

62. Correspondence with the author, June 2012.

63. The phrase specifically denotes the period from 1945 to 1960, when "gospel recordings flooded the market, many of surpassing excellence" (Heilbut, liner notes to *When Gospel Was Gospel* [Shanachie, 2005], 3).

64. Collins, *Black Feminist Thought*, 100. For Collins, safe spaces are not only places of refuge but also places in which to build resistance.

65. Tate, "Notes on the Invisible Women," 165–166.

66. The phrase comes from the subtitle of Heilbut's *The Gospel Sound*.

67. Werner, *Change Is Gonna Come*, xiv.

68. "Spook," in *Juba to Jive: A Dictionary of African-American Slang*, ed. Clarence Major (New York: Viking, 1994), 440.

69. In "Twentieth-Century Fiction and the Black Mask of Humanity" (written in 1946, published in 1953), Ellison cites Malcolm Cowley's designation of Hemingway, Hawthorne, Melville, and Poe as America's "haunted and nocturnal writers, . . . men who dealt with images that were symbols of an inner world," but Ellison argues for a social understanding of these authors' hauntedness, one that would see their degrading depictions of black people as signs of racial panic (in *Collected Essays of Ralph Ellison*, 95, 84–85). Ellison's argument anticipates Toni Morrison's, in "Unspeakable Things Unspoken: The Afro-American Presence in American Literature," *Michigan Quarterly Review* 28 (1989): 1–34, and, later, in *Playing in the Dark: Whiteness and the Literary Imagination* (New York: Vintage, 1992).

70. Robert G. O'Meally, introduction to *New Essays on Invisible Man*, ed. Robert G. O'Meally (Cambridge: Cambridge University Press, 1988), 10.

71. Ellison, "Twentieth-Century Fiction," 81.

72. Mahalia Jackson, "Mahalia Moans" (1949/1969), on *When Gospel Was Gospel* (produced by Anthony Heilbut).

73. Heilbut, *Gospel Sound*, 310.

74. Peter Antelyes, "Red Hot Mamas: Bessie Smith, Sophie Tucker, and the Ethnic Maternal Voice in American Popular Song," in Dunn and Jones, eds., *Embodied Voices*, 220–221.

75. Fred Moten, *In the Break: The Aesthetics of the Black Radical Tradition* (Minneapolis: University of Minnesota Press, 2003), 196.

76. See, for instance, Hemingway, "The Battler," in *In Our Time* (1925; repr., New York: Scribner, 2003): "He felt of his knee. The pants were torn and the skin was barked. His hands were scraped and there were sand and cinders driven up under his nails. He went . . . to the water and washed his hands. . . . He squatted down and bathed his knee" (53). See too *The Sun Also Rises* (1926; repr., New York: Scribner, 1956): "The beach was smooth and firm, and the sand yellow. . . . I swam out to the raft, pulled myself up, and lay on the hot planks. A boy and girl were at the other end. The girl had undone the top strap of her bathing-suit and was browning her back. The boy lay face downward on the raft and talked to her. She laughed at things he said, and turned her brown back in the sun" (238–239).

77. Ralph Ellison, "A Lament for Tod Clifton" (1968–1969), in *This Is My Best* (1970), Ellison Papers, Box 164, 2.

78. Lesley Larkin, "Postwar Liberalism, Close Reading, and 'You': Ralph Ellison's *Invisible Man*," *Lit: Literature, Interpretation, Theory* 19.3 (July–September 2008): 270–271.

79. Laura Doyle, *Bordering on the Body: The Racial Matrix of Modern Fiction and Culture* (New York: Oxford University Press, 1994), 197.

80. Boyer, *Golden Age of Gospel*, 89.

81. Goreau, *Just Mahalia, Baby*, 114–115.

82. Boyer, *Golden Age of Gospel*, 90, 88.

83. James Lee qtd. in Goreau, *Just Mahalia, Baby*, 114–115.

84. Mahalia Jackson, "I Will Move On Up a Little Higher" (parts 1 and 2) (1947), on *The Essential Mahalia Jackson* (Sony, 2004); "Move On Up a Little Higher" (1954), on *The Best of Mahalia Jackson* (Sony, 1995).

85. William Brewster qtd. in Bernice Johnson Reagon, "William Herbert Brewster: Rememberings," in *We'll Understand It Better By and By: Pioneering African American Gospel Composers*, ed. Bernice Johnson Reagon (Washington, DC: Smithsonian Institution Press, 1992), 201. (This source is cited in Guthrie P. Ramsey, *Race Music: Black Cultures from Bebop to Hip-Hop* [Berkeley: University of California Press, 2003], 52.)

86. Brewster qtd. in Reagon, "William Herbert Brewster," 201 (cited in Ramsey, *Race Music*, 53).

87. Ramsey, *Race Music*, 53.

88. Ibid.

89. Boyer, *Golden Age of Gospel*, 90.

90. Qtd. in Will Friedwald's liner notes to *Mahalia Jackson: Gospels, Spirituals, and Hymns* (Sony, 1991).

91. Mary Childers and bell hooks, "A Conversation about Race and Class," in *Conflicts in Feminism*, ed. Marianne Hirsch and Evelyn Fox Keller (New York: Routledge, 1990), 70, qtd. in Johnson, *Feminist Difference*, 3. hooks is specifically encouraging feminists to embrace contradictions within and between themselves.

92. Ralph Ellison, Drafts, Episodes, "Prologue," n.d., Ellison Papers, Box 146, folder 4.

93. Spillers, "Ellison's 'Usable Past,'" 79.

94. Ralph Ellison, introduction to *Invisible Man* (1981; repr., New York: Vintage, 1995), xx; Herbert Blau, *The Audience* (Baltimore: Johns Hopkins University Press, 1990), 42.

95. Blau, *Audience*, 5.

96. Ralph Ellison, "What America Would Be Like Without Blacks," in *Collected Essays*, 585.

97. Ibid.; Ellison, "Twentieth-Century Fiction," 90.

98. Ralph Ellison, "The Golden Age, Time Past" (1959), in *Living with Music*, 55.

99. Salaam, "Tok Tok Tok / 'Sometimes I Feel.'"

100. Kenneth Warren, *So Black and Blue: Ralph Ellison and the Occasion of Criticism* (Chicago: University of Chicago Press, 2003), 102.

101. For another excellent example of this tactic, see Jackson's performance of "How I Got Over," recorded live in Sweden in 1961; she restarts the song twice in the midst of the audience's applause (on *The Essential Mahalia Jackson* [Sony, 2004]).

102. Heilbut, *Gospel Sound*, 68.

103. Ibid., 71.

104. Jackson qtd. in ibid., 72.

105. Harry Belafonte qtd. in Alden Whitman, "Mahalia Jackson, Gospel Singer, and a Civil Rights Symbol, Dies," *New York Times*, January 28, 1972.

106. Heilbut, *Gospel Sound*, 70–71.

107. Ellison, "Lament for Tod Clifton," 2.

108. Heilbut, *Gospel Sound*, xxiii, xxxiii. Nathaniel Mackey cites this statement in *Bedouin Hornbook* (1986; repr., Los Angeles: Sun and Moon, 1997), 63; Fred Moten cites Mackey's citation in *In the Break*, 194.

3 / Understatement

1. I am thinking here of what Peter Szendy calls the *"responsibility of listening,"* as I explain in what follows (*Listen: A History of Our Ears*, trans. Charlotte Mandel [2001; repr., New York: Fordham University Press, 2008], 10, Szendy's italics).

2. Ralph Ellison, *Invisible Man* (1952; repr., New York: Vintage, 1995), 297.

3. In claiming Jackson and other black musicians for black listeners, Baldwin picks up a subtler thread in Ellison's own work. Ellison himself contrasts black and white audiences' understandings of Bessie Smith when he states that "Bessie Smith might have been a 'blues queen' to society at large, but within the tighter Negro community where the blues were part of a total way of life . . . , she was a priestess, a celebrant who affirmed the values of the group" ("Blues People" [1964], in *Living with Music: Ralph Ellison's Jazz Writings*, ed. Robert G. O'Meally [New York: Modern Library, 2001], 131).

4. Jean-Luc Nancy, *Listening*, trans. Charlotte Mandel (2002; repr., New York: Fordham University Press, 2007), 6; see, too, 36.

5. Studs Terkel, "An Interview with James Baldwin" (1961), in *Conversations with James Baldwin*, ed. Fred L. Stanley and Louis H. Pratt (Jackson: University Press of Mississippi, 1989), 3.

6. Ralph Ellison, "Brave Words for a Startling Occasion" (1953), in *Collected Essays of Ralph Ellison*, ed. John F. Callahan (New York: Modern Library, 1995), 152. Here

Ellison explains that understated novels such as Hemingway's were not viable models for him, since his "minority status rendered all such assumptions questionable."

7. James Baldwin, *The Fire Next Time* (1963; repr., New York: Vintage, 1993), 99.

8. Ibid., 41–42. This statement is rare among Baldwin's writings on music for addressing both ostensibly "happy" and ostensibly "sad" songs. As this chapter will show, Baldwin's writings on black women singers privilege seemingly happy songs that encode pain, not seemingly sad ones that encode pleasure.

9. Baldwin often strategically deploys pronouns to identify himself with a white liberal audience. While this strategy led Langston Hughes to lament that "Baldwin's viewpoints are half-American, half-Afro-American, incompletely fused," it was clearly intended to win over the "American" side of Hughes's equation (Hughes, review of *Notes of a Native Son* [1955], by James Baldwin, *New York Times Book Review*, February 28, 1956, qtd. in David Leeming, *James Baldwin: A Biography* [New York: Knopf, 1994], 101). See, for instance, the opening gambit of Baldwin's "Many Thousands Gone" (1951): "Today, to be sure, we know that the Negro is not biologically or mentally inferior; there is no truth in those rumors of his body odor or his incorrigible sexuality. . . . [Yet] up to today we are set at a division, so that he may not marry our daughters or our sisters, nor may he—for the most part—eat at our tables or live in our houses. Moreover, those who do, do so at the grave expense of a double alienation: from their own people, . . . [and] from us" (in *Notes of a Native Son* [Boston: Beacon, 1984], 26).

10. James Baldwin, "The Uses of the Blues" (1964), in *The Cross of Redemption: Uncollected Writings*, ed. Randall Kenan (New York: Pantheon, 2010), 58. Subsequent citations of this source refer to this edition and appear in the text as *U*.

11. For Baldwin's conflicted relationship with Wright, see Baldwin's "Everybody's Protest Novel" (1949), in *Notes of a Native Son*, 13–23; "Princes and Powers" (1957), in *Nobody Knows My Name: More Notes of a Native Son* (1961; repr., New York: Vintage, 1993), 13–55; and "Alas, Poor Richard" (1961), in *Nobody Knows My Name*, 181–215.

12. James Baldwin and Nikki Giovanni, *A Dialogue* (New York: Lippincott, 1973), 21. This book documents Baldwin and Giovanni's two-part conversation on the television show *Soul!*, which aired in December 1971.

13. *James Baldwin: The Price of the Ticket*, dir. Karen Thorsen (American Masters, 1989).

14. Douglas Taylor, "Three Lean Cats in a Hall of Mirrors: James Baldwin, Norman Mailer, and Eldridge Cleaver on Race and Masculinity," *Texas Studies in Literature and Language* 52.1 (Spring 2010): 85.

15. On the dubious value of suffering, we might note that Baldwin's work is in some sense an extended memorial for black men who either live with intolerable bitterness, like his father, or kill themselves out of despair (Rufus in *Another Country* [1962], Frank in *If Beale Street Could Talk* [1974]). Thus, while his writings celebrate black resilience, they also give the lie to the notion that what does not kill someone always makes one stronger.

16. Baldwin, *Fire Next Time*, 98.

17. Valerie Smith, "Black Feminist Theory and the Representation of the 'Other,'" in *Changing Our Own Words: Essays on Criticism, Theory, and Writing by Black Women*, ed. Cheryl A. Wall (1989; repr., New Brunswick, NJ: Rutgers University Press, 1991), 45. Smith cites this logic to critique scholars who use black female creative or critical

writers as a "historicizing presence" to "humanize" (and thus authorize) their work (45, 46).

18. James Baldwin, *Another Country* (1962; repr., New York: Vintage, 1993), 347. Subsequent citations of the novel are to this edition and appear in the text as *AC*.

19. Langston Hughes, "The Negro Artist and the Racial Mountain," *Nation*, June 23, 1926, 694.

20. James Baldwin, "Of the Sorrow Songs: The Cross of Redemption" (1979), in *Cross of Redemption*, 122. Subsequent citations of this source appear in the text as *SS*.

21. James Baldwin, "The Discovery of What It Means to Be an American" (1959), in *Nobody Knows My Name*, 5.

22. In an interview with Studs Terkel, Baldwin speaks in more technical (though rather vague) detail about how listening to Smith's records helped him write *Go Tell It on the Mountain*. See Terkel, "Interview with James Baldwin," 4–5.

23. In Baldwin's formulation, Smith is also implicitly made to bear the term "nigger," the force of which is mitigated neither by Baldwin's use of quotation marks nor by his matter-of-fact deployment of the term. Baldwin does not elaborate on his choice of the term here; the line thus threatens to read as a slur against Smith herself, as Baldwin defines the singer in and on his own terms.

24. Baldwin, "Alas, Poor Richard," 184.

25. James Baldwin, "The Black Boy Looks at the White Boy" (1961), in *Nobody Knows My Name*, 230.

26. Ibid., 231.

27. Ibid., 232.

28. Ibid.

29. Jack Kerouac, *On the Road* (1957; repr., New York: Penguin, 1991), 204, 180. The novel opens in 1947, when "bop was going like mad all over America," and the music embodies and spurs Sal Paradise's journey: "As I sat there listening to that sound of the night which bop has come to represent for all of us, I thought of all my friends from one end of the country to the other and how they were really all in the same vast backyard doing something so frantic and rushing-about. And for the first time in my life, the following afternoon, I went into the West" (12).

30. Kobena Mercer, "Skin Head Sex Thing: Racial Difference and the Homoerotic Imaginary," in *How Do I Look? Queer Film and Video*, ed. Bad Object-Choices (Seattle: Bay, 1991), 208.

31. Norman Mailer, "The White Negro: Superficial Reflections on the Hipster" (1957), in *Advertisements for Myself* (New York: Putnam, 1959), 341.

32. Ibid.

33. Baldwin's discussion of Smith in "Uses of the Blues" may also have ridden the new wave of publicity sparked by Edward Albee's play *The Death of Bessie Smith*, which opened in West Berlin in 1960 and which Smith's biographer Chris Albertson suggests was a main source of (mis)information about Smith's death (*Bessie* [1972; repr., New Haven, CT: Yale University Press, 2003]), 258). See note 35.

34. Baldwin's first lines echo W. E. B. Du Bois's "The Sorrow Songs," another essay that aims to recuperate and translate the legacy of African American song. Du Bois initially disclaims any specialized knowledge of musical form in order to advance another kind of knowledge: "What are these songs, and what do they mean? I know little of music and can say nothing in technical phrase, but I know something of men,

and knowing them, I know that these songs are the articulate message of the slave to the world" (*The Souls of Black Folk* [1903], in *Writings*, ed. Nathan Huggins [New York: Library of America, 1986], 538).

35. Smith, who died from wounds sustained from a car accident on a Mississippi highway, was long thought to have died on the way from a white hospital that turned her away to a black hospital that would treat her. Albertson convincingly dispels this myth in his biography of Smith, first published in 1972; he does so in part by relating the eyewitness account of a surgeon named Hugh Smith who contends that Smith's ambulance driver would never have thought to bring her to a white hospital in the first place (*Bessie*, 262–263).

36. The line "I know, I watched, I was there" recalls the quotation from Whitman's *Leaves of Grass* (1855) with which Baldwin frames *Giovanni's Room* (1956): "*I am the man, I suffered, I was there.*"

37. David Evans explains that, while "Backwater Blues" came to be "indelibly associated" with the Mississippi flood of 1927, Smith in fact recorded it two months before the levees broke. The song was released just as they did, however, and this coincidence fostered the popular assumption that Smith had written the song about the flood (while also yielding unprecedented record sales for Columbia) ("Bessie Smith's 'Back-Water Blues': The Story Behind the Song," *Popular Music* 26.1 [January 2006]: 99).

38. Here Baldwin refers to Smith's "Long Old Road," a blues she recorded in 1931.

39. Baldwin first uses this phrase in "Sonny's Blues" (1957), in *Going to Meet the Man* (1965; repr., New York: Vintage, 1995), 132.

40. "*The Black Scholar* Interviews James Baldwin" (1973), in Stanley and Pratt, *Conversations with James Baldwin*, 155.

41. Ibid.

42. Kenneth Burke, "Literature as Equipment for Living" (1937), in *Perspectives by Incongruity*, ed. Stanley Edgar Hyman (Bloomington: Indiana University Press, 1964), 100–109. This concept was frequently cited by Ellison; see, for instance, "What These Children Are Like" (1963), in *Collected Essays of Ralph Ellison*, 547. Abbey Lincoln also uses the phrase in her 1966 piece "The Negro Woman in American Literature" (*Freedomways* 6.1 [Winter 1966]: 11–13), as I discuss shortly.

43. Albertson, *Bessie*, 87, 274.

44. See Aldon Nielsen's introduction to Lorenzo Thomas, *Don't Deny My Name: Words and Music and the Black Intellectual Tradition*, ed. Aldon Nielsen (Ann Arbor: University of Michigan Press, 2008), 4.

45. Amiri Baraka (then LeRoi Jones), *Dutchman*, in *Dutchman and The Slave* (New York: Morrow, 1964), 34–35. Adam Gussow convincingly reads this moment through the lens of the white blues revival in "'If Bessie Smith Had Killed Some White People': Racial Legacies, the Blues Revival, and the Black Arts Movement," in *New Thoughts on the Black Arts Movement*, ed. Lisa Gail Collins and Margo Natalie Crawford (New Brunswick, NJ: Rutgers University Press, 2006), 229.

46. Larry Neal, "The Ethos of the Blues," *Black Scholar* 3.10 (Summer 1972): 42, qtd. in Gussow, "If Bessie Smith," 232.

47. Lincoln, "Negro Woman in American Literature," 12, 11, 13. Lincoln's piece is based on a panel discussion held at the New School in New York City in 1965. In addition to Lincoln, the panel included writers Sarah E. Wright, Alice Childress, and Paule Marshall, whose commentary is likewise reprinted in the Winter 1966 issue of

Freedomways. (See Farah Jasmine Griffin, *If You Can't Be Free, Be a Mystery: In Search of Billie Holiday* [New York: Ballantine Books, 2001], 174.)

48. Lincoln, "Negro Woman in American Literature," 13.

49. Gussow, "If Bessie Smith," 232.

50. Baldwin, "Sonny's Blues," 130, 132.

51. Szendy, *Listen*, 143.

52. When Vivaldo tells his friend Cass, a white woman, that because he grew up in a poor neighborhood "the same things have happened" to him that have happened to African Americans in Harlem, she points out, "[These things] didn't . . . happen to you *because* you were white. They just happened. But what happens up here [in Harlem] . . . happens *because* they are colored. And that makes a difference" (*AC*, 113–114).

53. Szendy, *Listen*, 2 (Szendy's italics).

54. Hortense Spillers suggests that we "draw out the emphasis on the female vocalist's art, rather than her biographies," in "Interstices: A Small Drama of Words" (1984), in *Black, White, and in Color: Essays on American Literature and Culture* (Chicago: University of Chicago Press, 2003), 166.

55. Bessie Smith, "Backwater Blues" (1927), on *Bessie Smith: The Complete Recordings*, vol. 3 (Sony, 1992).

56. Farah Jasmine Griffin, "Children of Omar: New Orleans, Resistance, Resilience & Resettlement" (talk presented at "Rites of Return: Poetics and Politics" Symposium, Columbia University, April 10, 2008).

57. Jackie Kay, *Bessie Smith* (Bath, UK: Absolute, 1997), 72–73.

58. Ibid., 10.

59. I owe this insight to Stephanie Ambroise.

60. Angela Davis, *Blues Legacies and Black Feminism: Gertrude "Ma" Rainey, Bessie Smith, and Billie Holiday* (New York: Vintage, 1998), 9.

61. Ibid., 137.

62. Ellison, "Blues People," 131.

63. Bessie Smith, "Preachin' the Blues" (1927), on *Bessie Smith: The Complete Recordings*, vol. 3.

64. Scott Saul, *Freedom Is, Freedom Ain't: Jazz and the Making of the Sixties* (Cambridge, MA: Harvard University Press, 2003), 31.

65. Billie Holiday with William Dufty, *Lady Sings the Blues* (1956; repr., New York: Harlem Moon, 2006), 43.

66. Robert G. O'Meally, *Lady Day: The Many Faces of Billie Holiday* (New York: Da Capo, 1991), 31–32.

67. Ibid., 30–31.

68. The extent to which the aesthetic of understatement has been coded male is reflected in Leon Forrest's description of Holiday's style. As Forrest writes, "Holiday's approach was more akin to that of certain modern writers, like Hemingway, Tennessee Williams, and later Baldwin and Mailer, in the essay form" ("Solo Long-Song for Lady Day," *Callaloo* 16.2 [Spring 1993]: 356).

69. Ibid., 365, 337, 357.

70. Billie Holiday, "Billie's Blues" (composed 1936, rec. 1944), on *The Commodore Master Takes* (GRP Records, 2000).

71. Willie Dixon's signature blues song "Built for Comfort" (1959) revolves around the opposite claim (Dixon and Memphis Slim, on *Willie's Blues* [Obc, 1991]).

72. Maya Gibson, "Alternate Takes: Billie Holiday at the Intersection of Black Cultural Studies and Historical Musicology" (PhD diss., University of Wisconsin–Madison, 2008), 125.

73. Teddy Wilson qtd. in ibid.

74. Gunther Schuller, *The Swing Era: The Development of Jazz, 1930–1945* (1989; repr., New York: Oxford University Press, 1991), 532. For an excellent analysis of Holiday's work with swing ensembles, see Kate Daubney, "Songbird or Subversive? Instrumental Vocalisation Technique in the Songs of Billie Holiday," *Journal of Gender Studies* 11.1 (2002): 17–28. Daubney argues that Holiday subverts the narrow role of "songbird," the female singer whose task is to convey lyrics to the audience (and look beautiful), by honing her skills via musical dialogue with instrumentalists.

75. Marisa Parham, *Haunting and Displacement in African American Literature and Culture* (New York: Routledge, 2009), 32–36.

76. Nancy, *Listening*, 7, 5.

77. In a tapped phone conversation between Holiday's manager-lover Louis McKay and Maely Dufty (the wife of Holiday's biographer), which is transcribed in Julia Blackburn's *With Billie* (New York: Pantheon, 2005), an enraged McKay threatens to beat Holiday, accusing her of spending his money and sleeping around (277–282). The association between the professions of singing and prostitution has a long history and a broad geography. Ann Petry represents this connection in her harrowing novel *The Street* (Boston: Houghton Mifflin, 1946). Lena Horne explains that her community considered singing an "unspeakable profession" for a woman, one that signaled sexual promiscuity, if not literal prostitution (*In Person: Lena Horne*, as told to Helen Arstein and Carlton Moss [New York: Greenberg, 1950], 13; see also 25–26, 41–43, 166–167). Angélique Kidjo states that "in Africa, if you are a little girl who dreams of making a career as a vocalist, it is very hard on you because the singing profession is considered like prostitution" (in *I Got Thunder: Black Women Songwriters on Their Craft*, ed. LaShonda Katrice Barnett [New York: Thunder's Mouth, 2007], 27).

78. James Baldwin, *Another Country* draft fragments, 1956–1959, Harry Ransom Humanities Research Center, University of Texas, Austin.

79. Eldridge Cleaver, *Soul on Ice* (New York: Delta, 1968), 14. See bell hooks, "Race and Sex," in *Yearning: Race, Gender, and Cultural Politics* (Boston: South End, 1990), 58–59.

80. hooks, "Race and Sex," 58–59.

81. In a 1972 interview with John Hall, Baldwin explains that it was important for him to depict Rufus as a character with agency rather than a victim of white society, in terms that are also relevant to his depiction of Ida: "Rufus was partly responsible for his doom, and in presenting him as partly responsible, I was attempting to break out of the whole sentimental image of the afflicted nigger driven that way [to suicide] by white people" ("James Baldwin, a *Transition* Interview," *Transition* 41 [1972]: 23).

82. Leeming, *James Baldwin*, 202.

83. James Baldwin, *The Devil Finds Work* (1976; repr., New York: Laurel, 1990), 122–123. For an incisive, extended reading of this concept, see Ryan Jay Friedman, "'Enough Force to Shatter the Tale to Fragments': Ethics and Textual Analysis in James Baldwin's Film Theory," *ELH* 77.2 (Summer 2010): 385–411.

84. Szendy, *Listen*, 10, 142 (Szendy's italics).

85. Ralph Ellison, "As the Spirit Moves Mahalia" (1958), in *Living with Music*, 94.

86. Baldwin explicitly links both women's deaths in "On Catfish Row" (1959), when he writes, "Out of [one] Catfish Row or another came the murdered Bessie Smith and the dead Billie Holiday and virtually every Negro performer this country has produced" ("On Catfish Row: *Porgy and Bess* in the Movies," in *The Price of the Ticket: Collected Nonfiction, 1948–1985* [New York: St. Martin's, 1985], 180).

87. As if to echo Ida's veiled engagement with Jackson in this scene, Baldwin closes the novel with a veiled (and inverted) allusion to "A City Called Heaven," a gospel classic that Jackson recorded in 1951. Jackson sings, "I've heard of a city called Heaven, and I'm striving to make Heaven my home." In the novel's last lines, Eric's French lover, Yves, arrives at a New York airport: Yves "strode through the barriers, more high-hearted than he had ever been as a child, into that city which the people from heaven had made their home" (*AC*, 436).

88. Saul, *Freedom Is, Freedom Ain't*, 72.

89. Larry Neal, "And Shine Swam On: An Afterword," in *Black Fire: An Anthology of Afro-American Writing*, ed. Amiri Baraka and Larry Neal (1968; repr., Baltimore: Black Classic, 2007), 645.

90. Quincy Troupe, "Last Testament: An Interview with James Baldwin" (1988), in Stanley and Pratt, *Conversations with James Baldwin*, 285.

91. Nancy, *Listening*, 36.

92. James Smethurst, *The Black Arts Movement: Literary Nationalism in the 1960s and 1970s* (Chapel Hill: University of North Carolina Press, 2005), 86.

93. Leeming, *James Baldwin*, 285.

94. Douglas Field, "Looking for Jimmy Baldwin: Sex, Privacy, and Black Nationalist Fervor," *Callaloo* 27.2 (Spring 2004): 468.

95. See Colm Tóibín, "The Last Witness," *London Review of Books* 23.18 (September 20, 2001): 19.

96. Henry Louis Gates Jr., *Thirteen Ways of Looking at a Black Man* (New York: Vintage, 1998), 12.

97. Ibid.

98. Cleaver, *Soul on Ice*, 107.

99. Baldwin cites Nina Simone and Aretha Franklin in "Of the Sorrow Songs," 123, 121; he invokes Simone in "*The Black Scholar* Interviews James Baldwin," 155, and Franklin in Baldwin and Giovanni, *Dialogue*, 79–80.

100. Nikki Giovanni explains her choice of Baldwin as the writer with whom she wished to speak on the television show *Soul!* in 1971 by stating, "He's the dean of American writing; it has to be Jimmy" (Tom Smith, "Public Radio Book Show: Nikki Giovanni" [1990], in *Conversations with Nikki Giovanni*, ed. Virginia Fowler [Jackson: University Press of Mississippi, 1992], 195).

101. Neal, "And Shine Swam On," 647.

102. Richard Wright, "Blueprint for Negro Writing" (1937), in *The Richard Wright Reader*, ed. Ellen Wright and Michel Fabre (New York: Harper and Row, 1978), 37–40.

103. "Farewell to Storyville" is a song performed by Holiday and Louis Armstrong in the 1947 film *New Orleans*. The song concerns the 1917 closure of Storyville, the famed New Orleans "red light district" that was a key birthplace of jazz.

104. Vaughn Rasberry, "'Now Describing You': James Baldwin and Cold War Liberalism," in *James Baldwin: America and Beyond*, ed. Cora Kaplan and Bill Schwarz (Ann Arbor: University of Michigan Press, 2011), 96.

105. Anthony Heilbut, *The Gospel Sound: Good News and Bad Times* (1975; repr., New York: Limelight, 1997), xxxiii.

106. Baldwin, "Many Thousands Gone," 24.

107. Baldwin, "Sonny's Blues," 139.

108. Ibid., 138.

4 / Haunting

1. Jones tells Michael S. Harper that "*Corregidora* . . . is a blues novel" in "Gayl Jones: An Interview" (1975), in *Chant of Saints: A Gathering of Afro-American Literature, Art, and Scholarship*, ed. Michael S. Harper and Robert B. Stepto (Urbana: University of Illinois Press, 1979), 360.

2. Toni Morrison, "Toni Morrison on a Book She Loves: Gayl Jones's *Corregidora*" (1975), in *What Moves at the Margin: Selected Nonfiction*, ed. Carolyn C. Denard (Jackson: University Press of Mississippi, 2008), 110.

3. Farah Jasmine Griffin, *If You Can't Be Free, Be a Mystery: In Search of Billie Holiday* (New York: Ballantine Books, 2001), 32.

4. Leon Forrest, "A Solo Long-Song for Lady Day," *Callaloo* 16.2 (Spring 1993): 336. Forrest uses some variation of the term "haunting" seven times throughout this essay.

5. Angela Davis, *Blues Legacies and Black Feminism: Gertrude "Ma" Rainey, Bessie Smith, and Billie Holiday* (New York: Vintage, 1998), 195.

6. See, for instance, Bernette Golden, review of *Corregidora*, by Gayl Jones, *Black World* 25.4 (February 1976): 82; and Paul Stoller, "'Conscious' Ain't Consciousness: Entering the 'Museum of Sensory Absence,'" in *The Senses Still: Perception and Memory as Material Culture in Modernity*, ed. C. N. Seremetakis (Chicago: University of Chicago Press, 1996), 109.

7. Bruce Simon, "Traumatic Repetition: Gayl Jones's *Corregidora*," in *Race Consciousness: African-American Studies for the New Century*, ed. Judith Jackson Fossett and Jeffrey A. Tucker (New York: NYU Press, 1997), 94.

8. Avery Gordon, *Ghostly Matters: Haunting and the Sociological Imagination* (1997; repr., Minneapolis: University of Minnesota Press, 2008), xvi.

9. Suzan-Lori Parks, "From Elements of Style" (1994), in *The America Play and Other Works* (New York: Theatre Communications Group, 1995), 9. Parks's concept resonates with Henry Louis Gates Jr.'s concept of "Signifyin(g)," which he defines as "repetition and revision, or repetition with a signal difference" (*The Signifying Monkey: A Theory of African-American Literary Criticism* [New York: Oxford University Press, 1988], xxiv). But whereas Gates uses "signifyin(g)" to theorize the process by which writers repeat and revise the work of other writers, Parks speaks of revising herself. Parks's idea is more germane here, as Jones and Holiday haunt by performing "incremental refrain" within a single work or across their own oeuvre.

10. Billie Holiday with William Dufty, *Lady Sings the Blues* (1956; repr., New York: Harlem Moon, 2006), 96. Subsequent citations of this source appear in the text as *LS*. Although some commentators believe cowriter William Dufty to be the sole author of this memoir, I nonetheless consider *Lady Sings the Blues* a richly suggestive resource due to the language it provides—a language that may in some cases be Holiday's own—for understanding Holiday's art. Maya Gibson offers the most extensive consideration of the status of *Lady Sings the Blues* in "Alternate Takes: Billie Holiday

at the Intersection of Black Cultural Studies and Historical Musicology" (PhD diss., University of Wisconsin–Madison, 2008), 15–62.

11. The notion that Holiday's singing voice offers her listeners intimate knowledge of her life may not be surprising, given Simon Frith's contention that "we hear [popular] singers as *personally* expressive" in general (*Performing Rites: On the Value of Popular Music* [Cambridge, MA: Harvard University Press, 1996], 186). However, this mythology is especially resonant with regard to Holiday's career, for the reasons I outline.

12. Griffin, *If You Can't Be Free*, 17.

13. Whitney Balliett, "Lady Day," *New Yorker*, November 4, 1991, 100, qtd, in *The Billie Holiday Companion: Seven Decades of Commentary*, ed. Leslie Gourse (New York: Schirmer Books, 1997), xxii.

14. Forrest, "Solo Long-Song," 340.

15. Nina Eidsheim, "Voice as a Technology of Selfhood: Toward an Analysis of Racialized Timbre and Vocal Performance" (PhD diss., University of California, San Diego, 2008), 239.

16. Harper, "Gayl Jones: An Interview," 357. *Lady Sings the Blues* offers an important account of the practice Jones evokes here. Glossing an interview in which cellist Pablo Casals explains that he must play differently every time because "nature is so. And we are nature," Holiday states, "So there you are. You can't even be like you once were yourself, let alone like somebody else. I can't stand to sing the same song the same way two nights in succession, let alone two years or ten years. If you can, then it ain't music, it's close-order drill or exercise or yodeling or something, not music" (53–54).

17. Another way in which Jones generates a sense of unstated complexity is by pruning information from the text. Versions of the novel available at the Howard Gotlieb Archival Research Center at Boston University show Jones omitting lines from subsequent drafts, such as when she revises the final scene, to enhance the novel's stark ambiguity (Gayl Jones Collection, drafts of *Corregidora*, Box 1).

18. Gordon, *Ghostly Matters*, 22.

19. Ibid., xvi, 203 (Gordon's italics).

20. In a "Postscript" to the book, Jones writes, "The preceding chapters . . . were completed in 1982," but does not explain the time lapse between composition and publication (*Liberating Voices: Oral Tradition in African American Literature* [New York: Penguin Books, 1991], 191).

21. Trudier Harris, foreword to *After the Pain: Critical Essays on Gayl Jones*, ed. Fiona Mills and Keith B. Mitchell (New York: Peter Lang, 2006), ix.

22. Ibid., ix, xii.

23. Morrison, "Toni Morrison on a Book She Loves," 109–110.

24. Jones tells Claudia Tate that a question Morrison asked her—"What about Ursa's past?"—"required that [Jones] clarify the relationships between Ursa and Mutt and Ursa and her mother. So [she] added about one hundred pages to answer those questions" (Claudia Tate, "An Interview with Gayl Jones," *Black American Literature Forum* 13.4 [Winter 1979]: 142). As Jones explained to Michael Harper, these hundred pages included "the scene where Ursa goes back and talks to her mother and . . . one about Ursa and Mutt before the incident of the fall down the stairs. Now, [both of those scenes are] very essential to the book" ("Gayl Jones: An Interview," 358). At the Howard Gotlieb Archive, one finds a handwritten draft without these episodes, as well

as handwritten "inserts" Jones later composed—about half of what is now part 2 of the novel and all of part 3 (Jones Collection, Box 1, folder 1).

25. Tate, "Interview with Gayl Jones," 142.

26. Ibid. Jones received tenure from the University of Michigan in 1982. She resigned due to controversy surrounding her late husband, Bob Higgins, who committed suicide in a confrontation with Lexington, Kentucky, police in 1998. See Peter Manso's article "Chronicle of a Tragedy Foretold," *New York Times Magazine*, July 19, 1998, http://www.nytimes.com/1998/07/19/magazine/chronicle-of-a-tragedy-foretold. html. This piece, which focuses on Jones's relationship with Higgins, is a rare source of information about her life.

27. Tate, "Interview with Gayl Jones," 146; Charles H. Rowell, "An Interview with Gayl Jones," *Callaloo* 16 (October 1982): 40.

28. Manso, "Chronicle of a Tragedy Foretold." The writing mentor who "sense[s]" Jones's "bottled-up black rage" is R. V. Cassill.

29. Harper, "Gayl Jones: An Interview," 357, 358.

30. Ibid., 359, 357. It is unclear whether Jones is referring to the drafts of *Corregidora* that are available at the Howard Gotlieb Archive, but these drafts do contain passages that Jones titles "Waking Song" and "Ursa's Song" (Jones Collection, Box 1, folder 1; see p. 91 and other unnumbered pages in following draft "inserts").

31. Harper, "Gayl Jones: An Interview," 359-360.

32. Gayl Jones, *Corregidora* (1975; repr., Boston: Beacon, 1986), 56. Subsequent citations of the novel refer to this edition and appear in the text as *C*. Blues-oriented critical approaches to the novel include Melvin Dixon, "Singing a Deep Song: Language as Evidence in the Novels of Gayl Jones," in *Black Women Writers, 1950–1980*, ed. Mari Evans (New York: Doubleday, 1984), 236–248; Katherine Boutry, "Black and Blue: The Female Body of Blues Writing in Jean Toomer, Toni Morrison, and Gayl Jones," in *Black Orpheus: Music in African American Fiction from the Harlem Renaissance to Toni Morrison*, ed. Saadi A. Simawe (New York: Garland, 2000), 91–118; and (especially relevant for my purposes) Alfonso Hawkins, "A Non-Negotiable Blues Catharsis: Billie and Ursa, *Lady Sings the Blues* and *Corregidora*," *Western Journal of Black Studies* 29.3 (Fall 2005): 656–665. Hawkins argues that "through the action statement of jazz, Billie Holiday . . . , like Ursa Corregidora, triumphs as a woman, African American, and singer" (656). Particularly interesting blues readings include Donia Elizabeth Allen, "The Role of the Blues in Gayl Jones's *Corregidora*," *Callaloo* 25.1 (Winter 2002): 257–273; and Cheryl A. Wall, *Worrying the Line: Black Women Writers, Lineage, and Literary Tradition* (Chapel Hill: University of North Carolina Press, 2005).

33. Critics who read the novel through the lens of trauma or repetition compulsion include Madhu Dubey, "Gayl Jones and the Matrilineal Metaphor," *Signs* 20.2 (Winter 1995): 245–267; Simon, "Traumatic Repetition," 93–112; Ashraf H. A. Rushdy, *Remembering Generations: Race and Family in Contemporary African American Fiction* (Chapel Hill: University of North Carolina Press, 2001); Elizabeth Swanson Goldberg, "Living the Legacy: Pain, Desire, and Narrative Time in Gayl Jones' *Corregidora*," *Callaloo* 26.2 (Spring 2003): 446–472; Christina Sharpe, *Monstrous Intimacies: Making Post-Slavery Subjects* (Durham, NC: Duke University Press, 2010).

34. This connection between revelation and submission runs throughout Jones's oeuvre. *Eva's Man* (1976) begins as the narrator, who has been convicted for killing her lover, resists the voyeurism of the police, the press, psychologists—and, by extension,

the reader (*Eva's Man* [1976; repr., Boston: Beacon, 1987], 3–5). The narrator of *Mosquito* (1999), Nadine, becomes increasingly suspicious of her readers, whom she calls "spies" and "rumormongers," and starts to withhold information from them: "I ain't gonna tell y'all all my business . . . I don't play that." As she tells her friend, "I patrols my own borders" (*Mosquito* [Boston: Beacon, 1999], 7, 8, 420, 136–137).

35. Tate, "Interview with Gayl Jones," 143, 147.

36. Jennifer Cognard-Black, "'I Said Nothing': The Rhetoric of Silence and Gayl Jones's *Corregidora*," *NWSA Journal* (National Women's Studies Association) 13.1 (Spring 2001): 41.

37. It is worth noting that the word "pluck" also features prominently in "Strange Fruit": "Here is a fruit for the crows to pluck . . ."

38. Jones Collection, Box 1, folder 1, 73–74 (my italics). Jones crosses out "your" and writes "their" ("their temples," "their eyes") in this version.

39. Ibid., 54. Here Jones removes quotation marks from three lines of dialogue in (an extended version of) the exchange in which Ursa tells her interlocutor that the blues help her "explain what [she] can't explain."

40. Hazel Carby, *Reconstructing Womanhood: The Emergence of the Afro-American Woman Novelist* (New York: Oxford University Press, 1987), 25.

41. Dixon, "Singing a Deep Song," 240.

42. Melvin Dixon, for instance, notes that Ursa's "reconciliation with Mutt . . . assumes the rhythm, structure, and tone of a blues stanza," and he takes this as "evidence for the *regeneration* that Ursa and Mutt experience" (ibid., 240–241).

43. See Holiday's performance of "Fine and Mellow" on the 1957 CBS special *The Sound of Jazz*: http://www.youtube.com/watch?v=YKqxG09wlIA.

44. Davis, *Blues Legacies*, 23.

45. Donny Hathaway, "I Know It's You," on *Extension of a Man* (Atlantic, 1973).

46. Esther Phillips, "Baby, I'm for Real," on *From a Whisper to a Scream* (Kudu, 1971).

47. Later neo-soul and pop examples of the "reassurance song" include the Roots and Erykah Badu's "You Got Me" ("Baby don't worry, you know that you got me") (The Roots, *Things Fall Apart* [MCA, 1999]) and Beyoncé's "Be With You" ("I ain't goin nowhere! I'm *happy* with you, you got me baby!") (*Dangerously in Love* [Columbia, 2003]).

48. A female singer also mediates a lover's sexual advance toward the narrator of *Eva's Man*. Eva first meets her lover, Davis, at a bar where a woman is singing: "'They call it the devil blues,' the woman was singing, low now. Davis looked back. 'She real fine,' he said, then he looked at me. 'I can tell something about you,' he said. 'You ain't been getting it, have you?'" (7).

49. Spike Hughes, *Second Movement: Continuing the Autobiography of Spike Hughes* (London: Museum Press, 1951), 260, qtd. in John Chilton, *Billie's Blues: The Billie Holiday Story, 1933–1959* (New York: Da Capo, 1975), 14, and in Gibson, "Alternate Takes," 73–74.

50. Ibid.

51. Jones Collection, Box 1, folder 1, 179 (typescript insert).

52. Amiri Baraka, "Billie," in *The Music: Reflections on Jazz and Blues*, ed. Amiri Baraka and Amina Baraka (New York: Morrow, 1987), 285. For an extended analysis

of Baraka's Holiday poems, see Farah Jasmine Griffin, "Baraka's Billie Holiday as a Blues Poet of Black Longing," *African American Review* 37.2–3 (Summer–Fall 2003): 313–320.

53. Forrest, "Solo Long-Song," 332, 351.

54. Despite this critique, I should note that Forrest has a great deal of value to say about Holiday's art, particularly as it relates to the work of writers as varied as Ernest Hemingway and Toni Morrison.

55. Griffin, *If You Can't Be Free*, 155–158.

56. See note 24. The only way we know that Ursa's visit to her mother occurs during the next twenty years—i.e., that it occurs significantly later than the main part of the narrative—is that Ursa states, "I was in my late thirties" at the time of this visit (*C*, 109). She is twenty-five when the novel begins. So Jones very subtly skips the narrative ahead ten to fifteen years for Ursa's visit to her mother, and explicitly skips ahead another ten years for the final part, which opens with the line, "It was June 1969" (*C*, 168).

57. Gibson, "Alternate Takes," 142.

58. John Hammond qtd. in David Margolick, *Strange Fruit: The Biography of a Song* (New York: HarperPerennial, 2001), 59.

59. Hammond qtd. in ibid.

60. Holiday qtd. in ibid.

61. Ibid., 68–69.

62. See Chilton, *Billie's Blues*, 160. The publisher opted for *Lady Sings the Blues*, despite the fact that Holiday had never liked being called a "blues singer" (ibid.).

63. Robert G. O'Meally, *Lady Day: The Many Faces of Billie Holiday* (New York: Da Capo, 1991), 21.

64. Another man's name, Frank DeViese, appears on Holiday's birth certificate— see Gibson, "Alternate Takes," 32.

65. Ruth Wilson Gilmore, *Golden Gulag: Prisons, Surplus, Crisis, and Opposition in Globalizing California* (Berkeley: University of California Press, 2007), 28.

66. Davis, *Blues Legacies*, 188–189.

67. Ibid., 190.

68. Ibid., 194.

69. Billie Holiday, "Strange Fruit" (1939), on *Billie Holiday: The Commodore Master Takes* (Polygram, 2000).

70. Gunther Schuller, *The Swing Era: The Development of Jazz, 1930–1945* (1989; repr., New York: Oxford University Press, 1991), 543.

71. Billie Holiday, "Strange Fruit" (1945), on *Ultimate Billie Holiday* (Polygram, 1997).

72. Billie Holiday, "Strange Fruit" (1956), on *Lady Sings the Blues: The Billie Holiday Story*, vol. 4 (Polygram, 1995).

73. This performance is featured in *Lady Day: The Many Faces of Billie Holiday* (dir. Michael Seig, screenplay Robert G. O'Meally [Kultur, 1991]). It is also available on YouTube: http://www.youtube.com/watch?v=h4ZyuULy9zs. For more information, see Griffin, *If You Can't Be Free*, 108, 114–115.

74. Amiri Baraka (then LeRoi Jones), "The Dark Lady of the Sonnets" (1962), in *Black Music* (New York: Quill, 1967), 25.

75. O'Meally, *Lady Day*, 30.

76. Shane Vogel uses this term to interpret Ethel Waters's performance of "Stormy Weather" in "Performing 'Stormy Weather': Ethel Waters, Lena Horne, and Katherine Dunham," *South Central Review* 25.1 (Spring 2008): 100.

77. O'Meally, *Lady Day*, 157.

78. Balliett, "Lady Day," 100, qtd. in *Billie Holiday Companion*, xxii.

79. Geoff Dyer, *But Beautiful: A Book About Jazz* (1991; repr., London: Abacus, 2007), 198.

80. See too *Lady Sings*, 160.

81. Barney Josephson qtd. in Donald Clarke, *Billie Holiday: Wishing on the Moon* (1994; repr., New York: Da Capo, 2002), 158; on Holiday's work with Teddy Wilson, see Gibson, "Alternate Takes," 130.

82. For an important discussion of singers' use of the language of personal feeling, see Lara Pellegrinelli, "The Song Is Who? Locating Singers on the Jazz Scene" (PhD diss., Harvard University, 2005), 265–285. Pellegrinelli suggests that we hear "I sing what I *feel*" as "I sing what *I* feel"—as a singer's assertion of control over and connectedness to her own repertoire. Given "the restrictions placed on [singers] by the publishing and recording industries, that statement can be read as a [powerful] assertion of freedom and agency" (283).

83. O'Meally, *Lady Day*, 167.

84. Schuller, *Swing Era*, 546, 528.

85. See Farah Jasmine Griffin, "When Malindy Sings: A Meditation on Black Women's Vocality," in *Uptown Conversation: The New Jazz Studies*, ed. Robert G. O'Meally, Brent Hayes Edwards, Farah Jasmine Griffin (New York: Columbia University Press, 2004), 107. Griffin refers to Eileen Southern's *The Music of Black Americans: A History* (New York: Norton, 1971).

86. Forrest, "Solo Long-Song," 340.

87. The sense in which analysis may enhance one's sense of wonder is clear, for example, when Gunther Schuller lists several facets of Holiday's art that he could only have detected through careful, analytical listening and yet describes them as "mysteries" (*Swing Era*, 537). To Schuller's list I would add Holiday's approach to musical timing, which is brilliantly analyzed by musicologists Hao Huang and Rachel V. Huang in "Billie Holiday and *Tempo Rubato*: Understanding Rhythmic Expressivity," in *Annual Review of Jazz Studies* 7 (1994–1995), ed. Edward Berger et al. (Boston: Scarecrow, 1996), 181–199. The authors seek to reconcile two popular yet contradictory accounts of Holiday's timing—that she was perfectly in time and that she sang off the beat—by explaining that both are true: Holiday keeps her own steady beat that is consistently out of sync with her accompanists, so she is "both with [her own] beat *and* off [the band's] beat" (188). Huang and Huang compare this technique with "tempo rubato," a concept associated with eighteenth-century Italian art music and literally meaning "stolen time" (195).

88. Rowell, "Interview with Gayl Jones," 45.

89. Jones, *Liberating Voices*, 17.

90. Ibid., 178, 54.

91. Amiri Baraka, "The Myth of a 'Negro Literature'" (1962), in *Home: Social Essays* (1966; repr., New York: Akashic Books, 2009), 124.

92. Larry Neal, "And Shine Swam On: An Afterword," in *Black Fire: An Anthology of Afro-American Writing*, ed. Amiri Baraka and Larry Neal (1968; repr., Baltimore: Black Classic, 2007), 653–654.

93. Jones, *Liberating Voices*, 90.

94. Ibid., 91.

95. Ibid., 186–187.

96. Amiri Baraka (LeRoi Jones), "The Changing Same (R&B and New Black Music)" (1966), in *Black Music*, 180–211.

97. Amy Ongiri, *Spectacular Blackness: The Cultural Politics of the Black Arts Movement and the Search for a Black Aesthetic* (Charlottesville: University of Virginia Press, 2009), 103.

98. Moynihan memo to Nixon qtd. in Peter Carroll, *It Seemed Like Nothing Happened: The Tragedy and Promise of America in the 1970s* (New York: Holt, Rinehart and Winston, 1982), 41 (cited in Rushdy, *Remembering Generations*, 13).

99. bell hooks, "The Chitlin Circuit: On Black Community," in *Yearning: Race, Gender, and Cultural Politics* (Boston: South End, 1990), 37.

100. Jones, *Liberating Voices*, 190. Jones's study generally demonstrates the challenge faced by many African American artists and intellectuals, as Madhu Dubey describes it, of "resisting essentialism while remaining invested in the project of authentic racial representation" (*Signs and Cities: Black Literary Postmodernism* [Chicago: University of Chicago Press, 2003], 39).

101. Baraka, "Dark Lady of the Sonnets," 25.

102. Marisa Parham, "Event Horizons: Notes on Memory, Space, and Haunting in African American Literature and Culture" (PhD diss., Columbia University, 2004), 15–16.

103. Michael Hardt, "Foreword: What Affects Are Good For," in *The Affective Turn: Theorizing the Social*, ed. Patricia Ticineto Clough with Jean Halley (Durham, NC: Duke University Press, 2007), x.

104. Gordon, *Ghostly Matters*, 163 (my italics).

105. Cathy Caruth, *Unclaimed Experience: Trauma, Narrative, and History* (Baltimore: Johns Hopkins University Press, 1996), 108, 9; Joseph Roach, *Cities of the Dead: Circum-Atlantic Performance* (New York: Columbia University Press, 1996), 2, 4–5, 80; Jacques Derrida, *Specters of Marx: The State of the Debt, the Work of Mourning and the New International*, trans. Peggy Kamuf (New York: Routledge, 1994), xviii; Gordon, *Ghostly Matters*, 17, 22; Gayatri Chakravorty Spivak, "Translating in a World of Languages," *Profession* (PMLA), 2010, 39 (my italics).

106. Cassandra Wilson qtd. in Margolick, *Strange Fruit*, 125.

107. Ibid., 126.

108. Cassandra Wilson, "Strange Fruit," on *New Moon Daughter* (Blue Note, 1996). In accordance with Wilson's remarks about singing "Strange Fruit," Etta James describes the aim of her own Grammy Award–winning Holiday tribute album: "to pay my respects to Billie, not by imitating her, but by singing in my own style." James also notes, "Billie Holiday haunts me to this day" (Etta James and David Ritz, *Rage to Survive: The Etta James Story* [1995; repr., New York: Da Capo, 2003], 262, 37).

109. Rowell, "Interview with Gayl Jones," 42.

110. Jones, *Corregidora* (1975; repr., New York: Bantam, 1976). The *New York Times* critic is Raymond Sokolov.

5 / Signature Voices

1. Cheryl Clarke is the only critic, to my knowledge, who sets Franklin in a Black Arts context—namely, through her brilliant reading of Franklin's version of "The Thrill Is Gone" (1970) (*After Mecca: Women Poets and the Black Arts Movement* [New Brunswick, NJ: Rutgers University Press, 2005], 7–10).

2. Amy Ongiri aptly characterizes many Black Arts theorists' evocations of soul and funk music as "ambivalent." Although these musical genres were more popular with black audiences than avant-garde jazz, writers like Baraka seemed to feel they were too mainstream and commercial to score a revolutionary movement. See Ongiri, *Spectacular Blackness: The Cultural Politics of the Black Arts Movement and the Search for a Black Aesthetic* (Charlottesville: University of Virginia Press, 2009), 131–133. Askia Muhammad Touré energetically rejects this ambivalent view of black popular music in "We Are on the Move and Our Music Is *Moving* with Us" (originally published as "Keep on Pushing," 1965), in *Black Nationalism in America*, ed. John H. Bracey, August Meier, Elliot Rudwick (1970; repr., Indianapolis: Bobbs-Merrill, 1980), 445–451.

3. The *Oxford English Dictionary* defines *signature* as the "name (or special mark) of a person written with his or her own hand as an authentication of some document or writing" (def. 2a, 2nd ed. [1989]). Giovanni and Franklin invite us to theorize a more nuanced relationship between "singing" and "signing" than that which Lindon Barrett proposes in *Blackness and Value: Seeing Double* (Cambridge: Cambridge University Press, 1999), 84.

4. Giovanni prefaced a reading of her "Poem for Aretha" in 1973 by telling her audience, "Somebody [an interviewer] asked me today if I could come back in another life, who would I come back as. I would come back as Aretha Franklin. I just space on Aretha! I would come back here in a long white dress with a big baby grand. You would probably laugh at me" (Lorraine Dusky, "Fascinating Woman" [1973], in *Conversations with Nikki Giovanni*, ed. Virginia Fowler [Jackson: University Press of Mississippi, 1992], 56).

5. Virginia Fowler, "A Conversation with Nikki Giovanni" (1991), in Virginia Fowler, *Nikki Giovanni* (New York: Twayne, 1992), 149.

6. Stephen Henderson, "Introduction: The Forms of Things Unknown," in *Understanding the New Black Poetry: Black Speech and Black Music as Poetic References* (New York: Morrow, 1973). For Henderson's discussion of "Black Music as Poetic Reference" (a section that includes analysis of Giovanni's poems), see 46–61.

7. Aretha Franklin and David Ritz, *Aretha: From These Roots* (New York: Villard, 1999), 109.

8. Sherley Anne Williams is one critic who advances the notion that the audience "assumes 'we' even though the blues singer sings 'I.'" See "The Blues Roots of Contemporary Afro-American Poetry," in *Chant of Saints: A Gathering of Afro-American Literature, Art, and Scholarship*, ed. Michael S. Harper and Robert B. Stepto (Urbana: University of Illinois Press, 1979), 124 (in which Williams credits Harper for codifying this concept).

9. Henderson, *Understanding the New Black Poetry*, 30.

10. Giovanni explained her decision to record her poetry to gospel music on *Truth Is On Its Way* as an attempt to reach older African Americans who, she feared, may

have been alienated by the militant politics of young black artists like herself. See M. Cordell Thompson, "Black Rebel with Power in Poetry" (1972), in Fowler, *Conversations with Nikki Giovanni*, 41.

11. Henderson, *Understanding the New Black Poetry*, 61.

12. John Seigenthaler, "A Word on Words" (1987), in Fowler, *Conversations with Nikki Giovanni*, 172. In a 2010 National Public Radio interview, Giovanni likewise highlighted the difference between rap lyrics and poetry—or, rather, supported poet Kwame Alexander's distinction between them. Alexander stated, "I think that if you look at a rap lyric and you put it down on the page, it may not resonate or connect as much as it does on the stage. And I think that a poem, as Nikki would like to say, a poem that 'behaves'... is going to resonate and connect on the page and the stage" (Michel Martin, "Poet Nikki Giovanni Out with 100 Best African American Poems," *npr.org*, December 22, 2010, http://www.npr.org/2010/12/22/132259083/ Poet-Nikki-Giovanni-Out-With-100-Best-African-American-Poems).

13. In claiming that Giovanni embraces textuality as much as music and other oral forms, I am departing rather dramatically from other critical approaches to her work. Even her most attentive critic, Virginia Fowler, contends that Giovanni expresses her "authentic" poetic voice by using forms like speech and music to defy white, Western conventions of printed poetry, whereas what I am calling Giovanni's "signature voice" *only* registers through the medium of writing (see Fowler, introduction to *The Collected Poetry of Nikki Giovanni, 1968–1998* [New York: Morrow, 2003], xxiii–xxv).

14. Amiri Baraka, *The Autobiography of LeRoi Jones/Amiri Baraka* (1984; repr., Chicago: Lawrence Hill, 1997), 337 (Baraka's italics). Baraka's position on this matter was not entirely consistent. Aldon Nielsen notes that, in a preface to a 1972 chapbook, Baraka critiques those who exalt orality over literacy on the assumption that African societies were oral *instead of* literate: "We were the first writers as well" (Baraka, "Introduction: Pfister Needs to Be Heard!," in *Beer Cans, Bullets, Things & Pieces*, by Arthur Pfister [Detroit: Broadside, 1972], 4, qtd. in Nielsen, *Black Chant: Languages of African-American Postmodernism* [Cambridge: Cambridge University Press, 1997], 19).

15. Larry Neal, "And Shine Swam On: An Afterword," in *Black Fire: An Anthology of Afro-American Writing*, ed. Amiri Baraka and Larry Neal (1968; repr., Baltimore: Black Classic, 2007), 655; Henderson, *Understanding the New Black Poetry*, 30.

16. Neal, "And Shine Swam On," 655.

17. Here I follow scholars such as Nathaniel Mackey, Aldon Nielsen, Brent Edwards, and Meta Jones, who encourage us to see the printed poem as a unique event in its own right, instead of as a poor substitute or score for oral performance. See Nathaniel Mackey, *Discrepant Engagement: Dissonance, Cross-Culturality, and Experimental Writing* (Tuscaloosa: University of Alabama Press, 1993), 122; Nielsen, *Black Chant*, 18ff.; Brent Edwards, "The Seemingly Eclipsed Window of Form: James Weldon Johnson's Prefaces," in *The Jazz Cadence of American Culture*, ed. Robert G. O'Meally (New York: Columbia University Press, 1998), 580–601; Meta DuEwa Jones, "Jazz Prosodies: Orality and Textuality," *Callaloo* 25.1 (Winter 2002): 66–91; Jones, *The Muse Is Music: Jazz Poetry from the Harlem Renaissance to Spoken Word* (Urbana: University of Illinois Press, 2011), 183. But again, I suggest that the "event" of Giovanni's poetry is not only to gesture toward an "absent music" that exists autonomously outside of the

poem (as Edwards's brilliant reading of the blues poem implies ["Seemingly Eclipsed," 596]), but also to re-create that music.

18. Phillip Brian Harper, *Are We Not Men? Masculine Anxiety and the Problem of African-American Identity* (New York: Oxford University Press, 1996), 53. See Michele Wallace's *Black Macho and the Myth of the Superwoman* (New York: Dial, 1979) for one of the earliest and most well-known critiques of Black Power masculinism and sexism.

19. Clarke, *After Mecca*, 2.

20. Harper, *Are We Not Men?*, 52. Harper uses Giovanni's "The True Import of Present Dialogue, Black vs. Negro" (in *Black Feeling, Black Talk*, 1968)—"Learn to kill niggers / Learn to be Black men"—to make this case (39–40). Michele Wallace charged Giovanni with black male identification much earlier, in her ungenerous reading of Giovanni's work in *Black Macho*, 166–169.

21. Examples of this approach include Clarke, *After Mecca*, and Cheryl Malcolm Alexander, "(Un)Dressing Black Nationalism: Nikki Giovanni's (Counter)Revolutionary Ethics," in *And Never Know the Joy: Sex and the Erotic in English Poetry*, ed. C. C. Barfoot (Amsterdam: Rodopi, 2006), 389–397.

22. Barbara Johnson, *The Feminist Difference: Literature, Psychoanalysis, Race, and Gender* (Cambridge, MA: Harvard University Press, 1998), 194.

23. That Giovanni and Franklin are (distant) friends who admire each other's work is evident from Giovanni's foreword to Matt Dobkin's *I Never Loved a Man the Way I Love You: Aretha Franklin, Respect, and the Making of a Soul Music Masterpiece* (New York: St. Martin's, 2004), xi–xiii.

24. Clarke, *After Mecca*, 23.

25. Amiri Baraka, "The Myth of a 'Negro Literature'" (1962), in *Home: Social Essays* (1966; repr., New York: Akashic Books, 2009), 125, qtd. in Lorenzo Thomas, *Don't Deny My Name: Words and Music and the Black Intellectual Tradition*, ed. Aldon Nielsen (Ann Arbor: University of Michigan Press, 2008), 123.

26. As Giovanni told Claudia Tate, "I just want to be clear on Phillis [Wheatley] because I think she gets a bad rap. People haven't read her and don't know a damn thing about her life and don't want to empathize with her life. I think she had a difficult life. If she could say she was delighted to be on these shores, then we have to look at that" (*Black Women Writers at Work*, ed. Claudia Tate [New York: Continuum, 1983], 63–64). Chapter 9 of Giovanni's memoir, *Gemini*, is an essay on Charles Chesnutt that aims to restore his place in the literary tradition by stating that black writers "sink or swim on his accomplishments" (*Gemini: An Extended Autobiographical Statement on My First Twenty-Five Years of Being a Black Poet* [1971; repr., New York: Penguin, 1983], 100). Nor is Giovanni's defense of unpopular writers limited to African American authors. When Yevgeny Yevtushenko asks her to confirm that "Black people don't like Harriet Beecher Stowe's *Uncle Tom's Cabin*," Giovanni answers, "No, they don't like it. But I like it. It was good propaganda in the 1850s. You can't judge a book outside of its context" ("Poet to Poet: Nikki Giovanni and Yevgeny Yevtushenko" [1972], in Fowler, *Conversations with Nikki Giovanni*, 20).

27. Harryette Mullen, "African Signs and Spirit Writing," *Callaloo* 19.3 (Summer 1996): 670–671.

28. Fowler, "Conversation with Nikki Giovanni," 145; Richard Wright, "Blueprint for Negro Writing" (1937), in *The Richard Wright Reader*, ed. Ellen Wright and Michel Fabre (New York: Harper and Row, 1978), 40.

29. Fowler, "Conversation with Nikki Giovanni," 147.

30. Ibid., 154.

31. Aaron Cohen, *Amazing Grace* (New York: Continuum, 2011), 13; Anthony Heilbut, *The Fan Who Knew Too Much: Aretha Franklin, the Rise of the Soap Opera, Children of the Gospel Church, and Other Meditations* (New York: Knopf, 2012), 93, 126.

32. Heilbut, *The Fan Who Knew Too Much*, 125.

33. Franklin's 1971 column for the *Amsterdam News*, titled "From Gospel to Jazz Is Not Disrespect for The Lord!," is quoted in Cohen, *Amazing Grace*, 28–29.

34. Aretha Franklin, "Amazing Grace," on *Amazing Grace* (Atlantic, 1972). This performance appears in the documentary *Aretha Franklin: The Queen of Soul*, screenplay by Nelson George, ed. Jody Sheff (A*Vision Entertainment, 1988). All citations of *Aretha Franklin: The Queen of Soul* refer to this film, unless otherwise noted.

35. David Llorens, "Miracle in Milwaukee," *Ebony*, November 1967, 29, qtd. in Phyl Garland, *The Sound of Soul* (Chicago: Henry Regnery, 1969), 194.

36. Charles Keil and Steven Feld, "Commodified Grooves," in *Music Grooves: Essays and Dialogues* (Chicago: University of Chicago Press, 1994), 306–307.

37. Angela Davis argues that blueswomen's work cannot be called "protest music" because these artists lacked an "organized political structure capable of functioning as a channel for transforming individual complaint into effective collective protest" (*Blues Legacies and Black Feminism: Gertrude "Ma" Rainey, Bessie Smith, and Billie Holiday* [New York: Vintage, 1998], 113). See too James Cone, *The Spirituals and the Blues: An Interpretation* (Maryknoll, NY: Orbis Books, 1972), 121.

38. Franklin and Ritz, *From These Roots*, 155; Williams, "Blues Roots," 124.

39. Fowler, *Nikki Giovanni*, ix.

40. Fowler, introduction to *Conversations with Nikki Giovanni*, xi. In a prescient 1986 essay, Margaret McDowell contended that Giovanni's literary reputation suffered due to disparaging reviews by male artists and critics who were alienated by the critiques Giovanni leveled at black male leadership in her 1969 essay "Black Poems, Poseurs and Power" ("Groundwork for a More Comprehensive Criticism of Nikki Giovanni," in *Belief vs. Theory in Black American Literary Criticism*, ed. Joe Weixlmann and Chester J. Fontenot [Greenwood, FL: Penkevill, 1986], 135–160).

41. Houston Baker, "Nikki Giovanni," in *The Norton Anthology of African American Literature*, 2nd ed., ed. Henry Louis Gates Jr., Nellie Y. McKay, et al. (New York: Norton, 2003), 2096.

42. "Special Issue: The 100 Greatest Singers of All Time," *Rolling Stone* 1066 (November 27, 2008). The sensational title of this survey does not accurately reflect its purview: voters selected their favorite pop, rock, and R&B singers of the twentieth century.

43. Heilbut, *The Fan Who Knew Too Much*, 125, 124. For Franklin's role as arranger-composer, see ibid., 131–133.

44. Dobkin, *I Never Loved a Man*, 194.

45. Recent scholarship on Simone includes Tammy Kernodle, "'I Wish I Knew How It Would Feel to Be Free': Nina Simone and the Redefining of the Freedom Song of the 1960s," *Journal of the Society for American Music* 2 (2008): 295–317; Shana Redmond, "Anthem: Music and Politics in Diaspora, 1920–1970s" (PhD diss., Yale University, 2008); Daphne A. Brooks, "Nina Simone's Triple Play," *Callaloo* 34.1 (Winter 2011): 176–197.

46. Guthrie P. Ramsey, *Race Music: Black Cultures from Bebop to Hip-Hop* (Berkeley: University of California Press, 2003), 157. Ramsey attributes this phenomenon to the "symbolic currency of 'soul music' . . . in black nationalist discourse" (ibid.).

47. Stephen Henderson, "Saturation: Progress Report on a Theory of Black Poetry," *Black World* 24.8 (June 1975): 15–16, 17. (This essay is reprinted in *African American Literary Theory*, ed. Winston Napier [New York: NYU Press, 2000], 102–112.) Critic and composer Carman Moore is the author of the 1972 *Village Voice* review of Franklin's album that Henderson cites. Henderson also invokes Franklin (as well as Bessie Smith) in his initial discussion of "saturation" in *Understanding the New Black Poetry*, 64. Williams, "Blues Roots," 124.

48. Giovanni qtd. in Cohen, *Amazing Grace*, 42.

49. Davis explains in her memoir that Franklin was ultimately unable to post the bail since she was out of the country when the moment to do so arrived, "and the money could not be released without her personal signature" (*Angela Davis: An Autobiography* [1974; repr., New York: International, 2008], 338).

50. Nikki Giovanni, "Poem for Aretha," in *Re:Creation* (Detroit: Broadside, 1970), 17–19. A prose version of this poem—what might better be called a re-creation of it—also appears as a "poetic insert" within Giovanni's review of Phyl Garland's *The Sound of Soul* in *Gemini* (113–121). Giovanni's reading of "Poem for Aretha," set to organ accompaniment and a gospel vocal of "Nobody Knows the Trouble I've Seen," is on *Truth Is On Its Way* (Right On Records, 1971).

51. Giovanni, "Poem for Aretha," 17, 19. Subsequent citations of the poem refer to the first (1970) edition and appear in the text as *PA*. I render the poem's line breaks as they appear in this edition.

52. Sterling Brown, "Ma Rainey," in *Southern Road* (New York: Harcourt, Brace, 1932), 62–64; Frank O'Hara, "The Day Lady Died," in *Lunch Poems* (San Francisco: City Lights Books, 1964), 25–26.

53. Johnson, *Feminist Difference*, 172.

54. Clarke, *After Mecca*, 66.

55. Giovanni, "Poem for Aretha," on *Truth Is On Its Way*.

56. Michael Awkward, *Soul Covers: Rhythm and Blues Remakes and the Struggle for Artistic Identity* (Durham, NC: Duke University Press, 2007), 46. It was commonplace for music journalists and industry insiders to draw analogies between Franklin and other female vocalists like Smith, Holiday, and Washington. Producer John Hammond deemed Franklin "the most dynamic jazz voice [he had] heard since Billie Holiday" (qtd. in Dobkin, *I Never Loved a Man*, 27). Janis Joplin repeated the compliment in her own inimitable way, calling Franklin "the best chick singer since Billie Holiday" (qtd. in Chris Porterfield, "Lady Soul: Singing It Like it Is," *Time*, June 28, 1968, 64). Phyl Garland stretched the comparison to its limit by describing Franklin as "the consolidated Bessie Smith–Billie Holiday–Dinah Washington of the day" (*Sound of Soul*, 191).

57. See Porterfield, "Lady Soul," 62–66. Awkward discusses this *Time* story and Franklin's putative responses to it in *Soul Covers*, 42–54.

58. Henderson, *Understanding the New Black Poetry*, 38.

59. The Temptations, "Message from a Black Man," on *Puzzle People* (Gordy, 1969).

60. Early Franklin classics that end in fade-outs include "I Never Loved a Man" and "Respect" (on *I Never Loved a Man the Way I Love You* [Atlantic, 1967]); "Chain of

Fools" (on *Lady Soul* [Atlantic, 1968]); "Think" (on *Aretha Now* [Atlantic, 1968]); and "Spirit in the Dark" (on *Spirit in the Dark* [Atlantic, 1970]).

61. Clarke, *After Mecca*, 66.

62. Kalamu ya Salaam, "Two Trains Running: Black Poetry 1965–2000," *Word Up* (blog), n.d., http://wordup.posterous.com/essay-two-trains-running-black-poetry-1965-20-0. Salaam associates "speech/music-oriented" poets with Black Arts writers, for whom "text was not the singular consideration but rather one of a number of considerations," and "text-oriented" poets with "academically-oriented" post–Black Arts writers.

63. See for instance Craig Werner, *Higher Ground: Stevie Wonder, Aretha Franklin, Curtis Mayfield, and the Rise and Fall of American Soul* (New York: Crown, 2004), 3; Dobkin, *I Never Loved a Man*, 204; Thulani Davis, "Aretha Franklin: Do Right Diva," liner notes to *Aretha Franklin: Queen of Soul, the Atlantic Recordings* (Rhino Records, 1992), 21.

64. While Franklin achieved superstardom just a few years before Giovanni published "Poem for Aretha" in 1970, it should be noted that she had released about a dozen albums by that time.

65. Clarke, *After Mecca*, 93.

66. Awkward, *Soul Covers*, 55.

67. Shane Vogel, "Performing 'Stormy Weather': Ethel Waters, Lena Horne, and Katherine Dunham," *South Central Review* 25.1 (Spring 2008): 96.

68. Aretha Franklin, "A Change Is Gonna Come," on *Never Loved a Man* (Atlantic, 1967).

69. Dobkin, *I Never Loved a Man*, 178–179.

70. This verse was included on the 1963 version of "Change" that Cooke donated to *The Stars Salute Dr. Martin Luther King,* an LP designed to raise money for the Southern Christian Leadership Conference. When it came time to release "Change" as a single, however, the song was about thirty seconds too long; Cooke's biographer Daniel Wolff suggests that RCA producers pressured Cooke to remove this particular verse (Wolff, with S. R. Crain, Clifton White, and G. David Tenenbaum, *You Send Me: The Life and Times of Sam Cooke* [New York: Quill, 1995], 314).

71. Nikki Giovanni and Margaret Walker, *A Poetic Equation: Conversations Between Nikki Giovanni and Margaret Walker* (Washington, DC: Howard University Press, 1974), 79, 80.

72. Lara Pellegrinelli, "The Song Is Who? Locating Singers on the Jazz Scene" (PhD diss., Harvard University, 2005), 285.

73. Aretha Franklin interview in *Aretha Franklin: The Queen of Soul.*

74. Pearl Williams-Jones, "Afro-American Gospel Music: A Crystallization of the Black Aesthetic," *Ethnomusicology* 19.3 (September 1975): 381.

75. Dionne Warwick interview in *Aretha Franklin: The Queen of Soul.*

76. Anthony Heilbut, *The Gospel Sound: Good News and Bad Times* (1975; repr., New York: Limelight, 1997), x.

77. Erik Leidal, "Aretha Franklin's 'Mary, Don't You Weep': Signifying the Survivor in Gospel Music," *GLSG Newsletter* 9.2 (October 1999): 5.

78. Franklin, "I Never Loved a Man."

79. Aretha Franklin, "I Say a Little Prayer," on *Aretha Now* (Atlantic, 1968).

80. Warwick interview in *Aretha Franklin: The Queen of Soul.*

81. Joseph Roach, *Cities of the Dead: Circum-Atlantic Performance* (New York: Columbia University Press, 1996), 2, 4–5, 80.

82. Charles L. Sanders, "Aretha: A Close-Up Look at Sister Superstar," *Ebony*, December 1971, 132–134 (emphasis in original). Franklin's statement is worth citing in full: "The Black Revolution certainly forced me and the majority of black people to begin taking a second look at ourselves. . . . It wasn't that we were all that ashamed of ourselves, we merely started appreciating our *natural* selves, falling in love with ourselves *just as we are*" (132). (Part of this interview is quoted in Cohen, *Amazing Grace*, 36.)

83. Nikki Giovanni, "Dreams," in *Black Judgement* (1969; repr., Detroit: Broadside, 1970), 21.

84. Davis, *Angela Davis: An Autobiography*, 161.

85. The Sweet Inspirations also recorded as a stand-alone group and achieved commercial success with songs such as "Sweet Inspiration" (1968). See Peter Guralnick, *Sweet Soul Music: Rhythm and Blues and the Southern Dream of Freedom* (New York: Harper and Row, 1986), 297–299.

86. Werner, *Higher Ground*, 134.

87. It should be noted that Franklin's backup singers are indeed there to back *her* up. None of her singers enjoy a moment in the spotlight akin to Hendricks's. Instead, when Franklin records "Night Time Is the Right Time" (on *Aretha Now*), she breaks down the "baby" herself in the third chorus and again, more dramatically, at the end of the song. Compared to Franklin's singers, the Raelettes play relatively central roles in Charles's songs: it is their vocals that dominate "Hit the Road, Jack" (1961), and a song like "Don't Set Me Free" (1963) is staged as a Charles-Hendricks duet. See *Ray Charles Greatest Hits* (ABC-Paramount, 1963) and *Ray Charles Live in Concert* (ABC-Paramount, 1965).

88. See Charles et al.'s 1958 Atlantic recording of "(Night Time Is) The Right Time."

89. M. Jones, "Jazz Prosodies," 67.

90. Nikki Giovanni, "Reflections on April 4, 1968," in *Black Judgement*, 7. Although subsequent editions of "Dreams" omit the "g" and render the phrase as "tal kin bout tal kin bout," Giovanni's initial spelling of the phrase in *Black Judgement* exemplifies my point that her depiction of the lyrics yields new meanings.

91. Henderson, *Understanding the New Black Poetry*, 52–53 (emphasis in original).

92. Clarke, *After Mecca*, 61.

93. Sonia Sanchez, "—a poem for nina simone to put some music to and blow our nigguh / minds—," in *We a BaddDDD People* (Detroit: Broadside, 1970), 60.

94. Sherley Anne Williams, "I Want Aretha to Set This to Music," in *Some One Sweet Angel Chile* (New York: Morrow, 1982), 53–55.

95. Nikki Giovanni, "The Way I Feel," in *The Women and the Men* (New York: Morrow, 1975), n.p.

96. Dick Gregory interview in *Aretha Franklin: The Queen of Soul*.

97. John Corbett, "Siren Song to Banshee Wail: On the Status of the Background Vocalist," in *Extended Play: Sounding Off from John Cage to Dr. Funkenstein* (Durham, NC: Duke University Press, 1994), 62.

98. Otis Redding qtd. in Guralnick, *Sweet Soul Music*, 332.

99. Otis Redding, "Respect," on *Otis Blue: Otis Redding Sings Soul* (Stax, 1965).

100. Patricia Hill Collins discusses this revision in *Black Feminist Thought: Knowledge, Consciousness, and the Politics of Empowerment* (1990; repr., New York: Routledge, 2000), 117.

101. Giovanni qtd. in Dobkin, *I Never Loved a Man*, 190.

102. Producer Arif Mardin qtd. in ibid., 167.

103. Leidal, "Aretha Franklin's 'Mary, Don't You Weep,'" 6.

104. In her memoir, Franklin claims that "Carolyn and I coined the phrase 'Sock it to me, sock it to me . . .' in the middle of 'Respect.' It became a household expression . . . , and we never got a dime of credit" (Franklin and Ritz, *From These Roots*, 111). In a recent interview, she tempers the claim by suggesting that she and Carolyn nationalized the phrase, previously in circulation around Detroit, but did not invent it (interview with Anthony Mason, *CBS Sunday Morning News*, May 8, 2011, available on YouTube, http://www.youtube.com/watch?v=rbYVkXnw8GA). As backup singer and composer of a number of Franklin's songs—including the devastating "Ain't No Way" (1968)—Carolyn Franklin was perhaps Franklin's most important collaborator. (Dave Marsh makes this point in "Gotta Find Me an Angel," liner notes to *Aretha Franklin: Queen of Soul*, 29.)

105. Franklin interview with Anthony Mason. Sherley Anne Williams underlines the point: when Franklin "went so far as to spell the word 'respect,' we just knew that this sister wasn't playing around about getting Respect and keeping it" ("Blues Roots," 124).

106. My reading of the backup singers' work partly responds to a published correspondence between ethnomusicologists Steven Feld and Charles Keil, in which Feld expresses discomfort with Franklin's use of backup singers in this song ("Respecting Aretha: A Letter Exchange," in *Music Grooves*, 220).

107. Feld phrases this question slightly differently: "Does 'Sock it to me' mean fuck me or fuck off?" (ibid.). Franklin and her sisters seem to have resolved the question by the time they record Dusty Springfield's "Son of a Preacher Man" in 1969. While Franklin sings, "He'd kiss and tell me everything is all right," the backup singers swell up around the phrase with a breathy, "Ohh, sock it to me" (on *This Girl's in Love with You* [Atlantic, 1970]).

108. Jerry Wexler interview in *Aretha Franklin: The Queen of Soul*.

109. For a striking visual representation of this hybridity, see Franklin and the Sweet Inspirations' appearance on *The Cliff Richard Show* in 1970. Franklin wears a dashiki-style minidress, Afro, and large jewelry, a new look for her. Her backup singers are styled as Franklin had been a year before: bobbed wigs, short dresses, and sweaters. A video of the women singing "Say a Little Prayer for You" can be viewed on YouTube at http://www.youtube.com/watch?v=STKkWj2WpWM.

110. Nikki Giovanni, "My Poem," in *Black Judgement*, 35; Harper, *Are We Not Men?*, 52.

111. See Heilbut, *The Fan Who Knew Too Much*, 155–156, on Franklin's 2011 performance at a same-sex wedding in New York and other more tacit gestures of support for gay rights—bold moves for a singer whose prominent supporters include antigay leaders like T. D. Jakes.

112. Clarke, *After Mecca*, 48; *Gemini* contains some striking moments of U.S. chauvinism and heterosexism (77-79, 43). Still, "Black Poems, *Poseurs*, and Power," an essay from this same early period, articulates a more expansive view of who belongs "in the circle" (in *Gemini*, 106–112).

113. Kimberly Benston, *Performing Blackness: Enactments of African-American Modernism* (London: Routledge, 2000), 155–159.

114. Michael S. Harper, "Dear John, Dear Coltrane," in *Dear John, Dear Coltrane* (1970; repr., Urbana: University of Illinois Press, 1985), 74–75. Thanks to Joshua Owsley and hari stephen kumar for this insight.

115. Sonia Sanchez, "a/coltrane/poem" (1970), in *We A BaddDDD People*, 69.

116. Ibid., 70.

117. Ibid., 71.

118. James Smethurst, *The Black Arts Movement: Literary Nationalism in the 1960s and 1970s* (Chapel Hill: University of North Carolina, 2005), 99.

119. Kimberly Benston names the Coltrane poem a discrete subgenre in "Performing Blackness," in *Afro-American Literary Study in the 1990s*, ed. Houston Baker and Patricia Redmond (Chicago: University of Chicago Press, 1989), 176, 192. Meta Jones analyzes what she calls the "post-soul Coltrane poem" in *The Muse Is Music*, 85–126.

120. Heilbut, *The Fan Who Knew Too Much*, 139.

121. Nelson George, *The Death of Rhythm & Blues* (1988; repr., New York: Penguin, 2004), 105.

122. Conversation with the author, June 22, 2012.

123. Heilbut, *Gospel Sound*, 66.

124. Robert Christgau, "Queen of Pop," *Village Voice*, March 17, 1998, http://www.villagevoice.com/1998-03-17/music/queen-of-pop/, qtd. in Dobkin, *I Never Loved a Man*, 11.

125. George, *Death of Rhythm & Blues*, 105. Peter Winkler provides an excellent account of the problem from a musicological perspective when he narrates his attempt to transcribe Franklin's "Never Loved a Man." He concludes that "the basic premises of our notational system may be inappropriate to [the] task" of transcribing Franklin's sound ("Writing Ghost Notes: The Poetics and Politics of Transcription," in *Keeping Score: Music, Disciplinarity, Culture*, ed. David Schwarz, Anahid Kassabian, and Lawrence Siegel [Charlottesville: University Press of Virginia, 1997], 186, 188).

126. Keil and Feld, "Respecting Aretha," 218–226; Dobkin, *I Never Loved a Man*, 189–190. Dobkin frames his book as a search for the secret of Franklin's art but ultimately eschews the question and concludes that "Aretha's music . . . is elemental, metaphysical. And to some degree, analyzing it detracts from its fundamentalness, from its 'realness' and hers" (ibid., 200). Even more unfortunate, but worth citing since it provides a limit case for the kinds of representations this book is designed to dismantle, is Dobkin's claim that "Aretha's singing emanates from her diaphragm—it may as well emerge from her loins—and resounds with glory and mystery, a sense of the unknowable. In that sense she is a kind of earth mother figure" (197).

127. Nikki Giovanni, "Foreword: A Song for Me," in Dobkin, *I Never Loved a Man*, x. ("Try Matty's" appears on *Spirit in the Dark* [1970].)

128. Tate, *Black Women Writers at Work*, 78.

129. James Baldwin and Nikki Giovanni, *A Dialogue* (New York: Lippincott, 1973), 20.

130. Mari Evans, "I Am a Black Woman," in *I Am a Black Woman* (New York: Morrow, 1970), 11.

131. Heilbut, *The Fan Who Knew Too Much*, 143, 156.

132. Franklin, "Spirit in the Dark."

133. E. Patrick Johnson, "Feeling the Spirit in the Dark: Expanding Notions of the Sacred in the African-American Gay Community," *Callaloo* 21.2 (Spring 1998): 399. Johnson convincingly points out that Franklin encourages "little Sally Walker" to "*ride*" the "spirit in the dark."

Epilogue

1. Sterling Brown, "Ma Rainey," in *Southern Road* (New York: Harcourt, Brace, 1932), 62–64; Sherley Anne Williams, "I Want Aretha to Set This to Music," in *Some One Sweet Angel Chile* (New York: Morrow, 1982), 53–55.

2. Amiri Baraka, "Sassy Was Definitely Not the Avon Lady" (1999), in *The LeRoi Jones/Amiri Baraka Reader*, ed. William J. Harris (New York: Thunder's Mouth, 1999), 567–570.

3. Mos Def and Talib Kweli, "Thieves in the Night," on *Mos Def and Talib Kweli Are Black Star* (Rawkus, 1998). Cf. Toni Morrison, *The Bluest Eye* (1970; repr., New York: Vintage, 2007), 205–206.

4. Nikki Giovanni, "Poem for Aretha," in *Re:Creation* (Detroit: Broadside, 1970), 18.

5. Anthony Heilbut, *The Fan Who Knew Too Much: Aretha Franklin, the Rise of the Soap Opera, Children of the Gospel Church, and Other Meditations* (New York: Knopf, 2012), 142.

6. For Franklin's performance of "Precious Memories," see ibid., 150.

7. "My Country 'Tis of Thee" (also known as "Let Freedom Ring") also plays a role in Mahalia Jackson's memoir. We might recall from chapter 2 that the song sparked a confrontation with a young African American woman who asked, "Miss Jackson, how can you sing 'My country, 'tis of thee, sweet land of liberty,' as if you believed it when you know the white people in America don't want us here? It's not our country." Jackson replied that "it *is* our country," and there are "better days ahead" (Jackson with Evan McLeod Wylie, *Movin' On Up* [New York: Hawthorn Books, 1966], 128–129).

8. Farah Jasmine Griffin, "When Malindy Sings: A Meditation on Black Women's Vocality," in *Uptown Conversation: The New Jazz Studies*, ed. Robert G. O'Meally, Brent Hayes Edwards, and Farah Jasmine Griffin (New York: Columbia University Press, 2004), 104.

9. Barack Obama, inaugural address, Washington, DC, January 20, 2009, available at http://www.whitehouse.gov/blog/inaugural-address.

10. As if to deny the vocal strain that this performance ostensibly betrayed, Franklin soon recorded "an excessively gospelized version of the anthem, complete with more high F-sharps than she had sung in years, amid double-timed [shouts] from her chorale" (Heilbut, *The Fan Who Knew Too Much*, 148), thus delightfully complicating notions of vocal transparency, as I have aimed to do in chapter 4.

11. Griffin discusses this performance in "At Last . . . ? Michelle Obama, Beyoncé, Race and History," *Daedalus* 140.1 (Winter 2011): 131–141.

12. "At Last" was composed by Mack Gordon and Harry Warren for the 1941 film *Orchestra Wives*. In calling it James's song, I refer to the fact that it became known as James's signature song in the early 1960s.

13. Beyoncé's starring role as Etta James itself marks a strange departure from other biopics of black women singers. Unlike Diana Ross's appearance as Billie Holiday in *Lady Sings the Blues* (1972), Aretha Franklin's ill-fated contract to play Mahalia Jackson in the Broadway play *Sing, Mahalia, Sing* (see Michael Awkward, *Soul Covers: Rhythm and Blues Remakes and the Struggle for Artistic Identity* [Durham, NC: Duke

University Press, 2007], 49–50), or Zoe Saldana's (and perhaps yet, as once rumored, Mary J. Blige's) appearance as Nina Simone in a forthcoming film, Beyoncé played James while James was alive. Angela Bassett's performance of Tina Turner in *What's Love Got to Do with It* (1993) and Theresa Randle's portrayal of Natalie Cole in the television biopic *Livin' for Love* (2000) are different, presumably less sensitive cases, since Bassett and Randle are not known as singers and because Turner and Cole both appear as themselves in these works. (James does not appear in *Cadillac Records*.)

14. See Sean Michaels, "Etta James: I'm Gonna Whup Beyoncé's Ass," *Guardian Online*, February 6, 2009, http://www.guardian.co.uk/music/2009/feb/06/beyonce-etta-james-barack-obama.

15. The inaugural ball of 2013 continued the trend of having a younger vocalist perform a soul legend's hit, as Jennifer Hudson serenaded the first couple with Al Green's "Let's Stay Together." Yet it seems that Obama (and the popular press) had learned something from Etta James's slight four years earlier. This time journalists asked, "Why didn't Al Green sing his own song, 'Let's Stay Together,' at the inaugural ball?" and *USA Today* reported that he had been asked to do so but had declined the invitation (Korina Lopez, "Al Green Turned Down President Obama," *USA Today*, January 23, 2013, http://www.usatoday.com/story/life/music/2013/01/23/inaugural-al-green-obama/1858005).

16. Trey Ellis, "The New Black Aesthetic," *Callaloo* 38 (Winter 1989): 235. Ellis lauds a group of second-generation college-educated black artists who embrace "a multiracial mix of cultures" and "shamelessly [borrow] and [reassemble]" them (237, 235, 234).

17. Etta James and David Ritz, *Rage to Survive: The Etta James Story* (1995; repr., New York: Da Capo, 2003), 37, 247. Subsequent citations of James's memoir appear in the text as *R*.

18. Heilbut, *The Fan Who Knew Too Much*, 153.

19. As James explains, "I'm not saying that to boast or shock, but just to be honest. That's who I was. The people I hung around were junkies and dealers. They accepted me and I accepted them. . . . I didn't feel judged, and I sure as hell didn't do any judging" (*R*, 198).

20. Here I should also mention the terrific R&B vocalist Leela James, who released an album-length tribute, *Loving You More . . . In the Spirit of Etta James* (Shanachie), in the summer of 2012.

21. Linda Susan Jackson, conversation with the author, June 22, 2012. This epilogue was intended in a similar spirit. However, when Etta James died on January 20, 2012, her passing instantly recast this closing discussion as an elegy.

22. Linda Susan Jackson, "Taste of Yellow," in *What Yellow Sounds Like* (Los Angeles: Tia Chucha, 2007), 37. Subsequent citations of this collection appear in the text as *Y*.

23. See Morrison, *The Bluest Eye*, 81–86.

24. Conversation with the author.

25. Methodologically speaking, the following analysis shows that we can compare musical-literary aesthetics even without the mediating nonfiction commentaries I have foregrounded in previous chapters.

26. Cf. *Sula* (1973), in which Toni Morrison uses the image of custard to figure Nel's shame and confusion at her mother's soft response to racism: "If *she* were really custard, then there was a chance that Nel was too" ([New York: Vintage, 2004], 22).

27. Etta James, "Trust in Me," on *At Last!* (Argo, 1961).

28. Etta James, "At Last," on *At Last!*

29. Etta James, "All I Could Do Was Cry," on *At Last!*

30. Jackson explained that, while she worked on this poem, she continually played recordings of Etta James, Abbey Lincoln, Dinah Washington, Carmen McRae, and others. She realized she was not only captive to but also captor of these singers: she needed them, but they also needed her; where would they be without her listening? (Conversation with the author.)

31. Etta James, "Something's Got a Hold on Me," on *Etta James Top Ten* (Argo, 1963).

32. Doi-Oing seems to have started the trend by sampling the song in "Good Feeling" (Brainiak Records, 1991); other notable tracks followed, for instance by Bachelors of Science ("Sometimes" [Breakbeat Lounge, 2005]). The most popular recent single to use this sample is Flo Rida's "Good Feeling" (Atlantic, 2011).

33. Jean Grae, "Threats," on *Jean Grae: Evil Jeanius*, prod. Blue Sky Black Death (Babygrande, 2008). It should be noted that Grae herself did not authorize the release of this track or the album on which it appears; nor did she receive money for sales. However, she does claim authorship of this work and asked to be cited as the composer of the song as it appears in this book.

34. Jay-Z, "Threat," on *The Black Album* (Roc-A-Fella Records, 2003).

35. Adam Bradley, *Book of Rhymes: The Poetics of Hip Hop* (New York: Basic Civitas, 2009), xix.

36. Jay-Z, *Decoded* (New York: Spiegel & Grau, 2010), 235, qtd. in Kelefa Sanneh, "Word," *New Yorker*, December 6, 2010, 84.

37. Sanneh, "Word," 88.

38. Wu-Tang Clan, "Can It Be All So Simple," on *Enter the Wu-Tang (36 Chambers)* (Loud, 1993); Kanye West, "School Spirit," on *The College Dropout* (Roc-A-Fella, 2004); Mocean Worker, "Sho Nuff Now," on *Candygram for Mowo!* (MoWo!, 2011).

39. Bradley, *Book of Rhymes*, xiii.

INDEX

Page numbers in italics indicate photographs.

ABOUT THE AUTHOR

Emily Lordi is an assistant professor of English at the University of Massachusetts, Amherst.

CPSIA information can be obtained at www.ICGtesting.com
Printed in the USA
BVOW08s0753270913

332256BV00004B/4/P